ADD/ADHD Behavior-Change Resource Kit

Ready-to-Use Strategies & Activities for Helping Children with Attention Deficit Disorder

GRAD L. FLICK, Ph. D.

JOSSEY-BASS
A Wiley Imprint
www.josseybass.com

Published by Jossey-Bass
A Wiley Imprint
989 Market Street, San Francisco, CA 94103-1741 www.josseybass.com

Jossey-Bass books and products are available through most bookstores. To contact Jossey-Bass directly call our Customer Care Department within the U.S. at (800) 956-7739, outside the U.S. at (317) 572-3986 or fax (317) 572-4002.

Jossey-Bass also publishes its books in a variety of electronic formats. Some content that appears in print may not be available in electronic books.

Library of Congress Cataloging-in-Publication Data:
Flick, Grad L.
ADD/ADHD behavior-change resource kit : ready-to-use strategies & activities for helping children with attention deficit disorder / Grad L. Flick.
p. cm.
Includes bibliographical references and index.
ISBN 0-87628-144-7
1. Attention-deficit hyperactivity disorder—Treatment—Handbooks, manuals, etc. 2. Attention-deficit hyperactivity disorder—Treatments—Handbooks, manuals, etc. I. Title.
RJ506.H9F62 1998
618.92'8589—dc21 97-42870

Printed in the United States of America
PB Printing 10 9 8 7 6 5 4

DEDICATION

This book is dedicated to our son, Marcus, and to all the children whose lives are filled with the challenges of Attention Deficit Disorders.

ACKNOWLEDGMENTS

The contributions of many persons need to be recognized for their assistance and influence in the completion of this book. First, my longtime friend, Nina Roland, typed much of the final manuscript and served as a reader, critic and consultant. I could not have completed this project without her. Much assistance with the typing of various forms, tables, etc. was contributed by Peggy Barbeau, Elise Everette and my office manager, Dianne Wilensky. Many thanks go to Lisa Russell, B.S., for her help in coordinating information and with scheduling. Technical assistance from our local computer consultant, John Senegal, has been greatly appreciated. Plaudits also go to Richard Scheidt, M.S., computer programmer, who contributed to the development of several of the attention training games described in this book. Lastly, I must recognize and gratefully acknowledge the technical assistance and enthusiastic support from my editor, Susan Kolwicz. She has provided on-going help, advice and encouragement throughout this project. She has also gone beyond the scope of the working on this book to give much needed relevant feedback and information.

Many individuals have influenced my views on ADD/ADHD. These include Russell Barkley, Ph.D., Sam Goldstein, Ph.D., and C. Keith Conners, Ph.D. I have been particularly impressed by the clinical approach of Christopher Green, M.D. My neuropsychological influence stems from Paul Satz, Ph.D.; Joel Lubar, Ph.D. has contributed greatly to my initial orientation to the neurophysiological aspects of ADD/ADHD. The works of Gerald Patterson, Ph.D., and Rex Forehand, Ph.D., have had much influence in the behavioral area; Daniel Cruse, Ph.D., has had influence on the more practical applications of behavior techniques. Lastly, much recent work in the area of behavior management has been based on the SOS Program by Lynn Clark, Ph.D. His program has been an excellent resource for clinical treatment programs and workshops on child behavior management. I would also like to recognize and extend my deep appreciation to Rene Duffourc, M.D., and Jule Miller, M.D., Board Certified Child Psychiatrists, for their critical reading and comments on the chapter pertaining to Medication Information for Clinicians.

A very special appreciation goes to my wife, Alma, who has been a long standing source of encouragement, offering nurturance and constructive comments when needed. Alma, who has an M.S. Degree in Social Work and a Doctor of Philosophy Degree in Clinical Counseling, has collaborated on clinical treatment programs for parents and on workshops for parents. She has shared not only technical information with parents but also some of the experiences of raising our adopted son, Marcus, who has ADD (although the term "ADD" had not yet been coined at the time we adopted him).

My last special thanks and my dedication goes, in fact, to my son, Marcus. Much of what I have learned about ADD—especially the practical aspects of daily living with ADD—came directly from Marcus.

ABOUT THE AUTHOR

Grad L. Flick received his Ph.D. in Clinical Psychology from the University of Miami in 1969 with APA-approved internship at the University of Florida Medical Center. A licensed psychologist since 1971, he has specializations in neuropsychology and biofeedback, along with certification as a biofeedback therapist. He has been certified in stress management, in employee assistance, and has Fellow and Diplomatic status from the American Board of Medical Psychotherapists. He has held positions in psychology at the University of New Orleans and Louisiana State University School of Medicine and has served as consultant to several hospitals in the New Orleans and Gulf Coast area. Since 1971, he has been in private practice and is currently director of Seacoast Psychological Associates, Inc., in association with his wife, Alma L. Flick, Ph.D.; they specialize in the evaluation and treatment of children, adolescents and adults with Attention Deficit Disorder, learning and behavioral problems. Dr. Flick is also the Director of the ADD Clinic (year-round and summer programs) for children, adolescents and adults with ADD where behavioral and cognitive therapies are offered as well as traditional psychotherapy, play therapy and various group therapies.

Dr. Flick has had numerous scientific presentations and publication credits, conducted many workshops for both parents and teachers on ADD, and has given lectures to various parent and teacher organizations on ADD and Child Management. He is the author of *Power Parenting for Children with ADD/ADHD: A Practical Parent's Guide for Managing Difficult Behaviors* (Center for Applied Research in Education, 1996). He has over 25 years' experience in both research and clinical practice with children who present attentional, learning and/or behavioral disorders. Grad and Alma have also parented a child with learning disability and Attention Deficit Hyperactivity Disorder.

ABOUT THIS RESOURCE KIT

This resource on ADD/ADHD presents comprehensive explanations of ADD/ADHD behavior, allowing professional and parents alike to have a good understanding of the nature of ADD/ADHD. In addition, the book details treatment options, covering many effective means of helping children with ADD/ADHD while documenting those procedures that are questionable. Teachers, parents, and counselors are seen as working together, and the book provides plans and strategies for doing so. As noted in my previous book, *Power Parenting for Children with ADD/ADHD* (1996), when individuals have a good understanding of the nature of ADD/ADHD, along with knowledge about the most effective techniques to deal with it, they feel a sense of empowerment. When there is increased confidence in dealing with difficult ADD/ADHD behaviors, and where there is consistent use of the most effective techniques, then opportunities for academic, personal, and other successes can be achieved for all individuals.

WHAT DOES THIS RESOURCE OFFER?

ADD/ADHD Behavior-Change Resource Kit first presents general information on the behaviors involved in the ADD/ADHD pattern, along with recent information on their biological bases. Behavioral descriptions, together with information from parents, teachers and the child, in the form of psychological test data, are integrated to form diagnostic impressions of ADD/ADHD along with its many co-morbid disorders and mimic syndromes. Typically, a medication approach is used, especially with more severe forms of ADD/ADHD, and information is provided in various forms to educate parents, teachers, and counselors about the variety of medications available. It is well known , however, that the best outcomes are obtained when a medication regime is combined with some form of behavioral intervention and other strategies. Many children with ADD/ADHD lack various skills, and it is clear that "pills don't teach skills." Consequently, this resource presents a host of exercises and strategies, utilizing some of the most recently developed technology to help the child with ADD/ADHD. For the most part, these techniques and strategies involve behavioral procedures, but many incorporate the use of commonly known sports games and recreational outlets, as well as some procedures that have been specifically developed for use with ADD/ADHD children.

ADD/ADHD Behavior-Change Resource Kit addresses common problems such as homework and social peer problems often encountered by children with ADD/ADHD. There are provisions for teachers, parents, and counselors to work individually with these children, and—more important—strategic plans for cooperation in monitoring and managing the child's behavior in combined home and school programs. The ultimate cooperation may result from integrative home, school, and clinic programs, where all parties involved are working to help the child. In general, the greater the combined effort, the more rapidly a child may show improvement and the faster she or he will acquire learned adaptive skills that will assist her or him in adjusting to the problems and difficulties manifested by attention deficit disorders.

Since ADD/ADHD behavior is often a greater problem in school situations, a comprehensive approach to accommodation strategies, adaptive techniques, and inclusion procedures is emphasized. This chapter covers general behavioral approaches as well as specific interventions geared toward managing problems that are mostly unique to the ADD/ADHD child.

Emotional problems are often associated with the pattern of ADD/ADHD behavior and contribute to a poor self-concept and low self-esteem. These problems are also addressed in some detail.

Last, there is some focus on the stress that is often associated with the management of ADD/ADHD behavior. Experienced by teachers and parents, such stress reactions may be quite significant and debilitating. Thus, this resource offers techniques to deal with that stress and to survive the critical periods of preschool, school-age, adolescent, and adult ADD/ADHD behaviors.

What the *ADD/ADHD Behavior-Change Resource Kit* offers readers:

- useful comprehensive information about the neurobiological nature of ADD/ADHD
- detailed reference materials on diagnosis and treatment, including medications and alternative behaviorally oriented programs
- presentation and analysis of many real-life examples of behavior problems
- specific exercises and activities to enhance knowledge of behavioral procedures to use with ADD/ADHD
- intervention strategies that address specific problematic behaviors for teachers and parents
- techniques to assist teachers and parents in becoming more effective and in maintaining their effectiveness in dealing with ADD/ADHD behaviors

WHO SHOULD USE THIS RESOURCE

Parents, teachers, and mental health professionals who must deal with ADD/ADHD behaviors directly at home, in school, or in clinical treatment centers will benefit from the information, exercises, strategies, and techniques offered by this resource. These three groups may use it differently, depending upon their own perspective and needs.

How Teachers Can Use This Resource

This book is an excellent and practical resource for teachers who must deal with ADD/ADHD behaviors in class and on school grounds. For teachers, the *ADD/ADHD Behavior-Change Resource Kit*

- provides detailed information about ADD/ADHD and the medications often used to treat it
- provides examples of rating scales frequently used by teachers to document the presence of ADD/ADHD behaviors
- presents programs for teachers working independently with the child with ADD/ADHD, as well as for teachers working in conjunction with parents and counselors
- provides forms and charts needed to construct and monitor behavioral programs for students with ADD/ADHD
- gives information about the most effective ancillary approaches to ADD/ADHD behaviors that utilize concepts of accommodation, adaptation, and inclusion

How Parents Can Use This Resource

Of particular interest to parents, the *ADD/ADHD Behavior-Change Resource Kit*

- presents a comprehensive overview of background information essential for parents to understand the nature of the behaviors of their child with ADD/ADHD
- explains concepts of behavior management in greater detail with special reference to ADD/ADHD
- provides more explicit illustrations of behavior management techniques
- gives practical evaluation tools for the parent
- teaches the parent behavior-specific exercises to practice so that behavior management techniques can be used successfully with the child
- provides many examples of the ideas and techniques discussed
- serves as an excellent reference for more detail about specific behavior management techniques and particular analyses of behavior problems
- provides many practical suggestions, using formats familiar to both child and parent (such as games)
- provides information on new instruments that may be used by parents to help the child

How Counselors and Other Mental Health Professionals Can Use This Resource

Mental health professional such as psychiatrists, psychologists, social workers, and licensed counselors may find this resource beneficial in the clinical evaluation and treatment of their clients with ADD/ADHD, as well as in their counseling, education, and training of these children's parents. For this group of professionals, the *ADD/ADHD Behavior-Change Resource Kit* provides

- up-to-date background information on ADD/ADHD and its co-morbid and mimic syndromes
- timely information on current concepts of assessment and treatment
- current medication strategies and coverage of controversial treatments
- extensive behavioral procedures and time-saving exercises that may be assigned by therapists working with parent training
- many procedures and strategies that may augment the therapist's own treatment program.

How Physicians Can Use This Resource

Family practitioners, pediatricians, and other medical doctors who see patients with ADD/ADHD may benefit from using this resource as a reference. It provides them with

- a comprehensive explanation of the nature of ADD/ADHD behaviors
- current concepts in diagnoses and treatments
- an up-to-date summary of the current medications used with ADD/ADHD, including some recent advances in combined pharmacology and newer medications available
- a review of current use of psychological tests in the description of the ADD/ADHD behavior pattern and how treatment plans may be based on such evaluations
- a review of behavioral concepts to familiarize the physician with alternative and adjunctive approaches, and how these may be combined with medication regimes
- information on educational plans, with their legal ramifications
- a discussion about how all professionals can work with parents to help the child with ADD/ADHD

General Format

The *ADD/ADHD Behavior-Change Resource Kit* offers three different types of information: (1) background information, diagnosis, and medications; (2) exercises designed to promote effective learning and practical application of the behavioral procedures; and (3) materials and strategies that are not necessarily behavioral in nature, but have been shown to be helpful in dealing with ADD/ADHD behavior.

The activities and exercises are designed to familiarize the teacher and parent with techniques, and at the same time, enhance awareness of underlying behavioral strategies and knowledge about materials that have helped the ADD/ADHD child. The teacher and the parent will be in a better position to help the child with ADD/ADHD when armed with knowledge of established behavioral techniques; they can then become more self-sufficient and independent in managing the child's difficult behaviors.

Grad L. Flick

CONTENTS

Chapter 1
ESSENTIAL BACKGROUND INFORMATION

Chapter 2
DIAGNOSIS AND TREATMENT OF ADD/ADHD

Chapter 3
LOOKING AT BEHAVIOR: THE A-B-Cs OF BEHAVIOR-CHANGE PROGRAMS

Chapter 4

MANAGING BEHAVIOR

Chapter 5
SOCIAL SKILLS

Chapter 6
HOMEWORK ISSUES FOR PARENTS

Chapter 7
EXPANDING HOME PROGRAMS TO INCLUDE SCHOOL BEHAVIOR

Chapter 8

EFFECTIVE BEHAVIORAL TECHNIQUES FOR TEACHERS

Chapter 9
GENERAL ACTIVITIES AND GAMES

Chapter 10
SURVIVAL TRAINING FOR PARENTS AND TEACHERS

APPENDICES

CHAPTER 1

Essential Background Information

WHAT IS ADD/ADHD?

ADD is an abbreviation for Attention Deficit Disorder; ADHD stands for Attention Deficit Hyperactivity Disorder. Many professionals use these terms interchangeably. Others distinguish between ADD, which is the basic inattentive pattern, and ADHD which is a generally more complex and serious attention disorder that involves the hyperactivity component. In this book, these terms are generally referred to as ADD/ADHD, one complex pattern of behaviors.

Three core behaviors contribute to the ADD/ADHD pattern:

1. Inattention
2. Impulsivity
3. Hyperactivity

In addition, a cluster of associated characteristics includes:

- disorganization
- poor peer/sib relations
- aggressive behavior
- poor self-concept/self-esteem
- sensation-seeking behavior
- daydreaming

- poor coordination
- memory problems
- persistent obsessive thinking
- inconsistency, the "hallmark" characteristic

CORE CHARACTERISTICS OF ADD/ADHD

The following looks at each of the core behaviors and associated characteristics of ADD/ADHD behavior in more detail and includes some typical related observations made by parents and teachers of children with ADD/ADHD.

Inattention

The most basic trait is lack of focused attention. It's not that children with ADD/ADHD don't attend—they attend to everything! All stimuli impinge on their senses with equal potency. Such students appear to satiate quickly on tasks, but, in actuality, they may get distracted by one of the other stimuli and go off on a tangent—failing to finish the task at hand. Their attentional processes are quite variable—some days the child may be "in tune" and finish all his work; other days he may seem to "be in a fog." Situation factors play an important part; in school, the child with ADD/ADHD may struggle to focus his attention on classroom assignments, but at home he may be the champion at video games. Exciting graphics, flashing lights, and bright colors may serve to attract and maintain the attention of the child with ADD/ADHD. Likewise, novel interesting tasks, including those spiced with humor, may help maintain the child's attention. Such children also have little difficulty focusing in a one-on-one setting, but when they're in the complex environment of a noisy classroom, they may have numerous problems with compliance and task performance. There is also one subgroup of inattentive children who may become distracted by their own internal thoughts and sensations, rather than by some external stimuli. These are the "quiet underachievers," kids who rarely create a behavioral disturbance in class—they simply go into a "trance-like" state and may focus on some internal creative thought process—in short, they daydream.

However, not all instances of inattention are attributable to ADD/ADHD. Some children may develop attentional problems secondary to a learning disability in language, reading, spelling, writing, or math. These children may become quite frustrated and overly stressed when asked to complete tasks that are difficult for them. Those asked to read and answer questions about a subject in which they have little knowledge and minimal interest may feel inadequate and experience sufficient stress to result in avoidance behavior, that is, not paying attention to the task at hand and doing something to remove themselves from the situation, or "tuning out." Similar conditions may exist for a child who may be overwhelmed with work beyond his/her capacity or developmental

INATTENTION

Parents may say:

When I tell her something it goes in one ear and out the other.

I know he can attend; he plays Nintendo© for hours.

He knows all the baseball players, but he can't remember what I said a minute ago.

Teachers may say:

Sometimes he just seems to be in outer space.

When I call on him, he never seems to have the right place in Reading.

She just has so much trouble following instructions.

level (e.g., a child with a developmental delay or mental retardation), or in other instances when a child has some preoccupation with depressive or anxious thoughts.

Impulsivity

This core symptom reflects a general lack of self-control. It is doubtful that children with ADD/ADHD plan their trouble-making behavior. Although they may be aware of right and wrong and may be able to cite a rule of the home or classroom, they often "think after they act." By this time, it's too late—they've already "done it" and are "in trouble" again. At times, it is perplexing to parents who wonder how someone of average or better intelligence can act so "stupidly" at times. While the child may feel quite guilty over his wrongdoing, this guilt is unlikely, by itself, to prevent future acting-out behavior. The average child who gets punched in line at school may first look to see if the teacher is watching before he punches back; the child with ADD/ADHD in the same situation responds impulsively and reflexively—and often gets caught and is thus labeled "the aggressor." Also, because of their impulsive style, children with ADD/ADHD have a higher incidence of "accident proneness." In conversations, such children can't wait to talk; they often interrupt and talk over others. Described as frustrated and impatient, they blurt out answers in class before raising their hands; and they frequently have a short fuse and may explosively vent their anger. These children start working on projects before learning all of the directions, rush through their work, and make many careless errors in the process. Socially and in play activities, these kids experience difficulty taking turns and problems with rules that involve control, and they are generally unaware of the effects of their action on others. Such children also learn slowly from their mistakes since their behavior is primarily reflexive and they are genuinely unaware of "how they get in trouble."

IMPULSIVITY

Parents may say:

He's 10 years old, but still interrupts my conversations.
He's got such a short fuse—you never know what to expect.
I'm afraid to let her ride her bike in the street; she's had so many accidents.

Teachers may say:

You really have to watch this preschooler all the time.
Other students tease him a lot—they know how to get him to react.
He has much difficulty waiting to be called; he often just blurts out an answer.

Hyperactivity

Perhaps the most salient behavioral characteristic in this ADD/ADHD symptom pattern is hyperactivity. Some mothers of children with ADD/ADHD have noted that hyperactivity was often present even before birth. Problematic hyperactivity may not be recognized as a real symptom until the first time a child is placed in a situation that requires some self-control of movement. Sometimes this doesn't occur until the child is in preschool or, most likely, kindergarten. While all youngsters are generally more active during the early years, those children with ADD/ADHD are apt to be described as restless and they find it especially hard to settle down for quiet activity such as reading or nap time. These children appear to be

HYPERACTIVITY

Parents may say:

He was overactive even before he was born.
This toddler is always in motion.
When we visit friends she has to touch everything.

Teachers may say:

He just can't stay seated very long.
She's always talking to her neighbor in class.
His drumming that pencil is really annoying.

"driven" and go from one thing to another, seemingly becoming easily bored and needing more stimulation. Enhanced self-stimulation such as humming, making noise and talking could come from excess overt motor activity. By the time the child is in a structured setting like a classroom, hyperactive behavior has become an obvious problem that often cannot be ignored.

ADDITIONAL CHARACTERISTICS

While this triad of symptoms (inattention, impulsivity and hyperactivity) is often used to describe the basic ADD/ADHD symptom picture, there are other characteristics that may vary considerably in degree but also contribute to the individuality of the overall pattern for each child. Here is a list of these additional characteristics followed by descriptions of each.

Disorganization

This characteristic may be manifested either in physical appearance or in the way the child keeps track of important things—or both. No systematic approach is used to remember notes from school, footballs, books, or other "important things." Deficiencies also abound in preparing for projects and tests (many of which are mentioned to the parent only the night before they are due). This lack of organization further contributes to the child's difficulty in completing tasks. Some children seem to overcompensate by developing an almost obsessive-compulsive routine in order to overcome their difficulty in organization.

DISORGANIZATION

Parents may say:

Her room is always a mess.
He's always losing things. He just can't get organized.
If I ask him to tuck his shirt in, even more of it is out when he's "fixed" it.

Teachers may say:

He can't even seem to find things that he needs.
Before doing classwork, she'll take out a pencil, put it away, try to find paper, take out another pencil and sharpen it. It takes forever for her to get started.
His desk is so messy he can't find anything.

Poor Peer/Sibling Relations

Despite their general sensitivity and strong desire to be accepted by others, these children often misread social cues and impulsively exhibit some socially inappropriate behaviors. It may be an inability to resist blurting out something insulting, whereas a similar comment may occur to another child who would think it over, realize that it's wrong, and refrain from verbalizing the insult. Blatantly intruding on others' games may cause rejection, a puzzling reaction to the child with ADD/ADHD who only exhibited what he perceived to be a strong desire to join a game. Even in a small group or a one-to-one situation, children with ADD/ADHD may be perceived as being too bossy or "always wanting to be first." While some of these children adapt and change their behavior somewhat over the years, during adolescence such interactive difficulties may re-surface as new social adjustments are required.

POOR SIB/PEER RELATIONS (SOCIAL PROBLEMS)

Parents may say:

She says she has no friends.

Before medication, he was the last one to be asked to a child's party.

When he's in a group, he acts like an idiot.

Teachers may say:

He's such a loner—no one seems to like him. Sometimes I think he doesn't finish his work so that he can stay in and avoid recess.

She gets so hurt when her classmates avoid her.

He has a real problem playing by the rules at recess.

Aggressive Behavior

This characteristic contributes to a generally long-term negative outcome for the ADD/ADHD child. When aggressive behavior is associated with ADD/ADHD, there is a poorer prognosis and it also makes it more difficult to deal with and to manage the child's behavior. Aggressive behavior often signifies the presence of a co-morbid condition such as Oppositional Defiant Disorder (ODD) or Conduct Disorder (CD). Such disorders do not respond well to medication intervention like other conventional symptomatic behavior associated with ADD/ADHD. Often, the presence of aggressive behavior requires a "multiple medication" schedule (i.e., more than one medication) and/or more intense behavior interventions.

AGGRESSIVE BEHAVIOR

Parents may say:

He's always picking on his brother.
She seems to defy me when I ask her to do something.
When this kid gets angry, he's like a wild person—you can't control him.

Teachers may say:

This child is so disrespectful to his teacher.
He gets so many discipline notices—I'm beginning to think he enjoys it.
When there is trouble, this kid is always involved.

Poor Self-Concept/Self-Esteem

Children with ADD/ADHD are very sensitive emotionally and neurologically to their difficulties and failures. Besides their personal frustration and awareness of failure, these children often experience harsh criticism and considerable negative feedback from peers, sibs, and—unfortunately at times—from adults as well. Their self-perceptions are poor, and over time such children may become increasingly more doubtful about their ability to cope with academic and social situations. In peer relationships, they are at times treated as "outcasts" and "misfits." Name-calling ("He's hyper; he's a retard; he's clumsy and can't throw a ball straight.") may elicit explosive angry retorts due to impulsivity combined with accumulated frustration and stress. These children are indeed

POOR SELF-CONCEPT/SELF-ESTEEM

Parents may say:

He says he's stupid.
He seems to get along better with younger kids and others that have problems.
She says she has no friends.

Teachers may say:

Nobody wants to play with this child.
He seems to give up so easily—he doesn't try anymore.
He makes fun of himself and gets laughs.

quite sensitive to comments from others and feel quite vulnerable, often inadequate, and, at times, even quite depressed as they go through life.

Sensation-Seeking Behavior

Fortunately, this characteristic in its more severe form is not present as frequently as the others. However, some children with ADD and especially with ADHD, are neurobiologically low-aroused (sleepy) and need more stimulation than would be forthcoming from typical hyperactive behavior. These children with ADD/ADHD—often during their teenage years—will seek out forms of excitement that can be described as "dangerous." Engaging in activities labeled as "surfing," these youngsters might ride on top of commuter trains or elevators, or grab on to moving cars or trucks to ride on skates at high speeds. Many of these stunts frequently result in serious injury or death. Less daring minor variations of these tendencies may be seen in those children who take more risks in their play behavior (e.g., doing wheelies in a busy street) or engage in activities that are still considered somewhat dangerous (e.g., jumping from the top of a garage, out of trees, or juggling sharp knives). Just like many other characteristics of ADD/ADHD, this one varies in degree. While most of these children will not engage in the very risky activities, many will seek out or create their own stimulation. For instance, it would not be unusual to find those children with ADD/ADHD coming to class with various toys in their pockets, in order to deal with what they perceive as a boring situation.

SENSATION-SEEKING BEHAVIOR

Parents may say:

I'm always catching him with things that are dangerous.
He's fallen out of trees trying to climb higher and higher.
This kid seems to live on the edge—he does a lot of stupid things.

Teachers may say:

This kid likes to push others to their limit.
He seems to invite others to fight with him.
She always seems to be the center of attention and excitement.

Daydreaming

This characteristic is associated with the child's underlying physiology. Since a child with ADD/ADHD will typically exhibit a general state of low-arousal in the nervous system, when in class or some other situation that might be perceived as boring, this child's tendency to engage in low-arousal "hypnogogic" or dream-like activity is reflective of the underlying degree of activation in the brain (i.e., a sleepy state). Many children with ADD/ADHD, especially when unmedicated, report a tendency to literally fall asleep in the classroom. Creating some type of excitement by talking, getting out of the seat, or disturbing the class with clowning behavior may thus represent the child's attempt (without his awareness) to adapt to the underlying (sleepy) brain-wave state.

DAYDREAMING

Parents may say:

She should be doing homework, but I catch her staring at some picture.
This kid can spend hours doing nothing.
Except when he plays Nintendo©, he looks half asleep.

Teachers may say:

His body is in the classroom, but I don't know where his mind is.
He looks spacey—I wonder about drugs.
I just know she must fall asleep in class sometimes.

Poor Coordination

Many children with ADD/ADHD have difficulty with fine motor tasks, especially handwriting. As a written assignment progresses, initial attempts at control often break down; thus written productions of such a child characteristically reflect a progressive deterioration of graphomotor performance. Increasing sloppiness, work overs, and crossouts are noted as the quality of work gradually erodes. These children often show many "battle scars" from various accidents associated with poor coordination which is, of course, combined with their impulsivity. While many of these children do have trouble with fine-motor coordination, they may have little difficulty with gross-motor skills

POOR COORDINATION

Parents may say:

He's so clumsy.
I've been told her coordination is OK, but she moves so differently.
It took a long time to learn how to bat a ball.

Teachers may say:

She's the last one to be picked for a game.
His writing is so messy, yet I know he does his best.
If there was one brick out on the playground, he'd trip over it.

and may actually excel in some sports. In such cases, their talents out of the classroom may serve as a balance for their many failures in the classroom.

Memory Problems

This characteristic is often reflected in difficulty with working memory, the memory function that is active and relevant for short periods of time (i.e., something that one wishes to say when it's his turn to speak, or remembering to bring the right key to unlock the tool chest). Other examples of this problem might be forgetting things in daily routines such as needed books or tools for a project, or even difficulty in recalling learned material and in memorizing. In some cases, these memory difficulties may be attributed to the child's being distracted and thus not remembering what he hasn't paid attention to.

> **MEMORY PROBLEMS**
>
> *Parents may say:*
>
> He's lost two footballs and his jacket.
> She can't seem to remember where she puts things.
> He's a magician—he does his homework, but it disappears before school.
>
> *Teachers may say:*
>
> I tell him the assignment and he does something else.
> If I send him on an errand, I have to write down what I want.
> She seems to lose information so quickly.

Persistent Obsessive Thinking

This characteristic implies that once the child gets an idea in his mind, there is difficulty in letting it drop. For example, if the child requests something to eat just before supper and is told no, he may continue to nag the parent with a number of similar requests. An almost endless number of requests, questions, etc., are made, continuing long after most children would have gotten the message to let it go and to go on to something else. This problem may be intimately tied into a child's difficulty in reading or in misreading social cues. In short, the child simply does not get the message from the parent even after numerous repetitions of saying "no" or providing answers.

Inconsistency

This is perhaps the hallmark characteristic of ADD/ADHD. Basically, a child is described by parents and teachers alike as having good days and bad days. On some days, he may complete all assigned work, on other days, none. Often, this pattern itself sets the child up for failure. Dr. Russell Barkley has eloquently stated, "The child with ADD/ADHD succeeds one time and we hold it against him for the rest of his life." Parents may often wonder if their child has a "split personality," since his performance is so inconsistent. Such fluctuations may coincide with the variability of underlying physiological processes, which, in turn, are affected by many factors both internal and external. Since inconsistency is a "hallmark" characteristic, it may come up in many situations; it will therefore be discussed in several sections of future chapters.

Related to this characteristic of inconsistency is the notion that these children also seem to have much difficulty with change and transitions. It is not uncommon for

PERSISTENT OBSESSIVE THINKING

Parents may say:

He never seems satisfied with what he gets.
She never stops asking questions.
He keeps asking for things one after another even when he is told no.

Teachers may say:

I sometimes hate to tell him about a special event; he drives me crazy with questions.
He's got a million questions, but they're on the same topic.
Once she has an idea, she can't seem to let go of it.

INCONSISTENCY

Parents may say:

He's got good and bad days.
I think he's got a Jekyll & Hyde personality.
I never know what to expect from her.

Teachers may say:

One day he does all his work; the next day, none.
Sometimes I think he missed his medication.
I don't know what to expect from one day to the next.

teachers to observe an increase in behavioral problems in a child who is generally well-controlled on medications but is experiencing change in his life:

1. significant changes in the family, such as marital separation or divorce
2. some seemingly minor change such as resetting the clock forward one hour for spring
3. change that might normally be perceived as "good" (e.g., One child became very upset and cried when his parents traded their old car for a new one.)

An interesting computerized program called ADD Mazement is offered by Goldstein and Cornacchio (1996). General information about ADD/ADHD is provided across various domains of home and school activities at different developmental levels. For example, a parent or teacher may review what behavior or problems may be expected from the ADD/ADHD child during activities such as sleeping, eating, or toileting (for pre-school children). Behavioral expectations for other developmental levels are illustrated. Resources and suggestions for coping with various problem areas are also provided.

BIOLOGICAL BASES FOR ADD/ADHD

Over the past 25 years, much has been learned about the neurobiological bases for ADD/ADHD, beginning with the early work of Satterfield and Dawson on psychological parameters, up to the current work on Brain Imaging. Integration of research from several disciplines, including genetic studies, neuroanatomical evidence, and neuropsychological findings all point to strong biological bases for ADD/ADHD that has a genetic cause.

The following summarizes what we now know about the biological bases for ADD/ADHD. Sources for the various studies cited are presented in the Bibliography at the end of the *Handbook* organized by chapter and topic.

Please note that the material in this section is of a technical nature and may be of interest to those readers who desire an update on neurobiological information. It is not, however, essential to those who are primarily interested in behavioral and other clinical techniques in diagnosis and treatment of ADD/ADHD.

Genetic Evidence

A comprehensive review by Lily Hechtman, M.D. suggested a genetic component for ADD/ADHD based on studies of twins, adopted children, and children in families where there is a history of ADD/ADHD. The importance of genetic factors was also noted by Cantwell, who reported that 35 percent of the parents of children with ADD/ADHD had a history of alcoholism, hysteria, and antisocial personality as compared to only 10 percent of normal controls. However, in the 1970s, hyperactivity was often confounded with Oppositional Defiant Disorder (ODD). In Cantwell's report, fathers and uncles of ADD children were implicated as having related ADD problems more than other relatives. Another early study by Morrison and Stewart found that 20 percent of the hyperactive children versus only 5 percent of controls had a parent with a childhood history of hyperactive behavior, but that approximately one-third of the parents of hyperactive youngsters carried a psychiatric diagnosis such as alcoholism, antisocial personality, and hysteria. While this suggested that ADHD is familial, there were questions about whether the association is genetically or environmentally based. Twin studies indicate greater concordance in monozygotic versus dizygotic twins for different behavioral characteristics of ADD/ADHD. In general, these twin studies support a genetic etiology. In studies of siblings with half sibs, Welner and associates found that hyperactivity was more common among brothers of hyperactive children than among brothers of controls. An early study found a significant difference between full and half sibs with about 50 percent of the full sibs having ADHD compared to only 10 percent of the half sibs.

Adoption studies also support a genetic linkage. Likewise, family studies suggest that confounding of ADHD with conduct disorder may be associated with greater related pathology in parents. Faraone and associates showed that the risk of a child having an antisocial disorder is much higher if the first-degree relative has conduct or oppositional disorders. A comprehensive family study by Biderman found a higher incidence of ADD, ODD and depression in first-degree relatives of ADHD children. There is also a surprising link between familial ADHD and anxiety disorders. A recent study by Roizen found increased rates of alcoholism (16 percent), depression (14 percent), substance abuse (12 percent), and learning disability (21 percent) in first-degree relatives of ADHD kids versus kids with Down's Syndrome who had no more than 4 percent of these problems. These findings do suggest family-genetic influences in the ADD/ADHD pattern.

However, there have been numerous criticisms and obvious limitations of these studies. Specifically, family studies must often depend upon reliable recall by participants and most of these cases may be biased with regard to selectivity factors. For example, more severe cases of ADHD may come to medical centers where these studies are conducted. Twin studies are limited in that results are difficult to generalize to nontwins. In addition, twins have increased prenatal risk and the shared fetal environment. Adoption studies also reflect a selectivity bias in that adoptive parents are often screened out for psychopathology, and with adopted children there may be unknown factors associated with poor prenatal care, low birth weight, diet, and so on.

With regard to the mode of inheritance of the ADD/ADHD behavioral complex, most theorize that the disorder is not due to a single gene effect. Several different genes, some of which interact—along with environmental factors—are believed to contribute to manifestations of the ADD/ADHD complex pattern.

Gaultheria has offered a "two stage model" to synthesize both genetic and brain damage factors. The first stage comprises children who have ADD due to genetic factors, primarily characterized by a polygenic inheritance pattern. This implies that a number of individual genes contribute to the condition, with severity also being a function of the number of genes involved. A second stage of this model has its etiology in brain damage associated with some type of birth trauma during the first year of life. These children, fewer in number than the first group, are similar to the genetic group behaviorally, yet some of their behaviors are thought to show a differential response to treatment and perhaps an adverse reaction to stimulant medication. However, as most clinicians surmise, it would be difficult to find pure cases of ADD/ADHD because there are so many variations and so many associated factors.

A genetic deficit known as the Fragile X syndrome has been associated with ADD. A fragile site on Q27 of the X chromosome has been found in Fragile X, a condition that has associated factors of learning disability, possibly mental retardation, and/or attentional problems. However, there is no direct evidence that this gene is also responsible for ADD characteristics in general. In 1993, a study on the Resistance to Thyroid Hormone (RTH) was initially thought to be the genetic link to ADD/ADHD. Hause found ADHD in patients with RTH. This study compared people in the families of those with ADHD to those without ADHD and noted that 70 percent of the children with RTH had ADHD, compared with 50 percent of the parents. However, RTH is a rare disorder and no one knew how many children with ADHD had RTH.

In molecular genetic approaches, an excellent candidate gene has been discovered. Irwin Wallman and others found preferential transmission of the Dopamine transporter 10 copy allele in ADHD combined type which was not found with the basically inattentive type (ADD). This is the first replicated linkage found in a childhood neuropsychiatric disorder. Wallman's study specifically pointed out that this gene previously described contributes less than 25 percent susceptibility to ADHD. Consequently, there are many other factors besides this identified gene to be considered.

In summary, genetic tests (when developed) may still not replace the behavioral criteria that are now used to diagnose ADD/ADHD. However, these genetic tests may help to clarify and subtype ADD/ADHD patterns and may eventually lead to novel and more specific treatments.

Neuroanatomical Evidence

In 1987, Mirsky noted that attention has distinct and separate aspects including focusing, executing, sustaining, and shifting. He indicated that each of these aspects of attention may involve different but interconnected regions of the brain that form a system. Problems with different aspects of attention may thus depend on where in this system of the brain the damage or dysfunction occurs.

Likewise, Flick, using the model of attentional processes formulated by Solberg and Mateer, states that "a child may have one or more of these difficulties (in focused, sustained, selective, alternating and divided attention) and there may be different complex neurobiological correlates for each condition." Numerous areas of the brain have been implicated as noted in a review of the literature. In recent years, technological advances have spawned a new wave of investigations. Early studies with CT scans using Xenon inhalation to demonstrate hypoperfusion in striatal regions of the brains in ADHD children, confirmed low striatal activity primarily in the right hemisphere. There was also less activity in the orbital prefrontal regions, again on the right side more than the left. These areas of the brain involving the striatum have been known to be important in the areas of attention as well as behavioral inhibition. Using newer technology that avoids use of ionizing radiation, studies have shown hypofusion in the right caudate which, upon optimal dose of methylphenidate, was reversed. Decreased blood flow has been found in the striatum as well as in prefrontal areas. See Figure 1.1 on page 16 to refer to specific areas of the brain mentioned in this section including the basal ganglia.* In a classic work, Zametkin studied glucose metabolism using positive emission tomography (PET) scans of 25 biological parents of hyperactive children, who gave retrospective histories of childhood hyperactivity. No medications were known to be given to this group in childhood. After normalization of glucose metabolic rates (to minimize individual variation of global glucose metabolism affecting ergional metabolism), the premotor and prefrontal cortex (left hemisphere only) showed significantly reduced glucose metabolism. Clearly, this study had methodological difficulties as diagnosis of ADHD (adults) was based only on retrospective reports.

As noted by Colby, damage anywhere in the system that provides direct or indirect cortical control over eye movements could produce the oculomotor symptoms found in ADD. He further points out that "visual hemi-neglect" is associated with deficits in eye movements." Recent studies indicate that children with ADD also show evidence of neglect."

Recent reports by Rapaport on brain imaging studies at the National Institutes of Mental Health indicate a smaller anterior frontal area and a lack of asymmetry in parts of the basal ganglia (caudate and globus pallidus). In normal children, the right side appears larger than the left; in hyperactive children there is a lack of this asymmetry. Hyperactives also reportedly have a smaller total cerebral volume. Predictive studies using these measurements alone have correctly identified, solely by the computer, with about 78 percent accuracy, correct group classification as normal or hyperactive. While these data may not be useful clinically, they are reliable and have been replicated. Dr. Rapaport has postulated that something may happen during early development of the brain of the ADD/ADHD child. Subsequent studies looking at those children who were on stimulant medication versus those who were not on stimulant medication revealed similar findings. This indicated that the use of stimulant medication did not affect the asymmetry of the basal ganglia and that this neu-

* Reprinted with permission from Van Zomeren & Branwer *Clinical Neuropsychology of Attention* (1994).

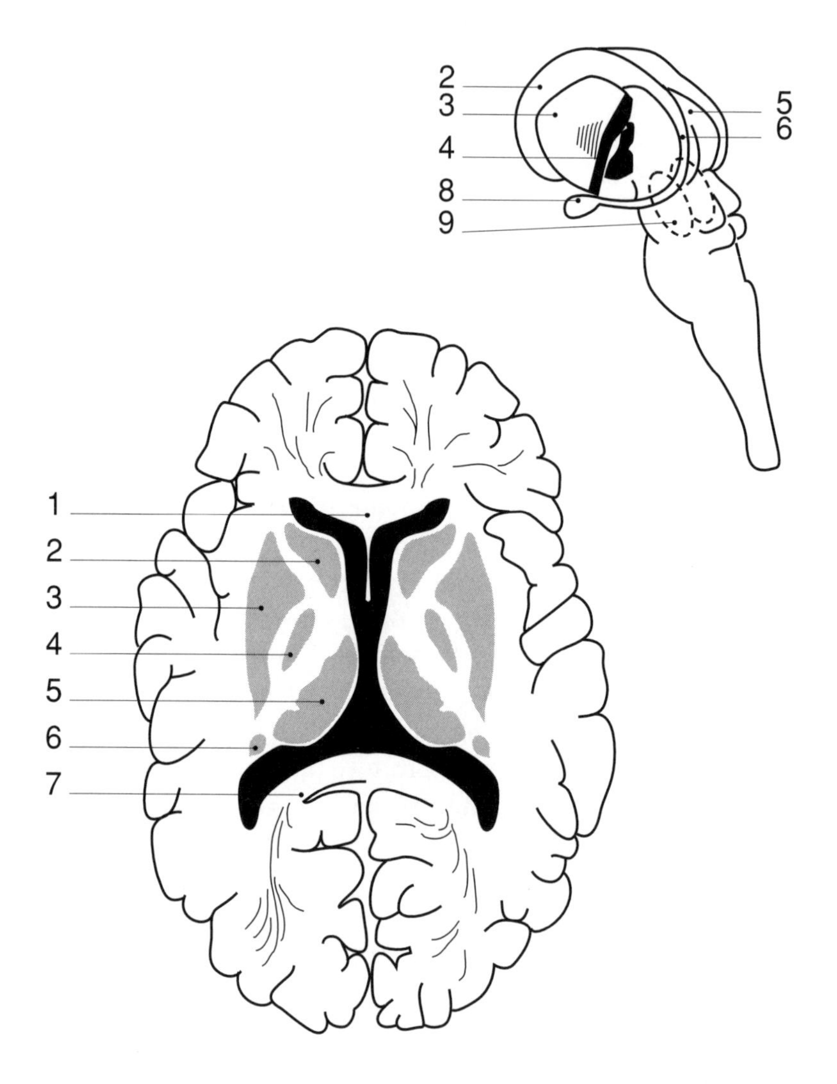

Figure 1.1* The basal ganglia, shown in a horizontal plane and in a three-dimensional view from the left. 1, genu of corpus callosum; 2, head of caudate nucleus; 3, putamen; 4, globus pallidus; 5, thalamus; 6, tail of caudate nucleus; 7, splenium of corpus callosum; 8, amygdala; 9, substantia nigra. Reprinted with permission.

---

*From *Clinical Neuropsychology of Attention* by Adriaan Hivan Zomeren and Wiebo H. Brouwer. Copyright © 1994 by Oxford University Press, Inc. Used by permission of Oxford University Press, Inc.

roanatomical difference appears to be generally characteristic of the ADHD pattern in males. Similar findings have been reported in females with ADD/ADHD. Additional studies have also revealed more space in the posterior fossa in hyperactive versus normal controls, and MRI studies of brain function while engaged in a reverse Continuous Performance Test (CPT) reveals activation in the prefrontal brain regions that occur during this behavioral inhibition task, that is, asking the child to refrain from pressing a button only when the target stimulus (the letter X) appears.

Castellanos and colleagues, using the MRI, discovered that normal boys showed a significant asymmetry of the caudate with the right side three percent larger than the left, on the average. In contrast, ADHD boys showed no asymmetry. Researchers also reported that the right prefrontal brain region was significantly smaller in ADHD boys compared to normals, while the left side was not different from normals. In addition, the globus pallidus was found to be significantly smaller especially on the right side. There have also been a number of reports of abnormalities in the corpus callosum. These studies reportedly support Heilman and colleagues' (1991) prediction of right sided abnormalities of the prefrontal basal ganglia circuit in cases of ADHD. In general, there is apparently a greater degree of dysfunction within the right hemisphere of the brain in ADHD. It is proffered that prior studies showing left sided differences may have reflected a higher percentage of co-morbid LD problems in those cases used.

Neuropsychological Evidence

Chelune noted that the prefrontal regions have reciprocal pathways with the reticular formation and diencephalic structures that mediate arousal and behavioral inhibition to irrelevant stimuli. Comparison of normal controls with children who manifest ADD/ADHD symptoms on the Wisconsin Card Sorting Test supported frontal lobe dysfunction in ADD/ADHD children. A battery of tests was used that not only looked at frontal lobe functions, but also included a variety of other measures of IQ, reading skills, and verbal memory, as well as an assessment of attentional and impulsivity factors. The postulate, that disturbances in frontal lobe functions may be related to impulse control and responsible for the kind of cognitive impairments typically found with ADHD, was supported. The conclusion was that inability to control, direct, and sustain attention appears as a core deficiency of ADHD and not impulsivity. Additional studies have also revealed deficits in children with ADD/ADHD that are compatible with frontal lobe dysfunction.

Neurochemical Evidence

Shaywitz and associates were first to propose a dopamine hypothesis for ADD/ADHD in 1977. A number of more recent studies support the involvement of dopamine in ADD/ADHD.

The noradrenergic system has also been implicated in ADD/ADHD. McCraken suggested that stimulant medication increases dopamine release and results in an increase in adrenergic mediated inhibition of the noradrenergic locus coeruleus. This interpretation allows for combined reaction of both dopamine and norepinephrine systems. There is little evidence for the involvement of serotonin in ADHD. In addition to dopamine and norepinephrine, other neurotransmitters may be involved in ADD/ADHD, but may be less important.

Castellanos (1997) has proposed a pathophysiological model of ADHD that is based on central dopaminergic systems and their regulation of prefrontal circuits. He and his colleagues believe that ADHD symptoms such as hyperactivity and impulsivity are associated with the relative overactivity of the dopamine circuit (extending from the substantia nigra to the striatum). "This nigral-striatal circuit is tightly regulated by inhibitory auto-receptors as well as by long-distance feedback from the cortex, and slow diffusion of therapeutic doses of stimulants via oral administration is hypothesized to produce a net inhibition of dopaminergic neurotransmission.

Offering an interesting conclusion, Castellanos (1997) notes that "the attention paid in this review to pharmacologic effects on neuronal circuits should not be interpreted as implying that ADHD is exclusively treatable with medications." He notes that, "Behavior Modification schedules increase the salience of socially sanctioned responses, thus increasing the likelihood that specific midbrain dopaminergic neurons will be activated, leading to better control of hyperactivity/impulsivity. At the cortical level, coaching cognitive strategies (Graham and Harris, 1996) can assist in the amelioration of executive dysfunction associated with the symptoms of inattention."

BRIEF HISTORY OF ATTENTION DEFICIT DISORDER

Prevalence

According to recent research, ADD and ADHD are reported to be the most frequently occurring neurobehavioral disorders of childhood. ADHD accounts for most mental health referrals of children, especially with associated Conduct Disorder (CD) problems. The incidence of this condition has been estimated in from 1 to 10 percent of *all* school-age children (where the prevalence rates are associated with the specific diagnostic criteria used). Some research estimates the incidence of ADHD as high as 20 percent of all school-age children. However, when using the criteria of DSM-III R and DSM-IV, the condition is estimated to occur in 3 to 5 percent of all school-age children (APA, 1987). In the prekindergarten and kindergarten age groups, Campbell noted that from 14 to 20 percent of the boys and approximately 5% to 7% of the girls have ADHD. Such variation in reported prevalence rates appears to reflect lack of standardization of the research reporting criteria indicating that (a) different diagnostic criteria may be used; (b) methods of assessment may vary; (c) cultural factors may not be considered; (d) age variation may not be recognized; and (e) sex variation may be ignored. ADD characteristics change with associated developmental changes of normal maturation from preschool age through adulthood. These changes in ADD characteristics also vary somewhat for each sex. It is interesting to observe that the greater reported incidence of ADHD in boys has been explained by noting that girls with ADHD show evidence of and cause of fewer problems than boys. Thus ADHD in girls may go unreported. Those children who create the most havoc in the classroom (most often boys) are the ones who get referred for evaluation. Barkley (1995) has further noted that the need to demonstrate these syndromes in two out of three environments "should go unheeded." This suggests a higher priority for those behaviors noted in school versus other situations.

Barkley has also noted some rather eye-opening statistics regarding ADHD. He notes that more than 20 percent have set serious fires, 30 percent have engaged in theft, 40 percent have used tobacco and alcohol at an early age, and 25 percent were expelled from high school due to their misconduct. Furthermore, he indicates that adolescents with ADHD were four times more likely to have serious auto accidents (causing bodily harm) and three times more likely to be cited for speeding.

Nosological Evolution

The term ADHD has literally evolved from its historical roots. Over time various terms have been used to describe the symptoms comprising ADD/ADHD, but this basic constellation of symptoms has been reported for many, many years.

HISTORICAL PERSPECTIVE

Descriptions of ADD/ADHD date to the Grecian Age. As noted by Goldstein and Goldstein (1990), "The Greek physician Galen was known to prescribe opium for restless colicky infants." In 1845 the German poet Hoffman published *Fidgety Phil* which described a child with impulsivity and motor overactivity. While such difficulties were noted in cases involving both trauma and other brain injuries, physicians noticed a similar pattern of inattentive, restless, and overaroused behavior in patients without a history of trauma.

At the turn of the century, an English doctor, G. R. Still, described the behaviors that we now call ADD/ADHD as "abnormal defects in moral control," and he attributed this to brain injury, genetics, or other environmental/medical conditions. He also noted a higher incidence in males. Dr. Still gave a poor prognosis for these children and recommended residential placement for many.

In 1908 Tredgold thought that children who experienced mild anoxia or brain damage at birth might later manifest problems when faced with the demands of the classroom. This concept of noting the effects of brain damage without its evidence was the precursor of *Minimal Brain Damage.*

Early in the 20th Century, following a severe outbreak of encephalitis in 1918, several researchers described problems of attention, impulsivity, and hyperactivity in many children who had encephalitis. In 1935, Childers attempted to differentiate the hyperactive child from those with brain damage. He reported that only a small number of hyperactive children actually suffered from brain damage.

During World War II, there were many patients with head injuries who manifested attentional problems, restlessness, and, at times, impulsive behavior. Research on such patients provided further evidence for the proposed link between hyperactivity and brain damage. Strauss and Lehtinen (1947) inferred brain damage from behavioral signs (e.g., hyperactivity) and made recommendations regarding special education procedures on this basis. Assuming that these children were flooded with stimulation resulting in an outflow of motor activity, they suggested making classrooms devoid of any stimulation. However, such sterile environments only *seemed* to make such children even more active.

In 1937, Bradley used the amphetamine Benzedrine™ to treat headaches, assuming that relief would come through increased blood pressure. However, he noted that there was a dramatic change in the behavior and school performance of many of these children. Their attention improved and the improvements were clearly dose dependent. Others reported improved performance on IQ tests for those children given Benzedrine™. However, at this time in the '30s, many doctors questioned such use of stimulant medications for hyperactive behavior.

Around 1950, when doctors began to recognize the potential for treatment of these behaviors with stimulant medications, there also began a primary focus on minimal brain dysfunction/damage (MBD). Hyperactivity was still the primary concern, with attentional problems and impulsivity being secondary. The MBD syndrome then came to be referred to as a "hyperkinetic-impulsive disorder." This was later shortened to "hyperkinetic syndrome" by the World Health Organization. In 1968, the American Psychiatric Association adopted the term "Hyperkinetic Reaction of Childhood" during the mid- to-late-1960s. Most researchers of that time felt that the disorder was no longer attributed solely to brain damage, although there was increasing interest in the underlying brain mechanism for the disorder.

During the 1970s, this disorder, once described primarily as a problem of overactivity, was now more broadly defined to include impulsivity, short attention, low frustration tolerance, distractibility, and associated aggressiveness. By the end of 1970, there were over 2,000 published studies in this area. In 1972, Virginia Douglas and Susan Campbell began the era of "Attention Deficit" and used that term when they reported research to the APA showing children who could experience problems with sustained attention even in the absence of distractions.

CURRENT DSM IV CRITERIA

The criteria established to diagnose ADD/ADHD are published by the American Psychiatric Association in the *Diagnostic and Statistical Manual of Mental Disorders,*

Fourth Edition. The formulation in the fourth edition represents improvement over that in the past edition (*DSM III-R*) with regard to the selection of specific items used. However, there still are problems since these diagnostic entities are formulated by a committee. As committees change so too do diagnostic criteria, items and nosology change. Many revisions in definitions have occurred and more are expected in future editions. There is also a problem in that Categories I and III, while different diagnostically, have been given the same diagnostic code. Clearly, the various ADD/ADHD behaviors are real; the diagnoses, however, have been created by consensus and majority rule. The preponderance of diagnostic descriptions about ADD/ADHD as well as most co-morbid conditions have been adapted with permission from the DSM IV.

DSM IV Diagnostic Features

There are three main behavioral dimensions of ADHD: inattention, impulsivity, and hyperactivity, although the *DSM IV* reduces them to two: inattention and hyperactivity/impulsivity. Diagnostic classification thus results from the presence of either one of these two dimensions or of both combined (Criterion A). In Criterion B there is a stipulation that these symptoms must be present prior to 7 years of age. To meet Criterion C these symptoms must impair one's functioning in more than one setting, that is, school, home, or work (adult). For Criterion D there must be evidence that one is impaired socially, academically, or occupationally. In Criterion E, the clinician must be able to rule out the presence of other disorders that might account for these symptoms, including—without limitation—pervasive developmental disorder, schizophrenia or other psychiatric disorder as well as mood disorder, anxiety disorder, dissociative disorder, and personality disorder.

Now further examine Criterion A wherein inattention, impulsivity, and hyperactivity may all be present.

Criterion A (1), inattention, involves the following:

a. Details may be ignored and careless mistakes are made. In some cases this may relate to a tendency to rush through work.

b. Attention span is short, often due to the tendency to be distracted. Tasks, or even play activities, are not completed, and the child or adult may shift from one incomplete activity to another.

c. Sometimes persons with ADD appear to be "in a fog," often failing to comprehend what is spoken to them. They may get bits and pieces of the message and respond inappropriately at times based only on the information they did get.

d. Although there is adequate understanding of a task and no general evidence of oppositional tendencies, there is difficulty following through with requests.

e. There is also difficulty with organization where planning, sequencing, and categorization are needed.

f. Major problems are noted on tasks requiring sustained effort, especially school or homework. Rushing to complete such work or deviously avoiding it are characteristic.

g. One avoidance technique is to lose things needed to complete homework or other tasks; however, noticeably this is not limited to unpleasant tasks.

h. There is also much difficulty ignoring nonrelevant stimuli; both relevant and nonrelevant stimuli appear to generate equivalent attentional responses.

i. Appointments are missed, or attended late; when appointments are kept, the person may forget critical material, for example, rushing out to go play football but forgetting where the ball is.

Criterion A(2), hyperactivity, refers to overactivity inappropriate for the child's age or developmental level, or for the situation. Hyperactivity has been characterized by the following: fidgeting or squirming while seated, getting out of one's seat; running or climbing in situations where it is not appropriate; having difficulty engaging in quiet leisure activities; appearing as if "driven by a motor," and excessive talking. Hyperactivity is sometimes difficult to assess in young children from behavioral observations alone. Adolescents and adults even with ADD alone (Attention Deficit Disorder Without Hyperactivity) typically show a diminished activity level but may manifest some hyperactivity in the form of restlessness (e.g., shaking leg) or having general difficulty complying with the requirements of the more sedentary activities.

Criterion A(2), impulsivity, basically means "acting before thinking." It may be exhibited when answers are blurted out before questions are completed or by impatience in having to wait one's turn in line, to play a game, or to express oneself. This interruption of someone's conversation or intruding on someone's work or play may create problems in play, academic, social, or work situations. Impulsive responding is a failure of self-control that often leads to social ostracism or to serious accidents caused by failure to pause and consider potentially dangerous consequences.

In novel and uncommon situations these behavioral symptoms may be minimal or even absent, for instance, while the child is engaged in interesting or stimulating activities, in one-to-one situations, or in highly unstructured settings. It is in the most common, everyday situations that these symptoms are most likely to occur, as for instance during group settings, where there are strict rules and where lengthy, and at times monotonous work may be required.

It is quite atypical for adults or children to exhibit ADD/ADHD characteristics only. Children show a wider range of associated features, and both adults and children sometimes exhibit co-morbid conditions or additional characteristics. (Co-morbid conditions are addressed later in this section.) Some additional characteristics associated with ADD are behavioral and physical features.

BEHAVIORAL FEATURES

Behavioral features exhibited with ADD/ADHD include low-frustration tolerance, temper problems, stubbornness, persistence, emotional liability, depression, peer rejection, poor self-concept and poor self-esteem—which ones and to what degree these are manifested vary according to developmental status and age, and with gender. Nonetheless, a common component seen in many ADD/ADHD children is devaluation and dislike of academics (probably because of the behavior constraints, though, not necessarily the learning process itself). Parents and teachers often perceive the ADD/ADHD child as lazy and lacking in responsibility; and that child is frequently known to be resistant to change—even a positive change. For such children, much conflict may occur with parents and other authority figures since much of their oppositional behavior is viewed inaccurately as outright disobedience. It is rare, however, for a child, especially an older child, to exhibit ADD/ADHD characteristics only. Because of the numerous problems encountered, the ADD child may also develop many *learned* inappropriate behaviors which then are associated with the biologically based ADD/ADHD behaviors.

PHYSICAL FEATURES

Most individuals with ADD/ADHD are unrecognizable by their physical features since so few physical features are actually characteristic of ADD. These minor physical anomalies include deviation in eye size from the norm (the eyes being either larger or smaller than average), low set ears, a highly arched palate, abnormal distance between the first and second toes, and abnormal palm creases. However, it should be emphasized that many children having these physical features do *not* manifest ADD. It has simply been noted that *with* ADD these physical features are often present. Consequently, such signs should only be used as supportive evidence.

CO-MORBIDITY/MIMIC SYNDROMES

Numerous psychological and medical/neurological conditions are often associated with ADD/ADHD and must be considered in making a differential diagnosis. Often these other conditions may share symptoms with ADD/ADHD or may involve ADD-like behaviors. Some of the potential overlaps with other diagnostic conditions are shown in Figure 1.2 on page 24. This list of overlapping symptoms demonstrates that quite often the clinician is presented with a very complex symptom picture. The clinician must be able to determine the primary condition and sort out what may be secondary or tertiary (i.e., co-morbid) conditions. The clinician must also be able to distinguish between ADD/ADHD symptomology and other conditions that mimic ADD behavioral symptoms. Following are two lists—one of medical conditions and the other of psychological conditions that may be co-morbid with ADHD or that may be considered in differential diagnosis. These lists are followed by in-depth discussions of ADD associated with medical conditions and ADD associated with psychological conditions.

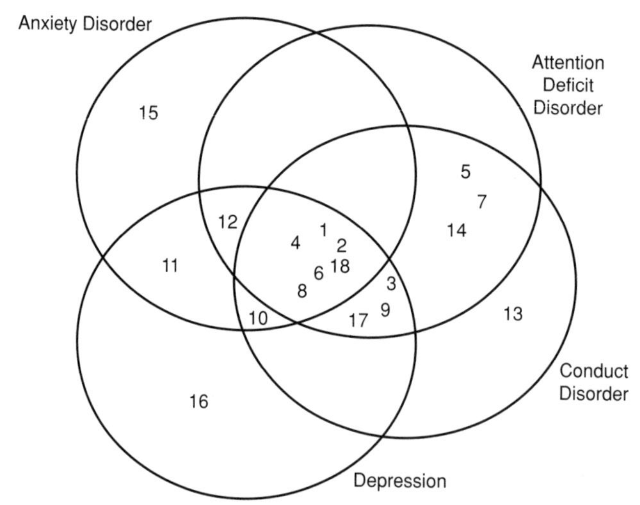

	Symptomatic Behavioral Characteristic	Attention Deficit Disorder	Anxiety Disorder	Depression	Conduct Disorder
1	Poor Concentration	X	X	X	X
2	Restless	X	X	?	X
3	Fails to Complete Tasks	X		X	X
4	Day Dreams	X	X	X	X
5	Impulsive	X			X
6	Poor Sleep	X	X	X	X
7	Aggressive	?		?	X
8	Mood Disturbance	X	X	X	X
9	Poor Self Concept	X		X	X
10	Quiet and Withdrawn	?		X	
11	Guilt Over Transgressions		X	X	
12	Memory Problems	X	X	X	
13	Stealing/Lying				X
14	Poor Social Skills	X			X
15	Fearful/Avoidance	?	X	?	
16	Crying	?	?	X	
17	Sensation Seeking (High Risk)	X		?	X
18	Difficulty Focusing on Task	X	?	?	?

Key: X = Symptom Usually Present
? = Symptom Possible
Blank = Symptom Not Usually Present

Figure 1.2 Overlaps with Other Conditions

*Mimic Syndromes and **Medical** Conditions Co-Morbid with ADD*

Reaction to Anticonvulsants (Phenobarbital/Dilantin)
Reaction to Theophylline (for Asthma)
Tourette's Syndrome
Movement Disorder—Sydenham's Chorea
Epilepsy
Narcolepsy
Structural Brain Lesion
Sleep Apnea
Head Trauma
Otitis Media
Anemia
Fragile-X Syndrome
Sinusitis
Pinworms
Thyroid Disorder
Isoniazid
Lead

*Mimic Syndromes and **Psychological** Conditions Co-Morbid with ADD*

Adjustment Disorder
Anxiety Disorder
Depression/Dysthymia
Bipolar Disorder
Mental Retardation
Learning Disability
Conduct Disorder
Oppositional Defiant Disorder
Obsessive Compulsive Disorder

ADD/ADHD ASSOCIATED WITH MEDICAL CONDITIONS

Numerous medical conditions and certain medications used to treat some medical conditions may cause impairment of attention (resulting in changes in one's degree of alertness) and movement functions (resulting in increased motor activity), or may compromise one's judgment (so as to make one's responses appear impulsive).

Some medications quite effectively treat a medical problem for a child without ADD, but exacerbate the ADD behavior in the child with ADD. *Anticonvulsants* may cause even more problems for the ADD child who also suffers from seizures. Phenobarbital and other anticonvulsants like clonazepam, phenytoin and dilantin, may further depress Reticular Activating System (RAS) activity and may generate more severe ADD behaviors.

Conversely, some drugs may cause ADD-like behaviors in a child without ADD. In particular, Isoniazid, an *anti-tuberculosis drug,* may cause a form of anemia and has effects upon the nervous system similar to lead toxins: In addition to dizziness, weakness, headaches, and nausea, its use may result in cerebral dysfunction, causing some ADD-like behaviors.

Allergy and asthma medications (e.g., Theophylline and Atarax) have been shown to sometimes cause or worsen attentional problems, hyperactivity and some behavior problems regardless of the presence or absence of ADD. These medications may also make ADD behavior worse in ADD children and they may generate ADD-like behavior in children who do not have ADD.

The Center for Disease Control has indicated that *lead* is the number one environmental health threat in the United States. However, in Conners' Risk Model, protective factors may counteract some toxic effects. Specifically, Conners points out that diets rich in calcium and iron may block the absorption of lead and thus prevent the typical hyperactivity that may result from ingestion of lead. The concept of the "risk model" may thus explain why some children exposed to toxic substances may not get sick or show a "typical" or expected response.

Medical conditions associated with ADD/ADHD include the following:

Tourette's Syndrome—One of the "tic" disorders that usually occur prior to 18 years of age and is characterized by sudden, involuntary and recurrent specific movements and vocalizations. These tic movements and vocal emissions may change over time and typically include such things as grunting, hissing, barking, whistling, sniffing, snorting, and clearing of the throat. Blatant cursing occurs in about half of these cases. ADHD occurs in about half of the children with Tourette's. Symptoms of Tourette's are sometimes brought on by the administration of stimulant medications used to treat ADHD symptoms. In other cases Tourette's Syndrome would have appeared whether or not stimulant medications were used.

Ear Infections—Clinically, many children with ADD/ADHD appear to have a history of ear infections with high fevers. When such ear infections occur within the first two years of life, there may be an interruption of development in the brain and nervous system for specific functions that relate to symptomatic ADD/ADHD behavior; motoric and attentional control problems may thus develop.

Narcolepsy—Narcolepsy is a disorder characterized by sleep attacks and symptoms of rapid eye movements occurring at inappropriate times during the day. This is considered an abnormality of the brainstem property of Rapid Eye Movement (REM) sleep and overrides the right-brain function of vigilance or wakefulness. An inherited disorder in children, this condition is different from the sleepy state often observed in ADD/ADHD children as shown by the lack of clinical manifestations of abnormal REM activity such as hypnotic hallucinations, sleep paralysis, and cataplexy (i.e., loss of muscle tone without loss of consciousness). However, it is interesting that the primary treatment for narcolepsy has involved the use of stimulant medications.

Anemia—This condition is defined by a reduction in the number of circulating red blood cells or in hemoglobin, or in the volume of packed red cells per 100 ml. of blood, or in a combination of two or more of these factors (*Taber's Medical Dictionary*). Symptoms of anemia may include dizziness, drowsiness, headache, as well as other autonomic nervous system symptoms that may appear as "arousal problems." As noted by Goldstein and Goldstein, studies have correlated anemia with "personality disturbance, conduct problems, feelings of inadequacy and immaturity."

Fragile-X Syndrome—This is a chromosomal disorder associated with a fragile site on the end of the X chromosome. It is the second most common cause of mental retardation with mostly males being affected and females as potential carriers. Associated learning and attentional problems have been noted clinically and reported by Hapermann and associates in a 1985 study. However, since only four cases were studied, little can be generalized to children with ADD/ADHD. Symptoms of Fragile-X include a prominent nose and jaw, long ears, and epileptic seizures along with impairments of interest, attention, and behavior.

Movement Disorders—A simple chorea, such as Sydenham's Chorea, is characterized by irregular involuntary movements of the face and extremities that may appear one to six months after a streptococcal infection. This condition may be accompanied by irritability as well as obsessive and compulsive symptoms, some of which could be confused with symptoms of ADD/ADHD.

Thyroid Dysfunction—Hyperthyroidism is caused by excessive secretion of the thyroid glands which increases the basal-metabolic rate. Symptoms of hyperthyroidism that may be mistaken for ADD/ADHD include tremor, increased nervousness (overactivity) and signs of autonomic nervous system activity (e.g., sweating and rapid heart beat).

Sleep Apnea—According to Stoudemire, there are two types of sleep apnea (SA)—obstructive SA and central SA. In obstructive SA, the pharyngeal walls collapse repetitively during sleep causing intermittent upper airway obstruction and cessation in ventilation or apneas. In central SA, cessation of ventilation is related to loss of inspiratory effort. The major symptoms of sleep apnea include loud snoring, pauses in respiration during sleep, daytime hypersomnolence, weight gain and disturbed sleep, and deficits in attention, motor efficiency, and psychomotor ability. Findley reported problems in concentration, complex problem solving and short term recall, all related to the severity of hypoxemia (insufficient oxygenation of the blood).

Sinusitis—Similar to sleep apnea, sinus infections may result in decreased airflow through the nasal passages and result in some of the same symptoms as those of sleep apnea. Likewise, one may expect to see decreased alertness manifested by poor attention and perhaps overactivity, due to hypoxemia.

Pinworms—Pinworms infect the lower small intestine and large bowel and often produce anal itching and result in restlessness or overactivity. Obviously, this may also serve as a distraction for the child making it difficult for him or her to engage in activities with sustained attention.

Head Injury—The National Head Injury Foundation defines traumatic brain injury as "an insult to the brain, not of degenerative or congenital nature, but caused by external force, that may produce a diminished or altered state of consciousness." Problems with attention have been noted in numerous studies on children and adolescents who have suffered head trauma. Likewise both hyperactivity and attention problems have been noted by parents of head-injured children. Problems with sustained attention and performance speed also have been noted. Of course, many other cognitive skills may be affected by a head injury, including intellectual performance, motor skills, visual-motor skills, language, memory and academic skills.

Epilepsy—Even when anticonvulsant medications are used appropriately to treat epilepsy, there is still the continuing possibility that seizures may recur. Seizure activity has been related to organic lesions, metabolic disorders, drugs, toxic substances, fever, infections, and vitamin deficiency—as well as head injury for both children and adults. Some seizures are also apparently genetically based, of unknown etiology (idiopathic). The common effects from seizure activity are some reported psychological changes, but more clearly there are associated changes in EEG activity generally observed over a period of time. There are various types of seizures. These have been listed in the International Classification of Epilepsies of Childhood.

TABLE 1.1 International Classification of Epilepsies of Childhood*

1. **Primary generalized epilepsies**
   - True petit mal
   - Tonic-clonic major seizures (grand mal)
   - Combined petit/grand mal
   - Primary myoclonic epilepsy
2. **Secondary generalized epilepsies**
   - Associated with diffuse brain disease, including epilepsies secondary to specific encephalopathies and nonspecific encephalopathies (infantile spasms and Lennox-Gastaut syndrome)
3. **Primary partial epilepsies**
   - With motor, sensorimotor, affective, or visual symptoms
4. **Secondary partial epilepsies ("lesional")**
   - With elementary symptomatology
     - with motor symptoms
     - with special sensory or somatosensory symptoms
     - with autonomic symptoms
   - With complex symptomatology
     - with impairment of consciousness only
     - with cognitive symptoms
     - with affective symptoms
     - with psychosensory symptoms
     - with psychomotor symptoms (automatisms)

Source: Gastaut 1983.

*From *Developmental Neuropsychology* by Otfried Spreen, Anthony H. Risser and Dorothy Edgell.

The material in this section is adapted (with permission) from Spreen. Most seizures involve motor activity. In the classic seizure there is a sequence of tonic and clonic movements. In *petit mal* seizures, there is a sudden interruption of activities that may be accompanied by nystagmus, slight muscle contractions with the head moving backwards along with brief loss of consciousness and dropping of the head. In *myoclonic* seizures, there is loss of muscle tone along with jerky movements of arms and facial muscles. With *absence* seizures there is a sudden loss of consciousness. *Focal* seizures (or *partial* seizures) frequently occur on one side of the body but can spread. With focal motor seizures, the precentral or motor gyrus of the brain may be involved, and symptoms of rigidity and clonic movements are seen (Jacksonian Epilepsy). In *complex partial* seizures (or psychomotor seizures) auras may involve complex experiences, mood changes, or even hallucinations. In some cases consciousness may be compromised; there may also be confusion that follows the seizure. *Temporal lobe* seizures are the most common of all partial seizures. Because of the close proximity and relationship to visual, auditory and limbic system structures, the disorder may involve complex auditory and visual experiences as well as automatic behaviors that would certainly affect sustained attention or concentration. Even during periods of no demonstrable seizure activity from behavioral observation, there may be some evidence of "kindling" where repeated subthreshold electrical stimulations in the brain may lead to subsequent development of seizures. Thus subclinical disorganized abnormal electrical activity may occur periodically and may result in some behavioral changes that appear as ADHD symptoms.

In 1978, Walt and Forsythe noted that almost one quarter of children with epilepsy may have ADHD as a co-morbid condition.

ADD/ADHD Associated with Psychological Conditions

Other disorders may have many symptoms that mimic ADD behavior. (See Figure 1.2. on page 24.) There are six diagnostic categories under this rubric that may be further described as either acute or chronic.

Adjustment Disorders—According to DSM IV, this category of disorders involves "the development of clinically significant emotional or behavioral symptoms in response to an identifiable psychosocial stressor or stressors. The symptoms must develop within three months after the onset of the stressor(s)." Obviously, the symptoms or the consequences of ADD behaviors are of course stressful; alternatively, a stressor (e.g., head trauma) might precipitate both the adjustment disorder and ADD behaviors. Also, adjustment disorders may be considered when ADD children experience significant stress in the classroom but do not manifest a pattern that would be consistent with a diagnosis of anxiety, depression, or other psychiatric disorder. Many clinicians may use this category to describe such secondary reactions to the neurophysiological condition of ADD/ADHD.

Anxiety—The essential feature of Generalized Anxiety Disorder is excessive worry (apprehensive expectation) about a number of events or activities occurring a majority of the time over a period of at least six months. Because severe anxiety may result in excessive agitated movement, impair one's attention and concentration, and cause errors of misjudgment in one's responding, some of these anxiety disorders may mimic ADD behaviors. Worry may appear similar to daydreaming, as one's fantasies to deal with anxiety-provoking stimuli may cause fixation of thought patterns and a generally introspective facade. Focusing on the child's fears, worries and possible source of anxiety may aid in the differential diagnosis. Because ADD and anxiety appear to be at opposite ends of the arousal continuum, there is an infrequent chance that the two may truly co-exist. There are many anecdotal reports of some people responding with panic while others remain calm and goal-oriented during emergencies. Perhaps this state of relative calm during emergencies represents a shift of arousal gears that occurs when the low-arousal ADD child encounters a highly stimulating situation that would overwhelm any normal person. For comparison of symptoms, again refer to Figure 1.2 on page 24. The two conditions of anxiety and ADHD may automatically manifest different somatic reactions to states of emergency with the same underlying process (i.e., an increase in arousal). While one state reflects overarousal and confusion, the other (ADHD) reflects an optimal arousal state and thus more effective reaction. Conners has cited evidence to suggest that ADHD and anxiety may interact with anxiety factors minimizing manifestations of impulsivity, hyperactivity, and aggression.

Depression/Dysthymia—Some ADD characteristics have been noted with depression disorders; depressive symptoms may be associated with ADD in teenage and adult years. With the presence of depressive symptoms, there may be interference with thinking, and certainly in some cases where one is preoccupied with depressive thought patterns, there may be an interference with sustained attention. Furthermore, in depressive states there may be sleep difficulties similar to that experienced in ADD. With agitated depression, there is the possibility of motoric restlessness similar to hyperactivity. With reference to the *DSM IV,* it would be unusual for ADD/ADHD children to meet the full criteria for depression/dysthymia. In *DSM III-R,* ADHD was listed as a predisposing factor for dysthymia; now it is simply noted that ADHD may be associated with dysthymia as well as other conditions such as learning disabilities or mental retardation.

Bipolar Disorders—In *DSM IV,* there are four categories of Bipolar Disorder (or Manic Depression). These include Bipolar I (marked by one or more Manic Episodes or Mixed Episodes), Bipolar II (marked by one or more major Depressive Episodes, accompanied by at least one Hypomanic Episode), Cyclothymic Disorder (marked by a chronic fluctuating mood disturbance involving numerous periods of hypomanic symptoms and numerous periods of depressive symptoms) and Bipolar Disorder (Not Otherwise Specified or NOS). In general, the presence of either manic or hypomanic symptoms defines Bipolar Disorders. During the manic phase there is irritable, expansive, or elevated mood with associated symptoms including hyperactivity (gross motor), racing thoughts, distractibility, and high-risk taking behavior. In hypomania, manic behaviors may be present within the context of a less severe mood disorder. The hypomania episode is marked by hyperactivity, silliness, giddiness, cheerfulness, distractibility, inattention, moments of rudeness and crudeness, and fluctuating cheerful to irritable moods. It should be noted that in *DSM IV* "ADHD and Hypomanic Episode are both characterized by excessive activity, impulsive behavior, poor judgment, and denial of problems." ADHD is distinguished from hypomanic episode by the characteristic early onset of ADHD (i.e., before age 7 years), its chronic rather than episodic course, its lack of relatively clear onsets and offsets, and the absence of abnormally expansive or elevated mood.

Mental Retardation—Mental Retardation (MR) is defined as below average intellectual functioning (IQ 70 or less) on an individually administered intelligence test together with deficits in adaptive behavior and having an onset prior to 18 years of age. According to DSM IV, "the most common associated mental disorders are ADHD, Mood Disorders, Pervasive Developmental Disorders, Stereotypic Movement Disorder, and Mental Disorders due to a general medical condition (e.g., Head Trauma)." According to Barkley, when an individual who is mentally retarded meets all of the diagnostic criteria for ADHD relative to his or her mental age, then the additional diagnosis is warranted.

Learning Disabilities—The degree of overlap with learning disabilities (LD) is significant for ADD. It has been estimated that about 10 percent up to 50 percent of ADD/ADHD children may have a learning disability. Goldstein and Goldstein point out that while attentional factors are necessary they are not sufficient for learning as the child with a learning disability has difficulty processing information. Thus, they contend that although medication stimulates the attention center deep within the brain, it may "have little effect on the cortical ability of the brain to process information." Consequently, both ADD/ADHD and LD children have academic problems but for different reasons.

Typically, a learning disability is defined as a significant discrepancy between the child's general level of mental ability and his or her academic achievement in such areas as reading, math, spelling, handwriting, and language development. Most of these LD types involve a verbal factor. Whatever their disability, when placed in the classroom, these LD children experience considerable frustration and may thus exhibit excess motor activity and poor attentional skills. Behaviors may be similar to those of the child with ADD/ADHD but are reactive (i.e., secondary) to the child's primary disorder—LD. Likewise, children with ADD/ADHD may have learning difficulties because of their difficulty in focusing and sustaining their attention; they may process only bits and pieces of information that is not sufficiently repetitive. Conners has also suggested that many children with LD exhibit ADD (i.e., no hyperactivity)—many of these are females who show some impairment of right hemisphere functions (e.g., poor organizational ability). In contrast, others have noted that those with ADHD (mostly males) have more frequent peer difficulties, fewer LD problems, but more conduct disturbance (CD) traits.

Conduct Disorders/Oppositional Deficit Disorder—It has been noted that in clinical settings, at least two-thirds of patients with ADD/ADHD also have oppositional defiant disorder (ODD) or conduct disorder (CD). Children who meet diagnostic criteria for both ADD/ADHD and CD/ODD reportedly tend to have an earlier age of onset, exhibit a greater total number of antisocial behaviors and display more physical aggression. Furthermore, it is noted that of all children with ADD/ADHD, those with co-morbid conduct disorders are virtually the only ones at risk for anti-social behavior and drug use as adults. The ODD category generally describes milder forms of chronic behavior problems than those seen in conduct disorder. However, children with ODD are seen as at risk for the development of a conduct disorder. Children with ODD display a pattern of stubborn negativistic, hostile, and defiant behaviors, but in contrast to CD, without serious violation of the rights of others. Roughly 40–65% of those with ADHD have ODD—the most frequently occurring co-morbid disorder. Many of the attentional problems of those with CD/ODD are associated with their persistent behavior.

It has become increasingly clear that while those with CD/ODD often exhibit some of the same behaviors as those with ADD/ADHD, these groups represent different types of disorders. According to Shaywitz and Shaywitz, the CD/ODD group seem to be found in older children who have experienced some psychosocial disadvantage. This group is similar to one described by Weinberg and Emslie of children who exhibited both ADD and CD/ODD characteristics. These children had evidence of repeated early abuse or neglect by multiple caretakers or inadequate or little parenting. The authors also describe two other groups, including one involving frontal lobe functioning and the other a family history of characterologic disorders. A third group is noted to be secondary conduct disorder, who manifest only behavioral disturbance during episodes of affective illness. They point out that some children with episodic conduct disorder, ADD, and affective irritability may develop a bipolar disorder.

Obsessive Compulsive Disorder (OCD)—OCD is characterized by recurrent and intrusive thoughts or images together with ritualistic behavior (e.g., hand washing), mental activity (counting, repeating words), and irresistible motor behaviors (touching, repeating others' behavior). These thoughts and actions are recognized as excessive, yet the person maintains contact with reality. Clearly such intrusive thoughts and behaviors may certainly disrupt one's ability to focus attention on task, and result in slower performance, missed information, and inappropriate responses due to lack of information. However, a common area of the brain, the orbitofrontal cortex, has been implicated in both ADD and OCD. It has been further noted that some compulsive behaviors have been produced by amphetamines and other psychostimulants.

DEVELOPMENTAL TRENDS: CHILD TO ADULT

According to Barkley, "up to 80 percent of school age children given a clinical diagnosis for ADHD will continue to have the disorder in adolescence, and between 30 and

65% will have it into adulthood, depending on how the disorder is defined in any particular study."

The Pre-School Child

Many mothers of ADD/ADHD children report that they noticed their children were more active even before birth. During infancy, the early ADD pattern may be characterized by unpredictable behavior, shrill crying, irritability, and overactivity. Sleep problems have also been noted as these infants show only brief periods of quiet sleep. Later, in the preschool years, these children begin to exhibit greater motoric restless behavior, rapid changes in mood, temper tantrums, continued poor sleep, a low tolerance for frustration, and a short attention span. Many of these youngsters also show speech and language problems and are described as more clumsy. They generally experience much difficulty in group settings, especially with aggressive behaviors, and as a result many of these children are sometimes "asked to leave preschool"!

The School-Age Child

By school age the behavior pattern appears to become worse as these youngsters enter the classroom and are expected to sit quietly, focus on their assigned tasks, and get along with others in the class. Problems are now likely to occur at home and at school. Homework, routinely assigned to children at an early age, becomes another potential battlefield. Additionally, these children, who have much difficulty with rule-governed behavior, find handling chores at home and completing assignments at school difficult. They experience either tolerance or outright rejection from others as social problems tend to increase. By late childhood social conflicts are well established. Barkley points out that "Between 7 and 10 years of age, at least 30 to 50 percent of children with ADD/ADHD are likely to develop symptoms of conduct disorder and antisocial behavior such as lying, petty thievery, and resistance to authority. Twenty-five percent or more may have problems with fighting with other children."

Adolescence

During this period of development it is not unusual for the symptom pattern to change, manifested by a marked decrease in hyperactivity but with other problems of attention and impulsivity remaining. By adolescence the child may have a history of failures in academic performance (about 58% according to Barkley) as well as marked difficulties in his/her social relations (25 to 30% displaying antisocial behavior, Barkley). Many of these teenagers in search of acceptance may then tend to associate with peers who have similar problems; this often results in the escalation of risk-taking behavior. Teens with ADD/ADHD are certainly more subject to peer pressures regarding the use of alcohol or other addictive substances (as many as 30% experimenting with or abusing alcohol and marijuana). Sadly, 35 percent of ADHD children quit school before completion. Depression appears to be more common for ADD/ADHD adolescents along with poor self-concept, low self-esteem and poor self- confidence, making future success seem unlikely and thus contributing to diminished motivation to complete school as well as much concern about social acceptance.

Adulthood

Symptoms persist into adulthood for over one half of ADHD children. Barkley notes that "only 10 to 20% of ADHD children reach adulthood free of any psychiatric diagnosis. They show a higher incidence of problems relating to achievement and vocational/work issues. Psychological problems and marital difficulties are more frequent and about 25% may even show antisocial characteristics and about 50% become alcoholics." In a long-term follow-up study by Borlund and Heckman on hyperactive children and their brothers, it was noted that despite similar ability and educational levels, the hyperactive group had a lower socioeconomic status and increased antisocial behavior, along with social and marital problems. Goodwin reported a relationship between early ADD patterns and later alcoholism. Weiss and Hechtman noted in their long-term follow-up study that 10 percent of ADD children later attempted suicide as adults and 5 percent died from either suicide or "accidental injury," an incidence higher than would be expected in the normal population of their controls. It is certainly now clear that ADD/ADHD is not simply outgrown, as was once thought in years past. We now know there is a higher incidence of more overall psychopathology and lower ability to function than in normal individuals without evidence of ADD/ADHD. It has also been found by researchers that the use of stimulant drugs for ADD/ADHD did not eliminate all difficulties in educational and daily living situations. Usage of these stimulant meds did, however, result in less social ostracism along with a general improvement in the feelings associated with their lives and others.

Adult ADHD with Antisocial Traits

From one of the most comprehensive of follow-up studies on "Hyperactive Children Grown Up" by G. Weiss and Lily Heshtman, it was concluded that "a higher percentage of hyperactive subjects than normal controls had a history of antisocial behavior . . ." and that "families of hyperactive children were found to have more psychopathology, particularly antisocial behavior, alcoholism, and hysteria, than normal controls." In studies of arrest rates of adolescents and young adults with ADHD, the ADHD subjects had significantly more arrests than did the controls. Also, it's been reported that young adults with ADHD are more likely than their matched controls to have been incarcerated. Considering the link between criminal conduct (i.e., conduct disorder) and ADHD, this diagnostic condition (ADHD) has been used with limited success as a criminal defense. The approach taken has either been one of a "biological deficiency defense" (similar to temporal lobe epilepsy—a brain disorder) and described as mental nonresponsibility (insanity) *or* as a "diminished capacity defense." While this stance, to date, has reportedly helped more during the sentencing phase, most courts do allow such evidence and the frequency of its use appears to have increased. A forensic neuropsychological evaluation of adolescents or adults with ADHD may therefore be quite helpful and may contribute to the legal process. An acceptable evaluation has been described in the section on neuropsychological testing and in the description of the model ADD Clinic (see Appendix E). Experienced clinicians who provide assessment and treatment of children, adolescents, and adults with ADHD would be essential for such an evaluation because of the complex array of factors (i.e., co-morbid conditions) typically involved in such cases.

CHAPTER 2

Diagnosis and Treatment of ADD/ADHD

MAKING A DIFFERENTIAL DIAGNOSIS

Many professionals believe that the diagnosis of ADD/ADHD should be made solely from the DSM IV criteria.* Using information supplied by the child's parents, a comprehensive developmental history is obtained. As part of that history, current behavioral characteristics are assessed. This information may be integrated with the developmental history to form the basis for a diagnostic impression. Most children with ADD/ADHD, however, present such a complex array of symptoms that they often meet the criteria for another diagnostic classification as well. There's a great deal of evidence for co-morbid conditions and the so called mimic syndromes (i.e., conditions that look like ADD/ADHD but are clinically different in their etiology, treatment, and prognosis). Consequently, the clinician must consider several sources of information besides the developmental history from parents to piece together the puzzle to sort out which characteristics are primary, and which ones may be secondary and tertiary problems. Such a multilevel analysis will frequently lead to a multicomponent treatment program that addresses each significant component. This process may be likened to the story of the three blind men who encounter an elephant and are asked to describe it. Each one bumps into a different part of the elephant so there are three quite different descriptions of the same object. Too narrow a focus on the ADD/ADHD child may similarly result

**Diagnostic and Statistical Manual of Mental Disorders: DSM-IV,* 4th ed., American Psychiatric Assn. Staff. American Psychiatric, 1994.

in an inadequate description, diagnosis and treatment plan. This seems to happen often in cases with children who have ADD/ADHD because they will often appear quite different in different situations and when dealing with different tasks.

In general, the evaluation process adopted at our ADD Clinic in Biloxi (see Appendix D for additional information on a Model ADD Clinic) begins with obtaining information from more than one source; for instance, from the child's parents, his teachers, and from the child himself. The child is also placed in different situations and given tasks to determine how he copes, whether he has co-morbid learning problems or co-morbid behavioral-emotional problems. Through such a comprehensive evaluation, a complete description may be provided of the child's abilities, achievements, specific visual, motor memory and auditory skills, and executive control skills. These test results may be considered along with the objective evaluation of attentional skills and social-emotional functions. The following explores each component that contributes to the overall differential diagnosis.

Background and Developmental History

It was once thought that ADD/ADHD was a problem of childhood that would eventually be outgrown. Now, it is generally agreed that the symptomatic ADD/ADHD pattern seen in childhood will typically persist even into adulthood, although somewhat modified in its overall appearance. While the basic ADD/ADHD pattern changes over time, there may be a host of other conditions that may evolve from it, or this ADD/ADHD condition may possibly serve as a catalyst for other disorders. Thus, depending upon the stage at which the person with ADD/ADHD is assessed, different clinical pictures could be obtained for the same person.

While ADD is primarily considered an inherited condition, ADD-like behavior can be acquired (e.g., via head injury), presenting a pattern quite similar to that exhibited when the condition is inherited. Family medical history, including psychiatric conditions on both sides of the family, is clearly very important to consider along with the child's medical history. A child whose parent had ADD could, for instance, also have experienced the cumulative effects of lead poisoning, and thus have a dual etiology for her disorder. The birth history may include indicators of neonatal distress, anoxia, maternal smoking and/or alcohol/drug use during pregnancy as well as other risk factors. Regarding effects during pregnancy, Barkley (1996) has reported that "nicotine from cigarette smoking and alcohol from drinking during pregnancy have been shown to cause significant abnormalities in the development of the caudate nucleus and the frontal regions of the brain in children." It has also been noted that the greater the number of complications during pregnancy the greater the risk of ADHD. A history of ear infections, especially with high fevers, may also be a contributing factor. Other possible significant medical conditions for the child include asthma, thyroid dysfunction, hypoglycemia, hearing defects, sleep apnea, encephalitis (brain infection), pinworms, mild brain damage (head trauma), and seizure disorders, to name just a few. Therefore, a comprehensive assessment of the child's background and developmental history alone with parental and family history must be obtained. Two excellent forms designed for this purpose include the "Childhood History Form for Attention Disorders" by Drs. Sam and Michael Goldstein (1985) and the "Conners-March Developmental Questionnaire" by Dr. C. Keith Conners and Dr. John March (1994).

Behavior Observations

In addition to the background and developmental history, three sets of observations are obtained about the child with ADD/ADHD during the assessment process. First, the parents present their observations which often seem to be mostly in the form of complaints regarding behavior difficulties and behavior differences (i.e., how their child is different from others). Second, teachers provide general behavioral descriptions from their viewpoint at the same time that the behavior ratings are obtained. In addition to narrative descriptions of problem behaviors by parents and teachers, both complete more formal rating scales that provide norm-referenced comparisons to other children the same age as the identified patient. Samples of these rating forms, such as the ACTeRS, Conners, ADHD Test, BASC Scales and others are found in Appendix C.

Information from these rating scales can be most helpful, especially those ratings from the child's teacher. The teacher may, in fact, be in the best position to rate the child as he or she has more information on behavior at various developmental levels; this information can be compared with that of other peers in general or of others in the child's class. These ratings not only help in the diagnostic process, but also serve as baseline observations to which the child's progress will be compared. Thus, these initial ratings may be periodically repeated to monitor the child's behavior during and after various treatment modalities. Since there will be increasingly more complex demands and rules with which the child must cope, it is useful to employ a standard set of observations on which the child can be compared across time. This will aid in determining additional needs for either medications and/or specific interventions to deal with changing rules and expectations.

A third set of observations is obtained from the psychological examiner. These observations serve as a context for the interpretation of the test results and provide basic information about how the child deals with the "assigned tasks." Many of these tasks are similar to the cognitive activities inherent in school subjects. Thus, a kind of "microclassroom" context is created so that the child's adaptive skills can be assessed.

Clearly, the way the child feels during the test session will affect test scores. Illness, lack of sleep, fear, depression, resentment, and lack of understanding of the purpose of the evaluation all affect the results.

Behavioral observations during the assessment tell the examiner much about how the child approached the task, what strategies may have been used, and how the child feels about her performance. Awkward pencil grip, blocking on verbal responses, long pauses, counting on fingers to solve math problems, word finding difficulty, restless behavior, excessive talking, and looking around at each noise and distraction, are just some of the many observations that the examiner may record. Some of these behaviors may be no surprise to the experienced examiner; however, some observations may be quite unique and highly individual, relating to something very specific about this particular child with ADD/ADHD. Much of this assessment of individuality in clinical presentation is quite helpful in planning a program of treatment. Since the child with ADD/ADHD often does well in a one-to-one situation, this performance on psychological tests with the examiner may be viewed like one that would be manifested in an ideal situation. Thus, the assessment reveals more about how the child might function in an ideal situation with maximum academic performance and assessment of abilities within the context of the child's natural physiological tendencies. Some children who are not yet on medication may essentially be untestable. Others may have little trouble with the test situation, especially because of its novelty (i.e., stimulation value). For some children who may already be on medication, an attempt may be made to see the child off meds. Later, a comparison may be made with his performance while on meds.

Psychological/Neuropsychological Assessment

There is no one specific test for diagnosing ADD. Recently, however, a test entitled "Attention Deficit/Hyperactivity Disorder Test" has been published. This test is helpful in gathering and organizing background information from the parents and is based solely on DSM IV Criteria, but it does not consider the child's performance on various tasks. It should not be assumed, because of its title, that this test alone is sufficient to diagnose ADD. Clinical observation, combined with the results of the child's performance on specific psychological and neuropsychological tests measuring verbal, nonverbal, visual-motor, fine motor, gross motor, memory, executive control, and attentional skills are all essential for the psychologist and/or neuropsychologist to describe the pattern of behaviors that the child presents and to formulate a diagnosis. Children who are mentally retarded or who experience brain injury may have basic difficulties with attention and concentration; however, ADD/ADHD is a condition that exists in children of average or above-average intelligence. Because of the complexities of the evaluation, a neuropsychological rationale will be proposed.

Rationale for Neuropsychological Assessment—The underlying assumption in the field of neuropsychology is that the brain mediates behavior. First, the behaviors that are part of the typical clinical picture of ADD are quite complex. It is highly unusual for the child being evaluated for ADD to have only ADD. In most cases the pattern may consist of secondary and even tertiary problem areas, in addition to the primary disorder—ADD. The usual approach of a neuropsychologist is to orchestrate a complex battery of tests to measure a complex array of symptoms. Then, through a process of ruling-in specific conditions and ruling-out others, the initial symptom picture becomes clearer. Since the child's behavior in her natural environment is of prime concern, the goal is to present neuropsychological tasks similar to those in which the child must ultimately function. In the case of the ADD child, measures of attention—both simple and complex—are essential. As noted by Barkley, "attention plays a critical role in the neuropsychological assessment of children with developmental, learning or other neuropsychological problems because it underlies the very capacity of children to undergo any form of psychological testing." Additionally, measures of *behavioral response inhibition* would also be needed to document the child's impulsive style. Furthermore, estimates of activity level, organizational skills, cognitive flexibility, social-emotional development, visual-motor skills, and a general capacity to adapt to situational changes are all important.

Second, in the history of working with ADD, it has been noted that some of the first cases identified as having "ADD" were those early post-encephalitic cases. Thus, a direct connection was made between some of the typical "ADD characteristics" and a brain disorder. While the type of organic involvement in such cases was nonspecific, there was a clear parallel of varied post-encephalitic symptoms with the current ADD symptoms such that a multivariate (i.e., many variables or symptomatic behaviors) approach to the assessment of neurophysiologically driven behaviors is warranted. Other forms of organic dysfunction may also involve attentional and behavioral response systems so that one may see ADD-like behavior in neuropsychological cases of epilepsy, head injury, structural brain lesions and others.

Third, several research reports have been written on the use of specific neuropsychological test batteries to evaluate children with ADD. These studies have focused on assessment of frontal lobe functions and other neuropsychological skills using simple measures such as the Wisconsin Card Sorting Test, verbal fluency tests, reading tests, and attentional (continuous performance, or CPT) tests. In one study, a battery of tests was used that not only looked at frontal lobe functions but included a variety of other measures of IQ, reading skill, and verbal memory as well as an assessment of attentional and impulsivity factors. The idea that disturbances in frontal lobe functions may be related to impulse control and responsible for the kind of cognitive impairments noted with ADHD was supported. The conclusion was that inability to control, direct, and sustain attention appears as a core deficiency of ADHD and not impulsivity. However, others believe that *behavioral inhibition* reflects the core difficulty and not attention problems. In a recently proposed theory, Barkley (1995) suggests that the problem of self-control may warrant renaming ADD/ADHD as a "Development Disorder of Self-Control."

Specific Tests vs. Test Batteries—As Barkley notes "over the past 50 years, the view of attention as a single, unitary construct has given way to theories of attention as being multidimensional." However, much of the early work in neuropsychology focused on finding a simple test that would detect organic brain disorders. Tests such as the Bender-Gestalt quickly became accepted as diagnostic instruments for "organacity," but with an abundance of research studies, it became clear that a simple test such as the Bender Gestalt should not be used as a screening instrument for organic dysfunction. It was, however, found to be a useful addition to a battery of tests where each test would assess a specific brain-behavior relationship. In the evaluation of complex organic problems, test batteries such as Reitan-Indiana Neuropsychological Test Battery and a later developed test battery, The Luria-Nebraska Neuropsychological Test Battery, may be more useful than single tests alone. Many variations of these batteries as well as numerous other very specific batteries have been developed. Other batteries have been proposed to evaluate patients exposed to toxic materials. To date, however, no specific battery has been developed for the assessment of ADD/ADHD. Various tests to measure attention have been discussed by Barkley, and Fennell has suggested basic domains of function that are typically assessed in a child neuropsychological examination. She has then listed commonly used neuropsychological tests in the evaluation of attention-deficit disorder within a broader context of learning disability. Many problems have been discussed with regard to the traditional static test batteries, which may be lacking in theory-based constructs as well as being poorly referenced to real-life criteria. Consequently, neuropsychological test batteries that cover a broad range of functions and have sufficient flexibility to include assessment of the many varied co-morbid conditions are preferred.

A Multidisciplinary Evaluation—It is clear that any neuropsychological evaluation that attempts to assess ADD/ADHD characteristics, must take into consideration the following factors:

1. ADD/ADHD is a complex disorder that has, in itself, many facets or variations.
2. ADD/ADHD has more basic subtypes than those described in *DSM IV.*
3. The concept of attention has several sub-categories; the concept of behavioral-inhibition may likewise be sub-divided.
4. ADD/ADHD is a developmental disorder that changes over the life span. Thus, for comparative purposes and to utilize the deficit approach to neuropsychological assessment, one must be familiar with normal neuropsychological and general behavioral development.
5. ADD/ADHD also involves situational components in which some of the variations are manifested such as when behavior problems appear only in school or just the reverse.
6. Knowledge of co-morbid conditions and adjunctive problems frequently associated with ADD/ADHD is essential.

A typical evaluation for ADD/ADHD may first focus on:

1. *The History*—A good developmental history that is provided by the mother or caretaker familiar with the child may be able to provide some of the pathognomonic signs of ADD/ADHD from background information.

2. *Rating Forms*—Information from both the child's teacher and the parent may be useful in detecting some of the behavioral signs exhibited either in school or at home.
3. *Specific Objective Measures of Attention*—There are several fairly well developed instruments (usually computer based) that have good and, in some cases, extensive normative data where a person's performance may be compared to one or more norms.
4. *Cognitive Measures*—Involving the assessment of abilities, achievements, memory, visual-motor, language, visual-spatial, sensory, motor, and executive control, and social-emotional skills are all needed to answer some of the questions regarding possible co-morbid conditions or additional facets that tend to make each ADD/ADHD pattern somewhat unique.

As Rourke has so eloquently pointed out, the current emphasis on neuropsychological evaluations (for the LD child) is not concerned with localization issues or even that there is demonstrable brain dysfunction. The primary concern in the evaluation of the LD child, as it would be for the child with ADD, is on documenting strengths and weaknesses as they relate to the real life issues of learning or adapting to one's environment. The patterns thus obtained on neuropsychological testing would shed some light on the direction and overall thrust of treatment and/or habitation for the child.

In the following sections, many of the currently accepted neuropsychological tests used for children are discussed.

Components of the Neuropsychological Assessment

The various tests that make up the neuropsych battery to assess children with ADD/ADHD may depend upon each clinician's choice. However, various categories of functions will be emphasized in the test battery. These specific functions relate to the various deficits and problems associated not only with ADD/ADHD, but also with the often found co-morbid disorders. Thus, a wide range of functions is assessed to allow the psychologist to not only rule in ADD/ADHD, but also rule out associated co-morbid disorders and mimic syndromes.

The following categories of functions are addressed: (1) Ability; (2) Achievement; (3) Executive Control (frontal lobe) Functions; (4) Visual-Motor Skills; (5) Motor Skills; (6) Memory; (7) Attentional Skills; (8) Self-Concept/Self-Esteem; (9) Social Skills; (10) Visual-Spatial Skills; (11) Language Skills; and (12) Behavioral-Emotional Assessment. Each of these areas is briefly discussed here. For a more in-depth discussion of the majority of these tests, see other references in testing such as the *Practitioner's Guide to Developmental and Psychological Testing* by Dr. Glen P. Aylward (New York: Plenum, 1994) or specific test manuals for additional technical information. Dr. Aylward's information on several of the tests listed is included in this section.

Assessment of Ability—The "gold standard" for assessment of abilities is the Wechsler Intelligence Scale for Children-III (ages 6 to 16 years, 11 months). It provides

Verbal, Performance (basically non-verbal/visual-spatial assessment) and Full Scale IQ Scores. The verbal subtests include information, similarities, arithmetic, vocabulary, comprehension and digit span. The performance subtests include picture completion, picture arrangement, block design, object assembly, coding, mazes and symbol search. Factor scores are: (1) Verbal Comprehension, (2) Perceptual Organization, (3) Freedom from Distractibility, and (4) Processing Speed. While some clinicians do look at the factor scores for problems with attention and concentration on the Freedom From Distractibility Factor score, others find much inconsistency and do not believe that this score provides a reliable and valid measure of attentional processes. Most clinicians do look for consistent patterns across various tests and will include this factor score as one measure to look at.

For clinicians who want a quick measure of the child's ability in short screening evaluations, the Kaufman Brief Intelligence Test (KBIT) is available. With estimates of verbal and non-verbal functions, as well as a composite score, these test scores correlate fairly well with other established measures of ability. There are some indications that WISC-III scores may be accurately estimated by KBIT scores in a sample of children with ADD/ADHD (author's unpublished data) and especially for children with average or above WISC-III scores. Other data show that in other populations, the KBIT fairly accurately predicts (i.e., estimates) WISC-III scores.

Assessment of Achievement—The Wechsler Individual Achievement Test (WIAT) was co-normed with the WISC-III, thus allowing for meaningful analysis of ability-achievement discrepancies important in the diagnosis of learning disabilities. It consists of subtests on (a) Basic Reading, (b) Math Reasoning, (c) Spelling, (d) Reading Comprehension, (e) Numerical Operations, (f) Listening Comprehension, (g) Oral Expression, and (h) Written Expression. There is a brief screener comprised of three subtests (a), (b), and (c).

Another comprehensive achievement test is the Woodcock-Johnson Psycho-educational Battery-Revised (WJ-R). Additional screeners for achievement include the Wide Range Achievement Test-3 (a revision of the popular WRAT-R), the Peabody Individual Achievement Test-Revised (PIAT-R), and the Boder Test of Reading/Spelling Patterns.

Assessment of Executive Control—While there are many available neuropsychological measures of frontal lobe functions, these three are helpful for use with ADD/ADHD children: the Trail Making Test, the Stroop Color Word Test, and the Wisconsin Card Sorting Test.

The Trail Making Test primarily assesses motor speed and mental flexibility. Sequencing is an obvious component of Part A where the child connects a series of numbered circles. In Part B, the task is more complex and requires the child to connect alternating numbers and letters in sequence. Thus, not only is motor speed involved, but also the child's ability to shift and to hold in working memory specific elements of two sequences.

The Stroop Color Word Test requires that the child inhibit competing information before making a response. An example would be to read names of colors printed in a different color (e.g., the word "red" printed in green). Vocal-motor speed and holding information in working memory are both needed to accurately inhibit competing information and respond appropriately on this test.

The Wisconsin Card Sorting Test requires again mental flexibility and conceptual problem solving. The child must be able to use feedback on her responses to formulate a concept of the correct response pattern based on color, form or number. This test has been one of the most useful in assessing frontal lobe functions and is used in most neuropsych batteries as well.

Assessment of Visual-Motor Skills—While the Bender-Gestalt Test has been the choice of clinicians for many years, it has limitations in use with children. For example, most children are able to complete the task by age 8 years. Older children may thus not be identified when their visual-motor problems are more subtle and therefore not detected by this test.

The Developmental Test of Visual-Motor Integration (fourth edition) has been normed on children 3 years to 18 years of age. It provides 24 drawing tasks that are developmentally sequenced in order of increasing complexity. A developmental age is computed as well as the visual-motor standard scores and percentile ranks. Useful supplemental tests allow the clinician to evaluate the relative contributions of visual perception and motor coordination. An overall profile of visual, motor, and visual-motor performance allows the clinician to sort out the relevant contributions of visual and motor functions.

Another useful test is the Minnesota Perception-Diagnostic Test which measures both visual perception and visual-motor skills. It was normed on over 4,000 subjects and can be used with children in the age range of 5-14 years. It can also be used with adults (over 16 years).

Assessment of Motor Skills—In most neuropsychological test batteries, motor speed is assessed by the Finger Tapping or the Finger Oscillation Test. However, there are other measures of fine-motor coordination that may also be useful in evaluating children with ADD/ADHD. Specifically, Barkley has suggested the Hand Movement Test, a subtest from the Kaufman Assessment Battery for Children. This test is well standardized and normed and, reportedly, was based on tasks reflecting frontal lobe functions in adults.

Another motor test typically used in neuropsych batteries is the Strength of Grip Test. This measure provides an estimate of motor strength that may reflect more significant problems than an ADD/ADHD pattern. Other measures of motor functions can be found in the SOMPA Physical Dexterity Tasks (for children 5 to 12 years old) and the Comprehensive Movement Assessment Battery for children (a 1992 revision of the Test of Motor Impairment or TOMI) for children ages 4 through 12 years.

A quick screening to identify motor problems is the "Movement ABC Checklist." There are four conditions where the child is rated involving whether the child is moving, or not, and whether the environment is changing, or not. For example, a child may be rated while he is walking around the classroom avoiding bumping into stationery objects or persons, or when the child is stationary and objects are passed down a line. A fifth rating on behavior problems that might relate to motor difficulties is provided to support valid interpretation of other ratings. This checklist is completed by the child's teacher. Cut-off scores for movement problems and being "at risk" for movement problems are provided for children ages 6 and above.

Assessment of Memory Functions—The Wide Range Assessment of Memory and Learning (WRAML) is a very useful test in the evaluation of a child with ADD/ADHD. The WRAML incorporates measures of both visual and verbal memory, some of which are very sensitive to attentional problems and is appropriate for children ages 5 to 17 years. The Sentence Memory and Number/Letter Memory along with Design Memory and the Fingers Windows visual memory subtests are especially sensitive. Another is the Test of Memory and Learning (TOMAL) used to evaluate children ages 5 through 19 years. It features verbal and nonverbal memory scores, as well as supplemental composite scores of an Attention and Concentration Index and a Learning Index. The Children's Memory Scale has just been published and there is no known data currently available on its potential use with children who have ADD/ADHD.

Assessment of Attentional Skills—The use of a continuous performance test (CPT) dates back to the late 1950s when Rosvold and colleagues used the CPT to evaluate attentional processes in epileptic patients. The original CPT was a noncomputerized version. Since then, several variations of the CPT have been developed; there are now an even dozen instruments, including one under development by the author.

One of the earliest computerized versions is the Gordon Diagnostic System (1987) or GDS, normed on over 1,300 children preschool age through age 16 years. Developed by Dr. Michael Gordon, this system consists of three distinctive tasks in a self-contained computerized unit. The first task measures self-control and is entitled the Delay Task; this procedure is unique to the GDS among all computerized attentional assessment instruments. For this task, the child is told that he can press a large blue button as quickly or as slowly as he wishes. He is informed that if he presses too fast, he will not earn points; but, at the right pace, he earns a point and a light comes on each time he presses the button with the appropriate delay. This provides a description, over a timed interval, of how the child is able to pace himself when *he* is in control of the task.

The second GDS task is entitled Vigilance and measures the child's ability to pick out a sequence of two numbers that are repeated periodically during the timed interval. On this task, the clinician is able to determine how well the child is able to accurately pick out the sequences and thus assess any attentional lapses. The clinician is also able to determine how impulsive the child may be by the number of errors she makes during the task. Impulsivity is reflected by the child's rapid pressing of the button when she sees the first number in the sequence without waiting to see if it is followed by the second number.

A third and similar GDS task is labeled the Distractibility Task. On this task, the child again must pick out the identified sequence (e.g., a five followed by a three), but now there are numbers flashing randomly on either side of the center screen. This is a very complex task that seemingly generates a state of high arousal. It is quite difficult even for adults and may provide important information about distractibility, primarily for older children with ADD/ADHD. Recently, an auditory module has been added to the GDS. The auditory vigilance task is identical to the visual vigilance task, except that the numbers are heard via headphones while the screen is covered.

A second computerized assessment procedure is called the Test of Variables of Attention, or TOVA (ages 4 years to over 80 years of age); it utilizes software for the IBM PC compatible computers and the Apple IIe. On this 22.5-minute visual CPT assessment, the child presses a firing button whenever a correct target stimulus is presented. There is a considerable body of research on this instrument which is purported to be useful in predicting appropriate medication, titrating the dose and monitoring medication patterns in ADD and other neurological conditions for children and adults. Developed by Dr. Lawrence Greenberg, this procedure is nonlanguage based (to differentiate ADD from learning disorders), requires no right-left discrimination and has negligible practice effects.

The author does, however, seem to overgeneralize in stating that the "TOVA may serve as a sensitive measure of inattention and impulsivity in clinical settings." Likewise, he describes a curvilinear pattern in the development of attention and impulsivity with age; rapid changes in early childhood and a leveling off during later childhood and early adolescence. An assumption that TOVA measures of attention and impulsivity are ecologically valid traits may not be tenable. However, perhaps the most glaring problem with the TOVA (as with most CPT measures) is the high number of false positives (i.e., indicating there are attentional problems—like in ADD/ADHD—when this condition is not present) in both nonclinical (28 percent false positives) or clinical (39 percent false positives) situations.

The Intermediate Visual and Auditory Continuous Performance Test (IVA)—age 5 through adult—was developed by Dr. Joseph Sandford and Ann Turner. All test instructions and test stimuli are presented visually and auditorily by the computer. This procedure takes 13 minutes and provides a computer report with measures of various parameters reflecting dimensions of inattention, impulsivity, and hyperactivity.

A unique form of computerized assessment of attention is the Conners Continuous Performance Test (6 years to adult) introduced by Dr. C. Keith Conners, originally developed in the mid 1970s. This procedure differs from others in that the child must press a key for any letter presented except the letter X. Thus, the focus of this CPT test is on "behavioral inhibition." The Conners' CPT takes about 14 minutes to administer. However, only visual attention is measured. A computer report provides for interpretation of scores and the overall summary compare scores to the general population norms (preferable) or to ADHD norms.

The Conners' CPT has been shown to be sensitive to medication (i.e., Ritalin). On medication, children's Reaction Times were faster, Standard Error measures smaller, and the percentage of hits higher compared to times when they were off medication. Reaction Times averaging over 900 msec were deemed slow. Attentional difficulties on the Conners' CPT are indicated by:

a. errors of omission

b. reaction times for hits

c. changes over time (i.e., atypical response speed)

Impulsivity is reflected by:

a. errors of commission

b. reaction time on hits

Other measures include:

1. d'—reflecting an individual's "perceptual sensitivity" or ability to discriminate targets from non-targets;
2. β—a measure of the person's "frequency of responding" (Conners notes that "risk takers" respond more readily than they should.)

Any T-score = or > 60 or any percentile = or > than 90 would be significant; the more measures that reach significance, the stronger the evidence for attentional difficulty. One of the most important features of the Conners' CPT is the variation of inter-stimulus interval; children with ADD/ADHD may often lose their attention on the longer inter-stimulus interval presentations and these intervals appear to be more dose sensitive, subject to deterioration in performance at too high a dose level.

Lastly, the Conners' CPT allows the clinician to compare a person's scores to either general norms or to ADHD norms. (Conners recommends the former for most clinical purposes.)

Assessment of Self-Concept/Self-Esteem—A child's perception of herself is an important component in the evaluation of children with ADD/ADHD, especially older children. Much of the information obtained in this area of assessment comes from clinical observation and report, as well as projective test data, for example, figure drawings, kinetic family drawing, sentence completion, and other similar projective test measures. However, there are some test instruments that may provide helpful information that is more objective.

The Multidimensional Self-Concept Scale (MSCS) assesses global self-concept and provides information on six areas of psychosocial functioning, including social competence, affect, academic, family and physical domains. It is administered in about 20 minutes for children ages 9 through 19 (grades 5 through 12). Results reflect overall classifications with percentile ranks and a profile of normative scale strengths and weaknesses. This instrument appears to have good psychometric characteristics and provides a clearer definition of self-concept that employs a behavioral rationale for the construct.

A second instrument, called the Self-Esteem Index (SEI) is a normative based measure reflecting how children perceive and value themselves and is thus closely related to the self-concept. It can be administered in about 30 minutes and is appropriate for children ages 7 through 18 years. In addition to the four basic scales reflecting Academic Competence, Family Acceptance, Peer Popularity and Personal Security, there is an overall Self-Esteem Quotient. The perceptions of Academic Competence, Family Acceptance and Peer Popularity are especially important measures to consider in the evaluation of the child with ADD/ADHD.

Assessment of Social Skills—In addition to information obtained clinically and from direct observation (e.g., BASC Direct Behavioral Observations or the ADHD School Observation Code), there are two instruments that may be helpful in assessing social skills.

The Social Skills Rating System (ages 3 to 18 years) utilizes ratings from parents, teachers, and the child (self-reports can be used in grades 3-12) to assess behaviors that affect the teacher-student relationship, peer acceptance, and academic performance. It also detects problems such as shyness, difficulty initiating conversations, and problems in making friends. Five positive social behaviors are measured, including Cooperation, Assertion, Responsibility, Empathy, and Self-Control on the Social Skills Scale. The Problem Behaviors Scale assesses behaviors that may interfere with the development of positive social skills, including Externalizing Problems, Internalizing Problems, and Hyperactivity. The Academic Competence Scale gives a quick estimate of academic functioning, motivation and parental support. A separate computerized program, the Assessment Intervention Record (AIR) allows the clinician to plan appropriate interventions.

A relatively new rating scale called the Walker-McConnell Scale of Social Competence and School Adjustment appears to target specific social skills on which the student needs instruction and practice. Completed by the classroom teacher, this scale is appropriate for children in kindergarten through grade 6 (elementary version) and grades 7 through 12 (adolescent version). The elementary version has three factor scales: Teacher Preferred Behavior, Peer Preferred Behavior, and School Adjustment Behavior. The adolescent version contains four factor scales: Self-Control, Peer Relations, School Adjustment, and Empathy. In general, this instrument is useful in obtaining information in two primary areas of adjustments in school: (1) *adaptive classroom behavior* and (2) *interpersonal social competence.* Both of these adjustments are seemingly critical to ultimate success in school as well as to the child's overall social development.

Assessment of Visual-Spatial Skills—The Minnesota Percepto-Diagnostic Test (ages 5 to 14 years) may be used for assessment of both visual-perception and visual-motor skills. Scores are corrected for both age and IQ. A "testing the limits" procedure is used and information is obtained to infer visual-motor, visual-perceptual or more complex integrative difficulties. However, while utilization of this one test may be efficient, it lacks some critical information on complex visual-perceptual processes.

The clinician may therefore find the Motor-Free Visual Perception Test-Revised (MVPT-R) test provides more detailed analysis, especially of visual-spatial skills. The MVPT-R is appropriate for children ages 4 through 11 years. Five areas of visual perception are assessed: Spatial Relationships, Visual Discrimination, Figure-Ground, Visual Closure, and Visual Memory. The MVPT was originally developed as an alternative to other measures of visual-perception which involve tracing or copying and therefore assess visual-motor integration rather than visual perception.

An additional test, the Jordan Left-Right Reversal Test-Revised (1990) has been especially helpful in evaluating a child's tendency to persist in reversing letters and numbers either individually or in word or sentence context. As a high percentage of children with ADD/ADHD also present evidence of dyslexia, this assessment of visual-spatial problems with letters and numbers seems relevant. It is appropriate for children ages 5 through 12 years.

Assessment of Language Skills—A comprehensive language evaluation may be provided by the Test of Language Development-Primary (TOLD-P:3) for ages 4 through 8 years, 11 months or the Test of Language Development-Intermediate (TOLD-I:3) for ages 8 through 12 years, 11 months.

TOLD-P:3 has nine subtests that measure Picture Vocabulary, Relational Vocabulary, and Oral Vocabulary. Additional subtests assess Grammatical Understanding, Sentence Imitation, and Grammatical Completion; supplemental tests include Word Articulation, Phonemic Analysis, and Word Discrimination. Not only are there measures of expressive and receptive modes of oral communication but there is a new composite "organizing" that has been included to reflect those linguistic abilities that mediate between receptive and expressive functions.

TOLD-I:3 has five subtests that measure various components of oral language. These include Generals (abstract relationships), Malapropisms (ridiculous sentences to correct) and Picture Vocabulary. Sentence Combining, Word Ordering and Grammatical Comprehension all assess different aspects of grammar. The TOLD-I:3 can be administered individually in about 40 minutes. This test measures various features of syntax and semantics along with listening and speaking systems of language that can provide a profile of a child's strengths and weaknesses in these areas of language assessment. The test also allows for analysis of receptive and expressive language differences.

A new edition of the Peabody Picture Vocabulary Test-III, Third Edition (PPVT-III) will be available in 1997 co-normed with the Expressive Vocabulary Test (EVT). Both tests are suitable for patients 2.5 to over 85 years of age, and both can generally be individually administered within about 30 minutes. These tests are, however, limited to receptive and expressive vocabulary, along with word retrieval.

Behavioral-Emotional Assessment—As noted by Aylward, "the Child Behavior Checklist (CBCL) often is considered the 'gold standard' in the assessment of children's behavior problems." This instrument is appropriate for ages 4 through 18 years. The parent form may be completed in about 20 minutes by any parent with a minimum fifth-grade reading level. A teacher form to rate children ages 6 through 18 and a Youth Self Report Form (for ages 11-18 years) are also available. The Social Competence Scale is categorized by activities, social and school-related items. The Behavior Problems Scale yields eight problem scales which are grouped into (1) Internalizing Behaviors, (2) Externalizing Behaviors, and (3) Neither (1) or (2). On the Teacher's Scale, an adaptive functions profile replaces social competence with factors including unpopular, inattentive, nervous-overactive, anxious, social withdrawal, self-distraction, obsessive-compulsive, and aggressive. On the Self-Report Form, there are only two basic scales: Competence and Behavior Problems. As Aylward points out, "the inattention scale also reportedly differentiates ADD with and without hyperactivity."

The Personality Inventory for Children (PIC), completed by parents, provides a description of personality characteristics applicable to children 6 to 16 years of age. It is developed along the same format as the Minnesota Multiphasic Personality Inventory (MMPI). The original version of the PIC contained 600 items, making it difficult for some parents to complete it within two hours. In its present form, 280 items allow for scoring of the 12 clinical scales, a general adjustment scale, and four factors including (1) Undisciplined/Poor Self-Control, (2) Social Incompetence, (3) Internalization, Somatic Symptoms, and (4) Cognitive Development. According to Aylward, "the PIC is useful in differentiating hyperactive, learning disabled and normal children, as well as learning disabled versus behaviorally disordered students."*

Additional Assessment Procedures—The Dyslexia Screening Instrument is a useful addition to the clinician's test battery, especially when a reading disability is suspected. This 33 item scale is rated by the child's teacher on characteristics that may be typically observed in the classroom. Appropriate for use with children ages 6 through 21 years, it is scored by computer using a *discriminate function* prediction of Pass, Fail (i.e., consistent with dyslexia), or Inconclusive Classifications.

Scales for Predicting Successful Inclusion is a recently developed norm referenced instrument designed to predict which students with disabilities will most likely be successful in a general educational setting. Appropriate for children ages 5 to 18 years, this scale focuses on four major factors associated with school adjustment: (1) Work Habits, (2) Coping Skills, (3) Peer Relationships, and (4) Emotional Maturity. Items on these scales represent essential behaviors needed for successful inclusion in a regular classroom. These scales may be rated by the child's teachers, parents, or others who are knowledgeable about her.

---

*Glen P. Aylward, *Practitioner's Guide to Developmental and Psychological Testing.* NY: Plenum Publishing, 1994.

A promising brief neuropsychological battery for children has been developed and will be published shortly. Based on advanced information provided by the Psychological Corp., the NEPSY is described as a comprehensive instrument for assessing neuropsychological development in children ages 3 to 12. This battery is divided into 5 domains:

- Attention/Executive
- Language
- Sensorimotor
- Visuomotor
- Memory functions

The NEPSY is validated for use on children diagnosed with LD (learning disabilities), ADHD, TBI (traumatic brain injury), Autistic Disorders, and Speech and Language impairment. Norms are based on a standardization sample of one thousand children. Administration time ranges from one hour (for preschool) to 2 1/2 hours (for older children). The subtest in the Attention and Executive Function category assesses inhibition, self-regulation, monitoring, vigilance, selective and sustained attention, maintenance of response set, planning, flexibility in thinking, and linguistic and figural fluency. In general, most of the subtests assess characteristics that are important in describing the child with ADD/ADHD. By combining this battery with other measures such as rating scales, CPT, personality and behavioral assessment, the clinician should be able to provide a comprehensive evaluation. The NEPSY is scheduled for release soon and should clearly receive much attention in studies involving children with ADD/ADHD.

Rating Scales

There are many rating scales for ADD/ADHD. (This rationale was previously discussed in the section on behavioral observations.) Some of the more frequently used rating scales that appear most helpful in comprehensive assessments are briefly reviewed here. However, it should be pointed out there is generally poor agreement between either parent or teacher ratings and performance on a CPT; specifically, there may be agreement in about one quarter of cases. (For more in-depth information, the clinician is referred to the section on Behavioral Assessment in Dr. Glen Aylward's *Practitioner's Guide to Developmental and Psychological Testing.*) The following rating scales can be completed by parents, teachers, and the child.

Parent Rating Scales—The most comprehensive is the Conners' Parent Rating Scales-Revised (CPRS-R) for children ages 3 to 17 years. The CPRS-R represents 30 years of research and development. Its reliability and validity stats exceed the original version. It includes eight scales and two indices: (1) Oppositional, (2) Cognitive Problems, (3) Hyperactive-Impulsive, (4) Anxious-Shy, (5) Perfectionism, (6) Social

Problems, (7) Psychosomatic, and (8) *DSM-IV* Symptom subscales, plus the ADHD Index (to distinguish ADHD from non-ADHD kids) and the Global Index (formerly the Hyperactivity Index), the latter of which has 10 of the best items from the original CRS and is especially sensitive to medication effects. The 80-item version is preferred, but when there are time constraints, a 27 item CPRS-RS that includes the first four scales along with the ADHD Index is useful.

The Home Situations Questionnaire-Revised (HSQ-R) contains 14 items that focus specifically on attention and concentration in a variety of situations both at home and in public. It is applicable for children ages 6 through 12 years.

Teacher Rating Scales—The Conners' Teacher Rating Scale-Revised (CTRS-R) contains 59 items which parallel the Parent Rating Scale, except for the Psychosomatic Scale, and was normed from ratings of over 2,000 teachers on children age 3 to 17 years. The shorter 28 item CTRS-RS covers the first three scales of the parallel parent form along with the Global Index. The 10 item Conners' Abbreviated Teacher Questionnaire is reportedly "diagnostically" sensitive not only to hyperactivity, but also to conduct disorder.

The recently published Spadafore-ADHD-Rating Scale, standardized on 760 students, is designed for use by teachers for children ages 5 to 19. It was reportedly intended not only to detect ADHD, but also to indicate the severity of problem behaviors. It consists of a 50-item behavior questionnaire (rating impulsivity, hyperactivity/attention, and social adjustment) and a 9-item ADHD Index. The latter ADHD Index includes criteria used to quantify on-task/off-task behaviors. The Behavior Scale is described as an effective screener that may be used to satisfy the assessment requirements of a 504 referral. However, this scale is also described as a "comprehensive evaluation" by the author, allegedly since the items cover a wide range of symptoms. Also, there is no available companion instrument for parents. An ADHD Observation Form is included to report results in five different categories and requires about ten minutes to complete. The Medication Monitor is comprehensive and may be useful by itself as a stand-alone measure that can be repeated over many weeks of treatment monitoring.

The ADD-H Comprehensive Teacher Rating Scale (ACTeRS) employs 24 items and 4 scales: Attention, Hyperactivity, Social Skills, and Oppositional Behavior. This rating scale provides separate norms for girls and boys (equivalent to ages 5 through 13). This scale is medication sensitive, and it appears helpful in distinguishing between ADD with and without hyperactivity. A recently developed parent form is now available with similar scales, as well as an additional scale focusing on early childhood behavior.

Since teacher ratings may be prone to halo and/or practice effects, some have recommended that two questionnaires be completed for a baseline measure as ratings often improve between the first and second administration without any intervention. However, Dr. Arnold Goldstein has also noted that some "teacher ratings of aggressive, disruptive, or acting out behaviors are very often erroneously high." A small number of disruptive behaviors may lead to a global impression of the child as a troublemaker or chronically aggressive.

Self-Report Ratings—The Conners Adolescent Self Report Scale contains 87 items on the following subscales: Family Problems, Anger Control Problems, *DSM-IV* Symptom Subscale, Emotional Problems, Conduct Problems, Cognitive Problems, Hyperactive-Impulsive, and the ADHD Index. A 27-item short form contains only the last four scales. This scale is very useful as symptoms clearly change with age and self report becomes more accurate as the child gets older. Also, co-morbid problems develop and become more consistent with age.

Combined Rating Scales—The Behavioral Assessment System for Children (BASC) is a newly developed comprehensive assessment of behavior and self-perception. It represents multi-raters with co-normed data from teachers, parents, and the children. About 10,000 children were rated by more than 2,000 teachers and more than 3,000 parents. It covers behavior, cognitive, and emotional data that are not only descriptive, but are also a diagnostic aid. The BASC reportedly measures "dimensions of behavior and emotions that are easily linked to the criteria in *DSM-IV* and the Individuals with Disabilities Act (IDEA)."

The BASC Teacher Rating Scale is subdivided by age with preschool (4-5 years), child (6-11 years), and adolescent (12-18 years) forms. It takes about 10 to 20 minutes to complete and provides four composites: Externalizing Problems, Internalizing Problems, School Problems, and Adaptive Skills. There is also an F Index, a validity check on "Faking."

The BASC Parent Rating Scale also has forms with three age levels using the same domains as those on the teacher scale, with the exception of the Learning Problems Scale on the School Problems Composite and the Study Skills Scale on the Adaptive Skills Composite. An F Index (to estimate Faking) is also included.

The BASC Self Report of Personality has two age levels: child (8-11 years) and adolescent (12-18 years). Four composite scores include (1) School Maladjustment, (2) Clinical Maladjustment, (3) Personal Adjustment, and (4) an overall composite—the Emotional Symptoms Index. This form requires about 30 minutes to complete. In addition to these rating scales, there is a Structured Developmental History which can be given in interview format by the clinician or may even be completed by the parent. There is also a Student Observation System—a form that can be used to observe and record classroom behavior directly for the identified child. This form allows for recording of both positive and negative behaviors. Overall, the BASC system is quite comprehensive and might even replace several instruments that may typically be used by the clinician. Its development and presentation appears to reflect good psychometric construction and appealing clinical utility.

The Diagnostic Process

The accompanying chart (Figure 2.1 on page 56) depicts the complex process used to make a complete and accurate evaluation of a child's presenting problems (at school and/or at home) and then to formulate a comprehensive individualized program for management of the child's behavior. There may be one or more presenting problems which significantly affect the child's performance and behavior in school and, perhaps, his behavior at home. While an important objective of this process is formulation of the primary, secondary and tertiary diagnoses, the evaluation process also gives the clinician an overall picture of the child's strengths and weaknesses which are incorporated into the individualized treatment program of behavior management and other clinical procedures. This treatment program will have behavioral modification components; it may or may not include a medication regimen; and it will include mechanisms to monitor and evaluate progress. Specific problem areas and symptomatic behaviors become targets for change.

To begin this process, it is essential for the clinician to obtain information from several sources including at least the child's parents and teachers (at school, at music lessons, in Sunday School, and coaches for sports activities, etc.) and, of course, from the child, him/herself. Observations during a direct interview and rating forms completed by the parents provide parental input. This information will include the child's medical history (e.g., seizures, head traumas, medications), developmental milestones, family medical history (e.g., regarding possible familial genetic disorders), and the child's academic history; all this information can be invaluable in raising suspicions about certain diagnoses or in making hypotheses to be considered and ruled in or out with test procedures. Then, combining this information with results from a wide range of test procedures, the clinician is able to formulate a pattern of strengths and weaknesses, assets and deficits that either support or negate "suspected" diagnoses. Independent observations in the classroom (or other school-like settings) would certainly help to diagnose and document the ADD/ADHD disorders since those settings tend to elicit many ADD-like behavioral symptoms.

Note that the self-reporting data and interview of the child one-on-one are especially critical when evaluating an older child or adolescent. As they get older, children can provide more valid and reliable information about their behavior, especially about externalizing (acting-out) problems. Direct behavioral observations during the testing session provide a wealth of information about how the child copes with easy or difficult material, whether a basic visual or hearing problem may exist, and information about many other issues related to general maturation, self-concept, attitudes toward academic tasks, coordination problems, arousal level, and potential neurological problems.

Assessment of behavioral and emotional characteristics provides the last component; such assessment reflects whether the child presents evidence of externalizing problems (e.g., aggression, defiance, conduct disorders) or internalizing problems (e.g., anxiety, obsessive compulsive tendencies, depression).

Once all the data and evidence have been gathered, a number of diagnostic conditions may be considered based on: the general background information; the parent, teacher, and self ratings; behavioral observations at home, school, and in assessment situations; and, of course, considering the neuropsychological test data. Typically more than one diagnostic condition is present; it is the exception for a child to manifest only

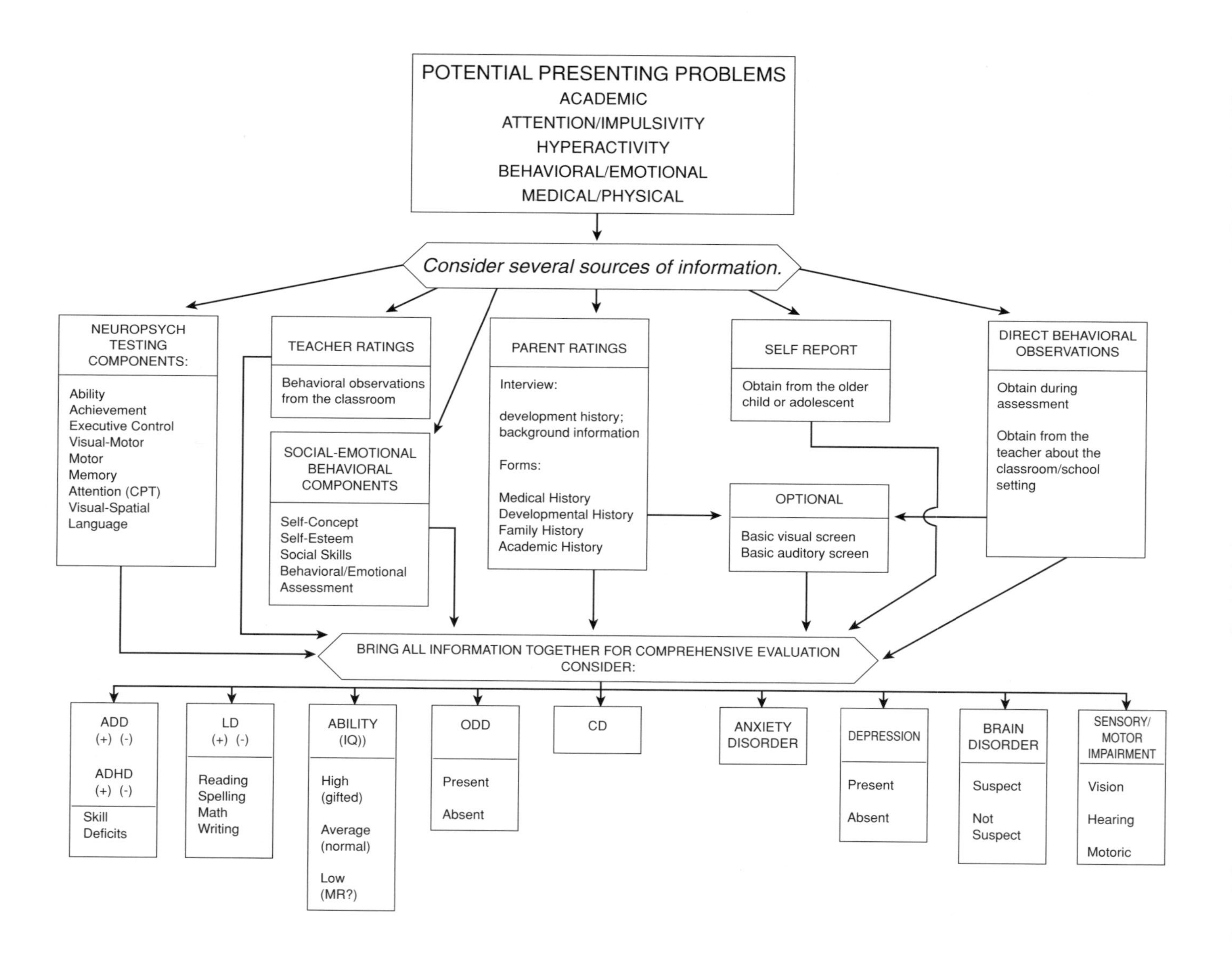

Figure 2.1 Diagnostic Process Flow Chart.

one condition. Thus, the implication for treatment is almost always that a multi-modal program will be needed to deal with a complex pattern of symptoms and problems.

The position assumed at the ADD Clinic in Biloxi, Mississippi, is that each separate component of the behavior/problem pattern must be addressed. While medications are often very helpful, they are generally ineffective with aggression problems of ODD (oppositional deficit disorder) and CD (conduct disorder). Likewise, medications have little effect on learning disabilities. Furthermore, "Pills do not teach skills" and ADD kids almost always need basic skills development through training. Specific behavioral training procedures (for parents and sometimes teachers as well as for the child) will be used to address some of these skill deficits.

Thus, an individualized, multi-modal treatment program will be developed to address the child's deficits (perhaps including organizational skills, learning strategies, training in following directions, development of social skills and study skills) and periodically to evaluate progress; this program will include use of appropriate and targeted *medications,* when needed, as well as appropriate targeted *behavioral interventions.*

Interpretation of Test Data

Much information is often collected in the evaluation of a child with ADD/ADHD. The first step in the interpretation of this data is to list all of the tests given with their respective standard scores or percentile ranks. This will allow for a direct comparison of the strengths and weaknesses across a variety of dimensions assessed and the development of a profile for this child. An example of this process of test data integration follows. The entire list of tests used and the neuropsychological report are presented in Appendix A.

Test Findings: Diagnosis and Description—This 7-year, 3-month old child who is in the second grade has academic and behavioral difficulties described as primary "concentration and memory problems." His neurologist wished to rule out a seizure disorder. An EEG and an MRI were essentially within normal limits. However, his developmental history revealed anoxia at birth (no Apgar scores were available). Subsequently, he has manifested learning, attentional, and behavioral problems.

Neuropsychological tests were selected to look for support of the ADD/ADHD behavioral pattern while also attempting to delineate additional manifestations of learning disability characteristics. As with many cases of ADD/ADHD behaviors, there are frequently associated co-morbid conditions. In this case, a learning disability was highly suspect, especially in light of the reported anoxia at birth. In addition, there were reported behavioral problems such that oppositional defiant disorder or perhaps even a conduct disorder would need to be ruled out. The test battery thus consisted of measures of basic abilities, achievements, language, executive control functions, motor, visual-motor attention, behavior and social-emotional functions. Specific emphasis was placed on frontal lobe function tasks as related to ADD/ADHD and executive control. Also important was an analysis of this child's ability to process and retain information presented through visual versus auditory sense modalities. Since there was no obvious organic lesion (from prior neurodiagnostic tests), it was important to describe patterns of neuropsychological dysfunction that might relate to his specific areas of difficulty. More important, these patterns might be used to formulate a series of interventions designed to address each problem area. In addition to the traditional neuropsychological measures, some assessment of behavioral and emotional issues was addressed as these problems were clearly interfering with his adaptive functioning. Test selection was thus based on these considerations. To provide this information there were more in-depth clinical interviews with parents and child, along with test procedures such as the Human Figure Drawings, Kinetic Family Drawing, Sentence Completion Test, Three Wishes, Animal Projectives Test, and the Personality Inventory for Children.

Interpretation of this child's test pattern was made with reference to his developmental history, medical evaluation, family history, and prior medical treatment. *First,* it appeared that the child was motivated to perform and exhibited a pattern of compensatory strategies similar to that used in school. Essentially, he tries hard to perform while experiencing much difficulty. This is reflected in his generally good achievements while having problems processing visual material. Considerable frustration and stress are encountered in this process. *Second,* while all of his deficits seem mild to moderate in degree of impairment, the total cumulative effect of all deficits combined seems to make it difficult for him to handle. *Third,* most problems are subtle, reflecting mild frontal lobe dysfunction and perhaps even some subcortical involvement. Other measures of executive control functions are consistent with the ADD pattern and with "frontal lobe characteristics" as well. Although this child does not present significant problems with regard to achievements, at present, it appears that he will have increasing difficulty as he proceeds to higher grade levels. *Fourth,* a combination of attentional problems, impulsivity, and hyperactivity—along with visual processing difficulty and slowed motoric responding—clearly make it hard for him to function adequately in the classroom. Accumulated frustration and stress further compound his problem with associated aggression and depression. With constant self-comparison to his brother (who is doing very well in school), there is poor self-concept and poor self-esteem.

Recommendation for Treatment Plan—Specific recommendations are made to address all problem areas with regard to clinical treatment approaches as well as practical recommendations that may be carried out at home or in school as part of his routine of daily activities. See Treatment Plan, Figure 2.2.

Inspection of the recommendations made in the neuropsych report indicates that additional general behavioral counseling will be needed with specification of several behaviors that will need to be incorporated into a Home and School Behavior Management Program. Other suggestions will involve more general activities that may assist not only in the direct remediation process but also in helping to generalize these skills that are trained in the clinic (e.g., visual-spatial and visual-motor skills).

TREATMENT PLAN		
Problem	*Program Goal*	*Outcome*
SELF-CONTROL	a. Development of improved impulse control using cognitive behavioral techniques b. Enhancement of self-control through relaxation and stress management c. Reinforcement of behavioral inhibition	1. Parent and teacher ratings 2. Direct behavioral observations 3. Performance on behavioral inhibition tasks
ATTENTIONAL SKILLS	a. Medication regimen b. Specific attention training exercises (e.g., ATG) c. Direct reinforcement of any improvement in attention	1. Direct behavioral observations 2. Parent and teacher ratings 3. Performance on attentional tasks
ANGER MANAGEMENT	a. Provide alternative strategies for dealing with frustration b. Develop relaxation training and stress management skills c. Use role-playing for the development of appropriate alternative behavioral strategies	1. Parent and teacher ratings 2. Self-respect 3. Direct behavioral observations 4. Psychological test data
SELF-CONCEPT SELF-ESTEEM	a. Through behavioral techniques, focus on developing more appropriate and desirable behavior with direct reinforcement b. Use self-motivation and self-talk procedures to enhance confidence in performance c. Use role-playing to develop increased competency in situations associated with feelings of inadequacy d. Generally increase positive stroking of desirable alternative behaviors	1. Direct behavioral observation 2. Parent and teacher ratings 3. Self-respect 4. Psychological test data

Figure 2.2 Treatment Plan.

TREATMENT PLAN		
Problem	*Program Goal*	*Outcome*
DEFICIENCIES IN FAMILY COMMUNICATON	a. Provide consistency and stability within the family with the establishment of rules, expectations, and clarification of targeted behavior problems	1. Direct behavioral observation 2. Parent ratings 3. Self-respect 4. Performance on specific psychological test measures
COMPLETION OF TASK ASSIGNMENTS	a. Reinforcement of comprehension of tasks b. Maintenance of tasks c. Task completion d. Use of successive levels of difficulty to enhance compliance	1. Periodic school consultation with teacher along with teacher ratings 2. Parent observation of task-related behavior 3. Psychological test data
DIFFICULTY WITH COMPLIANCE TO COMMANDS	a. Establish appropriate alternative cooperative behavior with nonreinforcement of non-compliance b. Develop appropriate use of contingency management both at home and at school	1. Parent and teacher reports 2. Behavioral observation 3. Psychological test data

Figure 2.2 *continued*

MEDICATION INFORMATION FOR CLINICIANS

The information in this section does not replace personal medical consultation. No change in medication schedule or dose should be made, nor should any medications be added to your child's medication regime without prior consultation with your child's physician. The author is also indebted to Rene Duffourc, M.D., and Jule Miller, M.D., both Board Certified Child psychiatrists, for their critical reading of the original manuscript on "Medication Information for Clinicians."

This section on medication information presents current concepts that may be helpful in guiding clinicians in the use of medications for ADD/ADHD. A medications handout that may be used to provide concise information on medications that are commonly used to treat ADD is presented in Figure 2.3 on page 62. A comprehensive review of many studies on medications that are typically used may be found in the special article, "Pharmacotherapy of Attention-Deficit Hyperactivity Disorder across the Life Cycle," appearing in the April 1996 issue of the *Journal of Child and Adolescent Psychiatry.*

The use of medication for ADD/ADHD began over 50 years ago. Stimulant medication was shown to be effective in 1937, but was not used to any large degree until around 1957 when methylphenidate (Ritalin) was introduced. Many carefully controlled studies indicated that this medication was *safe* and *effective.* Despite occasional attacks by the media and a strong campaign against Ritalin in the late 1980s by the Church of Scientology, this medication has survived both early and current attacks. Much fear was generated for parents of children with ADD/ADHD when Ritalin was implicated with brain damage, high blood pressure, confusion, murder, emotional disorders, Tourette's, neurologic seizures, agitation, depression, and suicide. Many doubts were created in the professional community with demands for medication by teachers described as unable to cope with their student's behavior and psychiatrists who were considered "money hungry." Problems still periodically surface, but it is now generally accepted that stimulant medications are often quite appropriate for some, absolutely needed by others, and basically safe. DuPaul and Stoner have noted that 750,000 children have been placed on stimulant medication. Also, the rise in use has been reportedly limited to those in the middle school and high school populations.

The Stimulants

There are three primary medications that fall into this category: (1) Methylphenidate (Ritalin®); (2) Dextrostat® or Dexamphetamine (Dexadrine®); and (3) Pemoline (Cylert®). A fourth medication containing Dextroamphetamine saccharate and sulfate with amphetamine aspartate and sulfate (Adderall®) was previously used in adults for weight control (Obitral) and recently FDA-approved about three years ago as a treatment option for ADHD.

MEDICATION CHART TO TREAT ATTENTION DEFICIT DISORDERS**

Drug	*Form*	*Dosing*	*Common Side Effects*	*Duration of Behavioral Effects*	*Pros*	*Precautions*
Ritalin® Methylphenidate	Tablets 5 mg 10 mg 20 mg	Start with a morning dose of 5 mg/day and increase up to 0.3–0.7 mg/kg of body weight. 2.5–60 mg/day*	Insomnia, decreased appetite, weight loss, headache, irritability, stomachache	3–4 hrs	Works quickly (within 30–60 minutes); effective in 70% of patients; good safety record	Not recommended in patients with marked anxiety, motor tics, or with family history of Tourette's syndrome
Ritalin-SR® Methylphenidate	Tablet 20 mg	Start with a morning dose of 20 mg and increase up to 0.3–0.7 mg/kg of body weight. Sometimes 5 or 10 mg standard tablet added in morning for quick start. Up to 60 mg/day*	Insomnia, decreased appetite, weight loss, headache, irritability, stomachache	About 7 hrs	Particularly useful for adolescents with ADHD to avoid noontime dose; good safety record	Slow onset of action (1–2 hours); not recommended in patients with marked anxiety, motor tics, or with family history of Tourette's syndrome
Dexedrine® Dextroamphetamine	Tablet 5 mg; Spansules 5 mg, 10 mg; Elixir 15 mg	Start with a morning dose of 5 mg and increase up to 0.3–0.7 mg/kg of body weight. Give in divided doses 2–3 times per day. 2.5–40 mg/day*	Insomnia, decreased appetite, weight loss, headache, irritability, stomachache	3–4 hrs (tablet) 8–10 hrs (spansule)	Works quickly (within 30–60 minutes); may avoid noontime dose in spansule form; good safety record	Not recommended in patients with marked anxiety, motor tics, or with family history of Tourette's syndrome
Cylert® Pemoline	Tablets (Long Acting) 18.75 mg 37.5 mg 75 mg 37.5 mg chewable	Start with a dose of 18.75–37.5 mg and increase up to 112.5 mg as needed in a single morning dose. 18.75–112.5 mg/day*	Insomnia, agitation, headaches, stomachaches; infrequently, abnormal liver function tests have been reported	12–24 hrs	Given only once a day	May take 2–4 weeks for clinical response; regular blood tests needed to check liver function

Figure 2.3 Medication Chart to Treat Attention Deficit Disorders.

Figure 2.3 *continued . . .*

Tofranil® Imipramine Hydrochloride	Tablets 10 mg 25 mg 50 mg	Start with a dose of 10 mg in evening if weight < 50 lbs. and increase 10 mg every 3–5 days as needed; start with a dose of 25 mg in evening if weight is > 50 lbs. and increase 25 mg every 3–5 days as needed. Given in single or divided doses, morning and evening. 25–150 mg/day*	Dry mouth, decreased appetite, headache, stomachache, dizziness, constipation, mild tachycardia	12–24 hrs	Helpful for ADHD patients with co-morbid depression or anxiety; lasts throughout day	May take 2–4 weeks for clinical response; to detect pre-existing cardiac conduction defect, a baseline ECG may be recommended. Discontinue gradually
Norpramin® Desipramine Hydrochloride	Tablets 10 mg 25 mg 50 mg 75 mg 100 mg 150 mg	Start with a dose of 10 mg in evening if weight < 50 lbs. and increase 10 mg every 3–5 days as needed; start with a dose of 25 mg in evening if weight is > 50 lbs. and increase 25 mg every 3–5 days as needed. Given in single or divided doses, morning and evening. 25–150 mg/day*	Dry mouth, decreased appetite, headache, stomachache, dizziness, constipation, mild tachycardia	12–24 hrs	Helpful for ADHD patients with co-morbid depression or anxiety; lasts throughout day	May take 2–4 weeks for clinical response; to detect pre-existing cardiac conduction defect, a baseline ECG may be recommended. Discontinue gradually
Catapres® Clonidine Hydrochloride	Tablets .1 mg .2 mg .3 mg Patches TTS-1 TTS-2 TTS-3	Start with a dose of .025–.05 mg/day in evening and increase by similar dose every 3–7 days as needed. Given in divided doses 3–4 times per day. 0.15–.3 mg/day*	Sleepiness, hypotension, headache, dizziness, stomachache, nausea, dry mouth, localized skin reactions with patch	3–6 hrs (oral form) 5 days (skin patch)	Helpful for ADHD patients with co-morbid tic disorders or severe hyperactivity and/or aggression	Sudden discontinuation could result in rebound hypertension; to avoid daytime tiredness starting dose given at bedtime and increased slowly

*Daily dose range
**Published with permission from Specialty Press (1995) and distributed by ADD Warehouse (1-800-233-9273)

How can medication help? There is emerging evidence to suggest that individuals with attention deficit disorders may have some form of dysfunction occurring in regions of the brain associated with the control and regulation of attention, arousal, and activity. The medications charted above fall into three classes: stimulants (Ritalin, Dexedrine, Cylert), antidepressants (Tofranil, Desipramine) and antihypertensives (Catapres). These medications have all been shown to be effective in increasing attention and reducing impulsivity and hyperactivity. However, each individual responds in their own unique way to medication depending upon the person's physical make-up, severity of symptoms, and other possible problems accompanying the ADD. Therefore, careful monitoring should be done by a physician in collaboration with the teacher, therapist, parents, and patient.

Medications to treat attention deficit disorders and related conditions should only be prescribed by a physician. Information presented here is not intended to replace the advice of a physician.

Miller (1996) has noted that a review of over 155 controlled studies with over 5000 children treated indicates that stimulant medications are effective about 70 percent of the time, with a range from 60 percent to 90 percent effectiveness. Compared to ADHD, the percentage of children with ADD (not hyperactive) showing a positive response is generally lower (55-65%). In general, these stimulants reduce restlessness (and general arousal), help children to maintain their work effort so they may complete tasks, enhance the accuracy of their work and their ability to plan tasks, and improve their overall productivity in the classroom; as Barkley (1996) has noted stimulants can increase a child's ability to show what he has learned. A decrease in impulsivity and disruptiveness, along with improved control of emotions (including aggressiveness), better interpersonal relations, better handwriting, and a general sense of calm have been observed. Some additional good side effects include more positive relationships with peers, sibs and family, along with enhanced self-esteem. Stimulants have also been shown to be helpful with retarded children who have ADHD symptoms, if the retardation is not severe.

It is, however, important to note here that no stimulant med will "cure" ADD. Currently, there is no cure for ADD. These medications help children with ADD/ADHD to more closely approximate their potential abilities and their capacity for social relationships. While these medications improve a child's present level of functioning, they do not have any apparent long-term effects other than to allow the child to better acquire the skills she will need in the future. There is evidence that many children who are treated with stimulants are better able to complete their education and probably have a lower risk of substance abuse in the future, but much depends upon the additional behavioral programs employed. Essentially, the child must perceive that he has the ability and skills to cope with problem situations. If a child has gotten the message that "what you need to do to improve your (school)work is to take this pill," an unfortunate association is established. It is clear that a "pill teaches no skill." It is essential that the child also be given structured learning experiences that focus on her abilities to cope and adapt to many situations both academic and social, and that these skills must generalize and be utilized in future vocational, work, and social areas. Medication should, therefore, be combined with behavioral procedures to provide the child with useful, adaptive skills that will be used throughout life.

In the past, there have been many concerns regarding the use of amphetamines for fear of "addiction dependency," or an increased risk for later substance abuse. First, the medications are used to enhance awareness and to improve attention and concentration ; in contrast, much addictive drug use focuses on escape from reality or distortion of one's awareness of it. Second, children with ADD/ADHD have been shown to exhibit a lower than normal level of arousal in the nervous system. Much of their hyperactive-restless behavior therefore makes sense—the child is simply attempting to increase activation in the brain to a normal level making the self-stimulation unnecessary. In short, when children with ADD/ADHD take an appropriate dose of stimulant medication, they do not get high—they get to feel "normal"—since the arousal level is increased to a more normal range.

Some concern has also been experienced over possible appetite suppression, along with weight loss and stunting of growth. This is generally not a problem when medication is taken with meals or shortly after a meal. Recent studies over a period of several years have revealed that these medications do not result in stunting of growth. Untreated children with ADD/ADHD have been found to be generally somewhat shorter prepubertal than normal. Growth does occur later, post pubertal, and the discrepancy disappears whether they are on or off medications. Actually, having ADD/ADHD affects their eating habits more than the medications. It has been reported that some youngsters eat better on medication as they can sit down at the meal and pay better attention to eating. While the medication does slow down the growth rate, it is highly variable. Also, larger children seem to be more affected than smaller ones. There is, however, no effect on puberty or rate of pubertal growth. Monitoring of height and weight is suggested on a monthly basis and not more frequently.

There are, however, some side effects that should be considered causes for concern. Some of these include becoming socially withdrawn, overfocused, lethargic, agitated, teary, and emotionally upset. Often these side effects may appear when the medication is first introduced to the child or when it is increased to a higher dose. They signal that the dose may be too high, but may resolve within a few hours after stopping the medication. When a stimulant causes these effects, the dose may be lowered or the child may be switched to another medication. The rebound effect may be observed when the stimulant begins to wear off. At some point, the child may become more irritable, crabby, teary, or hyperactive; this is basically related to a drop in level of arousal below that of the premedication level. This problem may be avoided by administration of a light dose of medication just prior to the time of rebound, or perhaps changing to a longer acting smoother stimulant.

The possibility of tics and the appearance of Tourette's Syndrome have been cause for concern in the past. ADD and Tourette's are fairly closely associated. While this may have been a contraindication for the use of stimulant medications in the past, it does not evoke as much concern today, and many physicians will proceed with stimulant medication, but perhaps with closer monitoring. It is estimated that about 50 percent of these children with tics also have ADD/ADHD; some researchers and clinicians believe these two disorders may be on the same gene. In many cases, the ADD/ADHD symptoms may be manifested first. Tics may appear later in the sequence. Many children who show these tics will improve, some showing tics at low doses only to disappear on a higher dose. Tics are fairly common between the ages of 6 and 12 years and when the child is under a high stress level. The stimulant Ritalin has, however, been known to lower the threshold for tics, thus increasing the probability of their occurrence.

Some children may report headache; this is generally rare and could be temporary or may necessitate a change of medication. Similar problems may occur with stomachaches, although this complaint is usually resolved if the child takes food with the medication. It also appears that the complaints are more like "butterflies" and may last only about 45 minutes.

A statement on the use of medication from the Academy of Pediatrics as of August, 1996, is as follows: "Medication may be indicated when difficulties clearly affect school performance, social adjustment, or are associated with a significant behavior disorder. These difficulties may result in academic failure, inability to fulfill potential and give poor self-esteem, or social maladaptive behavior. Medication is not a panacea or a cure-all and should not be continued unless there is clear cut benefit."

The Decision to Medicate—So many parents have voiced concerns over the use of stimulant medications that it is important to know who makes the decision on medications and on what basis the decision is made. Concerns have been raised even when parents understand the neurophysiological nature of ADD/ADHD and know the function of the medication. Knowing this, as well as the safety and effectiveness of these medications may still raise concerns and many parents express the wish that their child might not *need* the medication. Some children with mild ADD may be able to cope without medications using behavioral and cognitive techniques primarily. Some parents have even turned to remedies described as "natural" and found in health stores. One substance call Pycnegynol has many anecdotal claims, but absolutely no research to back its effectiveness or its safety for use with children. Consequently, none of these so-called natural remedies are recommended. However, the use of such substances does reflect the parents' needs for alternative treatments that are safe and effective.

When a decision is made to use a stimulant medication, it is done so with the parent's acceptance. In essence, *the parent makes the decision.* This decision will basically depend upon the seriousness of the ADD/ADHD condition and how it impacts upon the child's academic *and* social life. Frustration experienced by the child and by teachers who must deal with her behavior is critical in making a decision. It is most important that there be cooperation from all parties—parents, teachers, and professionals. Consideration must also be given to potential and actual side effects that may sometimes dictate whether a stimulant or some alternative medication should be used. While the presence of tics and even a seizure disorder are not absolute contraindications to the use of stimulant medication, the presence of glaucoma or cardiovascular problems may be clear contraindications.

Standard clinical practice also serves as a guideline for a decision on medication. Specifically, stimulant medications should not be used until a behavioral program is established. At that point, the need for medication is determined by residual problems and the impact they have. Medications should therefore be used, ideally, to manage any degree of problems not handled by the behavioral programs and educational adjustments. Ongoing studies at NIMH will perhaps shed some additional light on this issue of meds and behavioral components of treatment. However, many experts still indicate that stimulant medications exert greater behavior changing effects when combined with other effective treatments such as behavior modification. It has also been noted that such combined treatment may minimize medication dosage. Now, with the advent of technological advances, there may be more reliance upon use of electronic instruments in the classroom that filter background noise and/or improve signal-noise ratios in conjunction with behavioral programs. (See the section in this chapter on electronic assist devices.)

Some factors noted by DuPaul that appear to enter into the decision to medicate include:

- the apparent severity of the ADHD symptoms and the presence of disruptive behavior
- prior treatments (e.g., behavioral) that may have failed
- the presence of anxiety (which lessens the probability of stimulants being successful)
- the parents' attitude towards meds
- the adequacy and competency of adult supervision
- the child's attitude

Compliance may obviously be compromised by some of these factors.

Once a decision is made to use a stimulant medication, the only way to determine whether it will be successful is to conduct a careful *clinical trial.* Many physicians will not start medication at the beginning or end of the school year or during holidays. An *open* trial is typical where everybody knows that the child is on medication. A *double-blind* trial, where no one knows whether the child is getting a placebo or the actual medication, may be conducted if the results of the open trial are equivocal. It should be noted that about 10 % of children who have ADD/ADHD don't respond positively at first. It is also known that stimulant medications may help anyone to focus better. Therefore, response to medication should not be used as a diagnostic indicator of ADD/ADHD. Some physicians will also have access to the use of a continuous performance test (CPT), for example the Gordon Diagnostic System or TOVA, to aid in predicting response to a medication. However, the ultimate test is to have baseline ratings from teachers, start the medication and at some point, obtain repeat teacher ratings. Parent observation and ratings of behavior change, as well as side effects noted, is also documented. A copy of typical side effects and their monitor is found in Figure 2.4 on page 68. Often the physician begins medication on a weekend, and observations are noted. If there are no significant side effects, the medication may be given for a few days, stopped, and then readministered. When behaviors vary with the changes and behavior improvements are noted with medication, the doctor may then adjust the dose. The key here is to obtain maximum control while minimizing side effects, as well as any possible cognitive interference associated with some of the higher dose levels of medications. When the child appears overactive, irritable, weepy and more difficult to manage than prior to starting medication, this may be the *rebound* effect, especially if it occurs after four to five hours from the last dose in the case of methylphenidate, but later in the longer acting stimulants. Normally, this may be a problem when the child comes home from

STIMULANT DRUG SIDE EFFECTS RATING SCALE

Name ______________________________ **Date** ______________

Person Completing This Form ______________________________

Instructions: Please rate each behavior from 0 (absent) to 9 (serious). Circle only one number beside each item. A zero means that you have not seen the behavior in this child during the past week, and a 9 means that you have noticed it and believe it to be either very serious or to occur very frequently.

Behavior	*Absent*									*Serious*
Insomnia or trouble sleeping	0	1	2	3	4	5	6	7	8	9
Nightmares	0	1	2	3	4	5	6	7	8	9
Stares a lot or daydreams	0	1	2	3	4	5	6	7	8	9
Talks less with others	0	1	2	3	4	5	6	7	8	9
Uninterested in others	0	1	2	3	4	5	6	7	8	9
Decreased appetite	0	1	2	3	4	5	6	7	8	9
Irritable	0	1	2	3	4	5	6	7	8	9
Stomachaches	0	1	2	3	4	5	6	7	8	9
Headaches	0	1	2	3	4	5	6	7	8	9
Drowsiness	0	1	2	3	4	5	6	7	8	9
Sad/unhappy	0	1	2	3	4	5	6	7	8	9
Prone to crying	0	1	2	3	4	5	6	7	8	9
Anxious	0	1	2	3	4	5	6	7	8	9
Bites fingernails	0	1	2	3	4	5	6	7	8	9
Euphoric/unusually happy	0	1	2	3	4	5	6	7	8	9
Dizziness	0	1	2	3	4	5	6	7	8	9
Tics or nervous movements	0	1	2	3	4	5	6	7	8	9

Figure 2.4 The Stimulant Drug Side Effects Rating Scale, used to monitor side effects to stimulant medication. From *Hyperactive Children: A Handbook for Diagnosis and Treatment* by R. A. Barkley, 1981, New York: Guilford Press. Copyright 1981 by The Guilford Press. Reprinted by permission of the publisher.

school and this effect may make it very difficult to get homework completed. If the child is weepy, exhibits a dazed look, and is restless, this may indicate overmedication and typically appears after about two hours from the last dose. At these times, the child may also complain about "feeling weird."

Deciding on Which Stimulant to Use—As previously noted, there are options with regard to brand names and there are options regarding the length of time the medication is effective. For example, with the short-acting form of Ritalin or Dexadrine, a change may be noted after 15 to 30 minutes following ingestion of the medication. The improvement, if obtained, may last for about three to five hours and on the average four hours. This means that if the morning dose is taken with breakfast, by lunch time a second dose may be needed to allow the behavioral improvement to be maintained until the end of all classes. A third dose may, however, also be needed to obtain adequate cooperation and productivity during homework. There is a tremendous individual response to the medications and how they are metabolized. Thus, while many children are placed on three doses per day, others may require two and some need four. A fourth dose may sometimes be given at bedtime in lieu of an alternative medication. It may seem paradoxical that a child may go to sleep easier and more quickly with a light dose of stimulant medication, but clinically, this may be an effective alternative. (This is not surprising when one considers that many adults—perhaps with Adult ADD—are capable of rapid sound sleep just after having a cup of coffee.) Some factors that may influence the decision to use one stimulant over another include: (1) age—Some pre-teens and teens resent taking the dose at lunch and request a long-acting medication. While Ritalin SR (sustained release) is stated to be 20 mgs, only 12-15 are released over a period of 5-7 hours. Adderal is reported to last 8-12 hours and is a smoother medication; (2) rebound—Fewer problems are noted with Adderal vs. Ritalin; (3) depression—Ritalin has a higher rate of Dysphoria (an unacceptable side effect); and (4) tics—Ritalin appears to lower the threshold for tics.

When to Give Stimulant Medications?—Stimulant medications are just as effective when given with meals. Miller (1996) suggests not giving the medication with orange juice—it alters the effect. Since these medications do suppress appetite, it is best to avoid giving these medications in the two-hour period prior to a meal. If the child resists taking the medication, give the medication with applesauce or pudding.

Many physicians begin with either a half or a whole tablet (Ritalin is available in 5 mg, 10 mg, and 20 mg tablets; Dexadrine in 5 mg, 10 mg, and 15 mg tablets); Dexadrine equals one half to two thirds the dose of Ritalin. Some physicians use quarter tablet increases, especially for younger children. A child may show little effect on half tablet, experience side effects on one tablet, but may find that three-quarters tablet is optimal. Most of the difficulty with stimulants may be encountered in the beginning when attempting to regulate the dose, or when an increase is needed. Most practitioners believe that if the right dose is given up front, there should be little change required for most children. Although tolerance is not generally seen, some children may cease to show a positive response for some unknown reason. In these cases, the medication may be suspended and the child observed.

Some practitioners may start the child on a low single dose in the morning. If there is a positive change in behavior that disappears about four hours later, the effectiveness is confirmed. For a school age child, she begins at 5 mgs and then goes to a 10 mg or 15 mg dose. For the teenager, she may start on 10 mgs, then go to a 15 mg or 20 mg dose. For the preschool child, she may start at 2.5 mgs and go to 5.0 mgs or 7.5 mgs. Ritalin. The typical dose pattern is 10 mgs (A.M.), 10 mgs (lunch) and 5 mgs (afternoon).

Miller has noted that Dexadrine is not equivalent to Ritalin. It's estimated that 10 mgs Ritalin is equal to 5-7.5 mgs of Dexadrine, which equals 37.5 mgs Cylert. She notes that the PDR is incorrect in describing Cylert. Specifically, it takes 48 hours to start working and it has to be taken every day starting at 37.5 mgs, not 18.75 mgs. Sometimes Cylert may require a full week to build up in the body and get the full effect. It may also be noted that Cylert may last 2-3 days after the last dose is given (i.e., stopped).

What About Monitoring?—When a child is placed on stimulant medication, it is important to obtain a response rate every three to four months, according to Barren. He suggests that the patient be seen and given a physical exam each time. When on Cylert, some physicians may require a test of liver functions every 3-6 months. Barren also believes that it is important to use rating scales to provide information about behavior changes in the classroom.

After a child is placed on medication, behavior should be monitored on a weekly basis. It is often best to have the teacher rate the behavior and academic performance in school and the parents rate the side effects at home. A number of options exist for these ratings:

1. Combinations of the abbreviated forms of the Conners' Parent Rating Scale-Revised, Conners' Teacher Rating Scale-Revised, along with the Home Situations Questionnaire and the Academic Performance Rating Scale.
2. The BASC Monitor for ADHD (Teacher and Parent Ratings and a Student Observation System) combined with the Academic Performance Rating Scale.
3. The recently published Spadafore-ADHD Rating Scale Medication Monitoring Form that allows the teacher to rate ADHD symptoms, social symptoms, and academic and classroom behaviors. A Medication Side Effects Rating is combined on this form. The ADHD Observation Form may also be used for direct behavioral observations in the classroom. However, there is no companion parent form; a different parent rating scale would need to be selected.
4. The ACTeRS may be used for teacher ratings in combination with the Academic Performance Rating Scale and the abbreviated Conners' Parent Rating Scale-Revised. It is best to select instruments for monitoring that have been co-normed

and determined to be consistent with those used in the initial evaluation process so that the effects of test variability may be minimized. Consequently, the first two combinations (i.e., [a] and [b], above) now appear to offer greater benefits and ease of interpretation. It is, of course, best to remain consistent and use the same monitoring devices over time for more accurate comparisons and documentation of treatment effectiveness. While demonstrating adequate dose sensitivity, computerized CPT results may allow for interesting comparisons (and research), but these CPT measures are best considered secondary to the ratings.

5. Lastly, the clinician may wish to use Curriculum Based Assessment (CBA) to monitor changes in academic performance in specific areas of reading, spelling, arithmetic, and handwriting, as these assessments may have greater ecological validity in short-term comparisons that will reflect medication effects. An example of such a measure would be the number of words read correctly over a one-minute period. For details about this assessment procedure (CBA), see Roberts and Landau (1997).

The objective when placing a child on medication is not simply behavioral control. If a once-hyperactive child becomes passive but shows no other improvements in social interactions, completed work, or enhanced academic performance, then the current medication regimen/dose may be questionable. Many years ago it was noted that the optimal dose of Ritalin needed to manage social behavioral problems is higher than that required for adequate cognitive functioning. In addition to changing the dose and/or schedule, it is also clear that "pills do not teach skills." It is, therefore, essential to combine the medication regimen with other behavioral interventions such as skills training and perhaps adjunctive remediation programs. A child who continues to be unproductive academically, even when placed on medication may be suffering from an undiagnosed and unrecognized learning disability, dysgraphia, or neurological or emotional problems that impair his or her ability to function.

How Long Should Stimulants Be Given?—The answer to this question is both simple and complex. The simple answer is that medications should be administered as long as the child needs them. This may be six months or several years. As these medications become more accepted for adults, they may also continue to be used for a part of adult life, again as they are needed. The complex answer, however, is that a decision on the continuation of medication may depend on the severity of the ADD condition and the availability of viable alternatives to medications. Even now, there are electronic instrumentations that may enhance focusing, and in combination with or in lieu of behavioral techniques, there may be a much reduced need for stimulant medications.

Occasionally, a parent will forget to give the medication or runs out of it. If there is little effect upon behavior and/or academic performance, it is perhaps time to consider stopping the medication. To confirm the effectiveness, baseline teacher ratings are obtained while the child is on medications; the medications may then be suspended for two weeks, given in the second week, and then stopped again. This procedure should give sufficient evidence to continue the medication or to stop it. Some experts suggest stopping treatment annually for one or two weeks about one month after the beginning of a new school year to allow time for adjustment to going back to school (October is suggested for a trial stop). With stimulant medications, it is possible to stop and start the medication; with alternative medications used for ADD/ADHD, a gradual weaning off the medication is required, which, of course, needs to be done under medical supervision. Stopping some of the alternative medications abruptly or even missing a scheduled dose may be risky and clearly should be avoided.

What About Drug Holidays?—Some physicians recommend that stimulant medications be given only for school days or perhaps for significant social events. Others do not stop the medications as long as behavior is a significant problem. Some will argue that the medications are just as important for social interpersonal relationships and should be continued even during summer vacations. There is no evidence that continued use of medications is harmful, especially if they are monitored. Any decision regarding such "drug holidays" should be weighed against the potential harm that may result and the delay in development of critical skills that would occur without medications. This balance of possible benefits versus possible problems should be kept in mind with regard to the use of any medication. Any medication may have side effects and any medication may precipitate unique medical problems for a specific individual. It's important to remember, however, that this is true of any medication that one may be given, including the over-the-counter medications.

FACTORS INFLUENCING MEDICATION EFFECTIVENESS

1. *Generic Ritalin*—This has been reported to be less effective than the brand name. While some respond adequately to it, others will not. Miller has noted that only about 30 percent of ADD/ADHD kids do well on the generic form; it is estimated to be about two thirds as potent. If the medication appears to have stopped working, check to see if your pharmacy switched to the generic form.
2. *Allergies*—During the months in which allergies are more common (e.g., March), there may be a temporary need for more medication. When this allergy season passes, the child will return to his or her "pre-allergy" state. If medications were increased, they may now revert to their prior level. Another type of allergic reaction implicates the food coloring used in making some pills.
3. *Use of Sedating Medications*—Whether prescribed or over the counter, these medications may counteract the effect of the stimulant. Allergy and cold medications and some antidepressive medications may cause drowsiness. There will be a lack of stimulant-medication effectiveness until the sedating medication is changed or stopped.

continued . . .

4. *Ritalin with Orange Juice*—When stimulant medication is taken with orange juice, its effectiveness may be modified. There may even be increased stomach problems.
5. *Dramatic Events*—These events may change the need for stimulant medications. It is not unusual when highly stressful events or changes occur within a family (e.g., introduction of a foster child) that a child who was on a well-adjusted dose level now appears to show an increase in ADD/ADHD behaviors.
6. *Minor Changes or Transitions*—These can also disrupt the level of adjustment to stimulant medication. Such changes (e.g., a family move, getting a new car, or changes in time during spring or fall) can all trigger a reaction that makes the child appear unmedicated.
7. *Dose Level*—Some say that very few children respond to doses of 5 mg. A typical dose ranges from 10 mg to 15 mg.
8. *Young Children*—Very young children under 5 years of age don't respond as well to stimulant medications. Some of these difficult-to-manage youngsters may have pervasive developmental disorder or language problems. Behavior modification is a crucial need for this group. It is also anticipated that the rate of side effects will be higher in this group.
9. *Medications*—Some medications used for treatment of asthma (e.g., Theophylline) may cause severe behavior problems and worsen attention problems and hyperactivity. For stimulants to be more effective, it may be necessary to switch to another medication for asthma. Likewise, some medications for seizure disorders, such as phenobarbital and anticonvulsants like Clonazapem, Phyntoin, and Dilantin may generate more severe ADD behaviors making it more difficult to manage with the same level of stimulant that produced adequate control prior to introduction of one of these additional medications.
10. *Compliance*—Some children may have difficulty swallowing certain pills or may actively resist taking the medication either because they have been teased about it or because of the reaction they have to it. These problems must be sorted out and discussed with the child's physician.

The Antidepressants

The following antidepressant medications will be discussed:

- Tofranil®—imipramine
- Norpramin®—desipramine
- Pamelor®—nortriptyline
- Welbutrin®—bupropion

Alternate medications for ADD/ADHD may be used when there is a problematic reaction to a stimulant, significant side effects, or a lack of positive response. In many cases, this may indicate that the child is unable to tolerate stimulants. Other possible indications for the use of an antidepressant are the presence of significant anxiety or depression. It should be noted that these medications may be most useful for

ADD/ADHD symptoms and for enuresis—they are somewhat less useful for depression. According to Barren (1996), 30 to 40 percent of the children show a response to these medications. However, others report a response of up to 70 percent.

The antidepressants have several noticeable benefits. Decreases in impulsivity and hyperactivity have been observed, along with diminished emotional instability. While these medications have only limited effect on attentional processes, there is often observed improvement in mood and anxiety, as well as improved sleep. Other advantages as noted by Wilens (1996) include: (a) a long half-life; (b) they don't exacerbate tics; (c) there is no concern about growth problems; and (d) they are especially good when there is anxiety and/or mood problems present as well as ADD.

The typical side effects are dry mouth or constipation, sedation, dizziness or confusion, and changes in cardiac conduction. It should also be emphasized here that overdosing can be very dangerous.

Prior to the use of an antidepressant, it is critical to monitor and pretest for the following as suggested by Miller: (1) Syncope must be ruled out and it should be determined whether there is a family history of sudden death; (2) A baseline EKG should be obtained and repeated with each increase in dose; (3) Blood levels should monitor the metabolism of the medication and not the response; (4) A long QT syndrome (i.e. the QRST complex reflecting changes in heart rhythm) can be difficult to diagnose without an EKG baseline and a repeat EKG. Significant problems can result with slowing of the heart rate by medication.

To date, the most often used antidepressant medication for ADD/ADHD is Tofranil (Imipramine) which will be discussed in more detail. First, in general, the antidepressants are, as a group, less effective than stimulants. This group of medications is most often used when there is a mood problem (i.e., depression) associated with ADD/ADHD.

Tofranil is longer acting compared with stimulants. Its half life ranges from 10-20 hours and it also can be given once per day, typically at night so that sleep may also be improved. Some children develop a tolerance for Tofranil and the medication may be increased, but should additional increases be warranted, most physicians will turn to another medication.

For younger children (under 8 years) the dose may start at 10 mgs (night) and increase by 10 mg increments over a two-week period to a maximum of 20 mgs to 30 mgs per day. For older children, the dose may start at 10-25 mgs and increase by 10-25 mgs in increments up to 100 mgs per day. While distribution of doses during the day may provide more even levels of the medication, this must be weighed against sedation effects. This may be particularly evident in the beginning of treatment and may gradually improve; however, this effect can recur with each increase in dose. Sometimes behavior changes occur within a few days—in other cases it may take several weeks.

Sudden cessation of the medication may cause a flu-like withdrawal reaction with possible nausea, vomiting, headache, lethargy, and irritability or even emotional reactions like crying, sadness, or nervousness. Such problems can be avoided by a gradual weaning of the medication over several weeks. On rare occasions, heart rate and blood pressure can be affected. Plasma levels of the medication may be monitored, especially at higher doses. Some physicians will perform a routine electrocardiograph (ECG) as a precaution.

According to Wilens, Pamelor (nortriptyline) is given by the dose schedule of 2 mg/kg/day. His suggestion is that if this medication does not work, don't increase the dose, just terminate it.

According to Barren, Welbutrin (bupropion) may be helpful for those older adolescents and young adults in the 18-to-25 year age range. It has been reported to be mildly effective on aggressive and hyperactive behaviors. However, there have been complaints about "the way it makes the person feel." Wilens points out that it is somewhat like a stimulant and the dose must be started very low. Hunt notes that this medication is good for "Anergic Depression" where there is not much energy and there is a need to be activated. According to Spencer (1996), Dr. Keith Conners found this medication to be effective for kids. There is some reported risk of seizures (about 4 per 1,000 cases), but this is not significantly greater than that seen with other antidepressants (about 1 per 1,000 cases).

The Antihypertensives

The following medications make up this category:

- Catepres®—clonidine
- Tenex®—guanfacine

Antihypertensive medications benefit the child through decreases in overarousal, hyperactivity, and impulsivity. In addition, there is often a significant lessening of aggressive and oppositional tendencies, as well as some general improvement in socialization functions and sleep. There is, however, limited effect on attentional processes. A skin patch is available for a more even distribution of the medication as absorbed by the body.

Some of the pitfalls and drawbacks of these medications include sedation effects and occasionally contact dermatitis when the patch is used on a daily basis. In addition, a t.i.d. dose (i.e., given three times per day) is often needed with pills. Sometimes a fourth dose is given at bedtime. These medications, like the antidepressants, must be increased or decreased slowly and gradually.

Clonidine is perhaps the most frequently used medication in this category, but Tenex is fast becoming popular. Clonidine is useful with children who are hyperactive, impulsive, and aggressive. This medication has little effect on attention and distractibility; thus, a stimulant may often be combined with Clonidine. However, many physicians avoid using this combination because of concerns about possible cardiac side effects. Some physicians see Clonidine in combination with a stimulant as their first choice with the preschool child showing difficult behaviors. Most, however, use this medication as a second choice in preschool problems and their third choice for the older child.

If forthcoming, improvements may be seen within four to six hours with effects lasting up to 12 hours. Some sedative effects may be noticed during the first hour and a half after administration of this medication. A positive response may not occur until two weeks for some and the full peak effect may not be realized for up to two months.

Again, sedation with resulting sleepiness may be the primary side effect for this medication. This may improve over a period of several weeks for a small percentage of ADD/ADHD children. Use of the patch may still produce sleepiness, and it is sometimes difficult to keep the patch on. Some children may also have headaches, appear confused, or exhibit an increase in aggressive outbursts. Hypotension and hypoglycemia are potential problems, the latter of which can be controlled by taking the medication with food. Clonidine may also affect heart rate and thus exceeding the recommended dose can be *quite dangerous.* Stopping this medication should be done gradually over several weeks. Rebound hypertension may occur when stopping this medication suddenly and is potentially quite dangerous.

Many professionals report as many as 70 percent of the hyperactive, impulsive, aggressive children respond well on this medication. Since this medication is more likely to result in improved compliance, it is perhaps best used when such problems are greater at home that at school. Dr. Hunt believes this medicine may be most appropriate for those children with ADHD who are also very oppositional, defiant, or who present evidence of conduct disorder.

Tenex is less potent than Clonidine and thus considered to be a smoother medication. Given one to two times a day, it is less sedating. Reported dose levels range from .5-3.0 mg. per day and, when given one to two times a day, can last up to 10 hours in children. Wilens also reports that it is more effective on attentional processes and less effective on impulsive and hyperactive behaviors. Barren calls this a "more arousal modulating medication." The overall effect is to decrease arousal and increase inhibition. Hunt believes that Tenex, in combination with Adderal, may be safer than Clonidine. He explains that while the stimulant medication "increases the strength of the signal, Tenex decreases the noise." The overall result is seen in the improvement of the signal to noise ratio, making noisy classrooms less distracting and allowing the child to focus more clearly on the teacher's communications. As with Clonidine, an EKG is recommended on all patients being considered for this medication. Clonidine and Tenex are also useful when Tourette's Syndrome is seen with ADD/ADHD. These meds can help in treatment of the tics.

Medications Under Investigation

Many medications are currently being researched for their possible application to problems of the child with ADD/ADHD. These include:

1. **Serotonin Re-Uptake Inhibitors**

   Prozac®—fluoxetine: Barren believes that this medication does not help ADD/ADHD symptoms. He does, however, believe that it helps with symptoms of depression and anxiety and notes that some hyperactive behavior may be obsessive-compulsive behavior. One study, according to Spencer, showed it was helpful to depression associated with ADD/ADHD. This medication should not be used within six weeks of taking any MAO inhibitor such as Nardil, Parnate, or Marplan.

Zoloft®—sertraline: Leventhal (1996) notes that this medication has been helpful for depression in adolescents. Combined with a stimulant, it has been used in regulating mood and irritability.

Paxil®—paroxetine: When combined with a stimulant, it has been helpful in regulating mood and irritability, like Zoloft.

Effexor®—venlafaxine: Barren states that this medication should not be given to any child under 18 years of age. Leventhal indicates that this medication may be effective for ADD/ADHD, especially in those cases with depression.

2. **Mood Stabilizers**

   Tegretol®—carbamazepine: Barren notes that this anticonvulsant medication is used by more psychiatrists as a mood stabilizer. However, Leventhal believes that it is not especially effective for patients with ADD/ADHD.

3. **Neuroleptics**

   Mellaril®—thioridazine: According to Barren, this major tranquilizer is milder so that tardive dyskinesia (involuntary rhythmic movements of the tongue, jaw, or extremities) is lessened. He notes that it may be used in younger children after stimulants have been found to be ineffective. He further explains that this medication has been used with some aggressive children where other drugs haven't worked. In contrast, Leventhal does not recommend any antipsychotic medication for ADD/ADHD.

4. **Beta Blockers**

   Inderal®—propranolol: Barren indicates that this can be an antiaggressive medication, and that it has been useful with "post traumatic" aggressive children. However, continued and regular monitoring of heart rate and blood pressure is required.

5. **Atypical Anxiolytics**

   BuSpar®—buspirone: Barren notes that this medication is appropriate for adults and anxious teens. It addresses impulsive and restless behavior, plus anxiety. It is a good antianxiety medication and reportedly has helped some anxious or even aggressive ADHD children.

   Lithium carbonate—Barren notes that this medication has worked with some aggressive kids. In combination with a stimulant, it can be an antimanic mood stabilizer.

6. Other Medications

Auroix Maclobemide—Barren states that this MAO Inhibitor has been studied in Germany and appears to be a good second line medication. It reportedly helps most ADD/ADHD symptoms and shows some improvement with attentional problems. It is not known to be approved in this country at this time.

Depakote—This is a mood stabilizer according to Barren. Studies have shown that it sometimes helps aggressive behavior.

Haldol—Barren suggests that this medication may be used with Ritalin or Dexedrine when tics/Tourette's Syndrome (TS) are present. Leventhal suggests that the stimulant medication be used and determine if the tics get worse. In most cases, he reports that they do not worsen. This may be combined with a stimulant when both ADHD and TS are present.

Klonapin—Barren notes that this medication is different from Valium, but still similar. He notes that there are no problems with addiction and it can be used for panic attacks, tics, and aggressive attacks.

Resperidol—According to Barren, this medication has antiserotonin effects. It has been helpful for tics, but with longer duration of use, "kids seem to need more of it." He reports that it is not good for aggressive behavior and that there are no good studies of the medication in children.

Discontinuation of Medications

It is clear that most children with ADD/ADHD will require medications for years. If medications are stopped during the summer vacation, most feel it is best to start the new school year on medications. This procedure may thus avoid potential harmful effects of an unmedicated state. Difficulties may occur rapidly and it may be quite stressful trying to play "catch up" when putting the child back on medications. This is especially true of the nonstimulant medications which may not have their peak effect for up to two months. Parents should inform the teacher that their child is on medications or that there will be a medication change. Preparations may therefore be made to cope with the child's adjustment to the change. Baseline teacher ratings are essential. Additional ratings should be obtained on a periodic basis (every three to six months) and when there are changes in the child's medication schedule or therapeutic program. Follow-up medical visits should occur every three months.

What Children Should Know About Medications

Information about the purpose of the medications the child is taking is important for each child. It is essential that explanations be given that are consistent with the child's developmental level and his capacity to understand. It is critical to stress that the medication is used as an aid to help the child in areas that are important to her. School work, play activities, and homework are all areas in which the child must be made aware of problem behaviors to be dealt with. It is equally important to stress that it is not the medication that does the work; it is the child who should be given credit. Be sure to emphasize this point to the child by comparing the use of medications to other problems that need treatments. For example, one wears glasses to correct a problem with vision, or a hearing aid to hear better. Other medications may be shown to help with allergies or asthma and thus allow the child to function like everyone else. Conners has noted that the child may be encouraged by the statement "the real you" shows itself when the medication is working.

Another important point must be stressed. Medications are used as long as they are needed. While the child is taking medications, she may also be working on appropriate skills. Just as a child who must use crutches while he has a broken leg or a wheelchair while she learns to walk again, the same is true of the child with ADD/ADHD. The child should realize that there may be some point in time when she will no longer need the medications or may need less medication. The child must also be made to understand that medications should not allow the child to avoid consequences for inappropriate behavior. At times, some children may say, "I did it because I haven't had my medicine." There needs to be more recognition for positive behaviors and less emphasis on the negative ones.

Several good books for children and teenagers that describe the purpose of medications, their effects, and their use include *Otto Learns About His Medicine: A Story About Medication for Hyperactive Children* by Matthew Galvin, M.D. (New York: Magination Press, 1988), *Shelley, the Hyperactive Turtle* by Deborah Moss (Bethesda, MD: Woodbine House, 1989), and *I Would If I Could: A Teenager's Guide to ADHD/Hyperactivity* by M. Gordon (New York: GSI, 1991).

What Parents Must Know About Medications

Parents must know the purpose and general use of the medications that are prescribed for their child. Knowledge of the effects of the drug, side effects, and possible complications is important. The parent must know what to expect from the medication and when to expect it (i.e., time course for effectiveness of the medication). Parents must be good observers of their child. All changes, overt or more subtle, must be noted, and in many cases formally recorded. These observations may be very useful for the prescribing physician.

Parents need to know about adjustment on medications, possible changes, rebound effects, and other issues that may be addressed with medications. Parents should also be instructed in the primary purpose of the medications and that medication is not going to solve all the problems. They should know that "pills do not teach skills." Many children with ADD/ADHD are deficient with regard to specific skill areas that may impact upon the child's academic and social life. These deficiencies must be remediated through educational and therapeutic programs. Parents must remember that the best long-range outcome will be for those children who have not only had medications, but also have had behavioral programs and skill training.

Parents *must* refrain from making comments about a child's need for medication (e.g., "Boy, you sure need another pill now!" or "If you don't behave, I will have to take you back to the doctor for more pills."). It is also critical that parents think about these prescriptions as medication and not "drugs" in order to distinguish the prescribed substances from associations with effects of "street drugs."

It is equally important for the parent to remember that the medication is given for the child's needs and not the parent's needs. One child stated, "When I take my medicine, everybody else gets better." Those around the child do change, and may react differently to the child, but this is a secondary benefit. The child must also know that the changes are for her benefit and not the parents'.

What Teachers Need to Know About Medications

Many teachers seem to think that if a child is on medication for ADD, then nothing else needs to be done. It is important they know that even though medications may make it more likely that a child will stay "on task," there are many occasions when the child will not be on medication. Also, many behaviors are not influenced by the medications. Teachers should also be aware that some medications may help the child, but are useful only to a point; additional medication may actually interfere with learning. Thus, academic performance may be compromised at a dose level that is most effective in controlling unacceptable behavior. Lighter doses have therefore been generally more effective when combined with behavioral programs (Carlson et al., 1992). Sometimes less than a full dose of medication may be used. Research has also shown that more medication is not always better (Pelham et al., 1985) and that the dual approach of medications and behavior modification works as a very powerful combined program. Furthermore, research has consistently shown better outcomes when the child has had both a medication regime and a behavior modification approach (Pelham & Murphy, 1986).

It is also important to note that the child may rarely rely on medications indefinitely; having a learning component to improve "on task" behavior will thus be beneficial when the medication regime is terminated. It is possible, in some cases, to reduce or "wean" the child from medications with the assistance of the behavioral program. It is generally agreed that the less medications used, the better for the child. While most medications for ADD are safe, there is always some risk with any medication, and side effects should also be considered. Risk factors and side effects should, in fact, always be considered when designing the "dual-approach" treatment program. In some cases where children cannot take a certain medication because of a conflicting medication or simply because of a prior adverse reaction to the ADD medication, comprehensive behavior programs are essential.

Typically, the pediatrician evaluating for ADD will send out rating forms to both teachers and parents and should include a list of possible side effects when the child is placed on medication. In this way, the pediatrician may get feedback on what is happening with the child who is on a specific medication. See Figure 2.3 for a list of possible side effects.

OTHER TREATMENT OPTIONS

Nondrug Substances

Recently, there has been much advertising and promotion for a substance called Pycnogenol. Many anecdotal reports are available with testimonials from various professionals and lay persons on the "amazing results" with children who have ADD/ADHD. While "clinical studies" and "research" are mentioned in some of the literature distributed on this product, there is an apparent dearth of any available published research on this substance. In fact, to date, no research studies have been found. In short, the effectiveness and safety of this product are still in question; parents and professionals must therefore be cautioned about the use of Pycnogenol.

A second substance is called Pedi-Active ADD (where ADD stands for Advanced Dietary Delivery system). Clinical success of this substance is not sufficiently documented. Parents, teachers, or others contemplating use of either this substance or of Pycnogenol should consult a medical authority.

Innovative Therapies

Optimal Arousal Theory—This states that each individual has an optimal level of arousal that must be present to improve academic performance. For example, a study showed that by enhancing the difficult part of a word with color, the child with ADD learned the words better with the color helping to maintain the child's attention. Using bright colored pen markers can thus help maintain the child's attention while he/she is reviewing and studying words. Similar recommendations for using brightly colored mats on which the child may place materials for homework has been known for some time. A dissertation research study by Flick (1969) suggested that stimulus parameters of color, form, complexity, and brightness could be manipulated to enhance attentional processes in mentally disabled children.

Likewise, music can be used in the background while studying. For many normal children, rock music may be distracting. However, ADD kids may be more stimulated and may learn better with it. Other studies show that rock music was therapeutic for a small group of boys with ADD studied at the Oregon Health Sciences University. In the study, the researcher, F. Cripe (1986), hypothesized that the rhythmic beat increased central nervous system arousal (i.e., a kind of "driving effect" was achieved where the brainwave pattern becomes synchronized with the rhythmic beat), the music further masked other distractions, and its rhythmic beat), the music further masked other distractions, and its rhythmic beat also resulted in a reduction in tension, ultimately reducing overall motor activity for the student. The general consensus of the results was that most all of these boys improved their performance while studying under these conditions.

Other unpublished studies have shown that the use of auditory and visual stimulation may be most effective in creating a more normal internal neurophysiological state that would be more conducive to focusing and maintaining attention, thereby enhancing the processing of information and ultimately improving learning and performance.

Use of tapes with pre-recorded natural sounds or "white noise" has been known to be of benefit for the child both in the classroom as well as at home doing homework.

Biofeedback—Recent research using a type of computerized EEG, or topographic brain mapping, has supported the general notion of excess slow wave activity in the frontal central regions of the brain of children with ADD. The work of Joel Lubar, Ph.D. (1991) has indicated that when the ADD child increases activation in areas that he/she was once deficient, there is improvement in symptoms. Combined with the biofeedback sessions are EMG (muscle) relaxation training to control for movement along with tutoring to deal with areas of academic deficiencies. This research generally has been consistent with other biological research findings by Dr. Alan Zametkin, et al. (1990) indicating a slowing down of brain activity in the frontal central regions as reflected by PET Scans, a kind of brain imaging procedure where a radioactive substance along with glucose is injected. When the brain takes up glucose, more is used by the more active parts of the brain. During a task requiring concentration, ADD individuals showed less activity in the frontal regions of the cortex of the brain. Dr. Lubar and other colleagues have employed EEG biofeedback to modify the brainwave response in a more normalized direction.

While this work appears promising, it is expensive and had, in the past, required up to 80 sessions of training that must be combined with other procedures to be effective. On the positive side, the technique is one that can be documented quite well, correlating changes in the EEG pattern with changes in behavior. It is also promising in that a large percentage of those ADD persons, treated as children, have been followed through adulthood and have experienced continued success in school. Most recently the first control study has appeared (Rossiter & LaVaque, 1995), indicating that EEG biofeedback, or neurotherapy as it is now called, was just as effective as Ritalin for treatment groups with 23 patients in each matched by age. Additional studies forthcoming may indicate whether this approach now with more efficient training protocols has been reduced to about 20 therapy sessions over a four- to eight-week period. Replication of this study will determine whether neurotherapy may become a viable alternative to medication; it is, however, doubtful that other components of the treatment program (i.e., behavioral and educational) could ever be replaced. Thus, even if it should be possible to change the deficiency within the nervous system, there will still be a need for learned skills.

Hypnosis—From the limited research available on conventional hypnosis, there is little evidence to suggest that it would be a viable technique dealing with the complex pattern of symptoms exhibited by children with ADD. However, a recent report by Burte and Burte (1994) at the Milton Erickson Institute in Long Island, New York, indicates that use of Ericksonian hypnotic procedures can be a useful adjunct to the child's overall treatment program. The use of visualization techniques along with story metaphors may be used to address some of the behavior and feelings (such as impulsiveness, concentration problems, self-acceptance, and self-esteem difficulties that are often associated with ADHD) and have an impact on the child's academic and social skills. However, this represents only one component in a multi-modal treatment program that incorporates pharmacotherapy (medication), parent training/counseling, social skills, peer relations group work, and family counseling.

Using Ericksonian hypnosis, a very specific form of hypnosis, parents are aided in exploring their feelings and are assisted in "reframing" their perceptions of the child. Teachers, too, may be taught to reframe the ADD child's behavior of daydreaming, inattention, hyperactivity, and noncompliant behavior (as "boredom" or a "lack of stimulation"), and thereby devise ways of increasing "the child's stimulation or motivation" rather than punish the child. This may also include new materials, changing materials frequently, engaging the child more often, or utilizing the child's "imagination" more often. Hypnotic techniques with the child appear to involve primarily reinforcing "pro-social skills" taught during the group and employ the use of therapeutic stories (metaphor).

More specific treatment guidelines are needed to determine what part Ericksonian hypnosis actually plays in this overall program and what outcome figures are available. The authors state that the program is "still in its early stages, not yet systematically evaluated." It would appear impossible to determine the effectiveness of individual components and, unless more specific guidelines are made available for each component, it would be difficult to generalize results to any other setting. Perhaps future publications will present not only guidelines, but also outcome statistics so that, if clinically effective, those clinical practitioners who utilize Ericksonian hypnotic techniques may be able to make this available for the general public.

Habilitation—Neuropsychologists have, over the last ten years, been developing techniques to rehabilitate individuals (primarily adults, but some children) who have experienced some type of brain insult that produced impairments in specific skill areas involving attention, memory, visual motor skills, and other functions that have affected their adaptation to daily life routines. The emphasis in these techniques has been on rehabilitation as the attempt is made to regain or recover skills that have been lost or altered in some way. Some of these same techniques are beginning to be used with children who have ADD or LD (learning disabilities). While these children have not lost skills, they have failed to develop them. Consequently, their psychological test pattern looks similar to the adult or child with certain types of brain injury. While subtle differences in brain structure and function have been noted for children with the so-called "invisible handicaps" notably ADD and LD, no gross abnormalities of brain tissue or neurochemical processes have been fully "documented." "Documented" is emphasized as there are many sources pointing to a biological structural or neurochemical basis for the behavioral characteristics of ADD. There is a lack of definitive evidence. Nevertheless, there is such a similarity of behavioral characteristics with those individuals who have sustained actual brain injury that the application of cognitive neuropsychological remediation techniques to the child with ADD or ADD/LD seems clearly worthwhile. The bulk of outcome statistics are with individuals who have had actual brain damage, but these techniques have begun to be applied recently by several clinical researchers (including the author), and some results have been published.

One such program of training materials has been computerized and is entitled "Captain's Log.™" The program was developed by Dr. Joseph Sanford and R. J. Browne (1988). This system has been nicknamed a "mental gym." The explanation for this nickname is simple: The system provides a series of cognitive training exercises in several critical areas including modules for attention, visual motor skills, conceptual skills, numeric concepts/memory skills, and a newly added attentional program involving components that address visual scanning, concentration and inhibition, both visual and auditory attention (discrimination), as well as visual organization, memory, and attention to detail. The complete program is far too complex to explain in detail in this book and should be used only under the guidance of a clinical neuropsychologist familiar with such rehabilitation procedures. A recent study by Kotwal, et al. (1994) has shown that such training ranging from 20 to 35 sessions in the cited studies resulted in some improvement on the Connors' Parent Rating Scale and structured questionnaire, along with general improvement in grades.

A recent article in *CHADD* Magazine (Fall 1994) pointed out the value of using computers to help children with ADHD. Other computerized cognitive neuropsychological programs are also available (e.g., NeurExercise™) which primarily have been used, to date, with adult head-injured patients, but have more recently been applied to ADD behavioral symptomatology. No research studies have been found with the NeurExercise™ program that was developed by Dr. Marvin Podd et al. (1989). Future studies, including research by the author, look quite promising and may become a useful tool in planning a comprehensive treatment program for children with ADD. Perhaps some training exercises may also be extended for use with home and school computers. This would certainly help to increase generalization of learning skills to those critical environments in which the child must function. However, these home and school programs should perhaps best be used as adjuncts to primary training programs that are conducted under the supervision of a clinical neuropsychologist experienced in the use of neuropsych rehabilitation programs.

Electronic Assist Devices

An electronic device called the MotivAider®, invented in the early 1980s by Dr. Steve Levinson, can provide a signal or cue for the child to engage in some specific appropriate behavior. Looking very much like a beeper, it is worn on the belt or carried in the pocket. It can be set to deliver a two-second vibration (perceptible only by the child) that may occur from once a minute to once every several hours. The cue (the vibration) is directly associated with a special "private message" that only the child will know. For example, the child may be told that when she feels the cue, that is a signal to "pay attention" or "get back to work if you are off task," or perhaps something more general as to just "check to see if you are doing what you are supposed to be doing!"

With improvement, the device may be set to vibrate less frequently and may eventually be phased out. The MotivAider® appears to be a unique self-monitoring device that is appealing and "relieves teachers and parents of the need to nag."

Another more sophisticated and computerized system is called the Tickle Box™ manufactured by ADDAPTIVE Learning Company. This type of paging system that provides an external cue (vibration and a visual signal from the pager) for things on the child's "to do" list has some built-in goal rewards involving colorful graphic animations and audio feedback (e.g., "good job") when the child successfully completes a task. Weekly award certificates are built into the program for use as back up reinforcers for the child. Although no formal studies are available at this time, the device would seem to appeal to children; the authors state that "because paging systems are commonplace, the child does not feel ostracized by using this adaptive device." Wearing a pager would be quite unique, and might create a feeling of importance in the child. While the at-home software is fairly inexpensive, the addition of the pager (with activation fee and pager airtime) obviously poses a financial hardship for many potential users of this system.

The child with ADD/ADHD is quite sensitive to various sounds in the classroom. With hearing generally more sensitive than other children, they may be distracted by even subtle and soft sounds that are typically not noticed by normal children. An electronic device called the Easy Listener manufactured by Phonic Ear®, reportedly can help to create a better listening and learning environment by reducing the noisy distractions of air conditioners, squeaking chairs and chatting neighbors, and clarifying the teacher's voice with mild amplification. The overall result is an improvement of the signal-to-noise ratio. This device sounds appealing, but there are no available studies as yet to determine its effectiveness in actual classroom situations. The primary drawbacks, however, are that it is quite expensive and not only does the child wear a unit (receiver), the teacher must wear the transmitter. Another similar device is called HEARIT, and is promoted as a "new effective auditory tool for learning disabilities." It also reportedly reduces distractions to allow the child to stay on task more often and to sustain attention for longer periods of time.

HEARIT is described as a user-friendly "personal communicator" device that provides critical enhancement of higher consonant-range frequencies of spoken language. The child can reportedly "pluck out" speech in the presence of noise while sustaining auditory processing abilities. The device may be tested on an individual basis to determine whether it may be beneficial to try in other situations (e.g., the classroom). The benefits of using this device include:

- increased phonological awareness for improved focus and comprehension during reading
- reduction of distractions for improved on-task time
- improved auditory discrimination in remediating articulation errors

It is also noted that this device meets the demands of the Americans with Disabilities Act of 1990 to provide reliable accessible communication. There is, however, no known research on the use of this device with children with ADD/ADHD, and the high price would likewise limit its general use.

Another similar device is available at a much lower and reasonable cost. The Noisebuster Extreme™ from Educational Solutions reduces background noises. An electronic chip analyzes incoming offensive noise and a precise anti-noise sound wave is generated through the stereo headphones. This device provides 15 decibels of noise reduction canceling noise between the 20-to-1,500 Hz frequency range. There is also a slide bar adjustment to vary the amount of noise cancellation. It may be used in the classroom or at home during homework. The Noisebuster Extreme™ has been tested clinically and research evidence is reportedly forthcoming. However, the cost, design features, and technological basis for the instrument make it an interesting alternative to consider for some children.

Another unique device that is now commercially available is called TV Allowance™. Each child in the family is given a code number so that TV times and programs may be tracked for each child. With this device, the parent can easily provide extra time for cooperative behavior around TV time, while subtracting time for children's hassles over TV programs. One device can manage up to four children; each child uses her own code to view their programs. TV Allowance was designed to limit the amount of time children can watch television or play video games. See page 370 for ordering information.

Tape Recorders—Small tape recorders can be useful in school and at home. At home, the child may use one to record spelling words. It provides an additional sense modality (auditory) through which learning can occur. Thus, the child can write the words (kinesthetic mode of learning), visualize them (visual mode of learning), and hear them spelled out in his/her own voice (auditory sense modality of learning). This procedure may develop internal auditory cues that will be very useful when the child has a spelling test. As most spelling tests are dictated, associating the sound of the words with their visual and kinesthetic cues would certainly benefit the child. It is also a procedure that allows the child to practice writing and learning words in the same manner he/she will be tested.

Since many children with ADD have handwriting problems, they may find the tape recorder useful in recording stories and paragraphs that they are assigned to make up and write. This procedure of saying and reading words thus reduces the pressure of writing (which may slow down cognitive thought processes), frees the more relaxed creative right-brain thinking, and enables story construction to be more interesting. This technique, however, depends entirely on acceptance and approval of the use of the tape recorder by the child's teacher.

Another use of the tape recorder would be to have the parent (preferably in the father's voice as this has been shown to be more effective) record instructions or motivational comments or organizational plans, as well as cues for breaks (this use of the tape recorder would be in lieu of a timer to cue the child). All statements recorded should, of course, be in a positive framework and should not sound like drill-sergeant orders.

Computers—Kids appear more motivated when using computer programs to learn skills and tend to stay on task for longer periods of time according to research findings by Mary J. Ford, et al. (1993). A computer program called "Kid Works 2" produced by Davidson and Associates (see the References) allows the child to combine text and pictures to tell a story. The fascination of a computer that talks will certainly hold the child's interest. Children could, for example, type in reminders for rules or projects and have the computer tell them to carry out the instructions. It's like having a powerful parental ally on your side to back up your requests.

Mnemonic Devices—Memory aids have been very helpful for children with learning disabilities and can be used for children with ADD. For example, children may be taught to use visual images, rhymes, and songs to associate specific lists on chains of information. Another specific mnemonic procedure is termed the "write-say" method. This simply involves having the child *write* and therefore *see* misspelled words several times while spelling them *aloud.* In this procedure visual, auditory, and kinesthetic modes of learning are involved. Such multi-modal approaches have been quite effective not only for spelling, but also in learning multiplication tables in math.

Small electronic devices may also be used by the child to record important information in class for later replay at home. The only constraint is that such devices have limited capacity except for some of the more expensive ones.

Special Techniques and Procedures

A self-monitoring system designed by Dr. Harvey C. Parker to improve on-task behavior is entitled "Listen, Look & Think: A Self-Regulation Program for Children." It is available through the ADD Warehouse. This system features an endless loop cassette tape which plays an audible tone at variable intervals (every 30 to 60 seconds). As soon as the beep is heard on the headphones, the child marks a sheet to indicate whether she was on or off task. Depending on the length of the task, the child may mark the sheet 10 to 20 times. This procedure is based on research and although it may sound as if it would be distracting, it has worked well with many children to reduce off-task behavior as well as to control distractions. Perhaps wearing the headphones also reduces auditory distractions in the child's classroom, homework, or study environment. A copy of the recording sheet is found in Chapter 6.

Another device that has helped improve on-task behavior is the Attention Training System (ATS) devised by Dr. Michael Gordon and also available through the ADD Warehouse. This system has a small battery-operated electronic counter in a box that sits on the student's desk. The ATS automatically gives the child a point every minute. If the child gets off task, however, the teacher, using a remote hand-held unit, can deduct a point from the accumulated total and, at the same time, activate a small red warning light on the top of the box. It is claimed that the ATS "delivers unobtrusive but effective feedback, functions during regular classroom activities, circumvents the problem of treatment generalization, and has been shown to be as effective as stimulant medication in increasing attentiveness." Up to four student modules can be controlled with the teacher's hand remote so that four different children can be trained at the same time. The ATS is probably too expensive for many school budgets. An alternate procedure employs 3 × 5 cards numbered from one to thirty and placed on a flip-type recipe holder. This holder is preferably placed on the teacher's desk but within the student's view. Only one child can be monitored at a time to avoid confusion. At the beginning of the assignment, the child is told that she has 30 points. Each time the teacher observes that she is off task, a card is flipped over, thus deducting one point from her total. A clicker can also be used to signal the loss of a point. This system is reviewed with the child in advance so that she is clear about what to expect. It is not known whether any research-based comparison has been made between this inexpensive system and the electronic device. While the procedure is similar and falls within the "response cost" procedural category, it does lack the total nonverbal message delivered by the ATS. The only ways to give the child feedback on whether she was off task are to (1) call out the child's name and when she looks up, point to the cards as one is flipped, or (2) use a clicker and discuss what this signal means prior to using the system. These appear to be the only ways to inform the child she was off task and by the "loss of a point" the feedback may prompt her to return to work. Naturally, this system, as well as the ATS, needs to have some back-up consequences (i.e., rewards) other than just knowing how many of the total points were retained.

A procedure that is often helpful in academic work is called *self-instruction.* For example, a parent can teach this procedure to a child for use during homework. The parent simply models the way the child might "think out loud" using self-instruction (self-talk), verbalizing each logical step needed to solve a problem or to complete a task. Children not only learn that it is OK to talk to themselves while working, but they also acquire a process of asking questions about what the next step is and telling themselves, "What I need to do next is . . ." Having such self-talk appears to help the child who otherwise tends to rush through homework. This technique is especially useful for math problems and writing. Verbal descriptions of the task must be quite detailed—almost to the point where one can visualize the result simply by listening to the verbal description. This slow-down procedure helps to modulate the child's impulsive tendencies, while at the same time improving her attention to detail and accuracy—especially during written work.

Decision on Alternative Treatments

At present there is insufficient evidence on the recommended use of any alternative (non-drug) treatment with the exception of behavioral approaches to symptoms. Many parents who may feel desperate for some "quick fix" may be misled by anecdotal reports of success stories. Granted, some very promising approaches have employed scientific standards that must be considered even more rigorous than those used during the initial medication trials with Ritalin. Some of these novel procedures were, of course, not ever intended to be used as a sole treatment of ADD, and some would certainly be combined with other procedures in a typical multi-modal treatment program. With the incidence of other problems such as learning disabilities, depression, anxiety, and conduct disorders so high, it is necessary to address each problem. Thus, a multi-modal treatment program is a generally accepted standard.

THE PARENT-CHILD INTERACTION

Before parents obtain a fundamental understanding of how to manage ADD behavior, there must be a general understanding of the nature of the parent-child interaction process, as well as an understanding and an acceptance of ADD.

Some early research studies in clinical psychology once suggested that more aggressive children tended to have parents who were more punitive, more negative and less affectionate. There was clearly a correlation, but these studies erroneously concluded that aggressive children are that way because of the punitive style of their parents. Likewise, in early clinical practice, many clinicians, when presented with a child for evaluation, would tend to look for what the parents may have done wrong or failed to do in order to account for the child's problems. Then, and even today, many parents are often blamed and held responsible by others for their child's problems. It is not unusual to hear parents report that, "His teachers say I just need to be more firm with him," or relatives state, "My mother tells me I spoil her—she thinks I should not let her get away with all the things she does." Parents also tend to blame themselves when they say, "I know it must be something I've done. My child is not like others in the neighborhood." Such comments frequently lead parents to feel guilty, inadequate and depressed, with low self-esteem where their children are concerned.

Some of these early beliefs reflected the inaccurate notion that there was a *unidirectional* pattern in the parent-child interaction.

This belief placed the responsibility of the child's behavior solely on the parent. Inappropriate behavior was thus believed to be a reflection of inadequate parenting.

Today, we realize that a *bi-directional* view of the parent-child interaction is more accurate.

In this model, the *child* may have just as much an effect upon what discipline the parent uses as does the parent. Interactions are thus reciprocal. Within this model, which was originally proposed by Dr. Russell Barkley (1981), we can at any point in time view the outcome of the interaction as a function of the **constitutional, genetic, emotional, environmental,** and **learning factors** that abide in *each* person, parent, and child. This makes the nature of each interaction more complex and more difficult to understand. For example, it has already been noted that parents of children with ADD are more likely to show adult characteristics of ADD. Consequently, when the child acts impulsively, there may be a tendency for the parent to react impulsively with discipline, or just the opposite may occur if the parent is aware of these impulsive tendencies (i.e., he or she may take "too much time" to react or not react at all). In either case, the child may not benefit. There may be many factors outside of the parent-child interaction that may affect this interaction as has been noted by Barkley (1981). On the parent side, **financial, marital, stress,** and **health problems** may affect how the parent functions. ADD adults are, for example, more prone to stress-related/emotional problems. Such difficulties may modify the parent's threshold. All parents are aware that when stressed or drained, they may be less tolerant of a child's behavior and this may affect their reaction to the behavior. On the child's side, **school problems, peer problems, health,** and **stress problems** may also affect their behavior in the parent-child interaction. For example, the child who has experienced a fight in school or who was criticized in class because of his/her behavior may come home with a heightened level of suppressed anger (i.e., chip on the shoulder) that may be more easily displaced within the parent-child interaction.

Understanding and Accepting ADD

Understanding the nature of ADD behavior is critical for the parent to deal effectively with it. First, it is important to understand that the basic behavior is driven by this child's neurophysiology. This can alleviate much guilt and fault finding, self- and other-blame that many parents look to in their early attempts to deal with ADD behavior. Second, it is essential to understand that the most consistent finding about ADD behavior is its *inconsistency.* Thus, the child's good days and bad days, which may be so puzzling to both teachers and parents, may become more readily accepted. It is not at all unusual for parents to comment that, "His teacher said he did all of his work yesterday, but none today. If he did it one day, she knows he can do it." This inconsistency frequently sets children up for unreasonable expectations because of parents' and teachers' lack of understanding of the child's inconsistent work or behavioral pattern. The child's neurophysiology changes from one day to the next and may be affected by his/her stress events, food and drink intake, sleep patterns, environmental changes, and by both prescribed and over-the-counter medications. Whatever affects the child's neurophysiology also affects his/her behavior.

It is of paramount importance for the parent to learn to distinguish which behaviors are a function of the ADD and related conditions, and which behaviors are not. If a directive is given to a child (e.g., "Pick up your toys and put them in the closet"), and the child fails to do it, you may simply ask the child to repeat to you what you asked him/her to do. If the child is able to repeat the request, this is an example of outright *non-compliance,* **not** *inattention.* Many parents have been told their child is "just a normal child" or "don't worry; the child will grow out of that stage." Others comment that, "Well, the father said he was just like that when *he* was a child, and he'd get a beating every day." Parents are often confused by what others tell them and as a result sometimes deny that their child has a problem. This is indeed unfortunate, as the longer the problem goes untreated, the more difficult it is to deal with it. Older children and adolescents with ADD frequently have many additional problems to deal with including poor self-concept, a long history of failure in school, depression, and, at times, "acting out" of aggressive behavior. Ultimately, this may result in the child dropping out of school or necessitating some type of residential placement to impose limits and control behavior. Early understanding and acceptance of ADD will clearly have a greater effect on the success of treatment. It is critical to know that, at this time, there is no "cure" for ADD. It is a condition that can, however, be managed once it is recognized, understood, and accepted.

Behavioral Training Programs for Parents

Parent Training Programs developed over a ten-year period beginning in the early 1980s. These behavioral programs targeted the difficult to manage behaviors involving aggression, defiance and the *most difficult* conduct disorders. The addition of oppositional behaviors and/or conduct disorder behaviors make the typical child with ADHD even harder to manage. Since very few of these complex aggressive behavior patterns respond to medication, behavioral counseling or parent training programs in behavioral techniques have become increasingly more important. In part, this book as well as a prior one by Flick (1996), *Power Parenting for Children with ADD/ADHD,* addresses this need. In addition, workshops are offered through the ADD Clinic in Biloxi, Mississippi, on "Parent Training Issues." Other experts (e.g., Dr. Keith Conners and Dr. Russell Barkley) in this clinical area have also offered workshops and Parent Training Programs in their clinic work with children who present complex patterns of ADD/ADHD. Conners' program as well as Barkley's program is modeled after a program originally developed by Connie Hanf (1969). For example, in Conners' program parents receive 14 sessions over a 12-week period with "booster sessions" provided on a once-a-month basis. Group sessions utilize lectures, modeling and role playing. Information about ADD/ADHD is provided along with specific information on behavioral techniques, including those needed to set up a home token economy. Homework is assigned and telephone calls are made during the week to literally prompt parents to use the techniques.

In many hospitals, clinics and some schools, parent training programs are now offered to assist parents in understanding some of the special needs of the child with ADD/ADHD and to teach those techniques and general behavioral principals that have been shown to be helpful. While there has been an abundance of research and considerable clinical evidence that such parent training in behavioral techniques can be beneficial, it appears that the only measures of change have focused on the child. While this is certainly a critical point, there has been, to date, no instrument available to document changes in "knowledge of behavioral techniques" or general information about the use of such procedures with ADD/ADHD children.

An instrument has been developed by Dr. Grad Flick at the ADD Clinic in Biloxi, Mississippi, which provides a type of content-based assessment of such knowledge. This instrument, entitled *"Flick's Survey of Behavioral Practices & ADD/ADHD,"* assesses a wide range of information that is common to most all behavioral programs. It also assesses general factual information about ADD/ADHD. Although much of the information surveyed is based on the content as discussed in this author's book *Power Parenting for Children with ADD/ADHD,* the majority of this information would be commonly found in most all current books with material on either behavioral modification and/or the ADD/ADHD behavioral syndromes.

Some sample items are as follows:

T F 1. GOOD AND APPROPRIATE BEHAVIOR SHOULD BE REWARDED.

T F 2. BAD AND INAPPROPRIATE BEHAVIOR SHOULD BE PUNISHED.

T F 3. IT IS IMPORTANT TO REWARD A GOOD BEHAVIOR OR PUNISH A BAD BEHAVIOR AS SOON AS POSSIBLE AFTER IT APPEARS.

T F 4. PHYSICAL PUNISHMENT IS GENERALLY NOT EFFECTIVE IN THE LONG-RUN WITH CHILDREN WHO HAVE ADD/ADHD.

T F 5. USE OF TIME-OUT FOR BAD BEHAVIOR WILL ALWAYS WORK WITH THE ADD/ADHD CHILD.

This instrument is intended to be administered prior to parent training and then following the training. It might also be used prior to reading this book or *Power Parenting for Children with ADD/ADHD* and then taken again following completion of the book. Repeated assessments may also indicate where parents may wish to refresh their memories regarding certain techniques. Although it may be used, at present, as a measure of general knowledge of behavioral principles, it is anticipated that future research may allow for a description of a profile of practices so that parent training and/or behavioral counseling programs may target specific areas of weakness, thus saving much time and expense. Knowledge of remaining weakness or confusion regarding certain issues would certainly be best cleared up prior to the parent implementing behavioral programs as opposed to initially operating on the basis of misinformation. In summary, this instrument may improve the efficiency and the effectiveness of behavioral programs following various types of parent training or behavioral counseling programs.

Summary

Because of the many co-morbid disorders possible, it is not possible to include all treatment options to fully cover these disorders when combined with ADD/ADHD. However, many of the programs reviewed in this chapter do address some critical components of the complex patterns of ADD/ADHD conditions along with related symptoms and problems. The basic treatment orientation is to use a multi-modal approach involving parents, teachers, physicians, psychologists, and other professionals. The target goals of treatment focus on specific behaviors or problems (e.g., impulse control, improved cooperation with peers, staying on task, completing work, and controlling aggressive behavior—to name a few) and these goals will form the basis of a "symptomatic approach" to treatment. Review the chart in Appendix D to consider the various treatment options.

CHAPTER 3

Looking at Behavior: The A-B-Cs of Behavior-Change Programs

BEHAVIORAL PROGRAMS AND TRAINING EXERCISES

A typical behavioral program incorporates a very simple sequence of three components or events that together form the basis for development of a complete and comprehensive behavior management program.* These three consecutive components or events are:

A for Antecedent Events

B for Behavior

C for Consequences

This chapter provides a general review of each component or event and the type of training exercises appropriate for each of the three components. (First, we'll learn how the "A, B, C" sequence works, then each component event will be examined.)

A—ANTECEDENT EVENTS: What Comes First

The first in such a sequence of events is the *antecedent behavior*—the behavior that teachers and parents of children with ADD often lament about, making remarks such as:

*With one exception, all behavioral programs may be analyzed or broken down into these three components. (The one exception might occur when a behavior is spontaneously or capriciously emitted without any apparent antecedent event or trigger.)

"He just won't listen."

"She doesn't seem to remember what I tell her to do."

"If I tell him to do three things, he might follow through on just one of them."

Comments such as these from parents often are accompanied by body language and statements of frustration, anger and puzzlement.

Antecedent events are very important, for they are the *input* into the system. If this input is unclear or incomplete, then surely the outcome will be compromised. Antecedent events can be classified as

1. rules
2. expectations
3. communications

Together, they provide the basic structure (the input) in the child's family or in the school environment within which the ADD/ADHD behavior can be monitored.

Many teachers and parents may believe they have *rules,* but few rules are actually written down; most rules are so unclear (e.g., "Weekday chores must be done when you get home from school" could mean immediately, or after a snack, or before any TV, etc.) that it is not at all unusual for the child to be confused. Thus, an exercise to stimulate thought about rules and which rules are to be used would be extremely helpful for both parents and teachers.

Likewise, *expectations* also are often unclear, such as when a parent states, "Now, I'll expect you to behave yourself when we are visiting Aunt Sally," or when the teacher says "OK, class—'behave yourself' when we have a guest in the classroom." Even when a child nods appropriately, indicating apparent agreement, how does the child interpret "behave yourself"? The parental expectation or teacher's instructions given the child to "behave yourself" is unclear and certainly not specific. How can there be agreement when this is the case?

Lastly, when *communicating* requests, parents and teachers must not only be clear and concise, it is also critical that they have the ADD child's undivided attention when communicating: Eye contact is essential; the child must be oriented to you. This means that, with some children, you must gently hold their face or their shoulders so that they are directly in front of you when you give commands. While this may be difficult to do in a classroom, eye contact would be important. (See the section Developing Communication Skills on p. 103.)

It is also important to focus on the *style* of communication the parent or teacher uses. Both passive and aggressive styles are fraught with problems; an assertive approach, however, is most effective. More information about communication styles, including information on metacommunication, and a specific *communication style exercise,* are discussed in this chapter beginning on page 105.

B—BEHAVIOR: The Central Issue

Behavior is *what the child does.* Parents and teachers often make observations such as "He's lazy" or "He's just got a bad attitude" and believe they're truly describing behavioral problems that can be the focus of change. Not so; in all good behavioral programs, "Behavior" means something that is observable, countable, and of course changeable. Conversely, "Behavior" is *not* what the child *doesn't* do (i.e., "not doing work" is not a behavior). "Playing with a pencil" while not doing work may be "the behavior" that we wish to diminish. Having the parent or teacher list classes of behavior, such as desirable vs. undesirable, helps to provide a frame of reference for defining and working with these behaviors. The appropriate and inappropriate behaviors may be further subdivided into those that appear (a) at home, (b) at school, and (c) outside the home or school.

You will come to realize that, for the most part, problem behaviors fall into four basic categories:

1. relationship with parents
2. relationship with sibs
3. relationship with peers
4. relationship with self in personal areas pertaining to:
    a. safety
    b. morals
    c. habits
    d. emotional control and expression.

C—CONSEQUENCES: Reactions to Behavior

Consequences that are provided for these behaviors are of critical importance, and it matters not whether a behavior has been *elicited* by a specific request or *emitted* as a spontaneous variant of some behavior in which the parent or teacher has some investment.

Consequences may be classified as either *rewards or punishments.* There are many types of rewards, and also many variations of punishments. It is important to list consequences (both rewards and punishments and their subtypes), but it may be confusing, so let's look at a few examples.

First, let's look at rewards. There are two basic subtypes:

- giving a positive consequence
  a thing, an activity, a social reward
- taking away a negative consequence
  removal of a thorn from the child's foot

Likewise, punishments can take the form of either:

- giving an aversive consequence
  spanking
- removing something positive
  taking away a toy or privilege

Consequences can be structured so that there may be *contingencies;* for example a child can be told, "When you clean your room, then you can watch TV," or "When you finish your classwork you can have free time."

The antithesis of consequences, yet often also effective, is *no consequence* following a behavior. The absence of a consequence means that the behavior will not be strengthened or maintained. This, of course, is desirable (i.e., the absence of consequence) when we wish to weaken or extinguish certain inappropriate behaviors.

The last condition to consider in the areas of consequences is a concept called *shaping.* In this procedure, the behavior does appear to be an improvement (i.e., it is more like the final behavior the parent or teacher wishes to establish), although it is not yet the exact behavior that is desired. Since there is always some variation in how a behavior is exhibited, the parent or teacher need only wait until an even closer approximation to the desired behavior occurs and then reward it. This procedure is quite useful, too, in helping the child develop new behaviors or strengthen a desired behavior that exists in some immature form. The simplest example of this process involves the development of speech and language skills: As the child develops he receives positive feedback on the accuracy of his speech and over time he thereby shows more accurate productions.

Parents and teachers will find it quite helpful to develop an awareness of what is *rewarding to* and what is *punishing for* the ADD child. Even more specifically, it is a useful exercise to be able to subdivide these consequences as has been described earlier (the positive and negative rewards, and the positive and negative punishments). Listing specific behaviors that are appropriate for extinction (i.e., removal) and those that are targeted for *shaping* (i.e., improvement) is also helpful. In some cases, these will be opposite or alternative behaviors; in other cases they may be totally unrelated. Since social rewards are part of structured behavioral programs as well as informal ones, a special exercise focuses on the use and development of social rewards. In some families and classrooms, few forms of social rewards are used. However, it is possible for both teachers and parents to learn, practice, and develop skills in using social praise.

Using the A-B-C Sequence in Behavior Programs

If parents and teachers share a general background of basic principles of behavior, they will be in a better position to deal with behavior problems, even when faced with the so-called "difficult to manage behavior" of the child with ADD. The basic principles are as simple as A-B-C. Figure 3.1 outlines this sequence used in later discussions.

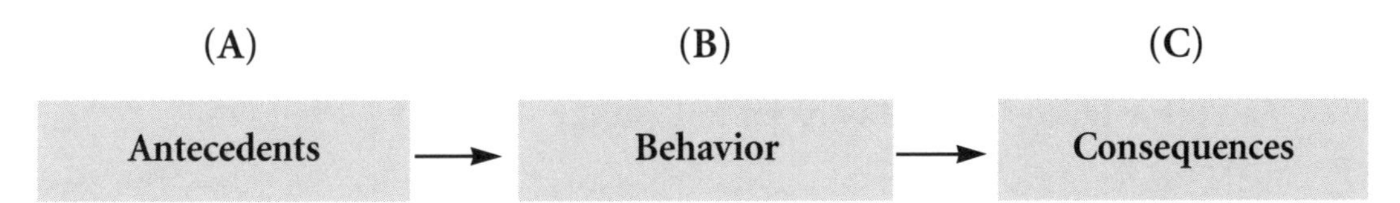

Figure 3.1 Antecedents-Behavior-Consequences

For appropriate and effective behavior management, it is essential to have a good understanding of these three components. The following pages of this chapter deal in detail with each of these three components.

Here we note that some behavior may seem to occur capriciously without any apparent cue or trigger. Even in this instance, appropriate consequences are necessary. However, our focus now is to understand and develop skills which bring specific behaviors under the control of a specific stimulus (e.g., a verbal request). In this process you will have helped the child develop a learned behavior. Ideally, the sequence might go like that shown in Figure 3.2.

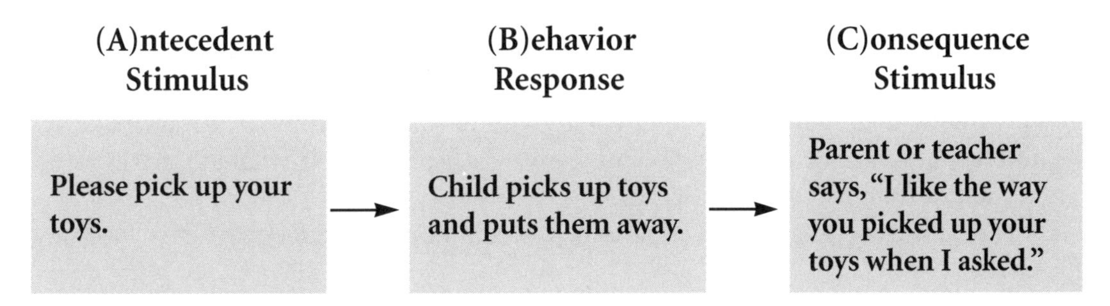

Figure 3.2 Stimulus-Response-Stimulus

The sequence may continue with the parent's or teacher's comment, which is a consequence, serving as a stimulus triggering another behavioral response from the child (child feels good or happy, exhibits new behavior, a smile), which behavior has the consequence (C) of being a stimulus for the parent or teacher who also responds (B) with a good feeling and a smile. Even without a technical analysis of this sequence, you can quickly see that more occurs than just a *learned response* to the request. The child and parent or teacher experience good feelings from the interaction. This is in marked contrast to a sequence where a child experiences pain, and the parent or teacher feels anger and frustration over the child's failure to comply. Using the basic behavioral principles in the A-B-C format can lead to enhancement of the parent-child or teacher-child interactions and, over time, to a more positive emotional bond between the parent and child, or an enhanced relationship between teacher and child.

ANTECEDENTS

The First Thing That May Need to Change

In the world of computers the acronym GIGO stands for "Garbage In—Garbage Out." It is quite relevant here to emphasize that if the wrong information is processed, the output may not make sense. Communications, rules, and expectations, and the manner in which these are presented to children may make the difference between compliance and noncompliance. This discussion of antecedents thus focuses on the basic structure of the family and even within a classroom. It provides the foundation on which behaviors result. If commands, directions, rules, and expectations are not clearly specified, the child's ability to respond appropriately is compromised.

Writing Rules and Developing Expectations

Rules are everywhere. Driving a car, working, or even playing games would be difficult without rules. In families, rules are seldom explicitly stated or written down. Most often rules are implied and seem to be discussed and stated primarily following the occurrence of some misbehavior. For example, when a child is caught jumping on the sofa, you may state, "You know the rules—no jumping on the sofa." Perhaps you assume that the child actually "knows the rules" but has probably not tested this assumption even in an informal manner. With ADD kids who respond on impulse, it may make little difference even if the rule could be cited. Also, rules often imply what the child should not do rather than what he should do.

The following is a list of situations where rule-governed behavior is typically found:

Awakening	Visiting
Talking	Dressing
Bedtime	Watching TV
Being home on time	Riding in the car
Eating	Homework
Chores	Expressing anger
Greeting others	Dinner time

Try your hand at writing rules for some or all of the situations listed above.

Exercise 3.1 WRITING RULES

1. ____________________
2. ____________________
3. ____________________
4. ____________________
5. ____________________
6. ____________________
7. ____________________
8. ____________________
9. ____________________
10. ____________________
11. ____________________
12. ____________________
13. ____________________
14. ____________________

After you have written your rules, check them against the following examples.

Exercise 3.1 WRITING RULES

1. Remain at the table while **eating.**
2. Wait turn to **talk;** don't interrupt.
3. Remain "quiet" and keep hands to self in **car.**
4. Keep feet on floor and off furniture while **watching TV.**
5. Keep hands to self when **angry.**
6. **Greet** others by saying, "Hello," or "Good morning."
7. First do **homework,** then go play.
8. **Bedtime** is 8:00 P.M.—no exceptions!
9. Be **awake** at 6:30 A.M.; **dressed** by 7:00 A.M.
10. When **visiting** always say, "Please," "Yes, Sir," and "No, thank you."
11. **Be home** by 5:00 P.M.
12. Do all **chores** on list each week.

Notice that all rules are clearly written and are specific as to what the parent wishes. Several of these rules might apply equally well to the classroom (e.g., #12 and #5). Others may be specified for the classroom only (e.g., "Raise your hand to ask permission to go to the bathroom" or "Remain quiet and listen carefully when the teacher is talking"). For children who may not fully understand the rules, role-playing may be used to model the appropriate behavior and/or cues may be provided in the form of pictures or cartoon drawings that depict the correct behavior associated with each rule.

Many rules could serve as the first statement in a *when-then* sequence. For example:

> "*When* you do all chores on your list for the week, *then* you may have weekend privileges" (that is, assuming there is no significant intervening punishment).

Note that not all of the preceding situations may be used. Some of these situations may be more appropriately discussed in terms of expectations for the child.

In some situations the parent or teacher may simply describe the desired behaviors. Somewhat different from rules, expectations may involve several components that describe a series of behaviors expected from the child. Expectations may vary with the age of the child as well as with the child's ability to comprehend and retain what is said. For example, the child might be told what is expected while at the shopping mall. The parent may say, "First, I want you to hold my hand while we're walking from the car to the mall. Next, I want you to stay right beside me while I shop in the store. Last, I want you to hold my hand on our way back to the car." A teacher might review expectations prior to entering a special event (e.g., a field trip). It is best to simplify these expectations and limit each to no more than three components.

Now write down some (at least three) sequences of events that involve some of your expectations for your child in Exercise 3.2. Remember, keep these simple, concise and straightforward. See the following examples on page 103 for some ideas.

Exercise 3.2 DEVELOPING EXPECTATIONS

1. ______________________________
2. ______________________________
3. ______________________________

Exercise 3.2 DEVELOPING EXPECTATIONS

1. While we are visiting Aunt Sally I will expect you to:
   a. Greet her when you meet (i.e., "Good morning, Aunt Sally.")
   b. Say "Please" and "Thank you" when you ask for something and get it.
   c. Keep your hands to yourself (i.e., no fighting with your cousin Bubba).
2. When you go to church on Sunday I will expect you to:
   a. Keep your hands to yourself while riding to church.
   b. Sit quietly during the service.
   c. Greet people you know saying, "Hello, ______"
3. While visiting the zoo I will expect you to:
   a. Hold my hand while walking through the zoo.
   b. Keep your other hand to yourself (no feeding the animals).
   c. Talk in a normal tone of voice (screaming will scare the animals).

These expectations may stand alone or be tied to consequences. In the preliminary stages of behavior management, these general expectations may be used to "test" the child to see if he or she is capable of compliance.

Rules and expectations provide important parts of the basic structure for behavior. However, the next important step is to communicate this information to the child. If the child doesn't get the right message, he can't make an appropriate response. Parents and teachers must not assume the child "knows better." This is equally the case with children who have ADD/ADHD. It is often discovered that the "message sent" is not necessarily the "message received." Teachers, parents, and professionals must therefore focus on developing good communication skills.

Developing Communication Skills

Getting the correct information to the child may be the most critical part of the entire behavioral sequence. As many ADD children are distractible and hear only parts of communications, it is most important to check out whether the child has gotten the entire message.

Some of the basic steps in the communication process are:

1. **Get eye contact.** Give your message facing the child and ensure that he looks at you. You may say, "Look here (while pointing to your eyes)."
2. **Speak clearly and distinctly in a normal tone of voice.** You don't have to shout or give these directives like a drill sergeant. Most children with ADD are, in fact, quite sensitive in their hearing.
3. **Present your command or directive in a simple concise manner emphasizing what you want the child "to do."** For example, "Pick up your clothes and put them in the dirty clothes hamper." Avoid giving negative commands (i.e., what you don't want).
4. **Verify that the child has heard what you said by simply asking him to repeat what you said.** If the child repeats it correctly, you have an opportunity to reinforce the correct perception of your words by saying, "That's exactly right. You got it right. Now do it." If the child has trouble repeating your words give him/her the correct words and ask again for him/her to repeat them. If the child still has trouble, it may be that the child really has a hearing problem or that the commands are too complex. Then you will need to simplify them or break them down into simpler components. In the preceding example the parent might first say, "Okay, now, pick up your clothes." Then, give the next directive, "Okay, good. Now put them in the hamper." Reinforce (stroke) each component successfully completed. Now we will focus on what a teacher or parent may actually say—the content of the message.

Exercise 3.3 DEVELOPING COMMUNICATION SKILLS

In this exercise, write down some of the commands, directions, requests, and instructions you use in communicating with ADD/ADHD children. Please limit your responses to ten items.

1. ______
2. ______
3. ______
4. ______
5. ______
6. ______
7. ______
8. ______
9. ______
10. ______

Now review some of the following examples below to compare with your communications. It sometimes takes a review of statements made orally—but now in written form—to determine how clear, concise, and positive the statements sound and how they might be perceived by the child. Are these clear to others? Ask yourself: Would they know exactly what to do after hearing these communications?

Exercise 3.3 DEVELOPING COMMUNICATION SKILLS

1. Put your dirty clothes in the clothes hamper.
2. Empty all the trash cans and put the garbage out.
3. Pour a glass of milk for your little sister.
4. Please turn off the lights in your room.
5. Would you help me put this ice chest in the car?
6. Put your life jacket on when you get in the boat.
7. Buckle your seat belt when you get in the car.
8. Put food and water out for the dogs.
9. Put all of your toys in the toy box.
10. Put the milk back in the refrigerator after using it.
11. Take your math book out of your bag.
12. Take out a pencil and writing pad for this next assignment.
13. Clear off all books on your desk and put them in your bag.
14. Write these pages down for your reading assignment.

Learning About Communication Styles

Dr. Harvey C. Parker, in *The ADD Hyperactivity Workbook,* has discussed three types of communication styles:

1. Passive
2. Aggressive
3. Assertive

Problems may be encountered in using the first two styles. The third alternative appears to work best for the parent. Try to obtain a copy of Dr. Parker's book in order to look at ineffective styles and then the style that is most effective with the majority of children, including children with ADD/ADHD. Dr. Parker's discussion of these styles of communication is right on target and they are summarized here in a modified form.

Passive Communication—Parents who use passive forms of communication typically have children who are manipulative and controlling. Such parents have difficulty stating rules and enforcing them. Recognizing that the child is in control, a typical communication might sound like, "Mary, it's your bedtime—do you want to go to bed now?" Of course, the parent hopes the child will say yes. If not, the parent might say, "Well, it's late but we can play one more game—then it's time for bed." This process may continue either until the child does get sleepy or until the parent becomes angry. If the latter should happen, the child knows exactly what to say: "Daddy, you're mean—you mustn't love me anymore." This statement will certainly "push a critical button"—i.e., now I've lost my child's love. Perhaps by this time the spouse enters, saying, "Why are you getting this child so upset at bedtime?" The parent in question now will fear rejection by the child and the conflict with his spouse. Future communications may thus be less authoritative, more evasive, and less believable.

Some examples of passive communication include:

1. Don't you think it's time to get ready for school?
2. How many times do I have to tell you to clean up your desk?
3. Don't you think you ought to be doing your work now?

Very often these passive communications are given in the form of a question with the decision resting upon the child. When one hears a communication like, "Young man, don't you think you should stop jumping on the sofa?" one expects to hear the child say, "No! I'm not ready to stop."

Aggressive Communication—Parents who use this form of communication may be manipulative and controlling of others. They tend to be exceedingly strict and may use threats, severe punishment, derogatory names, or any other technique to exert their power and control. Any resistance to their rules and regulations would be quite threatening and would typically be met with even greater force. Such forms of communication are often associated with severe physical punishment. The association of physical punishment with these communications will result in "temporary control" or control only in the presence of that person. Humiliating comments, name calling, or belittling may be made without regard for the child's feelings. While compliance may result in the short-term, in the long-term accumulated suppressed anger in the child may be expressed in a violent manner at some time, often quite unexpectedly.

Some examples of aggressive communication include:

1. You're lazy and no good—you're no son of mine!
2. You "crack head"—can't you think any better than that?
3. You never listen—do you know how to do that job I gave you (stupid is implied)?

Very often these communications are like "verbal darts." One can just imagine how the child might feel being on the receiving end of one of these communications. These communications are not limited to the home. Very often a teacher will create much embarrassment with questions such as, "Johnny, did you forget to take your medicine again (stupid is implied)?" Another teacher called a child "air head" since he couldn't possibly have any brains; if he did he would know his place in reading. These comments or communications do little in terms of constructive feedback and just simply devastate a child's already weak self-concept. While the child remains a victim, the aggressive communicator remains in control and "one up."

Assertive Communication—Parents who use this assertive form of communication are secure in their beliefs and can express their ideas, needs, and wishes in a clear and direct manner that is respectful of others' rights and feelings. These parents provide needed structure for their families by being explicit and fair in rules and expectations for their children. They are also capable of enforcing these rules and standards in a way that allows the child to think and act independently and to be responsible for his/her behavior. The parent is clearly in charge and assumes a leadership role in the family , modeling appropriate parental behavior for the child.

Some examples of assertive communication include:

1. When you finish your chores you can go out to play.
2. Name calling is against the rules. Stop it or get your consequence!
3. Stop arguing immediately or go to Time-Out!

In these examples, the parent is quite clear about consequences. Also, the responsibility for change is placed upon the child. The child can: (a) decide to stop arguing, or (b) go to Time-Out; it is his/her choice. Of course, if the child has to go to Time-Out, s/he will also be forced to stop arguing.

In a similar manner teachers may use the assertive form of communication. For example, providing a signal to a student who must then decide to (a) stop a behavior or (b) accept the consequence (pre-arranged). Should the child (self) control his behavior, he may be rewarded by the teacher who reinforces behavior change *and* maintains control in the classroom.

Now that you, the parent and teacher, have some familiarity with the Assertive Style you may go back and rewrite some of your typical communications in this format.

Exercise 3.4 WRITING COMMANDS IN THE ASSERTIVE STYLE

1. ____________________
2. ____________________
3. ____________________
4. ____________________
5. ____________________
6. ____________________
7. ____________________
8. ____________________
9. ____________________
10. ____________________

Some of the typical characteristics that distinguish the assertive style, illustrated by Dr. Parker, are adapted as follows:

1. Say what you mean and mean what you say.
2. Give commands politely, yet firmly.
3. Make eye contact with the child before a command is issued.
4. Follow through on your command with immediate supervision.
5. Don't ask the child to follow a command. Remind the child that the command *must* be followed.
6. If the child tries to talk you out of a command, stick to your guns.

Once you are able to communicate *clearly, concisely,* and *convincingly* (the three Cs) using the assertive style, move to the next step—determining which compliance problems may remain. In short, once you become more effective in communicating, some problem behaviors may literally "disappear." Essentially, these problems were probably related to ineffective communications.

Metacommunications

The term *metacommunication* refers to a communication about a communication—a higher level of communication that makes the original communication more complex. It may result in confusion on the part of the listener if conflicting messages are being sent. For example, when talking with a parent while his child is present, the teacher or counselor may ask the parent to deliver a command to the child. Even when the parent uses the appropriate content in the command, for example, "Please keep your feet on the floor," the manner or emotional tone in which the message is delivered will make a difference in how the message is perceived. This same message may be delivered while the parent is smiling (nonverbal metacommunication) or it may be delivered in a very soft voice. Either metacommunication may imply that the parent is not serious or perhaps is weak and ineffectual. With these perceptions the child may ignore the message even though the content is appropriate. On the other hand, extreme forms of metacommunication should be avoided (e.g., loud, booming voice and stern, threatening facial expressions). If the parent or teacher is to be effective with commands that have an assertive content, he or she must also present that content with an assertive style. The parent or teacher can practice some of the assertive commands by recording them and then replaying the tape for feedback on how he or she sounds.

Listening Behavior

Using the list of typical commands that are written in clear, concise and convincing terms, you are now ready to deliver these to the child to determine whether compliance is obtained. If you have had a major problem in getting the child to follow through with instructions (e.g., getting various things for you), then various things may be requested to determine how consistently the child will be in his response. While consequences will be discussed later in this chapter, concentrate at this point on the following:

1. Whenever the child complies, put a check by that item and reinforce the child for listening to you.
2. Whenever the child fails to comply, put an X by that item, but do not at this time give any other feedback to the child. You may, however, repeat the item at another time.
3. Once a child has complied with an item on three consecutive requests, you may feel relatively sure that this compliance will continue. Any lack of response or inconsistent response should be noted as they will require additional work.

Helping a Child to Pay Attention

Parents and teachers say "pay attention" many times with the average child and many more times with the ADD child. What does "pay attention" really mean? While many people inherently seem to "know" what is communicated, how can this be explained to the child?

It is sometimes obvious when a child is not paying attention by the position he/she assumes. The child's "body language" gives him/her away, despite the child's attempt to "look good" for the teacher or parent. While it is possible to use some type of psychological monitor to determine when the child is attending (in order to reinforce it), this would clearly be impractical in the home or classroom. There are several ways a parent or teacher could get some estimate; one is to simply ask the child; another is to have the child rate his/her attention on some attention-measuring scale. One such rating device, labeled "The Attention Meter," is provided in Figure 3.3 on page 110. A similar procedure has been described in detail by Garber, Garber, and Spizman (1990) in their book *If Your Child is Hyperactive, Inattentive, Impulsive, Distractible.* (No attempt will be made here to explain their procedure. The interested reader is referred to their chapter on "Stretching Attention Span" for details.) The purpose of the procedure outlined here is simply to promote greater *awareness* of the concept of "paying attention" and related issues of distractibility; no attempt will be made here to encourage the child to increase attention span over time. In fact, the most critical measure in this process is how well the child has processed information and been able to answer questions.

Employing the "Attention Meter," the child is given a story to read or to listen to on tape. Remember that children who have difficulty reading will tend to become distracted and will have more trouble answering questions about the story. If there are obvious reading problems, only use the tape version for this task. Using a stopwatch, begin timing when the child starts; temporarily stop the watch each time the child gets off task (i.e., looks around, begins playing with a piece of string, or some other behavior that might affect his/her ability to "concentrate" on the task) and then re-start it when he/she

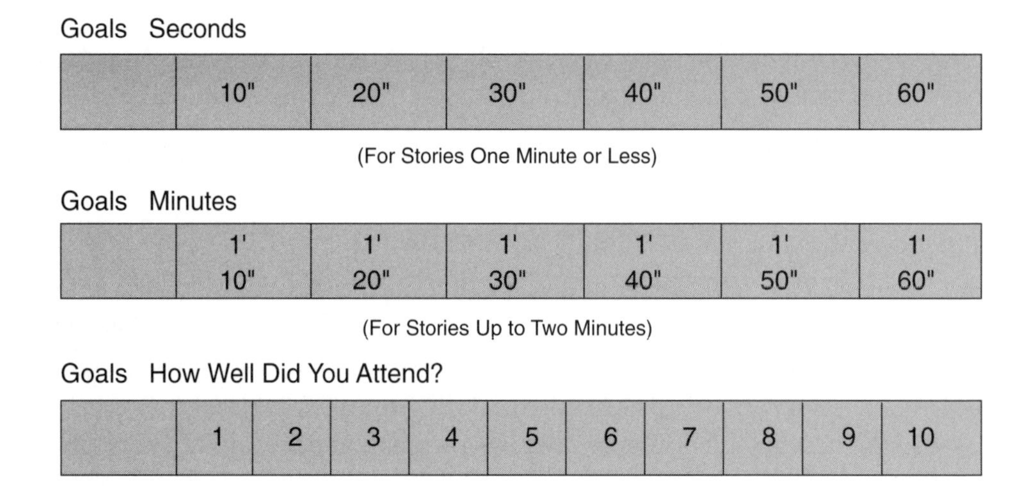

Figure 3.3 Attention Meter

returns to the task. The stopwatch will then show the accumulated time for the child's attention to the story. Selected stories, initially, should be very short (i.e., one to two minutes). Have a few questions (i.e., two to five) available for the child when using stories one to two minutes in length. For each story read or listened to estimate a goal of how long the attention span will be. Encourage the child to set a reasonable goal (e.g., at least 40 seconds on a 1-minute story, or 1 minute and 30 seconds on a 2-minute story). When the goal is set low enough, the success will be optimized. Suggest to the child that goals may be increased with each success. It is also useful to estimate a rating of how well the child thinks he/she can do with regard to his/her attention to the story before (on a 10-point scale) and then again after the story is read (on a 10-point scale). Subsequently, the actual time is recorded. The chart in Figure 3.4 will be useful in monitoring awareness of attention.

Date	*Story Read on Tape*	*Goal M/S*	*Actual M/S*	*Rated B Goal*	*Rated A Actual*	*No. of Questions Answered*

Figure 3.4 ("Goal" and "Actual" are to be expressed in minutes and seconds (M/S). "Rated *B* Goal" means the goal before the process "Rated *A* Actual" means the actual time. These ratings should reflect how close the child actually came compared to the goal he/she set.)

At the far right of this chart is a place to indicate how many questions a child was able to answer (e.g., ?/2 for short story, or ?/5 for the longer stories). This will perhaps be the most useful information as the child can certainly be reinforced for improvement in the percentage of correct answers over time. Attention span per se would be much harder to estimate from the child's performance.

A third method is to model the behavior you wish to establish. This alternative procedure, in general, will be covered in greater detail in Chapter 7. In this situation a parent can demonstrate the notion of "paying attention" versus getting "off task" to the child. (See Figure 3.5) For example, a story might be recorded on tape so that the total story time can be determined; the parent could then demonstrate attending by first listening and then periodically engaging in other behavior, e.g., playing with a pencil, looking around the room, etc. It will be the child's task to judge when the parent is attending or not attending. The accuracy of the child's perceptions may be determined by using the stopwatch to time the parent's time "on task" and then calculating the parent's time "off task" by subtracting the recorded time "on task" from the total time of the story (i.e., minutes as indicated).

Date	*Story*	*Minutes*	*Paid Attn/Time "On Task"*	*Did Not Pay Attn/Time "Off Task"*

Figure 3.5

The child may then reverse roles and it will be the parent's turn to see how much the child is on or off task. Again, this type of exercise with parent and child would be more beneficial in promoting greater *awareness* of when the child is attending (on-task) and not attending (off-task) rather than having the effect of expanding attentional processes directly. Finally, a more direct form of attention training, the Attention Training Game, will be discussed in Chapter 9.

Simply telling a child to pay attention or stay on task does not appear to be effective. If it were, parents and teachers would not need to say that as often as they do. Sometimes, adding a nonverbal component to the attention process may make it more exciting or game-like for the ADD child. For example, when Johnny appears to be "daydreaming" during homework or class work, a parent or teacher might have a prearranged cue to get the child back on task and attending. The child may be told that, "When I tug on my ear that will mean I want you to listen to what's being said." This nonverbal cue may also avoid some embarrassment and self-esteem problems for the child who may get comments to "pay attention" many times during the day. Questions such as, "Now what is it that everyone needs to be doing at this time?" also avoid focusing on one child and stimulate all children to question themselves.

Cues may be provided for rule-governed behavior in many other ways. In addition to posters, notes can be placed in strategic places; a wrist alarm watch with daily reminders can be used; and there is a non-verbal tactile cue (similar to that of a beeper) that can be set to vibrate at a certain time (the MotivAider®). This device was invented by Dr. Steve Levinson in 1980 and produced by Behavioral Dynamics, Inc., since 1988.

Remember, *antecedent* stimuli are crucial for obtaining appropriate behavior. When the child knows what to do, he/she has the opportunity to do it.

BEHAVIOR

Behavior is observable, countable, and changeable. Simply stated, behavior is what the child does. Behavior can fall into two basic categories: desirable (appropriate), or good behavior, and undesirable (inappropriate), or bad, behavior. Your goal is to *increase* the frequency and number of desirable behaviors and to *decrease* the frequency and number of undesirable behaviors.

The first step in any behavioral program is to *identify* problem behaviors and *identify* appropriate behaviors the child may exhibit. Often, the number of inappropriate behaviors may far exceed the number of appropriate behaviors, and at times it may seem as though there are no appropriate behaviors. However, all children will exhibit behaviors in each of these categories; it may take some time, but you will be able to make a list of both desirable and problem behaviors.

Listing Behaviors

In Exercise 3.5, fill in the "Behavior" columns only (the ratings will come later). List the child's behaviors that fall into the two categories of desirable (appropriate) and undesirable (inappropriate) behavior.

Right now, you may believe that you have exhausted all behaviors to be listed, but put the list aside for at least a few minutes—or perhaps a whole day—and then come back to it. Now, add to the list any behaviors that you remembered.

Once you have finished listing the behaviors (still ignoring the ratings), refer to the following examples of the Child Behavior List on page 114 which gives examples of desirable and undesirable behaviors. When you have compared your list to the examples, you may wish to go back and revise some items or put even more items on your Child Behavior List.

Exercise 3.5 LISTING BEHAVIORS

Child Behavior List			
Desirable (Appropriate) Behavior	*Rating 1-5*	*Undesirable (Inappropriate) Behavior*	*Rating 1-5*

Exercise 3.5 CHILD BEHAVIOR LIST

CHILD BEHAVIOR LIST

Now that you have your list of your child's desirable and undesirable behaviors and their ratings, you may compare your list to the sample list below.

Desirable (Appropriate) Behavior	*Rating 1-5*	*Undesirable (Inappropriate) Behavior*	*Rating 1-5*
Helps to clean up room	4	Hits brother	5
Mows grass	3	Hits sister	5
Bathes without prompting	3	Curses	5
Keeps room/desk neat	3	Steals money from Mom	4
Takes out trash	1	Tears pages from magazine	4
Fixes own lunch	3	Marks on crossword/books	3
Combs hair neatly	1	Creases pages in books	1
Puts cap on toothpaste	1	Resists (i.e., argues) completing homework	4
Puts toilet seat down	2	Hides *Playboy* under bed	3
Says "please"	3	Grabs toys/games	4
Says "thank you"	3	Gets "off track"	2
Greets strangers	4	Forgets tasks/assignments	2
Stays "on task"	4	Breaks toys/others' property	5
Talks in normal tone	3	Makes sexual gestures	5
Cares for valuables	3	Yells/screams	4
Plays cooperatively/shares	4	Is bossy	4

This list is certainly not exhaustive; there are numerous other behaviors that could have been added. However, the list will give some idea of the range of behaviors that you may expect to deal with. The ratings enable you to make judgments as to the importance of each behavior, whether it be desirable or undesirable. The sample ratings are quite subjective, but do give the conceptualization of a scale of importance for each behavior on the list.

Now, go back through each behavior, desirable and undesirable, and rate each on a five-point scale with 1 representing the weakest behavior and 5 representing the strongest behavior. As a guideline, the strength of the behavior may be directly proportioned to how often the behavior is exhibited. Thus, you would expect a behavior with a rating of 5 to be seen almost daily; in contrast, those behaviors with a rating of 1 may be seen once weekly or less.

These ratings will be useful to you in selecting desirable behaviors to strengthen and undesirable behaviors you want to weaken. The ratings may also be especially useful when constructing point systems (see Chapter 4), as well as helping you to develop priorities for specific behavioral approaches.

Listing Alternative Behaviors

Next, you will have the opportunity to develop a list of alternative behaviors for each undesirable behavior you have listed. There is an alternative behavior for every undesirable behavior that you could imagine, and you can list these alternative behaviors by thinking of what the opposite of each undesirable behavior would be. Some simple examples are:

Undesirable Behavior	*Alternative Behavior*
Fighting	Playing cooperatively
Getting “off track”	Staying “on task”
Hogging toys	Sharing toys

A more extensive list is provided at the end of this chapter, but before looking at those examples, fill in the behaviors (no ratings yet) in Exercise 3.6 on page 116. Specify an Alternative (more desirable) behavior opposite each undesirable behavior you have listed for the child.

Once you have completed this listing of behaviors, rate each of the alternative behaviors as to its strength. In all probability, these alternative behaviors will be weak (or less frequently observed), yet if any of them are moderate-to-strong behaviors (rating of 3 or better), they will be easier to strengthen even more. If an alternative behavior you have listed does not exist yet, then give it a 0 (zero) rating. This indicates that the child has never shown this behavior and that it will have to be taught to the child through modeling and imitation learning. For now, just identify these behaviors. Refer to the Alternative Behavior Checklist on page 117 for a model.

Exercise 3.6 LISTING ALTERNATIVE BEHAVIORS

ALTERNATIVE BEHAVIOR LIST			
Undesirable Behaviors	*Rating 1-5*	*Alternative Behaviors*	*Rating 1-5*

Exercise 3.6 ALTERNATIVE BEHAVIOR LIST

Undesirable Behaviors	*Rating 1-5*	*Alternative Behaviors*	*Rating 1-5*
Interrupts others	4	Waits turn to talk	0
Fights with siblings	5	Works/plays cooperatively	1
Destroys toys	5	Cares for toys	2
Hurts pets	5	Strokes/cuddles pets	2
Talks back to parents	5	Listens to parents	0
Ignores commands	4	Carries out trash	1
Ignores others	3	Greets others	1
Hogs toys	2	Shares toys	1
Acts out anger inappropriately	5	Controls anger	0
Acts before thinking	4	Thinks before acting	0

Compare your list with this sample. Note that in the example there are a number of undesirable behaviors with ratings above 3. This would suggest that these behaviors are of great concern and have probably existed for some time. Looking at the alternative behaviors, we can see that several have "never been observed" (i.e., they have a "zero" rating). This would also indicate that these behaviors will require a more complex program that will probably involve such techniques as *modeling* and *shaping.* Two desirable behaviors do exist to some degree (i.e., cares for toys, strokes/cuddles pets). This is a good sign and such behaviors—even when only moderately established—may respond immediately to a positive reinforcement program.

Next, to get an idea of how widespread some of these behaviors are, a parent should complete the Home Situations Questionnaire (Barkley 1987) in Exercise 3.7 on page 118. This covers a number of common situations when inappropriate behaviors may typically occur for the ADD child. A Home Situations Questionnaire–Revised is also available. There is a comparable School Situations Questionnaire–Revised for teachers to complete. An example of both is provided in Figure 7.5 on page 228.

Exercise 3.7 HOME SITUATIONS QUESTIONNAIRE

Child's Name ______________________________ Date ______________

Name of Person Completing This Form ______________________________

Instructions: Does your child present any problems with compliance to instructions, commands, or rules for you in any of these situations? If so, please circle the word Yes and then circle a number beside that situation that describes how severe the problem is for you. If your child is not a problem in a situation, circle No and go on to the next situation on the form.

Situations	*Yes/No (Circle one)*		*Mild*		*If yes, how severe? (Circle one)*						*Severe*
Playing alone	Yes	No	1	2	3	4	5	6	7	8	9
Playing with other children	Yes	No	1	2	3	4	5	6	7	8	9
Mealtimes	Yes	No	1	2	3	4	5	6	7	8	9
Getting dressed/undressed	Yes	No	1	2	3	4	5	6	7	8	9
Washing and bathing	Yes	No	1	2	3	4	5	6	7	8	9
When you are on the telephone	Yes	No	1	2	3	4	5	6	7	8	9
Watching television	Yes	No	1	2	3	4	5	6	7	8	9
When visitors are in your home	Yes	No	1	2	3	4	5	6	7	8	9
When you are visiting someone's home	Yes	No	1	2	3	4	5	6	7	8	9
In public places (restaurants, stores, church, etc.)	Yes	No	1	2	3	4	5	6	7	8	9
When father is home	Yes	No	1	2	3	4	5	6	7	8	9
When asked to do chores	Yes	No	1	2	3	4	5	6	7	8	9
When asked to do homework	Yes	No	1	2	3	4	5	6	7	8	9
At bedtime	Yes	No	1	2	3	4	5	6	7	8	9
While in the car	Yes	No	1	2	3	4	5	6	7	8	9
When with a babysitter	Yes	No	1	2	3	4	5	6	7	8	9

——————————-For Office Use Only——————————-

Total number of problem settings ______ Mean severity score ______

Now, compare your responses on the Home Situations Questionnaire to the following example on page 119 for interpretive guidelines.

Exercise 3.7 HOME SITUATIONS QUESTIONNAIRE

Child's Name ______________________ Date ____________

Name of Person Completing This Form ______________________

Instructions: Does your child present any problems with compliance to instructions, commands, or rules for you in any of these situations? If so, please circle the word Yes and then circle a number beside that situation that describes how severe the problem is for you. If your child is not a problem in a situation, circle No and go on to the next situation on the form.

Situations	*Yes/No (Circle one)*		*If yes, how severe? (Circle one)*								
			Mild								*Severe*
Playing alone	Yes	No	1	(2)	3	4	5	6	7	8	9
Playing with other children	Yes	No	1	2	3	4	5	6	(7)	8	9
Mealtimes	Yes	No	1	2	3	4	(5)	6	7	8	9
Getting dressed/undressed	Yes	No	1	(2)	3	4	5	6	7	8	9
Washing and bathing	Yes	No	(1)	2	3	4	5	6	7	8	9
When you are on the telephone	Yes	No	1	2	3	4	5	6	7	(8)	9
Watching television	Yes	No	1	2	(3)	4	5	6	7	8	9
When visitors are in your home	Yes	No	1	2	3	4	(5)	6	7	8	9
When you are visiting someone's home	Yes	No	1	2	3	(4)	5	6	7	8	9
In public places (restaurants, stores, church, etc.)	Yes	No	1	2	3	4	(5)	6	7	8	9
When father is home	Yes	No	(1)	2	3	4	5	6	7	8	9
When asked to do chores	Yes	No	1	2	3	(4)	5	6	7	8	9
When asked to do homework	Yes	No	1	2	3	4	5	6	(7)	8	9
At bedtime	Yes	No	1	2	3	4	5	6	7	8	(9)
While in the car	Yes	No	1	2	3	4	5	6	(7)	8	9
When with a babysitter	Yes	No	1	2	3	(4)	5	6	7	8	9

——————————For Office Use Only——————————

Total number of problem settings ______ Mean severity score ______

The Home Situations Questionnaire. From *Defiant Children: A Clinician's Manual for Parent Training* by R. A. Barkley, 1987, New York: Guilford Press.

You should note several things about the example. First, in this scenario there is much more difficulty with the child's behavior when he is in a group. Second, there is a very high rate of inappropriate behavior, probably with "interrupting" occurring mostly with the mother, as disruptive behavior is not repeated when the father is home. Third, there are times when behavior is more appropriate and the child does not have greater difficulty when in the presence of others (except for their children). Fourth, tasks appear to present some difficulty as disruptive behavior arises with chores, but especially with homework. Last, bedtime is somewhat of a problem, and riding in the car (when without Dad) presents significant problems. Overall, the most significant problem areas include playing with peers, doing homework, and behaving appropriately while Mother is on the phone and while riding in a car. Organizing your child's range of behavior problem areas, as in this exercise, can help you to get a better overview of the vastness of noted problems.

So far, certain specific behaviors of the child have been listed and classified as desirable or undesirable, and the list of undesirable behaviors has led to a list of alternative desired behaviors. Next we will discuss problem behaviors.

Major Problem Behaviors

Problem behaviors fall into four basic areas. These four areas include:

1. Relationship with parents
2. Relationship with siblings
3. Relationship with peers and
4. Relationship with self in personal areas covering
   a. Safety
   b. Morals
   c. Habits
   d. Emotional controls

With Exercise 3.8, you will be able to categorize problem behaviors to determine in which area(s) the child presents the most problems. You will again be asked to rate each problem behavior with regard to its perceived severity, where 1 represents a behavior that is considered least severe and 5 represents a behavior you consider most severe. Using this range of 1-5, you may see these problem behaviors as at either extreme or somewhere in the middle.

Exercise 3.8 MAJOR PROBLEM BEHAVIORS

MAJOR PROBLEM BEHAVIORS	*Severity 1-5*
Relationship with parents	
a..	
b.	
c.	
d.	
e.	
Relationship with siblings	
a.	
b.	
c.	
d.	
e.	
Relationship with peers	
a.	
b.	
c.	
d.	
e.	
Personal area: Safety (engaging in high-risk activities)	
a.	
b.	
c.	
d.	
e.	

continued . . .

MAJOR PROBLEM BEHAVIORS	*Severity 1-5*
Personal area: Morals (other high-risk, including stealing and lying)	
a.	
b.	
c.	
d.	
e.	
Personal area: Habits (eating/elimination/hygiene/appearance/dress)	
a.	
b.	
c.	
d.	
e.	
Personal area: Emotional (control and expression)	
a.	
b.	
c.	
d.	
e.	

Once the exercise is completed, you may compare your responses with those in the examples provided on pages 123-124. Since almost all behavior problems occur in relationships with others, this exercise will also demonstrate how widespread the child's problems are and how severe you perceive them to be. In the earlier exercises, you rated behaviors according to *frequency*, but here you are asked to rate *severity* (also on a scale of 1-5, where 1 represents least severe and 5 most severe). Evaluating this list with the prior ones will allow you to address problems that are not only most frequent, but also ones that vary in severity.

Exercise 3.8 MAJOR PROBLEM BEHAVIORS

MAJOR PROBLEM BEHAVIORS Comparisons of your listings of behaviors with the sample provided will aid you in arriving at a final set of problem behaviors on which you may focus.	*Severity 1-5*
Relationship with parents	
a. Hits parents	5
b. Curses parents	5
c. Says "no" to commands	5
d.	
e.	
Relationship with siblings	
a. Hits sibs	5
b. Breaks sibs' toys	4
c. Calls names	3
d. Fights over being "first"	2
e.	
Relationship with peers	
a. Fights with peers	5
b. Calls names	3
c.	
d.	
e.	
Personal area: Safety (engaging in high-risk activities)	
a. Jumps out second-story window	5
b. Lights fires (burned self)	5
c. Plays with knives (cut off finger)	5
d. Throws objects at others	4
e.	

continued . . .

MAJOR PROBLEM BEHAVIORS	*Severity 1-5*
Personal area: Morals (other high-risk, including stealing and lying)	
a. Plays with penis by sister	5
b. Takes other's games/toys	3
c. Lies about where he's been	4
d.	
e.	
Personal area: Habits (eating/elimination/hygiene/appearance/dress)	
a. Burps at dinner table	3
b. Leaves hands dirty	3
c. Sloppy dresser	3
d. Flatulates in public places	4
e.	
Personal area: Emotional (control and expression)	
a. Quick temper	5
b. Hurts small children and pets	5
c. Runs into street when excited	5
d.	
e.	

This overview of problem behaviors will aid you in developing the most appropriate techniques to deal with each problem and to assign priorities in your approaches. Such exercises will also give you a greater awareness of the child's ADD/ADHD behaviors. Thus, multicomponent programs may be set up, encompassing all identified problem areas.

Comparison of the behaviors you listed in Exercise 3.8 with the sample behaviors will give you a good foundation to establish the final set of problem behaviors you wish to deal with in your behavioral management program.

Final Behavior List

In the Final Behavior List, Exercise 3.9, one column denotes the unacceptable behavior (to be gotten rid of) and the other column represents acceptable behaviors (to be developed).

Exercise 3.9 FINAL BEHAVIOR LIST

FINAL BEHAVIOR LIST	
Remove These Unacceptable Behaviors	*Develop These Acceptable Behaviors*

Compare your list to the following examples:

Exercise 3.9 SAMPLE FINAL BEHAVIOR LIST

SAMPLE FINAL BEHAVIOR LIST

At this point, you, the parent, should have a good conceptualization of behavior, both desirable and undesirable, developed and undeveloped. The next step is to list:

1. those behaviors that should be removed from the child's behavior repertoire, and
2. those that should be developed.

Remove These Unacceptable Behaviors	*Develop These Acceptable Behaviors*
Fighting with others	Good dinner-time behavior
Noncompliance	Work/play cooperatively
Name-calling	Improve judgment in face of danger
Cursing	Care for other's property
Destroying property	Better self-control
Sexual gestures	Truth-telling

In some cases, more generalized behaviors have been listed, since it would be far too cumbersome to list every behavior that is to be addressed.

Listing Behaviors to Be Ignored

If attending to a behavior is rewarding and strengthens that behavior, then ignoring a given behavior (paying attention to something else) is mildly punishing and weakens the behavior in question. In other words, ignoring a behavior helps to extinguish or get rid of the behavior. Your attention—and a parent's attention, in particular—has quite a powerful impact on a child, especially during the early years and throughout the preteen years. Unfortunately, this generally does not hold true for adolescence, although many adolescents still crave much attention, especially if an early pattern of "attention to appropriate behavior" was developed and maintained over the early years. Of course, many ADD/ADHD children have a history of receiving a substantial amount of negative attention for their inappropriate behaviors (e.g., as class clown), and these will have to be modified. However, the fact that the child is responsive to any kind of attention will be an asset in behavior management. In Exercise 3.10, list behaviors to be ignored, but prior to deciding which behaviors should be ignored, look at the general category of those behaviors that will best respond to the ignoring procedure. Generally these behaviors are: (a) behaviors that are annoying; (b) behaviors that do not involve acting out of anger; (c) behaviors that interfere with the achievement of a goal.

Exercise 3.10 LISTING THOSE BEHAVIORS TO BE IGNORED

BEHAVIORS TO BE IGNORED (EXTINCTION PROCESS)	
1.	11.
2.	12.
3.	13.
4.	14.
5.	15.
6.	16.
7.	17.
8.	18.
9.	19.
10.	20.

Once you have completed your list of Behaviors to Be Ignored, refer to the examples below for Exercise 3.10 to obtain some feedback. Remember that these sample listings of behavior are for comparative purposes; they are not meant to be exhaustive. There may be many behaviors (some unique to your situation) that are quite annoying and are not included in the example; the specific behaviors listed are intended to help you understand the kinds of behavior referred to and to serve as a guide for you.

Exercise 3.10 SAMPLE BEHAVIORS TO BE IGNORED

Behaviors to Be Ignored (Extinction Process)

The last list provided illustrates those behaviors which are best ignored as a way of removing them. This following sample list is provided for you to use as a guideline. Ignoring does not imply avoiding dealing with the behavior. It is, instead, a viable technique to weaken and remove these behaviors.

1. Whining	11. Swearing (for reaction)
2. Pouting	12. Inappropriate noises
3. Repetitive demands	13. Repetitive questions
4. Repetitive requests	14. Clowning
5. Burping	15. Inappropriate eating (occasional noise)
6. Passing gas	16. Rolling eyes (when punished)
7. Screaming	17. Stamping feet (after being punished)
8. Temper tantrums	18. Baby talk
9. Crying (demanding)	19. Complaining
10. Sulking	20. Begging

Typically, ignoring these behaviors on a consistent basis will weaken them sufficiently so that eventually the (undesired, unacceptable) ignored behavior becomes extinct. The key words are *consistent* and *ignoring*, and you must monitor the behavior to determine if the frequency (i.e. strength) does actually change.

During the actual process of ignoring the behavior, you must expect that the behavior *may get worse* before it gets better, and you must stay focused on the procedure; once a behavior is selected to be ignored, you must consistently ignore it over a reasonable period of time. This period may range from two to eight weeks, depending on how strong the behavior is initially. If you give in to the child, you will very often not only reinforce the behavior at an even higher level of intensity, but you may also reinforce a pattern of persistence that will make it even more difficult to change the behavior in the future; use the "self-talk" procedure (discussed in Chapter 4) during the ignoring technique to counter some of the difficulties that arise. Specifically, to avoid giving in and attending to the inappropriate behavior (e.g., whining), you must constantly use self-talk such as, "OK, I know this behavior is going to get worse—what I must do is to keep reading this paper. I know that he's going to try something else to get my attention. I must focus my attention on this paper; I know I'm not really going to get anything out of attempting to read at this time; it's just important that I keep giving it my attention. I don't have to give in to his demands (etc.)."

Some of these listed behaviors to be ignored may already have become too well established to be handled with the ignoring technique alone. A very good option here is to attend to the alternative behaviors (i.e. opposite, appropriate behaviors) while using the ignoring procedure. For some other behaviors on the list, an entirely different approach may be needed. In all behavioral programs, there must be a constant *analysis* and *evaluation* of whether the program is working. If it is not, there are many other approaches that can be employed.

CONSEQUENCES

In behavioral terminology, the word *consequences* refers to *whatever follows a particular behavior.* These events may be generally classified as either "rewards" or "punishments." A *reward* is a positive reinforcer that either increases or maintains the strength of a behavior so that the positively reinforced behavior will be *more likely* to be exhibited. A *punishment* is a negative reinforcer that will decrease or weaken the behavior it follows so that this negatively reinforced behavior will be *less likely* to be exhibited.

A Special Note About Physical Punishment

Research and clinical experience regarding the excessive use of physical punishment (spanking) is that it is generally ineffective since it never tells the child what *to do,* only what *not* to do. In addition, there are several undesirable "side effects" that may result from physical punishment, according to Azrin and Holz (1966):

1. A tendency to withdraw from social contacts, in general
2. Aggression turned back towards the punisher—either active (hitting) or passive (resistance or tuning out)
3. Modeling of aggressive behavior (often as inappropriate solutions to problems)
4. Disruption of the social relationship with the authority figure who imposes the punishment (typically a tendency for the child to distance him/herself from that person)
5. A failure of the control imposed by the punishment to generalize to other situations

6. Selective control where the child may inhibit an inappropriate behavior only in the presence of the one authority figure who punished him/her
7. Stigmatizing the self-concept with feelings of being worthless and deserving of such treatment

Rewards can be classified into three basic categories:

1. Tangible (goods)
2. Activities (privileges)
3. Social (praise)

A punishment can be categorized as either:

1. An aversive event—presentation of some negative stimuli to the child, evoking pain, discomfort or displeasure; or
2. A deprivation event—withdrawal of positive stimuli, taking away from the child for a short period of time something she perceives as pleasant or pleasurable.

Note, however, that all events that modify behavior (i.e., consequences) may not clearly be classified as a *reward* or a *punishment.*

Exercise 3.11 focuses on the rather surprising effects of *simply monitoring behavior.* The phenomenon of noted change in behavior as a result of merely counting (monitoring) the behavior is almost universally acknowledged, but poorly understood. Nonetheless, counting inappropriate behavior may result in decreases in such behavior while counting appropriate behavior may result in increases. Even when counting is the only consequence, there is very often a change.

Why Should Behavior Be Monitored (Counted)?

The simple answer is that we need something to compare with (a *baseline measure*) when behavior does or does not change. With baseline measures, we can state whether the behavior in question has improved or gotten worse. This information is crucial in our ongoing analysis of our behavioral program to determine what, if any, changes may be needed.

Exercise 3.11 MONITORING BEHAVIOR

Select a Specific Behavior You Wish to Change

This may be a behavior that you would like to see:

—more often (i.e., increase in frequency of occurrence), or

—less often (i.e., decrease in frequency of occurrence).

The former, a *desired behavior,* would be an *appropriate though weak behavior;* while the latter, an *undesirable behavior,* would be an *inappropriate behavior of mild strength.*

These behaviors in question should not be the ones of primary concern to you; however, the behaviors must clearly need to be dealt with at some point in the overall program. Dealing *continued . . .*

with these secondary behavior problems may make some of the more significant behavior problems actually easier to handle.

Write down the specific behavior to be monitored (counted) and recorded: ____________

Now Record the Selected Behavior at Some Regular Interval

How do you decide what interval (observation unit) to select?

If a behavior occurs a great deal, you may select a daily recording or even a specific period of the day (e.g., from 2 P.M. to 6 P.M.).

If the behavior occurs infrequently, you may wish to use a two-day observation unit.

However, a typical starting point may be to record daily.

The behavior must be very clearly defined, be observable, and be countable. That way, for example, it will be clear how many times the child says "please" in making a request. Alternately, it will also be clear each time the child throws dirty clothes on the floor rather than putting them in the hamper, for example. In each case, you can see or hear the selected behavior; thus, the selected behavior can be counted each day (or other interval).

Remember to select only one behavior at a time to monitor when you are just beginning to learn these behavioral techniques.

The number of times the behavior occurs is then recorded for each interval (observation unit).

Exercise 3.11 BEHAVIOR MONITOR

SELECTED BEHAVIOR

*Number of Times Selected Behavior Is Noted**	SUN.	MON.	TUES.	WED.	THURS.	FRI.	SAT.
50							
45							
40							
35							
30							
25							
20							
15							
10							
5							
INTERVAL	**SUN.**	**MON.**	**TUES.**	**WED.**	**THURS.**	**FRI.**	**SAT.**

* This scale may change depending upon the frequency of the behavior under observation.

When you have accumulated monitoring data for at least one week, see the following sample graph, for some feedback on this exercise.

Exercise 3.11 BEHAVIOR MONITOR

SELECTED BEHAVIOR

Number of Times Selected Behavior Is Noted	SUN	MON	TUES	WED	THURS	FRI	SAT	SUN	MON	TUES	WED	THURS	FRI	SAT
25														
20														
15														
13														
11														
9														
7												•	•	•
5								•		•	•			
3					•	•	•		•					
1	•	•	•	•										
INTERVAL	SUN	MON	TUES	WED	THURS	FRI	SAT	SUN	MON	TUES	WED	THURS	FRI	SAT

What this sample graph shows is:

1. There is probably some finite limit to the improvement (i.e., you have only so many chances to say "please" in one day).
2. There is general improvement (i.e., the number of times "please" is verbalized increases over 14 days).
3. There is some variation in the number (e.g., after one week there is actually a decrease).

This behavior monitoring exercise simply shows that by observing and keeping a record of some behavior, the frequency and underlying strength of that behavior may change. This occurs without any formal consequences.

Understanding Rewards and Punishments

How do you know what is rewarding or punishing for a child? One way to find out is to ask the child. The other way is to note which things, activities, or other events the child prefers to have or to do—*as much as possible* or *as often as possible.* Thus, the *frequency* in which a child engages in an activity or shows preference for a toy is directly proportional to the *reward value* of that toy or activity.

Sometimes it is difficult to make judgments about what a child says; he might distort the truth slightly if he has some awareness of how this information is going to be used. However, it is rare that distortion appears in the frequency a child engages in play with a particular toy or engages in some play activity. Specifically, if a child plays with Nintendo© every chance he gets, or rides his bike daily, then it is apparent that these are rewarding events.

Another method of determining a child's likes and dislikes is to give the following questionnaires to the child as an exercise in awareness of what's rewarding and what's punishing for your child.

Exercise 3.12 AWARENESS OF REINFORCERS

The four questionnaires listed here are provided for the child to complete (or for a parent to fill in the answers the child gives, if the child is too young to perform this task on his or her own). Please note that some parents may be able to complete the *likes* and *dislikes* part without using a questionnaire, and some parents will need to give only some of these questionnaires. The questionnaires are provided so that parents and others working with the child may learn some additional reinforcers to use with the child. Counselors and teachers may not know the child's likes and dislikes as well as the parent does.

1. The Children's Reinforcement Survey Schedule
2. The Reinforcement Menu
3. The Response-Cost Survey Schedule
4. The M-R Incomplete Blank (Modified)

Once these are completed, review the child's answers and make two lists:

1. Things/activities the child likes
2. Things/activities the child dislikes

Now, see the examples for this exercise on the following page.

Exercise 3.12 AWARENESS OF REINFORCERS

Likes	*Dislikes*
Playing Nintendo©	Making models
Baseball Cards	Giving reports in front of class
Fishing on weekends	Time-out
TV shows about cops	Math, Spelling, Handwriting
Money	Fixing broken things

The questionnaires with one child's responses appear at the end of this chapter, starting on page 139.

Getting the Message from Rewards and Punishments

Sometimes what the child says does not really reflect his or her underlying feelings and thoughts. For example, if the child says in response to an item in Exercise 3.12, "I like spankings!" what does this mean? This next exercise is actually designed to improve communication with the child. Statements like the preceding one may suggest one of the following:

1. The child would prefer a spanking to "get the punishment over" because she dislikes some other form of punishment even more.
2. The child is stating that he is tough—that he cannot be hurt.
3. The child is attempting to manipulate the parent into using some other form of punishment, trying to convince the parent that spanking would certainly be ineffective.
4. The child may simply be asking for the parent's time and attention; she may realize at some level of awareness that negative parental attention is all that is available.

Perhaps none of these assumptions would be tenable and none may be validated by the child, yet when unusual or inappropriate responses are made, there is some underlying reason. By writing down some possible interpretations in Exercise 3.13, you may come to realize what the child is trying to communicate about underlying needs, positive strokes (rewards), and negative strokes (punishments).

Exercise 3.13 GETTING THE MESSAGE

1. Note each apparently unusual response the child gave in Exercise 3.12.
2. Write a list of possible interpretations (as was just illustrated) for each.
3. Compare these with the examples on p. 149.

Focus on Social Rewards

Social rewards consist of nonverbal actions, gestures, and touch along with specific verbal forms of approval as discussed by Barkley (1987). These verbal and nonverbal social rewards may initially be associated with a structured behavior program, and as that structured behavior program is gradually faded out, the use of these social rewards becomes a primary reinforcer to maintain and further develop appropriate behavior. Clearly, the parent's or teacher's attention is still quite powerful in effecting behavior change.

Sometimes, however, such actions or words of kindness may be lost in a sea of confusion, frustration, and anger—perhaps because a parent relies on physical punishment to attempt to manage behavior, even though it isn't effective. Sadly, too, some parents may never have tried using kind words or actions—modeling the way they were treated by their own parents, by making comments such as, "Well, my parents never thanked me for doing *my* chores," or "Why should I praise my child for doing what he *should be doing*?" It may be difficult to convince these individuals that a new, different, kinder approach is needed; it sometimes seems especially hard to accept a kind and gentle approach when the old approach hasn't worked. While the habit of using new verbal and nonverbal feedback with the child may be difficult for a parent or teacher to acquire—it may even feel quite awkward at first—the most important step at this stage is the willingness to try.

Exercise 3.14 is designed to make you more familiar with these verbal and nonverbal social rewards. See the examples for this exercise on page 149.

Exercise 3.14 SOCIAL REWARDS

For each category, list those verbal and nonverbal forms of social rewards you use or may learn to use.

Nonverbal Social Rewards

1. ______________________
2. ______________________
3. ______________________
4. ______________________
5. ______________________
6. ______________________
7. ______________________
8. ______________________
9. ______________________
10. ______________________

continued . . .

Verbal Social Rewards

1. ______________________	11. ______________________
2. ______________________	12. ______________________
3. ______________________	13. ______________________
4. ______________________	14. ______________________
5. ______________________	15. ______________________
6. ______________________	16. ______________________
7. ______________________	17. ______________________
8. ______________________	18. ______________________
9. ______________________	19. ______________________
10. ______________________	20. ______________________

As Barkley (1987) has also noted, it is important to:

1. Give these social rewards *immediately* after a good behavior
2. Be *specific* about what you liked
3. Never give a backhanded compliment ("It's about time you cleaned your room. Why couldn't you do that before?").

Also note that verbal and nonverbal components together make the most powerful and natural social rewards; for example, while patting the child on the back, state exactly what you liked about his behavior ("I really liked the way you did all of your chores without a reminder."). See the list of social rewards on p. 150.

WRITING INSTRUMENTAL BEHAVIOR PLANS

Behavior that leads a person to obtain a specific reward is termed *instrumental behavior.* The simplest example of instrumental behavior in a parent-child relationship is the age-old saying: "First you eat your dinner, then you get your dessert." Eating dinner is thus "instrumental" in getting dessert. Instrumental behavior plans should:

1. be written in a positive framework—for example, "When you clean your room, you may go out to play" instead of "If you don't clean your room, then you can't go out to play."
2. use *when* instead of *if,* leaving no doubt that the work will be done—for example, "*When* you do your homework, then you can play."

These *when-then* plans in Exercise 3.15 can be used equally well in the school setting. For example, "When you finish this assignment, you can have free time."

Exercise 3.15 WRITING INSTRUMENTAL (WHEN-THEN) PLANS

To get a feel for what these are like, write a sample of five plans using the following format:

1. When you ______________________________,

   Then you may ______________________________.

2. When you ______________________________,

   Then you may ______________________________.

3. When you ______________________________,

   Then you may ______________________________.

4. When you ______________________________,

   Then you may ______________________________.

5. When you ______________________________,

   Then you may ______________________________.

Review your written examples and compare them to the examples shown below. Be sure yours meet the two basic criteria (i.e., positive approach and "when-then"). Remember, *never* allow the child to have what she or he wants based on a promise from the child to complete the desired behavior at a later time. Some parents, especially parents of children with ADD, often say, "You can watch TV, but you have to promise to complete your homework." To the parent's dismay, the homework does not get completed since there is not enough time left after the TV program. There is one additional point to make at this time. Children with ADHD experience some difficulty with "delay of gratification." Typically, a child with ADHD would prefer to do a small amount of work for a small "immediate" reward than a larger amount of work for a much larger reward at some later time. Thus, large rewards offered for good grades at the end of a semester or year will be ineffective.

Exercise 3.15 WRITING INSTRUMENTAL (WHEN—THEN) PLANS

1. When you finish your homework,
   Then you may go out to play.
2. When you take out the trash,
   Then you may have a treat.
3. When you clean your room,
   Then you may watch TV.
4. When you help clean the garage,
   Then you may go to the teen dance.
5. When you wash the car,
   Then you may play Nintendo©.

DEVELOPING A SHAPING PROGRAM

Sometimes a desired behavior does not exist. More specifically, a desired behavior may not exist in the form we want—maybe because of a developmental delay, or perhaps as a result of a physical impairment. A procedure termed *shaping* may be used to develop this desired behavior. It doesn't matter whether we are referring to a vocal response (word), motor response (motor coordination), or an emotional response (e.g., inhibition of anger), the process in each case is very similar. What you must do is establish a step-by-step plan stating what behavior will be reinforced at each step. You can facilitate this process by *modeling* appropriate behavior; then when the child imitates this or at least "does it better," a reinforcement (praise, pat on the back, chips, or some other event significant for the child) may be delivered.

A simple example might involve a child's developing vocal-language skills with words (e.g., the word "water").

Primitive	*Intermediate*	*Final*
wa-wa	wa-er	water

Some children may skip an intermediate step (or two) and go directly to the final form. This is no problem—both you and the child will have saved some time and effort. When the child uses the primitive form "wa-wa," wait for an improved response after modeling the appropriate response. If you get improvement over the primitive form, say, "That's much better, you said that word much better than before!" Keep repeating this until the final form is obtained. When you get the final form, say, "That's exactly right; very good."

Don't be surprised if the child regresses at times, even after getting to the final form. If this regression occurs, simply say, "Try again to say *water.*" When the child pronounces "water" correctly again, repeat the final form response to the child. This should be reinforced periodically thereafter to maintain the final form response.

Assuming that there are no structural or neurophysiological impairments that could block the development of a behavior, the shaping procedure may allow for maximum development of that behavior. Should progress not be forthcoming, such training should cease in order to avoid excessive stress and frustration for the child (and you!). Let us turn our attention now to Exercise 3.16—Shaping Behavior.

Exercise 3.16 SHAPING BEHAVIOR

First, select a behavior that the child may exhibit in some primitive form. This may be word, action, or some higher level behavior. Now see if you can fill in the three basic levels of response: (a) Primitive Form (b) Intermediate Form (c) Final Form.

continued . . .

Behavior	*Primitive Form*	*Intermediate Form*	*Final Form*
Word			
Action			
Higher Level			

Compare your responses to the examples below for shaping. In general, one can easily define the primitive response and the final form. While the intermediate stage may assume many different forms, most individuals working with the child will be able to recognize: (1) improvement, and (2) the final stage. Here are some examples of each stage:

Exercise 3.16 SAMPLE SHAPING BEHAVIOR

Behavior	*Primitive Form*	*Intermediate Form*	*Final Form*
Word	wa-wa	wa-er	water
Action	picks up large coins	picks up med-size button	picks up small bead
Higher Level	impulsive acting-out of anger	pauses before acting out	inhibits angry retort

"TOP TEN" TAKE-CONTROL TIPS FOR PARENTS AND TEACHERS

The following suggestions summarize information on consequences and are adapted from the materials in *Power Parenting for Children with ADD/ADHD.* These general recommendations may be used by parents and teachers.

1. Tell the child what you want him or her to do; avoid saying what you don't want.

2. Be specific about the behaviors you like instead of saying "good boy" or "good girl."
3. Model the desired behavior you wish to establish instead of waiting for this behavior to appear.
4. Reward with social praise and touch; avoid the use of physical punishment.
5. Build on small changes in behavior; don't expect major changes.
6. Withdraw attention to some inappropriate behaviors, but do pay attention to the behavior you are trying to get rid of.
7. Reward appropriate behavior and punish inappropriate behavior; never reverse this.
8. Reward and punish immediately after respective appropriate or inappropriate behavior.
9. Provide a consequence (i.e., punishment) for inappropriate behavior, instead of using threats.
10. Use mild punishment for inappropriate behavior and avoid using physical punishment for aggressive behavior.

EXAMPLES FOR EXERCISES 3.12, 3.13 AND 3.14

In Exercise 3.12, Awareness of Reinforcers, (see page 133) information is obtained from the *child* regarding those things that may be rewarding or punishing to him or her.

Information for awareness of reinforcers is derived from:

1. Children's Reinforcement Survey Schedule (c)
2. Reinforcement Menu
3. Response-Cost Survey Schedule
4. The M-R Incomplete Blank

Based on the pattern of responses from the child, we can determine two lists (page 133):

1. Things or activities the child likes, and
2. Things or activities the child dislikes

CHILDREN'S REINFORCEMENT SURVEY SCHEDULES (C)

Schedule C

Name ______________________________ Date ______________

Age ______ Sex: Boy ______ Girl ______

School ______________________________ Grade ______________

This is a list of many different things or activities. Explain how much you like each choice by making an X in the appropriate box.

If you dislike the choice, make an X in the box under Dislike:

Dislike	Like	Like very much
X		

If you like the choice, make an X in the box under Like:

Dislike	Like	Like very much
	X	

If the choice is something that you like very, very much, make an X in the box under Like very much:

Dislike	Like	Like very much
		X

	Dislike	Like	Like very much
1. Do you like candy?		✓	
2. Do you like fruit?		✓	
3. Do you like soda?			✓
4. Do you like cooking?	✓		
5. Do you like to make models?	✓		
6. Do you like to play with model cars and trains?		✓	
7. Do you like to draw and paint?	✓		
8. Do you like to do crafts?	✓		
9. Do you like carpentry and woodworking?	✓		
10. Do you like making things out of clay?		✓	
11. Do you like working with motors?	✓		
12. Do you like puzzles?	✓		
13. Do you like fixing broken things?	✓		
14. Would you like to have sports equipment of your own?		✓	
15. Do you like to play on playground equipment?		✓	
16. Do you like to go bike riding?		✓	
17. Do you like to go swimming?		✓	
18. Do you like to go skiing?	✓		

	Dislike	Like	Like very much
19. Do you like hockey?	✓		
20. Do you like baseball?			✓
21. Do you like football?			✓
22. Do you like basketball?		✓	
23. Do you like kickball?		✓	
24. Do you like camping?		✓	
25. Do you like gocarts?			✓
26. Do you like mini-bikes?			✓
27. Do you like listening to music?		✓	
28. Do you like singing?	✓		
29. Do you like learning how to play musical instruments?	✓		
30. Do you like cartoons and comic books?			✓
31. Do you like fairy tales?	✓		
32. Do you like science fiction?		✓	
33. Do you like mysteries?	✓		
34. Do you like biographies (stories about people's lives)?	✓		
35. Do you like to sell things?	✓		
36. Do you like to go shopping?	✓		
37. Do you like to watch TV?		✓	
38. Do you like to go to different, faraway places on vacation?		✓	
39. Do you like to eat out in a restaurant?	✓		
40. Do you like to go to the movies?		✓	
41. Would you like to go to a circus or a fair?		✓	
42. Do you like going on field trips at school?		✓	
43. Do you like outdoor recess?		✓	
44. Do you like it when your teacher buys materials that you especially like?		✓	
45. Do you like being a leader in your class, such as being a class officer?	✓		
46. Do you like giving reports in front of the class?	✓		
47. Do you like creative writing (making up stories or poems)?	✓		
48. Do you like science?		✓	
49. Do you like math?	✓		
50. Do you like spelling?	✓		
51. Do you like playing with dogs?		✓	
52. Do you like playing with cats?	✓		
53. Do you like to go to the zoo?		✓	
54. Do you like taking care of the pet animals?	✓		
55. Do you like to play with some children younger than you?			✓
56. Do you like to play with some children older than you?		✓	
57. Do you like to play with some special grownups?		✓	
58. Do you like being alone rather than being with other people?	✓		

	Dislike	Like	Like very much
59. Would you like to talk to a sports star you know about?		✓	
60. Would you like to talk to a TV or movie star you have seen?		✓	
61. Do you like going to parties?	✓		
62. Do you like to stay overnight at a friend's house?		✓	
63. If your friend is sick, do you like to take some things to your friend's house to make your friend happier?			✓
64. Do you like earning money?			✓
65. Do you like to be praised for your good work?			✓
66. Do you like your parents to ask you what you did in school today?	✓		
67. Do you like to be the winner of a contest?	✓		
68. Do you like to have your teacher ask you to help?		✓	
69. Do you like getting the right answer?			✓
70. Do you like to show your good work to other people?		✓	
71. Do you feel good when you have just finished a project or job you had to do?		✓	
72. Do you like it when all the other kids think you are terrific?		✓	
73. Do you like having a birthday party and getting presents?		✓	
74. Do you like someone to take care of you when you are scared?		✓	
75. If you are sick, do you like people to take care of you?		✓	

76. What do you think is the best thing about you? I like to help my mom.

77. What do you daydream about ? Being a policeman.

78. What do you do for fun? Play Nintendo.

79. What would like for your birthday? Nintendo Games.

80. Do you have any collections? Yes If so, what do you collect? Baseball Cards

REINFORCEMENT MENU (C)

Name ______________________________ Date ______________
Age ______ Sex: Boy ______ Girl ______
School ______________________________ Grade ______________

Below are activities you could do when you are bored or instead of something you are not supposed to do. Circle the ones you would enjoy doing. On the empty lines at the end of the list, fill in anything you like to do that isn't already on the list.

1. Listening to the radio
2. Listening to the stereo (circled)
3. Watching television (circled)
4. Riding a bicycle (circled)
5. Going for a walk
6. Shooting baskets (circled)
7. Ice skating
8. Playing a game by myself
9. Reading a book
10. Going to the store
11. Working on a hobby
12. Riding on my skateboard (circled)
13. Jogging
14. Playing school
15. Playing dolls
16. Coloring
17. Drawing pictures
18. Playing with clay (circled)
19. Cooking
20. Baking cookies
21. Writing a letter
22. Building something
23. Making pudding or Jello
24. Painting
25. Playing with jacks
26. Jumping rope
27. Doing a crossword puzzle
28. Helping the teacher
29. Playing with cards (circled)
30. Playing with toy people
31. Going to a friend's house
32. Talking on the phone
33. Playing in the sandbox
34. Playing in the bathtub
35. Playing cards with someone
36. Helping mom or dad
37. get baseball cards
38. get more Nintendo Games
39. Go to McDonalds
40. ______________

From *Forms for Behavior Analysis with Children* (page 137) by J.R. Cautela, J. Cautela and S. Esonis, 1983, Champaign, IL: Research Press.

RESPONSE-COST SURVEY SCHEDULE (C)

Name ______________________________ Date ____________
Age ______ Sex: Boy ______ Girl ______
School ______________________________ Grade ____________

How much would it bother you to *lose* the following things or privileges? Put an X in the box that tells best how you would feel.

	Not at all	A little	Very much
1. A favorite toy		✓	
2. My allowance			✓
3. The chance to watch my favorite television program		✓	
4. The chance to watch television for the evening		✓	
5. Playtime after school		✓	
6. Playtime on Saturday			✓
7. Playtime after dinner		✓	
8. Playtime on Sunday	✓		
9. Playtime in my room	✓		
10. The chance to stay up until my regular bedtime			✓
11. Dessert		✓	
12. My snack		✓	
13. Going to a friend's house			✓
14. Going out for a treat such as ice cream with my parents		✓	
15. Going out to eat with my parents	✓		
16. Going to the movies with my parents	✓		
17. Going to the movies with a friend			✓
18. Going to the zoo with my parents	✓		
19. Going to a a. football game			✓
b. basketball game	✓		
c. hockey game	✓		
d. baseball game			✓
e. soccer game	✓		
20. My bicycle		✓	
21. My favorite game			✓
22. The chance to watch cartoons on Saturday morning		✓	
23. Money a. 5 cents	✓		
b. 10 cents	✓		
c. 25 cents		✓	
d. 1 dollar			✓
e. 5 dollars			✓

How much would it bother you to be assigned the following jobs? Put an X in the box that tells best how you would feel.

	Not at all	A little	Very much
24. Washing the dishes		✓	
25. Vacuuming			✓
26. Dusting the furniture			✓
27. Changing the sheets on my bed		✓	
28. Cleaning the inside of the car	✓		
29. Washing the windows		✓	
30. Washing the kitchen floor			✓
31. Cleaning the bathroom			✓
32. Washing the floor			✓
33. Raking leaves		✓	
34. Taking the garbage out	✓		
35. Drying dishes	✓		
36. Cleaning my room	✓		
37. Weeding the garden		✓	

38. Please write down (or tell me) other things or privileges you would not like to lose or jobs you would not want to be given. ______________________________

____

____

____

____

Name ______________________

Date ______________________

School ______________________

M-R Incomplete Blank

1. My favorite grown-up (adult) is My Mom

   What do you like to do with her/him? Play Nintendo games

2. The best reward anybody can give me is Baseball cards

3. My favorite school subject is Recess

4. If I had ten dollars I'd Buy some baseball cards

5. My favorite relative in a city or town close by is My uncle

6. When I grow up I want to be A policeman

7. The person who punishes me most is My Dad

   How? Spankings

   Effectiveness? Not good

   Other punishments used? Take privileges away

   Which works best with you? I don't know

8. Two things I like to do best are (1) Play Nintendo and (2) Get to go to baseball card shows

9. My favorite adult at school is The assistant principal

10. When I do something well, what my mother does is Hugs me and sometimes I get money to save for baseball cards

11. I feel terrific when My Mom hugs me

12. The way I get money is Do chores

13. When I have money I like to Buy baseball cards

14. When I'm in trouble my father Spanks me

15. Something I really want is Go to a baseball card show

16. If I please my father, what he does is Nothing

17. If I had a chance, I sure would like to Play football

18. The person I like to reward me is My Mom

How? Hugs, money, kiss

19. I will do almost anything to avoid A spanking

20. The thing I like to do best with my mother is Play Nintendo

21. The thing I do that bothers my teacher the most is Yell out answers

22. The weekend activity or entertainment I enjoy most is Going fishing

23. If I did better at school I wish my teacher would Tell me

24. The kind of punishment I hate most is Time-out

25. I will do almost anything to get A spanking

26. It sure makes me mad when I can't Get a spanking

27. When I am in trouble, my mother Tells me

28. My favorite brother or sister in a city or town close by is Bob

29. The thing I like to do most is Play Nintendo

30. The only person I will take advice from My Mom

31. Not counting my parents, a person I will do almost anything for is My teacher

32. I hate my teacher to Yell at me

33. My two favorite TV programs are (1) NYPD Blue (2) Cops

34. The thing I like to do best with my father is Go fishing

Subject's Ranking of Reinforcers

Exercise 3.13

Based on a review of the child's responses on the questionnaires in Exercise 3.12, some interpretive statements may be made. The following are derived from the information on the four questionnaires in Exercise 3.12.

In the following examples, some observations are provided about the sample responses given by this child with ADD.

First, on the Children's Reinforcement Survey Schedule, it is obvious that the child either: (1) forgot the instructions, or (2) had difficulty reading the instructions, or (3) deliberately changed the requested response from placing an "x" to indicate his preference to placing instead a (✓). (This latter tendency may suggest oppositional tendencies that may be supported by other information.)

Second, it is clear that the child does not prefer activities in which some facility with hand-eye coordination is needed (e.g., building models). There is also an aversion to writing (which also requires good hand-eye coordination) and to giving reports (speaking) to the class (perhaps a sign of poor self-concept and lack of confidence with academic performance).

Third, specific reinforcers are indicated: sodas, football, baseball, riding go-carts/minibikes, comic books, playing with younger kids, money, being praised, helping a friend, and, of course, getting right answers to questions. Specific games (Nintendo©) and activities (collecting baseball cards) are mentioned. It also seems that this child has a more positive interaction with Mom, as he prefers that she play the games with him.

On the Reinforcement Menu, this child again lists some favorite reinforcements, adding (a) trip to McDonald's, (b) riding skateboard, (c) shooting baskets, and (d) listening to stereo (watching TV). Preference for "playing with clay" may also suggest that there is difficulty with fine-motor coordination. It is far easier and less demanding to work with clay than with models that have many small parts to assemble.

The Response-Cost Survey Schedule indicates what the child would not like to have. Again, there is some misinterpretation of the instructions on the last set, as he initially checks (✓) everything. Further questioning allows the parent to record the child's correct opinions (indicated by "x" marks).

On the M-R Incomplete Blank, the child again states his favorite things and activities. Although his favorite grown-up is Mom, he apparently does one thing with his father—goes fishing on the weekend. He states that he likes to have contact with his mom as hugs and kisses are reinforcing, as is money. The child further states at one point that he actually enjoys spankings. This may be a playful attempt to get attention, a misinterpretation of the incomplete statement, or it may be that he actually prefers a spanking to "get his punishment over." Further explorative questioning of the child may isolate his true answer. Specific TV shows are also given as ones he would probably not want to miss. These would certainly have some motivating power.

Exercise 3.14 SOCIAL REWARDS

The following is a list of social rewards as noted by Barkley (1987).

- *Nonverbal signs of approval*
  - Hug
  - Pat on the head or shoulder
  - Affectionate rubbing of hair
  - Placing arm around the child
  - Smiling
  - A light kiss
  - Giving a thumbs-up sign
  - A wink
- *Verbal approval*
  - I like it when you . . .
  - It's nice when you . . .
  - You sure are a big boy/girl for . . .
  - That was terrific the way you . . .
  - Great job!
  - Nice going!
  - Terrific!
  - Super!
  - Fantastic!
  - My, you sure act grown up when you . . .
  - You know, six months ago you couldn't do that as well as you can now—you're really growing up fast!
  - Beautiful!
  - Wow!
  - Wait until I tell your mom/dad how nicely you . . .
  - What a nice thing to do . . .
  - You did that all by yourself—way to go!
  - Just because you behaved so well, you and I will . . .
  - I am very proud of you when you . . .
  - I always enjoy it when we . . . like this.

This list is fairly comprehensive; it certainly is not exhaustive. There may be many highly personal individualized verbal and nonverbal forms of communication that convey your approval to a child.

For those who are not accustomed to using these positive verbal and nonverbal expressions, it will take some personal preparation, rehearsal, and practice before one becomes comfortable with these verbal and nonverbal expressions. Remember, you may wish to adapt the language of these sample verbal expressions to conform with your own personal jargon. In any case, with practice, expect to gradually become more comfortable with these forms of positive feedback so that eventually they become automatic when you "catch" the child in some appropriate behavior.

Remember, it is critical to:

1. Make these comments *immediately* after observing the good behavior.
2. Be *very specific* about what you like—for example, "I like it when you follow my instructions."
3. Remember to give the positive feedback *without any negative component.* Additional statements like, "Why can't you do that all the time?" diminish the reward value of the compliment.

It may be important at this time to review some of the possible negative components that you may have said or done, or even thought of saying or doing, to guard against using them in the future. It's always important to listen to yourself and be aware of any such negative comments so you can avoid them in the future.

CHAPTER 4

Managing Behavior

All children must learn appropriate behaviors at home, in school and in other situations. Whenever you wish to develop a new behavior, consider the child's age and physical capabilities, and whether there are any interfering behaviors. Behaviors that are inappropriate may be physiologically determined or may be learned or acquired in association with behaviors that are physiologically determined.

DEVELOPING NEW BEHAVIORS

Listing Alternative Behaviors Opposite to ADD Behaviors

Evidence from clinical research indicates that behavioral programs that focus solely on punishing inappropriate behaviors may work only for a short time. Mild punishments are necessary for some inappropriate behavior, but when the entire focus is on punishment (mild or severe) for inappropriate behaviors the negative focus may backfire, bringing about results contrary to our wishes. Thus, you must focus on developing more appropriate behavior through a positive orientation. The first step in this process is to list appropriate behaviors that are alternatives to the ADD behaviors typically exhibited.

Exercise 4.1 on page 152 focuses on listing behaviors that are opposite (alternative behaviors) to typical ADD behaviors. When writing these alternative behaviors, think of the appropriate behavior you would like to see in place of the typical ADD behavior (e.g., if interrupting others is typical, then waiting one's turn to talk is desired). Try your hand at writing these, then check the example for feedback.

Exercise 4.1 LISTING ALTERNATIVE BEHAVIORS

Characteristic ADD Behavior	*Alternative (Opposite) Behavior*
Short attention span	______________________
Rapid shifts in attention	______________________
Gets off task	______________________
Forgets to do tasks	______________________
Acts too quickly	______________________
Acts before thinking	______________________
Overactive—moves around	______________________
Talks excessively	______________________
Ignores peers/Siblings	______________________
Shows anger to peers/siblings	______________________
Hogs toys	______________________
Acts out anger	______________________
Is defiant of authority—says no	______________________

Now, refer to the following examples:

Exercise 4.1 LISTING ALTERNATIVE BEHAVIORS

Characteristic ADD Behavior	*Alternative (Positive) Behavior*
Short attention span	Sustained attention
Rapid shifts in attention	Focuses on one thing
Gets off task	Stays on task
Forgets to do tasks	Remembers to do tasks
Acts too quickly	Delays response (waits)
Acts before thinking	Thinks before acting
Overactive—moves around	Remains still
Talks excessively	Remains quiet
Ignores peer/siblings	Greets peer/siblings
Shows anger to peer/siblings	Plays cooperatively with peer/siblings
Hogs toys	Shares toys
Acts out anger	Controls angry responses
Is defiant of authority—says no	Is respectful to authority—Says Yes Sir, No Ma'am

continued . . .

Study the alternative (positive) behaviors listed to see how they really are just the opposite of some of the undesirable ADD characteristics. The objective of this exercise is twofold: to provide some items for formal (i.e., points/tokens) and informal (i.e., with normal use of verbal and nonverbal social reward) behavior programs and to help you to begin to think more about alternative (positive) behaviors in general. This is extremely important in the development of balanced behavioral programs for the ADD child.

Note that for every inappropriate behavior in the example there is an alternative appropriate behavior. Incorporating these in your behavioral program will make for a more powerful program. This will be discussed more fully in the section Writing Successful Behavioral Plans.

An Exercise to Generate More Appropriate Behavior

Most children learn through imitation on some occasions in their life. Unfortunately, some role models demonstrate little appropriate behavior. Bizarre, inappropriate, and crude social behaviors are sometimes exhibited by athletic role models, who often receive substantial media attention, and are often even rewarded by publication of their books and increased exposure on national TV. A TV reporter recently stated that a young child (6 years old) had received a great deal of media attention following an incident at school where he had head-butted another child; he was promptly handcuffed by a policeman who was on duty nearby. This incident followed very closely one on national TV in which a professional basketball player had head-butted a referee and received repeated exposure. This is a good example of bad modeling. There was also much public outrage that a 6-year-old, an ADD child who was on Ritalin, was handcuffed. It should also be noted that despite any attempt to explain such behavior or to offer a reason for it, when such behavior is modeled, it will influence the child—not the later explanation.

When you wish to develop an appropriate behavior that has not as yet been demonstrated by the child, modeling, imitation, and shaping may be involved. In Exercise 4.2 on page 154, write a brief descriptive statement to develop a modeling procedure for several different behaviors. Please be as specific as you can because these detailed behavioral descriptions will serve as a script, detailing your part in training the child to exhibit certain behaviors.

Once these are completed, check your descriptions against the following example. These ten situations will not cover every event where an appropriate behavior is needed, but the samples provide guidelines for modeling other behaviors not on the list. When you model a behavior, the next step is to strengthen that behavior when it is imitated.

Exercise 4.2 MODELING BEHAVIOR

What You Wish the Child to Do	*How You Will Model This Behavior*
1. Stick to a task	________________
2. Sit quietly	________________
3. Take turns	________________
4. Play cooperatively	________________
5. Ask questions of adults	________________
6. Share toys	________________
7. Handle frustration	________________
8. Be polite	________________
9. Ask for things appropriately	________________
10. Raise hand to answer	________________

Now, refer to the following examples:

Exercise 4.2 MODELING BEHAVIOR

What You Wish the Child to Do	*How You Will Model This Behavior*
1. Sticking to a task	1. Work on project until complete
2. Sitting quietly	2. Sit without talking
3. Taking turns	3. Exchange toy with child after brief play (10-15 min.)
4. Playing cooperatively	4. Play with one child by rules while another watches
5. Asking questions of adults	5. Tell child, "OK, I'm going to show you how you can ask me a question." Explain how one waits for a break in conversation, then says name and asks question.
6. Sharing toys	6. Set stage by saying what you will do, for example, "OK, now, after a short while (few seconds) I'm going to let you play with this toy." Exchange toys with child.
7. Handling frustration	7. Explain, "If I'm having trouble doing something, then I'll need to take a break or take a deep breath before going back to it."
8. Being polite	8. Demonstrate asking for something saying "Please," saying "Thank you" when getting it, and answering questions with "Yes Sir" or "No Sir."

continued . . .

What You Wish the Child to Do	*How You Will Model This Behavior*
9. Asking for things appropriately	9. Demonstrate asking, "May I have another piece of cake?" Instead of "Can I" or the usual "Give me another piece of cake!" or "I want another piece of that cake!"
10. Raising hand to answer	10. Demonstrate how the child can ask the teacher questions or give answers by raising a hand first (use a routine question, for example, "May I be excused?")

Note that it is important to show the child exactly what should be done in each situation; this is an example of modeling or role-playing. In many cases, a child learns a behavior at home and then may transfer it to another situation (at school). When the child imitates your behavior, be sure to reinforce it with statements such as, "Good, that's exactly right—that's the way you need to raise your hand to answer a question in the classroom." Always be specific about what you like; avoid saying, "Good boy" or "Good girl." If the child does not imitate the behavior exactly right reinforce her attempt, saying, "Well, that was a good try, let me show you again how to . . ." After a second demonstration, say, "OK, now try it again." If there is poor repetition over these trials, either the child is not ready to learn this behavior or she is not in the appropriate state to learn (i.e., she may be tired, angry, too excited or playful) to carry out the task. Simply say, "OK, let's try this another time." As most people know, habits require repetitive practice to become established. It is also not unusual for those with ADD/ADHD to require more repetitive practice than most other children. Depending on the current strength of the habit, the behavior may need to be practiced daily or only occasionally. Remember that all learning takes time; practicing a behavior several hundred times a day will not work. Practicing for short time periods over many days will be more effective and less stressful for parents, teachers, and the child.

Practice Rewarding One Behavior vs. Another

When a behavior that is close to what you want is either imitated or spontaneously emitted, it is important to pay attention to it, comment about it, and provide some social or tangible reward for the child. In most cases, the use of social praise, touch, and direct feedback on the appropriateness of the behavior is all that is needed. However, many younger children (e.g., preschool age) may need some tangible reward. *Differential reinforcement* simply involves reinforcement of one behavior over another, and hopefully the more desired behavior. *Shaping* occurs when the behavior exhibited gets closer and closer to the desired behavior. This is a slow process and goes like this: A child may exhibit cooperative play by taking turns playing with a toy. This change (i.e., taking turns with another) should be reinforced with touch and praise, for example, "I like the way you are playing more cooperatively with your brother." However, you note that the child grabs the toy when it's her turn. Now, either model appropriate "taking of the toy" or wait for a positive variation in behavior and reinforce that behavior. Modeling saves time and provides a basis for immediate learning to occur. Thus, when the child takes the toy appropriately, you can say, "Now I like the way you guys are playing cooperatively, and I especially like the way you took the toy easily instead of grabbing it." This statement should also be given with touch (perhaps rubbing the child's back while saying it).

Exercise 4.3 is a very general one, but it is useful in thinking about how some behavior may be acceptable, yet still not the most desirable. The intermediate step may have a component that is still a problem behavior. When you have finished the exercise, see the following examples for this exercise.

Exercise 4.3 USING DIFFERENTIAL REINFORCEMENT

Current Behavior	*Some Improvement*	*Most Desirable (Goal)*
Fighting over toy	________________	________________
Fighting over seating (car, table, etc.)	________________	________________
Asking permission rudely	________________	________________

Exercise 4.3 USING DIFFERENTIAL REINFORCEMENT

Current Behavior	*Some Improvement*	*Most Desirable (Goal)*
Fighting (physically) over toy	Not hitting, but angry	Playing appropriately & cooperatively with toy
Fighting over seating (Car, Table)	Complaining about seating but complying	Taking turns for preferential seats
Asking permission rudely, "I wanna go out!" (Demanding!)	Saying, "Can I go out?" in whining tone	Saying, "May I go out to play?" in a normal tone

It is important to reinforce each step of the child's progress with feedback that lets the child know he's on the right track. This reinforces him for making a change even though it may not be *the* most desirable change. Some reinforcement keeps the child responding—providing motivation so that eventually when *the* most desirable behavior is shown, you can excitedly say, "Yes, that's exactly right. That's the appropriate way to ask permission for something." By your excitement and tone of voice, the child will know that he has pleased you. It should again be noted that the child with ADD/ADHD generally seeks stimulation and excitement. Thus, when you provide consequences (i.e., reinforcement) in an excited tone of voice, the reception of the feedback is better and overall learning more efficient. If you appear excited, the child is more alert and the information is processed better, and he will seek out this excitement from you in the future.

Now you have a number of procedures to promote and develop new and more appropriate behaviors. Do not think only of punishing inappropriate (bad) behavior. When this happens, the child may associate punishment with the sole occasions she gets attention. Such cases simply result in an increase in inappropriate behavior and the general impression that the punishment may be ineffective. What is needed here is a balanced behavioral plan, involving both rewards and punishments.

Writing Successful Behavioral Plans Involving Reward and Punishment

Simply stated, punishment alone is not effective for a number of reasons. First, it tells the child only *what not to do.* Second, punishment is associated with pain and results in distancing in the relationship. Third, the child is confused, never knowing exactly what he should do. From extensive clinical research, it is clear that the most powerful behavioral program will come from a combination of mild punishment of the "bad" behavior and positive reinforcement for the "good" behavior. To illustrate the effects of a positive approach, a procedure labeled "Time-In" is shown in Exercise 4.4a.

Exercise 4.4a BALANCED BEHAVIORAL PLAN—"TIME-IN"

The purpose of this exercise is to show you the general effects of positive reinforcement alone. By itself, it can be very powerful; when later combined with mild punishment, it can be even more effective.

Instructions (for parents)

For three days, simply *observe* the child's play during play time (that is, the same period each day, e.g., 3:30-5:30 P.M.) and note for each half-hour segment whether the child was: (a) playing appropriately, or (b) playing inappropriately.

These observations are made after the half-hour at 3:30, 4:00, 4:30, 5:00, and 5:30 P.M., on each of the three "observation" days.

Over the next four days, *approach* the child at least three times during each half-hour period; if he is playing inappropriately, turn your back and walk away. If he is playing appropriately—or at least is not doing anything inappropriate at the time—go over and make physical contact, and if there is something to praise (e.g., appropriate sharing, cooperation, etc.), then give the appropriate verbal praise.

For the next three days, return to the observation mode; simply observe and again record the number of times the child was: (a) playing appropriately, or (b) playing inappropriately during the five observation times.

You will probably notice that the number of appropriate behaviors will have increased and the number of inappropriate behaviors will have decreased during this second observation period, since it follows the four-day period where you have intervened and given the child positive feedback for appropriate behavior and ignored her inappropriate behavior.

Exercise 4.4b WRITING A BALANCED BEHAVIORAL PLAN—POSITIVE REINFORCEMENT AND PUNISHMENT

For each of the inappropriate behaviors listed, write a positive reinforcement approach (reward) and a negative reinforcement approach (punishment).

Behavior	*Reward*	*Punishment*
Fighting	________________	________________
Cursing	________________	________________
Disrespectful talk	________________	________________
Failure to do chore	________________	________________
Temper tantrum when told no!	________________	________________

After completing Exercises 4.4a and 4.4b, see the following examples for feedback on the behaviors listed. Note that this exercise, while written for parental observation of after-school play time, can be used with equal ease in the school setting. Following the establishment of a combined *reward-for-appropriate-alternative-behavior / punishment-for-the-inappropriate-behavior,* it will be clear that *both* are needed for punishment to be effective. When punishment is the sole approach, there is very little positive outlook for desired results, and depression, along with either "emotional shutdown" or acting out of anger, occurs. The balanced approach is especially important for the child with ADD/ADHD because some forms of punishment (e.g., physical punishment) are totally ineffective, and thus often lead to a deprivation of positive feedback for appropriate behavior.

Exercise 4.4a BALANCED BEHAVIORAL PLAN—"TIME-IN"

OBSERVATION TIMES					
	3:30	4:00	4:30	5:00	5:30
First Three-Day Observation Period					
Appropriate	1	0	0	1	0
Inappropriate	2	3	3	2	3
Next Four Days: Positive Intervention					
Second Three-Day Observation Period					
Appropriate	2	1	3	3	3
Inappropriate	1	2	0	0	0
NET RESULTS					
Appropriate	+1	+1	+3	+2	+3
Inappropriate	–1	–1	–3	–2	–3

continued . . .

This record shows general improvement on all five time periods over a short period of time. The intervening four days of rewarding appropriate behaviors and not rewarding (ignoring) inappropriate ones has a dramatic impact on the child's behavior. During the second three-day period there was improvement on twelve of the fifteen observations, a satisfactory percentage of improvement. By adding a punishment (mild) or some type of "fine" for inappropriate behavior, this behavioral system may be made even stronger.

Exercise 4.4b WRITING A BALANCED BEHAVIORAL PLAN—POSITIVE REINFORCEMENT AND PUNISHMENT

Behavior	*Punishment*	*Reward Alternative*
Fighting	Loss of all privileges for one day	Working/playing cooperatively—Gets to stay up 1/2 hour later
Cursing	Loss of favorite activity (e.g., bike riding) for one day	Mark down good talk during occasion when child would have cursed; every three marks earn special reward, e.g., favorite dessert
Disrespectful talk	Loss of TV/Nintendo© for one day	Record good talk to parents/others; every five marks, rent a Nintendo© game
Failure to do a chore	Must do extra chore (and original one) to restore privileges	Praise when child performs chore and make contact—pat on shoulder/back
Temper tantrum when told no	Ignore temper tantrum—if excess, delay all privileges one hour	Praise when child complies with requests first time. Keep record; after five marks, gets special treat.

As punishment weakens the inappropriate behavior and positive reinforcement strengthens the opposite (alternative) behavior, behavior change (and improvement) occurs more rapidly than by using either one alone. Remember that when punishment becomes the sole means of behavior management, the child often becomes *confused* (punishment never tells him what to do), *depressed* (as he loses more and more privileges), or *frustrated and angry* (with less hope of regaining lost privileges, the child may give up and act out even more).

GETTING RID OF UNWANTED BEHAVIORS

Behavior that is annoying, disrespectful, or hurtful to the child, to another child, or to others is clearly inappropriate and unwanted. The problem for many parents and teachers is to get rid of such inappropriate behavior in a manner that will be beneficial for the child and others. While this may sound simple, it is often complicated by misunderstandings, distortions in perceptions, and rigid, inflexible attitudes regarding discipline.

Behaviors become weaker (a) when they are followed by no consequence whatsoever or (b) when they are followed by some negative consequence (i.e., punishment). Both research and clinical practice have documented quite well the notion that physical punishment is clearly not effective for children with ADD/ADHD. There are, however, many procedures that do work well, and these are classified as mild punishments. The first step for parents and teachers is the selection of behaviors that they wish to change.

Selecting Behaviors to Weaken or Remove

Parents and teachers often agree on behaviors that need to change. First, it is clear that those behaviors that are dangerous to the child or others are of prime concern; they include aggressive behaviors such as hitting, pushing, wielding dangerous objects (e.g., knives) and high-risk behaviors such as running into the street, jumping from high places, or using dangerous objects inappropriately (e.g., trying to catch a sharp knife thrown in the air). Second, other behaviors, while not intrinsically dangerous in a physical sense, may be hurtful to others or simply annoying. These behaviors include such actions as temper tantrums, making noises, inappropriate gestures, disrespectful back talk, whining, and annoying verbal comments and actions such as name calling. Noncompliance may also be included in this category.

You have probably already made lists of all undesirable behaviors. However, it will be advantageous to review these in Exercise 4.5. List those that fall into *Category A* (Physical Aggression/Dangerous Behaviors) and those that belong in *Category B* (Annoying and Noncompliant Behaviors). This will help sort out behaviors that vary in severity and make it easier to decide which techniques may be applied to change them.

Exercise 4.5 SELECTION OF UNWANTED BEHAVIORS TO CHANGE

Category A (Physical Aggression/Dangerous Behaviors)

1. ______________________________
2. ______________________________
3. ______________________________
4. ______________________________
5. ______________________________

continued . . .

Category B (Annoying/Noncompliant Behaviors)

1. ____
2. ____
3. ____
4. ____
5. ____

Ignoring Some Behaviors

Sometimes parents or teachers feel they cannot ignore inappropriate behavior, believing that if the misbehavior is ignored the child has "gotten away with something." However, it is now well known that many children, and especially children with ADD/ADHD, will often emit some behaviors that are certain to attract attention, "hook" the parent or teacher, or create some desired effect (stir up some excitement). Often such behaviors are shocking behaviors that involve some taboo (e.g., sexual gesture or curse word). The child often expects a response and when there is one, albeit negative, the response may simply reinforce the behavior; giving attention to such misbehavior may serve only to maintain it. A simple comment such as "That's a no-no" or "Stop that immediately" may inform the child that he has indeed "hooked you" and though the behavior may stop at that time, it is likely to recur soon.

Attention from a parent or teacher is extremely powerful and may be used to reinforce many behaviors. Some parents and teachers state that they give equal attention to appropriate and inappropriate behaviors, which results in no change in the balance of these behaviors. Instead, a shift in the positive direction is needed, that is, withdraw attention to the annoying behavior while attending more to a desired behavior that is opposite to the annoying behavior (a more appropriate behavior). This procedure will result in a balanced program.

Developing a Plan to Ignore Some Behaviors—Once you have categorized the undesirable behaviors, select one annoying behavior to ignore. Follow this sequence of steps:

> **STEP ONE:** Be Prepared. This old Scouting motto is good advice. Know what to expect when a (mis)behavior is ignored. For example, if whining is selected as the annoying behavior, talk to yourself (silently) about the child's reaction; have an internal dialogue. Say, "I know that by withdrawing my attention, Sally is going to become increasingly more frustrated and angry, and her whining will become more intense. I will have to continue to talk to myself so that I don't make the mistake of giving in to her."
>
> **STEP TWO:** Say, "I know that once I choose to ignore a behavior, I'll have to continue ignoring it until it is under control. If I attend to Sally while she is engaged in more intense whining, I know it will be exacerbated because of her frustration and

anger over being ignored; then I will simply reinforce her whining at a more intense level and also reward her for persisting in misbehavior (continuing to whine for longer periods in the absence of getting attention for it). Continue self-talk to avoid falling into the trap of reverting to attending to the behavior. Much will depend on how well you prepare for this stage of the process and your emotional state. If you are overstressed, drained, or too involved with personal problems, it will indeed be difficult to withstand the child's behavior. Remember that the child is usually quite skilled and experienced at getting attention from you, and you are accustomed to giving it. Change will not come easily.

STEP THREE: Once you achieve success in riding out the child's behavior, provide self-reward and recognition for the way you handled the child's behavior. Continue self-talk to say, "Good, I did a good job of controlling myself and the situation. I am in control." This self-talk is especially important for a parent who also has a history of ADD/ADHD and who may exhibit a tendency to react impulsively and with anger toward the child. Anytime behavior changes in an appropriate direction, it is important for that behavior to be rewarded whether it comes from the child, parent, or teacher. Most behavioral changes are quite difficult, and ultimate success often comes in small steps. Reward each of these steps. Once the child's behavior changes and whining decreases, point out (more frequently right after the change) that the child's behavior is now more appropriate. Reinforcement frequency may be tapered off as the behavior change becomes more stable and consistent. However, in the beginning stages of change, it is important to notice even subtle or minor improvements. For example, you might say, "I really like the way you reacted when I said you couldn't have an extra piece of pizza; you didn't even whine. I really like the grown-up way you handled that."

Time-Out for Misbehavior

Much like ignoring, the time-out procedure removes the child from any potential positive reinforcement; in the case of ignoring, positive reinforcement is withheld from the child. Time-out is very much like the old "go sit in the corner" punishment. Kids reportedly hate time-out—and especially kids with ADD/ADHD. They say that it's boring; many ask for another punishment rather than be put in time-out. Also, the child with ADD/ADHD wishes to get the punishment over quickly.

What is time-out like? If a child just hit his sister, he might be told "No hitting; go to time-out, now!" He is then sent to a boring place—usually a bathroom or a hallway at home. He is not sent to his room—a place that may be either full of positive reinforcements (stereo, TV, games, etc.) or a place where he could easily fall asleep (in the bed); either of these consequences would not be punishing. The time-out place should be devoid of all reinforcements. A kitchen timer is used and set for the child's age (i.e., one minute for each year). This and other criteria are in accordance with recommendations from Dr. Lynn Clark (1985). He also recommends that you use no more than ten words or ten seconds to get the child to time-out. Once in time-out, the child is basically ignored until the timer rings. *This is important.* No one, parent, other child, teacher, or another student should pay attention to, talk to, or otherwise provide rewards for the child in time-out. The child cannot take a toy to time-out, and you should not get hooked into attending to the behavior of a child in time-out. Some children are quite adept at getting into a hassle, particularly with a parent, while in time-out. It is not surprising in such cases to hear the parent say, "Time-out does not work; he misbehaves even more now." If time-out is used incorrectly, the misbehavior may become worse, as the child is actually getting rewarded (by parental attention) for getting into the time-out.

Immediately when the timer rings, time-out is over, and the child is asked, "Now Jimmy, tell me—why were you sent to time-out?" If the child says, "Because I hit my sister," the parent says, "That's right." If the child says, "I don't know," he is given the answer and allowed to resume his activities. It is best to avoid giving much attention just after time-out and, of course, it is not recommended that the child receive a hug, kiss, treat, or anything special—or he'll get the impression that time-out really pays off! The child also should not receive a lecture after time-out, and should not be asked to promise never to exhibit that behavior again. However, it is not unusual that the child may engage in some more appropriate behavior after time-out. When this occurs, it should not be ignored. Any time behavior changes in a more positive direction, it is best to point this out to the child. When the child shows an improvement in behavior after time-out, *do* reinforce this change and point out to the child that you are pleased to see this behavior. It is also useful to state the process that changed, for example, "You really have much better control over yourself now; I like the way you are sharing that toy with your sister."

Listing Behaviors Appropriate for Time-Out—Now that there is a general understanding of the time-out procedure, it is important to consider when to use time-out—and that may depend on what behavior is shown. A list of specific acting-out behaviors (adapted from Dr. Lynn Clark's 1985 list) follows:

Hitting others, threats to hit
Temper tantrums
Hostile teasing
Sassy talk, back talk
Angry screaming
Toy grabbing
Toy throwing
Destroying toys
Kicking others
Biting, threats to bite
Hair pulling
Throwing objects at others
Mistreating, hurting pets
Obnoxious, loud crying
Slapping
Pinching
Scratching
Dangerous acts
Cursing
Pushing others (hard)
Damaging property
Mocking parents

Choking others
Spitting, threats to spit
Persistent interrupting:
- Adult conversation
- After a warning

Loud complaining, demanding
Name calling
Making faces at others
Disobeying a command to stop a misbehavior

Time-out is best used for behaviors that would be classified as aggressive, or acting out behaviors. Whining, pouting, fearful, seclusive, timid, irritable, and grumpy behaviors, for example, would not be appropriate for time-out. Note that passive behavior, such as failing to perform some chore or forgetting to do something, is not appropriate for this procedure. Not doing something is not an acting-out behavior. Resisting bedtime would not be appropriate for time-out; this would only delay his bedtime and give him what he really wants (i.e., in addition to control).

Developing a Time-Out Plan—It is important to understand and practice time-out before actually using it. This means that you must review and make decisions regarding some critical issues. Also, a plan should be in place to deal with any problems encountered in time-out. Now consider the following issues.

1. **Select Target Behavior(s).** It is important to use time-out for specific acting-out behaviors and to avoid using it for every misbehavior. Parents who learn this procedure often use it for everything, which reduces its effectiveness, as there is a lack of balance such that punishment (time-out) may become a prime source of getting attention.

   In Exercise 4.6, list those behaviors that you will consider for time-out.

Exercise 4.6 BEHAVIORS FOR TIME-OUT

1. ______________________________
2. ______________________________
3. ______________________________
4. ______________________________
5. ______________________________

Select two from your list to target for time-out (put a star next to these).

2. **Select a place for time-out.** Use anyplace that is boring, where the child will not receive attention from those passing by, and one where she has no access to rewards. A bathroom, hallway, or corner will suffice. Do not lock the child in a closet or use any place that may generate fear. If the bathroom is used, the door should be left partly open, as it is important for the child to hear the timer ring.

Outside the home, the back seat of the car, a bench in the shopping mall, or facing a wall may be used. In the school setting, the ideal place is probably a corner. Separating or segregating the child is not advisable. A special place may be set aside in the classroom and designated as a time-out zone—a place for calming down and regaining control.

3. **Determine how much time in time-out.** This is usually set according to the child's age (i.e., one minute for each year)—a 10-year-old may receive a ten-minute time-out. When there are several children in the family or school setting, a specific number of minutes may be used (three minutes, five minutes, etc.). The total time for any time-out should not exceed twelve minutes.

4. **Measure the time.** Be consistent and use a kitchen timer. This avoids having the child continually yelling, "Can I come out now?" The timer cannot be manipulated, rushed, or avoided. The child needs to know that she can come out of time-out only when the bell rings. This structure allows the child to know what to expect and avoids troublesome situations; responsibility is not placed on the parent or the child to decide when enough time is spent in time-out.

5. **Withdraw attention while the child is in time-out.** This cannot be emphasized enough. Parents and teachers often make the mistake of lecturing or continuing a hassle with the child, which simply makes time-out ineffective. A child may yell, "This isn't going to work" or continue yelling, screaming, or crying, complain of pains, or even plead to use the bathroom (not a problem if the child is already in the bathroom). All of these behaviors should be *ignored,* unless a real physical danger is obvious. Any destructive behaviors during time-out may result in added punishment, such as a behavior penalty, and having the child "clean up" or "pay up" for any mess or damages incurred.

6. **Establish the connection after time-out.** Ask, "Why were you sent to time-out?" as suggested by Clark. If the child answers correctly he is allowed to go back to the prior activity. If the child answers incorrectly or doesn't know, she is informed of the behavior that precipitated the time-out. It is important to clarify the connection between her behavior and the time-out. It is especially important to make the child aware of the "cause-effect" sequence when there is lack of awareness and weak internal cognitive recognition about which behaviors will bring about negative consequences. The child must know what the consequences will be for certain misbehaviors. She will learn this for the behaviors selected but only after much practice and review.

   There is no need for lecturing after time-out, nor should the child be forced to "promise never to do it again." Such promises do not result in improvement, and entrap the child for any future transgressions.

When you spend an inordinate amount of time with a child immediately after time-out, you give the child a message that certain behaviors can really get you upset or excited. When the child with ADD needs to "stir up some excitement," she will certainly know which buttons to push!

General Comment Regarding Time-Out—It is important to note that time-out, like many other forms of punishment, is often overused by parents, and usually slightly less so by teachers. So much emphasis has been placed on dealing with behavior that is inappropriate, that very little time is spent focusing on which behaviors a parent or teacher wishes to see more often. Remember, punishment never tells the child what "to do"—only what "not to do." Balance your reward and punishment techniques. (This does not necessarily mean an equal number of rewards and punishments.) Focus on using positive reinforcements for appropriate behavior as much as or even more than using negative reinforcements for inappropriate behaviors. Skill development through reinforcement of appropriate behavior is crucial for the survival of the ADD/ADHD child.

Rehearse time-out before you use it. Before you use time-out, you need a kind of "dress rehearsal"—to ensure there will be no surprises when time-out is actually employed, and to allow each participant—child and parent or teacher—to review his or her role. Present time-out in the following way, saying, "For some time now, we have had hassles over name calling. This is not much fun for me or for you. So, when you 'name call' you will be sent to time-out." A general explanation should be given regarding the sequence of events in time-out, appropriate for the child's age. Then run through the procedure, saying "OK, now let's suppose you have just name-called; that's a time-out for name calling—go now!" The child knows where to go and that a timer will be set for a specific number of minutes; it will be placed where the child can hear it. The child comes out of time-out and you ask, "Why were you sent to time-out?" If the child states the reason, say, "That is exactly right." If not, the child is told. This rehearsal is quite important and ensures that parent or teacher and child are ready. Be aware that, as Goldstein (1988) has noted, the first few times that a child is placed in time-out, there may be a "time-out burst" where a heightened degree of aggressiveness may occur. These outbursts will usually subside, especially if the parent or teacher adds to the duration of the time-out the number of minutes that the outburst lasts.

Time-Out Procedure at Home and at School—In general, time-out will be used more frequently at home. There has been much controversy over its use in school and it has generally been difficult to set up a time-out in the school setting. Because of these difficulties, time-out has not received as much emphasis in overall behavior management programs in schools. It can also backfire—as when the child is sent outside the classroom; it is often rewarding for the child, not punishing. Consider a child who is having difficulty doing a task, and becomes easily distracted to engage in some aggravating behavior with her neighbor (e.g., pinching his arm). Should this child be sent out of the room? She may actually be taken out of an unrewarding and boring task; therefore, she is rewarded for acting out and will probably repeat the behavior in the future. In normal discipline programs, when this occurs a number of times, she may be suspended and forced to leave school. What a punishment! Such a procedure of suspension from school may work for many normal children who would, for varying reasons, find it unpleasant to be sent out of the class or to be sent home. It would not, however, be effective for most children who experience behavior problems.

Typically, when time-out is used in the school, the child simply goes to a designated place and must still follow the lesson or continue working. A modified time-out is a time to "calm down," "refocus," or "redirect" activities to a different situation.

At home there may be different types of time-outs as well:

1. *Time-out for two.* Frequently, when siblings fight, rather than playing detective and discover "who started this," both children go to time-out. Either an average of their ages or a preset number of minutes (e.g., five minutes) may be chosen. When the questioning to "get to the bottom of this fight" is avoided, the effectiveness of time-out is enhanced. Remember that it is important to deliver consequences of behavior immediately following the behavior. If they are delayed, a parent may get confused over what started the fight and the siblings win. Punish both by saying, "Both of you have a time-out for fighting—go now." When they come out of the time-out, ask both why they were sent to time-out. More important—ask them, "Now, can you think of another way you could have solved your problem without fighting?" Here both siblings will compete for a "good answer" and this process will aid in the development of problem-solving concepts. Both siblings are now learning to develop cognitions that may mediate aggressive behavior in the future. When the child knows other options, and is reinforced for using them, coping skills can improve. The impulse-oriented (ADD) child learns cognitive mediating techniques that essentially involve "thinking before acting" as a means of controlling his impulses.
2. *Time-out for toys.* When a child misuses a toy or acts out destructively with it, or when the toy is a source of conflict between two siblings, the toy may be placed in time-out for a specified time. The parent may say, "You are not playing appropriately (or cooperatively) with this toy. It goes in time-out." For high-interest, frequently used toys, it is necessary to use only a short time-out (about 15 minutes). Other toys may be put in time-out for a day or two. Again, it is important to use reasonable time-outs. Many children with ADD/ADHD report that they have lost toys completely, that they have been thrown away; one mother even decided to play with the toy herself in front of the child as "an added punishment." Excessive and cruel punishments are not only ineffective; they may create other problems such as depression and hopelessness. Instead, reward good behavior by giving the toy back sooner, thus "time off for good behavior" may be used for any toy that would otherwise be in time-out for at least one hour.

3. *Time-out for the young child.* For children less than two years of age, some special provisions can be made. Instead of sending the child to the bathroom, a straight-back chair may be used as recommended by Clark. Sometimes, even a time-out of very short duration (i.e., one minute) may be effective. Sometimes it may be necessary to hold the child to prevent him from escaping. No attention is given to the child in this situation other than to remind him that once he complies he will be released. So often, power struggles develop with the young child, and there is resistance to a change in control. However, it is important to win this power struggle if you are to be effective with the child in other situations requiring discipline.

Planning for Problems with Time-Out—Some children comply immediately with time-out; others resist. The easiest way to deal with resistance to time-out is to add additional minutes. The young child may be held in the chair; no excessive force should be used. The child should be told that when he calms down and the timer rings he can come out of time-out. It is important not to let the child out if there is severe misbehavior. No lecturing or scolding need be given. It is also important to withdraw visual attention and not look at the child who is in time-out.

With an older child, simply add additional minutes to the time-out for each instance of resistance (i.e., failure to go) as suggested by Clark, but this should not exceed five minutes. If the resistance continues, a behavior penalty may be given (i.e., withdrawal of a privilege).

WRITING A BEHAVIOR PENALTY PLAN

Behavior penalty or response cost involves taking a privilege away from the child for a short period of time. There are some advantages to the use of behavior penalty. Outside the home, time-out may be more difficult to employ. A behavior penalty does not require a special place; it can be administered anywhere, anytime. Misbehavior while riding in a car, in a shopping mall, or while visiting a friend can easily be dealt with using a behavior penalty.

The following are general guidelines for the use of a behavior penalty:

1. Make a list of those behaviors that may be difficult to deal with using other techniques (maximum of three).
2. Inform the child which behavior will result in a behavior penalty.
3. Make a list of privileges that can be taken away for a behavior penalty.
4. Remember to review with the child the consequences for one of these misbehaviors, as well as to note the consequences for appropriate behavior. If misbehavior has occurred while riding in the car in the past, the child is informed which privilege will be lost should the misbehavior occur and what the reward will be

should the child show alternative appropriate behavior instead. This technique, called *priming,* will increase the effectiveness of the consequences and provide some cognitive link of past consequences to behavioral control at present. There will be some internalization of what consequences will follow either misbehavior or appropriate behavior. It is also assumed that, given a choice, the child would prefer the positive consequence (reward) for appropriate behavior.

5. It is wise to give the child some predetermined signal (preferably nonverbal) to serve as a warning and to allow the child to develop self-control, which may subsequently be rewarded. One signal might be to hold up two fingers for the child to see. This will serve as a signal for the child to decide either: (1) to change the current misbehavior, or (2) to accept the consequences. All of this is reviewed with the child prior to being in these situations and you can even have a rehearsal similar to that previously discussed for time-out.
6. Once the signal is given, say, "Children, look here" (while holding up two fingers), and give the child a few seconds to respond. It will be far better for the child to develop and gain control over his or her behavior.
7. If control is achieved, you may say, "John, I'm very proud of the decision you made to stop teasing (annoying, hitting, or anything else) your sister. I like the way you are sitting quietly with her. As I said, for your good behavior we will stop for an ice cream." If you have set up a point system (as in the next section), then points may be given instead of the ice cream. The child should, however, be reminded that you will be pleased to see good behavior continue and disappointed should the child lose the reward for any misbehavior that might surface on the way to getting the reward. Remember, the last behavior prior to a reward is the one that is strengthened. If the child were to misbehave prior to getting an ice cream, such misbehavior would then (erroneously) be rewarded.
8. Be consistent and follow through with the procedure. If you don't, the child will see that you often say things you don't mean. It is important to provide the reward as soon as possible. Any significant delays may result in frustration and some angry, acting-out behavior. Parents, especially, may wish to time the reward (ice cream) using verbal praise to maintain behavior and the ice cream notice given just before driving up to the ice cream shop.

DEVELOPING AN EFFECTIVE GROUNDING PROCEDURE

Grounding has almost universal stature in discipline, especially among teens, even though its effectiveness is often questionable. There are so many complications surrounding this procedure that it often does not work. One common problem is that when the child is grounded, so, too, is the parent who must supervise him or her. The parent may wish to terminate the grounding and let the child go; this is often done capriciously and does not follow any appropriate behavior. If there is some reason to terminate, be sure the child performs some task or chore prior to termination. A second problem is that often the child may be restricted to the home but have privileges intact (e.g., stereo, TV, Nintendo©). If so, the situation is not that unpleasant. Third, grounding is often far too severe. As with any punishment, the best way is to use limited time. If too lengthy, thc child may develop a hopeless feeling about remaining privileges, and this may simply lead to additional misbehavior, which in turn leads to additional grounding. The vicious cycle almost never ends and neither does the misbehavior.

If a child is to be grounded, use a short term plan. In addition, don't allow the child to just hang around the house. Select three extra chores for the child to perform; when they are completed, the grounding may end (assuming no other misbehavior has occurred). When appropriate behavior appears, the termination of grounding will serve to reinforce that appropriate behavior. The purpose is not just to weaken the undesirable behavior but to facilitate the development and maintenance of alternative desirable behavior. During the period of grounding there should be no privileges (TV, telephone, etc.) allowed.

PRACTICING APPROPRIATE BEHAVIOR HABITS

One assumption often made when misbehavior occurs is that the "child simply doesn't know better." Thus, if a child slams a door closed when entering a room, a parent or teacher may assume that the child doesn't know how to close the door. Although this is a very simple concept, it is really quite complex. For example, you may first ask the child, "Do you know how to close the door?" If the child says "Yes," say, "Well, show me the proper way to close the door." If the child does it correctly, say, "Yes, that's exactly right, but apparently you need a bit more practice doing this so that it will be automatic." Then the child is asked to go out and come in, closing the door appropriately each time for ten practice trials. This is called "positive practice." If the child does not initially demonstrate that he or she knows how to close the door, you then model this for the child saying, "Let me show you the proper way to close the door." Following the demonstration, go through the practice steps, having the child close the door appropriately ten times. If during one of those trials the child slams the door, then three more additional practice trials are added.

On some occasions, a child's misbehavior may be disrespectful to you. In this case, he or she might go through the "positive practice" phase and then have to provide "restitution" to you for speaking in a disrespectful manner. Restitution may involve having the child perform an added chore. This general procedure has been termed *overcorrection with positive practice and restitution.* If the child requests something in a disrespectful manner, then following the overcorrection procedure, the child is allowed to ask for the requested item or favor in an appropriate manner. At this time, say, "Yes, that is the appropriate way to ask. You may have. . . ."

POINTS AND TOKENS

A behavioral system involving points or tokens is a kind of *token economy,* which sets specific behavioral goals to be met using well-defined rewards (points or tokens) and punishments (fines or loss of points or tokens). It is fairly objective, does not require a great deal of decision making for the parent or teacher (once set up appropriately), and presents well-defined guidelines for the child who may previously have thought it impossible to get rewards and privileges on a consistent basis. Many children, both normal and those with ADD, have worked successfully with these programs. The ADD child, however, often has the most difficulty with such programs—particularly in school—and often becomes frustrated and angry or depressed when he or she never reaches the desired goal. This can happen when ADD children are placed in competition with non-ADD children in the classroom. Clearly, the ADD child is unlikely to reach the criteria set for most non-ADD children.

Point and token systems are excellent balanced behavioral programs, as they focus on both reward and punishment. It is also possible to deal with several behaviors (appropriate and inappropriate) at the same time, but don't attempt to deal with too many behaviors at once. If you do, the system becomes too complex and, with frustration for both you and the child, the program is dropped. A point and token system provides the child with valuable experience that will be important later in life, for example, checking account. The system also provides the child with opportunities to plan ahead (i.e., to determine how many points are needed for an array of privileges) and to make decisions (i.e., with only so many available points, the child may have to choose which privileges are to be selected). Of course, these experiences provide an excellent introduction to events in adult life where similar decisions must be made. The point or token behavioral system may provide a wide range of experiences that have an impact on the child's life as an adult.

Practice for the Point or Token System

First, let's look at a few age guidelines for these systems. Token systems are generally used with younger children ages 3 years to 6 years. These guidelines may change with the child's estimated mental age. For example, a very bright 2-year-old may be able to work with the system if simple communication skills are adequate, and a child older than 6 years may still use tokens up to perhaps 8 or 10 years of age if the mental age is lower. Second, let's consider some guidelines in the use of fines. With very young children, 3 to 4 years of age, there should be no loss of tokens (fines) for inappropriate behavior. Those in the 5- to 6-year range, whether mental or chronological, may be candidates for some limited fines (i.e., loss of tokens for inappropriate behavior). However, the general principle for younger children is to utilize a purely positive approach in developing new and more appropriate behavior; other techniques may be used to deal with that child's inappropriate behaviors.

Listing Behaviors for Rewards and Fines

Basic to all point and token systems with older children are the following:

1. Listing the behaviors we wish to see more of—for the rewards.
2. Listing behaviors we wish to see less of—for the punishments (fines).
3. Listing the privileges and fines—the source of motivation for the program.

Exercise 4.7 helps you begin the process.

Exercise 4.7 LISTING BEHAVIORS

Desirable and Appropriate (1A)			*Undesirable and Inappropriate (1B)*		
Behavior	Frequency (Rating)	Importance (Rating)	Behavior	Frequency (Rating)	Importance (Rating)
1.			1.		
2.			2.		
3.			3.		

This exercise is similar to one completed earlier. It provides you with a list of behaviors that you may use in setting up a program. However, it is important that these behaviors be ranked according to (1) how frequently the child exhibits the behavior, and (2) how important it is that the behavior be developed. Go back and rate each behavior by frequency on a 1-5 scale, with 1 being the lowest frequency and 5 the highest. The scale is developed as follows and on the next page to help you rate each behavior:

Frequency Rating		*Description*
High	5	Seen most of the time—almost every day
	4	Seen much of the time—every other day
Medium	3	Seen a fair amount of time—once weekly
Low	2	Seen a little of the time—once every other week
	1	Seen very little of the time—once a month or less

continued . . .

Importance Rating		*Description*
High	5	Very important
	4	Important
Medium	3	Somewhat important
Low	2	Of little importance
	1	Of very little importance

These two ratings are clearly important in determining which appropriate and inappropriate behaviors to select for the point or token system. For example, a high frequency rating for an *appropriate behavior* means that you have little concern over that behavior and may not even need to include it on the behavior program, except where there is a need to guarantee some success. "Don't mess with a good thing." However, having a high frequency rating on an *inappropriate behavior* indicates that you should put it in the system. The ranking of importance will also give input as to whether a behavior makes it in the system. As an example, a behavior that is inappropriate may be relatively minor (with a rating of 1 or 2) compared with the child's other presenting behavior. These ratings simply provide an organized and systematic approach to the selection of behavior (both appropriate and inappropriate) to work with in the behavioral system. Refer to the examples for Exercise 4.7 on the following page.

The rankings will be used not only to select appropriate behaviors that you wish to improve through reward but also to decrease and remove those inappropriate behaviors through punishment. As you get more experience in designating the behaviors you wish to work with, some of these steps may be eliminated (e.g., ratings). Formal ratings may therefore be eliminated should you have a good subjective impression of the behavior to be included in the behavioral program. Following selection of appropriate and inappropriate behaviors, the next step is to set the reward value (points) so the child knows what the payoff will be for exhibiting those appropriate behaviors, and what punishment, or fine, will be encountered should he or she exhibit the inappropriate behavior. See the sample on the following page.

Privileges are the tangible rewards, social interactions, and specific activities that the child finds enjoyable and that serve to reinforce the behavior that allowed for them. Privileges are the known reinforcers that provide an incentive or motivation to perform behaviors that may seem difficult or even unpleasant. You probably have a pretty good idea of what is reinforcing for a child, as the child will typically engage in that activity every chance he or she gets.

Exercise 4.7 SAMPLE LISTING BEHAVIORS

Desirable and Appropriate (1A)			*Undesirable and Inappropriate (1B)*		
Behavior	**Freq**	**Imp**	**Behavior**	**Freq**	**Imp**
1. Plays cooperatively with sibs	1	5	1. Hits sibs	5	5
2. Complies with requests	2	5	2. Noncompliance	4	5
3. Greets others	3	3	3. Ignores others	3	3
4. Brushes teeth (2 minutes)	5	5	4. Leaves cap off toothpaste	3	1
5. Completes chores	1	5	5. Leaves before completing chores	4	5
6. Dresses for school at 7:45 A.M.	3	5	6. Remains in bed after alarm	3	5
7. In bed by 8:30 P.M.	1	4	7. Whines about going to bed	5	4
8. Puts dirty clothes in hamper	2	2	8. Throws dirty clothes on floor	4	2
9. Home by 6:00 P.M. for supper	1	4	9. Late for supper	4	4
10. Makes bed	1	2	10. Leaves trash in bedroom	5	5

By completing these lists, you focus on all behaviors that need to change—either to develop and strengthen the appropriate ones or to weaken and remove the inappropriate ones. While this example is of behaviors at home, a similar list can be made of school behaviors. By making these lists, you can organize your thinking about these two categories of behavior and make it easier to select those behaviors to be included in the more formal behavioral programs.

If you have completed Exercise 3.12, you already have an abundance of information obtained from several sources to indicate the things and activities that the child likes or dislikes. Of course, you must avoid those items on the "dislikes" list of activities and things, but such a list may be used to formulate extra chores for inappropriate behaviors that fall outside the structured behavioral system established. Those "likes" list of activities, things, and social interactions may be formulated as a final list of privileges (Exercise 4.8). Some parents may find this exercise superfluous, as they have a good idea of how privileges may be ranked in order of preference; others may wish to complete the exercise simply to compare with their impressions of privileges for their child. List these privileges now and note their frequency and importance to the child alongside each one. Use prior descriptions of frequency and importance ratings.

Exercise 4.8 SELECTING PRIVILEGES

Privilege	*Unit of Time/Money*	*Frequency Rating*	*Importance Rating*	*Composite Rating*	*Rank*	*Points*
1.						
2.						
3.						
4.						
5.						
6.						
7.						
8.						

Now, refer to the following examples:

Exercise 4.8 SAMPLE SELECTING PRIVILEGES

Privilege	*Unit of Time/Money*	*Frequency Rating*	*Importance Rating*	*Points*
1. Riding bike	Per 1/2 hour	5	5	5
2. Watching TV	Per 1/2 hour	4	3	3
3. Playing Nintendo©	Per 1/2 hour	5	4	4
4. Fishing trip	Day trip	1	3	15
5. Skating trip	Per trip	2	3	15
6. Eating at pizza restaurant	Per trip	5	4	20
7. Playing board game	Per game	3	2	2
8. New fishing lure	Max $5.00	2	3	15
9. Renting movie	About $3.00	4	2	10
10. Getting favorite snack	Max $2.00	4	2	10

In addition to listing the privileges, you must also describe the unit of time or how much money may be involved in that privilege. This unit of time or money will also be important in determining the points required for that thing. Teachers can compile a similar list appropriate to the school setting.

continued . . .

In determining the initial point values for each one, use the rating of importance to the child to guide you. For example, in the list provided, "riding the bike" rated at 5 (tops) so we allow 5 points per half hour, whereas "watching TV," rated at 3, is assigned 3 points per half hour.

For extended events and for those things that cost money, we can roughly estimate the number of points required for that thing at 10 times the rating divided by 2. Thus "eating at pizza restaurant" would be 10 times 4 divided by 2 = 20 points. This does not, however, apply to regular high frequency high importance events (e.g., riding bike). Throughout all of these behavioral programs where points or tokens are used, it will be essential to keep the points assigned to behaviors, fines and privileges as low as possible to make it easier for the parent to run the program. It is also important to remember that these points assigned to privileges are only our initial estimates. It will be important to determine how many points the child is generally able to earn and then to make sure that some of the privileges are able to be obtained. Our points assigned to behaviors, fines and privileges can be revised once we know what the child can earn. It should also be remembered that some privileges are daily while others are week-end (e.g. fishing trip). It is most critical that the child be able to earn the daily ones.

After listing the privileges, go back and rank each one with regard to how often the child wishes to engage in that activity (or to have that thing) and how important the privilege is to the child (as perceived by you). Multiply these two rankings to get a composite rating, and then look through the list and give a rank order for each privilege. For those privileges that have the same composite score, rank the one with a higher frequency ahead of the others; this provides you with a list of privileges rank ordered in a systematic way. It will therefore make sense to assign point values to privileges based on their rank. Several factors will, however, determine the point value in the system in addition to their rank. While it may not be necessary to go into this much detail for many children, using the most powerful motivators of behaviors will be essential for the success of the program. Once you have done this exercise, these estimates may be used in future programs.

As DuPaul and others have noted, it is important to use reinforcers that are viewed as "necessities" by the child (e.g., TV, playing video games, riding his bike), rather than reliance on "luxury" items the child could live without (e.g., eating lobster at a fine restaurant, or a trip to Disney World). Carr (1981) has some suggestions regarding identification of significant reinforcers for the child:

1. Observe the effects of the reinforcer on the child. Something may be reinforcing if:
   - the child asks for that reinforcer again;
   - the child seems happy during the time he has the reinforcer;
   - the child seems unhappy when the reinforcer ends; and
   - the child is willing to work to earn that reinforcer.
2. One may note the child's choices on various questionnaires regarding reinforcers. These are discussed fully in Chapter 3.

Planning Point or Token Systems for Children of Different Ages

Programs may be modified according to the child's chronological age or mental age. Variations in the point and token systems will be discussed here.

Tokens—This system will be used primarily for preschool-age children (ages 3-6). You can use plastic poker chips in red, white, and blue. At ages 3-4 years, chips may be used interchangeably; at 5-6 years—and assuming the child is able to discriminate colors—the red, white, and blue may assume different values, with blue representing *good;* white representing *very good,* and red standing for *excellent.*

Use a clear jar or bank so that the child sees chips building up. Have a list of behaviors that will be reinforced with tokens and from that list select one behavior to start the program. The child is told that when the jar is full (small jar that can be filled with ten chips) he or she will receive a privilege (an activity or a thing). It is very important that even young children begin to think about what is expected of them. The payoff is defined for each occasion, for example, a chip, and when the goal is met—the jar is full of chips—the child receives a small toy. Instead of a jar with chips, you might also use a drawing of a thermometer and red stars instead of tokens. You can post the thermometer sheet in a central location and allow the child to place the red star on it. When the stars reach the top (i.e., main goal), a special reward is given. Other rewards (sub-goals) may be marked on the way to the top. The thermometer, Figure 4.1 on page 178, can be duplicated for use with different behaviors.

When using tokens or stickers, it is important to follow some basic rules.

1. As soon as the child shows the appropriate behavior, give the token or sticker.
2. When presenting the token or sticker, say exactly what you liked; that is, state how pleased you are that he showed that behavior. For example, "Mark, I really liked the way you sat down while you ate. Here's a token."
3. Go to the thermometer sheet or jar with the child and put the token or sticker there. Say, "Miranda, you're really doing well, you'll have that special treat very soon; keep up the good behavior."
4. When the inappropriate behavior occurs, it is important to (a) not attend to it, (b) select another specific privilege to withdraw, (c) withdraw a token (least desirable alternative), or (d) analyze the behavior to see if you expected too much of the child. You can then revise the expectation or program.

If there was sufficient preparation and you observed that the child was capable of meeting the expectation, then the occasional inappropriate behavior may be ignored. If something has changed and the inappropriate behavior continues, some revision of the program and the expectations must be made.

Points—A point system may be used with children ages 6 through 12 years. Again, keep in mind that these are simply rough guidelines. Some very effective programs have

Figure 4.1 "Thermometer" to document progress on sub-goals on way to main goal.

been conducted with immature adolescents. Also, while children ages 6 to 8 years may have only appropriate behaviors in the system (i.e., no fines) (Exercise 4.9a on this page and page 181), children 9 to 12 years of age may work with both appropriate and inappropriate behaviors (Exercise 4.9b on pages 180 and 183).

Exercise 4.9a Point System (Ages 6-8)

Behavior	Points	Mon	Tues	Wed	Thur	Fri	Sat	Sun
1.								
2.								
3.								
4.								
Total Points Earned								
Privileges	**Pts Used**	**Mon**	**Tues**	**Wed**	**Thur**	**Fri**	**Sat**	**Sun**
1.								
2.								
3.								
4.								
Points Used								
		MON	TUES	WED	THUR	FRI	SAT	SUN
NET POINTS								

Notice that there are no fines in Exercise 4.9a. As with younger children, fines are not recommended. In some cases, and especially where the child is very bright, some withdrawal of a privilege, time out, or suspension of privileges for a short time (maximum one day) may be used. Once you have made an attempt to construct this program, look at the examples on page 181.

If the child is older (9-12 years of age), let's take a look at a behavioral program for that age level. The major difference will be that of adding inappropriate behaviors to the lists; they will receive fines. Also, you may be able to work with a few additional behaviors; however, start with a fairly simple program, especially if you are a novice at setting up and managing such programs. Other behaviors can always be added—still within limits. On the Home-School Behavior Chart, notice that there are several places to put appropriate behaviors for development, but only a few spaces for the inappropriate behaviors that will be fined. The reason is simple; you want to avoid emphasizing the negative, the inappropriate, the undesirable behavior. Unless you do, a child may be burdened with so many fines that a negative balance of points is obtained, and this should never be allowed to happen. A negative point balance might occur due to carelessness or other unusual circumstances, but this condition should never be allowed to continue. If it is, a runaway system is the result, where a child may begin to feel hopeless, depressed, angry, and a failure. This may clearly affect his self-concept and self-esteem. This type of system is undoubtedly faulty in design; terminate such a program immediately. Note that many parents will probably not be able to set up and manage this type of behavioral program; they will need direct supervision and guidance from an experienced behavior therapist.

Exercise 4.9b POINT SYSTEM (AGES 9-12)

Home School Behavior Chart

Behavior List	Points	Monday	Tuesday	Wednesday	Thursday	Friday	Saturday	Sunday
Followed Inst.	0-4/T	8	6	8	8	8		
Complete Work	0-4/T	8	8	8	8	8		
Obey Class Rules	0-4/T	6	4	8	6	8		
Got Along Peers	0-4/T	4	6	8	8	8		
Ready by 7AM	5	5	5	5	5	5		
Bring HAS/Ret. Home	5	5	5	5	5	5		
Complete Homework	10	10	10	10		10		
In Bed by 9 PM	5	5	5	5	5	5	5	5
Bonus	2	// (4)	/// (6)	//// (8)	///// (10)	/// (6)	////// (12)	/////// (14)
Total Points		55	55	65	55	63	(163) +17 180	(120) +19 139
Points Used/Fines		45	35	10	20	20	60	100
Net Points/Day		10	20	55	35	43	120	(savings)* 39
Fines List	**Points**	**Monday**	**Tuesday**	**Wednesday**	**Thursday**	**Friday**	**Saturday**	**Sunday**
Name Calls 5.6	10	/// (30)	/ (10)	—	—	/ (10)	/ (10)	—
Talks Back	5	/ (5)	/ (5)	—	—	—	—	—
Fails to Comp. HW	20	—	—	—	20	—	—	—
Totals		35	15	0	20	10	10	0

Savings in brackets.

Once you have finished setting up your point system, see another example of this type of program on page 183. Use the suggestions provided to modify your program where needed. Remember that the only criterion is that the child be successful at the program.

Exercise 4.9a POINT SYSTEM (AGES 6-8)

Point System (Ages 6–8)

BEHAVIOR	PTS EARNED/ HATCH MARK	MON	TUES	WED	THUR	FRI	SAT	SUN
complies w/requests	2	///	//	///	////	//	///	///
dressed by 7:50 A.M.	5	/	/	/		/		
plays coop'ly w/sibs	3	//	///	//	/	///	//	//
does chores	3	/		//	//	//	//	//
POINTS EARNED		20	18	23	17	24	18+ 38 =56	18+ 8 =26
PRIVILEGE	**PTS USED/ HATCH MARK**	**MON**	**TUES**	**WED**	**THUR**	**FRI**	**SAT**	**SUN**
riding bike ½ hr	5	//	//	/	/	//	///	//
eating at pizza place	20						////	
playing Nintendo©	4	/		//	/	//	//	//
POINTS USED		14	10	13	9	18	48	18
NET POINTS		**MON**	**TUES**	**WED**	**THUR**	**FRI**	**SAT**	**SUN**
		6	8	10	8	6	8	[8]*

**Savings in brackets.*

You can indicate with slash marks how many times a behavior was observed or how many events of privileges were used. At the end of the day, or any time the child wishes to use privileges, the point totals may be calculated. Points used are subtracted from points earned to give net points for that day. The child starts each new day with *zero points.* However, the remaining *net* points from each day will carry over to the weekend (Sat and Sun) where he may have fewer opportunities to earn points. This will be especially true when many of these points are earned in school. Note that on Saturday the total points come from (a) points earned that day and (b) net points left over from each weekday. The child will also need to develop the idea of saving some points on Saturday so that she will have points to use on Sunday; otherwise, the child may repeatedly ask for something that could be done for points.

Another possible way for the older child to earn extra points is the use of *bonus points,* awarded for *special good behaviors.* There will be sufficient incentives to motivate the child to earn more points. This may also carry over into future weeks of the program, as the child may wish to have an abundance of points—especially on weekends. Any points left over at the end of the week will go into "savings." (See the bracketed points in Exercises 4.9a & b.) With young children, you must continuously provide guidance and cues to develop the idea of savings. ADD kids will resist delaying gratification and have a strong tendency to use all points *now.* The concept of savings must be taught and developed. At some point, you state, "OK, you've worked hard for several weeks and you have (X) points in savings. I think it's time to use these points for something special." For example, a parent can then arrange for a special trip (e.g., a movie), a special event (e.g., renting a Nintendo© game), or anything that the child enjoys, within some reasonable limit. The question of how long the program should run is often asked. There are no exact rules, but in general continue the program until there is at least 80 percent improvement—when a behavior is shown eight times in ten possible situations. Remember that perfection is not the goal. A program may be continued if other behaviors were not originally addressed but now seem more important, or when a new behavior must be targeted and included. When it is time to stop a program, have a kind of "graduation party." This will emphasize again how well the child has done. Although the formal program may be stopped, continuing feedback on the child's behavior must be provided in the form of praise and touch. Providing verbal praise and touching the child (e.g., a pat on shoulder or back) will be crucial in allowing for a continuation of improvement.

In this system you are reinforcing several appropriate behaviors and punishing (i.e., fining) a few inappropriate behaviors. It is always important to list more appropriate behaviors than inappropriate ones. For several of the behaviors, there is an inappropriate behavior and its opposite, alternative appropriate behavior. This will provide a very powerful program to get some of the inappropriate behaviors under control fairly quickly. Typically, during the beginning phase of the program, there is considerable variability; it may even seem as if some inappropriate behaviors get worse. The child will often test the system to see if you mean what you say. This will especially evident when the child, faced with a low number of points, plans how he or she will earn a sufficient number to have access to desired privileges. Again note that on Friday the net points carry over to Saturday and Saturday's net points carry over to Sunday. This is the only time that the points will carry over. During weekdays, each day starts at zero points. If a child gets a number of fines, it is best to set a maximum number (e.g., five). If that number is exceeded, there is total loss of privileges for that day. It is essential, however, that you avoid negative point balances. If they occur, reassess the program and start over with new point values assigned. The sole criterion for these point or token systems is that they be successful. If a parent does not have success in three attempts, he or she should request professional consultation and cease all such behavioral programs. Just as in the first example, all points remaining from Sunday go into savings (in brackets). After a period of time and accumulated points these "savings" may be used in a special celebration.

Exercise 4.9b POINT SYSTEM (AGES 9-12)

Point System (Ages 9—12)

BEHAVIOR	**(Pts Earned)**	**M/**	**T/**	**W/**	**TH/**	**F/**	**S/at**	**S/un**
Playing cooperatively with sibs	5 each	/// (15)	// (10)	/// (15)	// (10)	/// (15)	// (10)	/// (15)
Complying with requests	5 each	/// (15)	/// (15)	/// (15)	//// (20)	/ (5)	/ (5)	//// (20)
Completing chores	2 each	// (4)	// (4)	// (4)	//// (8)	//// (8)	// (4)	//// (8)
Putting dirty clothes in hamper	5	5	5	5	5	5		
Home for supper by 6 P.M.	5		5	5	5	5	5	
Total Points Earned		39	39	44	48	38	53+24 =77	13+43 =56
Fines	**(Pts Lost)**	**M/**	**T/**	**W/**	**TH/**	**F/**	**S/at**	**S/un**
Hitting sibs	5 each	/ (5)	/ (5)		/ (5)		/// (15)	/ (5)
Noncompliance	5 each	/ (5)	/ (5)		/ (5)		//// (20)	/ (5)
Late for supper (Past 6 P.M.)	5	/ (5)					/ (5)	
Throws dirty clothes on floor	4						/ (4)	
Total Points Lost		15	10	0	10	0	44	10
Pts. Available to use		(24)	(29)	(44)	(38)	(38)	(33)	(46)
Privileges	**Pts Used**	**M/**	**T/**	**W/**	**TH/**	**F/**	**S/at**	**S/un**
Riding bike (½ hour)	5	/ (5)	// (10)	// (10)	/// (15)	// (10)	/ (5)	// (10)
Playing Nintendo (½ hour)	5	// (10)	// (10)	// (10)	/// (15)	/ (5)	/ (5)	
Skating trip	15							
Selecting movie to rent	10						10	
Eating at pizza place	20			20				20
Special fishing trip	15							
Total (Points Used)		15	20	40	30	15	20	30
Net Points		9	9	4	8	23	13	[16]*

**Savings in brackets.*

CHAPTER 5

Social Skills

Fitting into today's society is a challenge for many children, and especially so for those with ADD/ADHD. Being accepted by one's peers is vitally important not only for older children and adolescents but also for young preschool children. Children with ADD/ADHD often are rejected by their peers due to their *impulsive* and often *aggressive* style of interaction, along with their general *difficulty in "playing by the rules."* Children with ADD/ADHD often experience

- frustration
- anger
- feelings of inadequacy
- helplessness over the lack of good coping skills
- loneliness
- depression because of frequent isolation from their peer group

ADDRESSING SOCIAL BEHAVIORS

Sometimes, some of the ADD child's difficulties seem to be made better by medication; though it takes the collaborative and persistent efforts of those working with the child, it is certainly desirable for him or her to learn and develop social and coping skills. Such skills help the child accept responsibility for her social experiences and these learned skills benefit the child in pervasive ways throughout her life. Social graces (saying "Yes, sir," offering a chair to an elder, etc.) are part of the learned social skills, along with the more basic life skills. (See the section Developing Social Graces in this chapter.)

Most of the essential social skills fall into one of these five categories:

1. Listening
2. Following instructions and rules
3. Sharing
4. Working and playing cooperatively
5. Problem solving and anger control

Today, our society faces many problems, and perhaps the most serious is the escalation of violence. It is not uncommon to hear of children physically hurting other children, their parents, or their teachers—an ineffective and destructive way of "problem solving" that relies upon hostility and aggression. Such violence is often matter-of-factly presented in the media, and surely influences children.

What can parents and teachers do to manage, control, and gradually eliminate undesirable social behaviors in children, while at the same time establishing, developing, and maintaining appropriate social behaviors? The following programs address these issues generally, and in more structured approaches. Some social skills discussed here will have ecological relevance and should receive priority in development; others may simply be desirable behaviors to develop. In any case, emphasize positive social skills as the child cannot exhibit both appropriate and inappropriate behaviors at the same time.

Essentially, parents and teachers will be most concerned about the development of more appropriate behavior that relates to the child's social acceptance—behavior skills that enable the child to control aggressive styles of social interaction. Our primary focus is necessarily on the development and maintenance of each social skill within the home context, but these learned social skills may be generalized to the school context. The home situation is the ideal starting place, since parents can structure the child's home and family activities to include all the elements necessary to establish essential social skills. Also, the home setting typically involves the child's siblings and friends, thereby providing a "practice arena" for developing social skills. Barkley has suggested videotaping play interactions. When viewing the tape one can then pick out the appropriate behaviors to reinforce, and at the same time pick out one or two inappropriate behaviors that would be good candidates for teaching prosocial skills (e.g., listening, cooperation, sharing, etc.).

DEVELOPING LISTENING SKILLS

A critical element of "paying attention" involves listening—hearing and then processing auditory input from others. Listening skills are vital for academic work (gathering information, following directions, understanding assignments, etc.), and being able to really listen contributes to effective social interactions as well. Often, when the child with ADD/ADHD misinterprets something said by another child and acts or responds based on his misinterpretation, the stage is set for negative interactions, conflict, and aggression. Such situations most often occur within a group (peer) context—not in a one-to-one situation. Peers often observe the ADD child's inappropriate response and do not understand that the ADD child may have misinterpreted what was said. They see only the overt response—usually aggressive behavior—and quietly record this as another bit of evidence to "avoid that child." Following such an incident, even if the ADD child is told accurately what was initially said to him (as contrasted to what he "heard"), he may still appear confused, and may even develop the belief that he is "misunderstood" by others.

Exercise 5.1 DEVELOPING LISTENING SKILLS

Exercise goal: Develop listening skills.

Players: Initially: parent and child, then teacher.

Frequency: Daily—for all ages.

Time required: Up to about age 10:
initially—approximately 5 minutes;
as toleration builds—10-15 minutes.

For older children:
less structured time (see notes).

Basic exercise:
- Hear auditory stimulus.
- Learn to pay attention to stimulus immediately.
- Process verbal information presented.
- Show understanding by verbalizing same information.

Complexity level: Begin at a level where child can experience success from the beginning.
Gradually increase complexity, allowing time for many successes.

Reward: Social praise and touch.

Punishment: None—use *only* positive reinforcement.

Notes:
- Child's responses can guide parent as to tolerance for longer sessions and complexity.
- Do not attempt to force the child to sit for longer sessions than she can tolerate—counterproductive.
- Eye contact is desirable but not essential.
- Have child's full attention.
- Choose or structure a time when there will be no interruptions (not even using the bathroom).

continued . . .

- Avoid negative comments like, "You sure are stupid. That's not what I asked you to do." Be positive.
- In more advanced stages, *priming* speeds learning these skills. As noted in a prior chapter, *priming* brings into awareness what positive consequences (i.e., rewards) will be given or experienced when the skill is used. For example, say "It sure will be fun to work with your team on that project" or "I'll bet you and your friends will really enjoy the new video games we'll have for your party next month."

Example for young child:

- Read short story appropriate to child's mental development.
- Ask child to retell in own words.
- With success, give social praise and touch (e.g., pat on back).
- If child has difficulty retelling, simply give a shorter story or one paragraph, or even repeat simple words of the child.
- Use a level that allows for success.
- After success is experienced by the child, gradually increase difficulty level and complexity, using child's success or lack of it as your guide.

Example for older child:

- May not require such structure.
- Parent will often just ask, "What did I just ask you to do?"
- As child successfully remembers and is able to follow requests, increase complexity, perhaps using a sequence of requests: "Please put your dirty shoes in the washroom; put your dirty football uniform in the washer, along with the dirty towels on the floor, and hang up the clean shirts in your closet."
- If the child has difficulty with such a complex task, it can be broken down into two or more components.
- Let the child serve as a guide to how much complexity she can handle.
- Each time there is success in processing and recalling the request (i.e., being able to tell you what was requested), praise the child by saying, "Good, you got all of that request."

After listening skills have been learned and practiced at home, it's time to generalize these skills to the classroom setting. The teacher can follow the same process to verify that communications were heard accurately. Thus, the teacher, too, might ask, "What did I just ask you to do?" The teacher gives immediate feedback (verbal praise) to the child for accurate response statements and provides the parent on a daily or weekly basis with a record of the number of requests and the number of the child's accurate responses. This short-term record keeping is needed only for about two weeks and may be replaced by frequent praise from the teacher in the future. When formal reports are given to a parent, these improving listening skills may become part of the child's behavioral (point system) program, or—as the child's classroom listening performance stays at 90 percent correct or better—she will receive some agreed-upon reward. The parent's or teacher's use of priming each morning, to remind the child of the potential reward, often results in faster learning of these listening skills.

DEVELOPING A PROGRAM FOR FOLLOWING INSTRUCTIONS

Only after a child has well-established listening skills can he be expected to follow instructions well. Training in these two skill areas (listening, following directions) can even be done together as in Exercise 5.2. Complying with requests or following directions is something a child is expected to "do" as compared with things he "should not do." As such prosocial skills become stronger and more frequent, there is a corresponding reduced probability of inappropriate behavior. When the child is doing what he's supposed to—following directions or rules—he cannot be doing what he's not supposed to do.

Exercise 5.2 DEVELOPING A PROGRAM FOR FOLLOWING INSTRUCTIONS

Exercise goal: Increase compliance with instructions, rules, requests.

Players: Initially: parent and child, then teacher, bus driver, Scout leader.

Frequency: Structured exercise—daily until habit and ability to follow instructions are established.

Unstructured exercise—occurrences in real life used as often as opportunities present themselves.

Time required: Initially—5-10 minutes with structured exercise.
As developed—depends on complexity and difficulty of instructions.

Basic exercise:

- Verbally give the child a sequence of three or fewer tasks.
- Model the expected response while repeating each step.
- Have child complete sequence while verbalizing each step.
- Give positive feedback.

Complexity level:

- Appropriate to child's mental age and severity of beginning inability to process and retain information and ability to act on it.
- Simplify this exercise so that the child can experience success.
- Build from child's success.

continued . . .

Reward:	Verbal praise for each correct step. Bonus for correctly performing entire sequence.
Punishment:	None. Do not give criticism. Simply repeat the process another time when child is not successful.
Notes:	– Child learns through modeling and imitation. – Child learns as correct steps and procedures are rewarded with praise, touch. – Child learns through repetition. ADD/ADHD child needs much repetition and reinforcement because he is easily distracted and has a short attention span. – Information is processed and understood best when presented in more than one sense modality. – Rewards may be offered both for listening to instructions and completing the steps.
Example:	Parent: "I want you to set the dinner table tonight. First, put the placemats on the table; second, get the silverware and napkins and put them where they belong; third, get glasses for drinks and plates for food. Like this." (Parent repeats instructions as he models the expected behavior.) Parent may also write the steps and review them with the child via reading them aloud together. Praise each correctly done step. Extra praise for entire sequence.

You may use many other tasks for this exercise. Remember, any request given may bring about a reward for *listening* (i.e., knowing what do to), and for *carrying out the request(s)* (i.e., doing it). Completing the task may thus result in additional praise and touch (i.e., pat on the back). You may certainly include both skills (listening and following directions) in a behavioral point system.

When such behaviors are included on a home-school note, it will facilitate learning of the skill and enhance generalization of the skill. As the child is reinforced for his use of this compliance skill in more and more situations, the skill becomes stronger. Following rules in class, on the playground, in the lunchroom, and on the school bus are all situations in which the skill may become generalized. Successfully generalizing the compliance skills does, however, take cooperation among parent, teacher, bus driver, and others, and consistency of consequences to strengthen the skill. Inappropriate behaviors (e.g., breaking rules) may be reinforced when the child is able to manipulate attention from the bus driver or the person monitoring the lunchroom. Predictable consequences must be in place for misbehavior—as well as recording and relating of appropriate behavior (i.e., following the rules). Keep in mind that it is far more important to teach the child a prosocial skill that emphasizes what he needs "to do" rather than what he "should not do." Reminding the child of what the rules are in different situations, and stating the consequences for adhering to or violating them (priming), will further improve the child's ability to be successful.

DEVELOPING SHARING BEHAVIOR

At some point in life, everyone has had an experience of having to share with others. It is quite normal to share as part of developing friendship—and certainly siblings are often asked to share food, toys, and time with their parents. The child with ADD/ADHD may develop a sense of being the less favored child—or even the "black sheep" of the family. Often feeling victimized, such a child will at times resent having to share, resent being second, and ultimately resent his siblings. This situation generates conflict and leaves parents frustrated and frazzled in seeking peaceful solutions to hassles between and among their children. It is, at times, quite difficult to know where to begin.

Since there is often competition over, and difficulty with, sharing of a toy, begin training on this social skill with an exercise aimed at teaching the concept of sharing to one or more siblings or playmates. Conflict over a toy with subsequent fighting may, of course, result in placing the toy in time-out. However, this does not teach the child about sharing or playing cooperatively; it may only serve to discourage fighting. What is needed is the prosocial approach. First, explain to both children that you have noticed that there is difficulty in playing with this toy. Tell the children that you will expect them to share this toy and say, "I would like to show you what I mean by sharing." Then model what is meant by sharing, showing that "I can play with the toy for a while and then I can offer it to you." Depending on the age of the children, the time spent with the toy may vary, using briefer periods for younger children. After modeling sharing, say, "OK, now I would like to see each of you share this toy. I'm going to use a kitchen timer; each of you will be able to play with this toy for one minute." Set the timer for one minute and when the bell rings say, "OK, I liked the way you played with the toy and (to the other child) I liked the way you played with something else while you were waiting for this toy." Now, allow the other child to play with the toy, again setting the timer for one minute. Repeat the praise for the second child as was done for the first child. If there is any hassle while the first child plays with the toy, warn the second child that fighting for the toy will result in the first child's having the toy for an additional minute. Any further hassles over the toy result in the toy's going in time-out, as you say, "OK, we'll need to try this another time. This toy goes in time-out for ____________. (The time may be estimated. For something really desirable, 15 minutes may be sufficient; one hour or one day may be used for other, less desirable toys.) As with most programs, the really important factor is not the punishment, but rather the opportunity to develop more appropriate prosocial skills. Return to this training quickly and often for most efficient learning to occur.

A common situation in the family with an ADD child involves sharing the TV or taking turns watching a preferred show. A parent may suggest a solution stating, "You watch your program this week and your brother will watch his next week at this time." In some cases, a favorite show for each may occur on the same day. In this case, tell one child, "You watch your favorite show at 3:30 P.M. and your brother can watch his favorite show at 4:00 P.M."

There are fewer opportunities in school to observe and reinforce sharing or taking turns, but some occasions can be found—especially for younger children. Often youngsters working on projects together at a table may be faced with the problem of taking turns with materials. This behavior may be monitored by the teacher and reported to the parent, as well as directly reinforced in the classroom. For example, on a Recording Sheet for Social Skills (see Figure 5.1) the teacher may demonstrate sharing and taking turns to the child and then say, "When I see you sharing and taking turns I'm going to mark the paper so that you can show your parents(s) at home how well you can do with this behavior." If fights break out in the classroom, the teacher may cue the child with the question, "What should you be doing instead of fighting over that ________________?" This allows the child to develop some cognitive awareness of the appropriate behavior (i.e., sharing). When the child changes his behavior and begins to share, the teacher may praise and give a pat on the back saying, "I'm going to put that good mark on your report." As with other skill training, this information may be used equally well in the classroom and at home in a behavior (point) system.

Figure 5.1 RECORDING SHEET FOR SOCIAL SKILLS

SOCIAL SKILLS
RECORDING SHEET

Social Skill	M	T	W	TH	F	Totals
Listening						
Follow Rules						
Sharing						
Work/Play Cooperative						
Problem Solving						
Anger Control						
Totals						

DEVELOPING COOPERATION IN WORK AND PLAY

This area has been of prime concern to parents of children with ADD/ADHD. As with other appropriate behaviors, it is not possible for the child to play cooperatively and fight at the exact same time. Thus, more frequent reinforcement of cooperative behavior should result in a decrease in fighting or aggressive behavior. Have a plan for dealing with fighting. This may involve a time-out or a specific behavior penalty, and the child should be informed of this prior to the start of a game or task. Priming reminds the child of what to expect for appropriate as well as inappropriate behaviors. These reminders need not be directed toward one child (with ADD); they may be quite general. Remember, it takes two to fight.

To develop this social skill, suggest that the ADD child and her sibling or playmate play a game. To encourage this skill, pick a game where the child with ADD will not be at a disadvantage. For example, don't choose checkers for this, as there are too many chances for the ADD child to give impulsive and poorly planned responses. Instead, pick a game where success is more dependent upon chance (e.g., Candyland®). This will ensure more opportunities to reinforce cooperative behavior. Once the game is selected, tell both children, "You know that it has sometimes been difficult for you two to play together without fighting. I'm going to be looking for times when you two get along in play without fighting. When I see this, I'll let you know, but I'll also put a mark on this card (Behavior Check Card, Figure 5.2). When you reach ten marks, we will have a celebration by going somewhere (or doing something) that you both like."

Figure 5.2 BEHAVIOR CHECK CARD

Behavior	*Mon*	*Tues*	*Wed*	*Thurs*	*Fri*	*Sat*	*Sun*
Working Cooperatively							
Playing Cooperatively							
Cumulative Totals							
Date	Point Total Goal This Week						

In this structured situation, neither child will know when you will be observing; this kind of random check results in far greater consistency in exhibiting appropriate cooperative behavior. If necessary, model cooperative behavior for a game (i.e., playing by the rules) and even show the child which behaviors would be inappropriate. Explain further what will happen if inappropriate behavior occurs. You can develop a signal to warn the child when such behavior occurs. The signal may be holding out two fingers, communicating that the child has two choices: (1) change the inappropriate behavior, or (2) accept the consequence for that behavior. Both children are told that if inappropriate behavior occurs (e.g., name calling, hassling, fighting, etc.), the game will be stopped and put in time-out. However, by giving the child a chance to change his behavior by himself, you shift the responsibility for the consequence totally on the child. Remember that it is far better to promote positive, prosocial behavior than to simply punish an inappropriate behavior. As the children get better at earning points for cooperative behavior and the point totals increase, set higher goals to get the same payoff. Some children will voice complaints over the increase in expectation (i.e., higher points), but you may lessen their concerns by stating, "Yes, you do need a greater number of points to get the reward, but you are getting so much better at cooperation that it's much easier for you to get the points; you know I'm really proud of the progress you have made."

During the school year it is sometimes difficult to arrange a sufficient number of situations in which social skills can be trained. However, a summer camp experience can provide numerous situations to work on prosocial skills as well as other skills. In Pittsburg, Dr. William Pelham has conducted a summer day treatment program for kids with ADHD since 1980. His program provides intensive individual treatment centered around a point system. A variety of social skills are taught including social skills, group problem solving skills as well as computer-assisted instruction. Parents are taught behavior management techniques. Follow-up treatments at the end of the summer include:

- a Saturday treatment program that is similar to the summer program
- school interventions in the class
- additional parent training

A program similar to this one is also available through the ADD Clinic in Biloxi, Mississippi and is described in the section on "A Model ADD Clinic" (Appendix D).

DEVELOPING SOCIAL GRACES

Children with ADD/ADHD who are also aggressive are clearly deficient in problem solving. Such children have difficulty in coming up with alternate solutions to their problems, fail to foresee the consequences of their behavior and have difficulty addressing the complexities of conflict situations. Clearly, there is difficulty in reflecting on behavioral alternatives. In fact, children with ADD/ADHD may have difficulty with all four basic steps of problem solving, that is, identification of the problem, thinking of solutions, foreseeing consequences, and being able to develop a plan of action to achieve a goal (conflict resolution).

You may approach this with firsthand knowledge of some of the past problems and conflicts the child has experienced, or the child may be asked to discuss a recent problem encountered at home or at school. Say "OK, let's take the time you hit a boy who teased you and called you some name just because you got a short haircut." You can then model for the child how to go about problem solving. Many children with ADD fail to recognize the problem. Some might say the problem is "I got in trouble for hitting." You can give feedback saying, "Well, you got in trouble because hitting is against the rules in school." Continue saying, "It seems to be that the problem was that you got very angry over being teased and called names. It certainly wasn't appropriate for that boy to do that, but you got caught breaking a school rule." Then say, "Can you think of some other ways that you might have handled that situation? Other than hitting? Let's write them down." List whatever the child says, allowing any and all solutions. After all are listed, go back through each one saying "OK, now let's look at what the consequences might be for each of these." You may wish to give some additional solutions if all of the consequences for the child's solution are poor.

It is important to select problem solving situations that do not arouse anger. For example, say, "Remember when you saw that group of boys playing down the street? You weren't sure how to get invited to play. I remember that you just went over, introduced yourself, and asked if you could play a game with them. I remember that they told you no and you were really disappointed. I wonder what other approaches you might have taken in that situation? Let's go over that one because that's a situation that may come up again."

Where the child with ADD/ADHD has a problem with aggression, there are almost certainly poor peer relations. When impulsive children are quick to anger and respond in an explosive manner, they are often either shunned and avoided, or teased and prodded into acting out often to see them "get in trouble."

To begin, note that everyone has been angry at some time, but not everyone knows what anger looks or feels like. The first question may be What does anger look like? What are the outward signs of anger? Next, it can be pointed out that anger not only has outward signs, but there are also inward signs. See if the child can relate what it feels like inside to be angry. Last, it is helpful to explore some of the possible consequences to expressions of anger—what things might happen when we act out or show anger.

Explore some of the triggers for anger both at home and at school. At school, the child may be frustrated and angry over being rejected and left out of social groups and play activities. In the neighborhood, the child may become angry over being teased because he is poorly coordinated and called names like "Spaz."

Each one of these situations may then be explored. In the latter example, in cooperation with the child, develop potential ways to handle teasing and name calling. Second, it's important that the child be aware of internal cues, as feelings may intensify over time. You and the child may role-play the situation. As the child assumes the role of the "teaser," you reflect on your feelings and thoughts commenting "I'm beginning to feel my muscles tensing up—my heart is beating faster—I need to relax—I need to just ignore him." Then ask, "What else could I do besides ignore him?" A list could be generated. You can add the following: You could also count to 10, look at something, think about something else.

An interesting "turtle technique" has been described by Dr. Arthur Robin (1976) to help control anger. Children with ADHD were taught to "play turtle" when teased and angered. "Going into their shells" would be a protective strategy to ward off teasing and other forms of verbal aggression.

While those problem areas are critical for the child with ADD/ADHD with regard to the development of peer acceptance, the social niceties are also desirable behaviors for social relations. The Social Graces Checklist in Figure 5.3 incorporates such behaviors as greeting others, saying thank you, introducing others, giving and receiving compliments, offering to help others, being sensitive to what others are feeling, and apologizing. A record of the frequency of each behavior may be kept for one week. Should you determine that one or more of these behaviors would be useful to develop further, a behavior (point) system may be used. Through the use of modeling, imitation, shaping, and consistent reinforcement—especially at home—such behaviors may be developed and maintained.

Tracking the totals by social skill and by day of the week should be helpful in determining which skills or situations may need to be addressed in greater detail.

Figure 5.3 SOCIAL GRACES CHECKLIST

DATE: ______________________

NAME: ______________________

Social Skill	*Mon*	*Tues*	*Wed*	*Thurs*	*Fri*	*Sat*	*Sun*	*Totals by Skill*
Greet others								
Say goodbye								
Say thank you								
Introduce others								
Give compliments								
Thank for compliments								
Offer to help								
Recognize others' feelings								
Apologize								
Be neat/clean in appearance								
Totals by Day of Week								

SELF-CONCEPT AND SELF-ESTEEM

The ways a child perceives himself or herself constitute self-concept, and a child may have several differing views of that "self." A child with ADD/ADHD may realize she has poor social skills and poor math skills, but she may also realize that she performs as an excellent soccer player. Such varying awareness is, indeed, fortunate; otherwise, the child with ADD/ADHD could be devastated by her many difficulties, making such comments as, "I'm really stupid in school," or "I really am a weirdo; I can't get along with anyone." Such a child exhibits a lack of understanding of the important fact that she is a "person" and thus distinct from "what she does." The essential message to convey to this child is, "You are not your behavior." Don't criticize or put the child down; be aware of the child's internal dialogue regarding such a negative message. Over time, children can accumulate quite a number of negative messages; the effect is a progressive erosion of self-perception to the point of a generally negative self-concept.

Self-esteem represents how the child feels about himself. It's a generalized feeling that develops over time and reflects the impact of his life experiences. Often, this feeling state is based not only on what the child perceives but also on the expectations others may have of the child. A child with ADD/ADHD who is having a problem completing a task may be told, "I know you can do this work; you completed it yesterday." Such performance inconsistency (characteristic of the ADD/ADHD pattern) sets the child up to fail to meet the expectations of others, and thereby creates another negative weight on the self-esteem scale. The greater the number of failure experiences, the more negative, or lower, will be the child's self-esteem. Despite their effort in school, little is achieved. Even though there is a tremendous desire to be popular, many are treated like annoying outcasts. Although some do well in sports, others are banished to the sidelines and often criticized when they do play. Since the child may encounter failures and disappointments in many areas of his life besides in the academic area, there is a general tendency for that child to develop a poor self-image, or self-concept, and to have many negative feelings (low self-esteem). Remember, too, that most children with ADD/ADHD are exceptionally sensitive emotionally, as well as neurologically. When children with ADD/ADHD begin to believe that they are retarded, lazy, or losers, these beliefs may become associated with feelings of hopelessness and a perception that putting forth effort in school, or in other situations, does no good. When this leads to a pervasive sense of being "defective" there may be significant loss of motivation. Positive strokes are clearly needed.

Give Positive Strokes

It is most important that parents and teachers of children with ADD/ADHD provide numerous and frequent positive strokes to counteract the numerous negative ones they receive. Exercise 5.3 on page 198 will help you develop an awareness of those things the child does well so you can use this information to provide positive strokes.

Exercise 5.3 POSITIVE STROKES

List all of the things the child with ADD/ADHD does well.

1. ______________________________
2. ______________________________
3. ______________________________
4. ______________________________
5. ______________________________
6. ______________________________
7. ______________________________
8. ______________________________
9. ______________________________
10. ______________________________

If you have not named ten things, go back and add those "parts of" things the child does well (even if the overall activity would not be described as done well). In other words, if only a single component of an activity is performed well, list that component. For example, child works very hard on tasks (once these have been organized and put into proper sequence). This list will serve you later as a resource to provide positive strokes for the child.

The following is a list of sample positive strokes regarding what the child does well:

Exercise 5.3 Sample Positive Strokes

These written strokes give feedback to the child.

1. I really liked the birthday card you made for me—that was a very caring thing to do.
2. I appreciate the way you helped to clean the house.
3. You are really helpful to me in taking care of your little brother.
4. You know, you're very good at drawing those pictures of race cars.
5. I was really impressed by your play in the baseball game—two home runs—wow!
6. Thanks for folding the clothes so neatly.
7. I can really count on you to take out the trash on Monday night.
8. You're doing so well with your drum lessons—even our neighbors have commented.
9. I really like the way you have organized your baseball card collection—it's really impressive and shows that you've put a lot of work into it.
10. I know that math isn't easy but I am really impressed by the way you've accepted extra assignments to work on. It's really going to pay off.

Improving Self-Esteem

Parents of a child with ADD/ADHD need to be almost superhuman to remain positive and supportive in the presence of the child's difficulties and failures. The child's perception of self-worth is influenced by the reactions of others. Parents, teachers, and others significant in the child's life provide a mirror that shows the child how he or she is appreciated; based on this, self-image is shaped. To maintain adequate self-esteem, the significant people in the child's life must be aware and constantly emphasize the positive in what is said to the child if he or she is to enjoy success.

You can affect self-esteem by the words you use and by how those words are used. Intonations of the voice, lack of interest in activities, failure to listen to what the child says, backhanded compliments, and statements that question competence may all erode the child's self-esteem. Eventually, your perceived lack of interest may result in reduced or even closed communications with the child. Remember that the child with ADD/ADHD is quite sensitive to remarks of others. Accusations such as "You really annoy me" or "You always make such a mess" focus directly on the child and not on his behavior. It *is not OK* to focus your criticisms on the child; it *is OK* to state how you feel about his or her *behavior,* for example, "I really get upset when you interrupt my conversation." Sometimes a parent or teacher, who is aware that the child has previously exhibited dangerous behavior and may simply want to "protect" him, may, in the very act of being (over)protective, inadvertently say things that recall to the child his incompetency. For example: "Don't climb that tree. You know you always fall," or "Don't try to do that by yourself. You know you'll hurt yourself." Sometimes it is really difficult to balance the need to protect the child with allowing him to feel trusted in becoming more independent.

You must be careful to avoid comparisons with other relatives and classmates—and when the child with ADD/ADHD shows improvement and does her best work ever, it's important to *note that improvement* and avoid finding fault. Don't give backhanded compliments.

Example of backhanded compliment:

> "This is a really neat and organized math homework page. You are really improving. Maybe next time you'll get all the answers right."

Example of sincere, reinforcing compliment:

> "This is a really neat and organized math homework page. You are really improving. Look, you've even gotten more answers right this time than last."

The language used is most important. Critical comments and destructive words (like dumb, stupid, pest, and worse) can all depress the child's self-esteem. Everyone has negative qualities, but adults are allowed to promote their assets and hide their weaknesses; children with ADD/ADHD are often forced to expose their difficulties in front of a class or on the ballfield. If these children are to feel good about themselves, they must receive more attention for what they *do well now,* for their *effort,* and for their *improvements* in all that they do. Listen to this child, acknowledge what she says, and be genuinely interested in her conversation.

Do focus on any positive characteristics and emphasize improvements when they appear. For example, writing may be messy and words may be misspelled, but the child's story may have good content. It's important to point this out, saying, "I really like the story you wrote." These children must experience a sense of competency and be allowed to think and act in a more independent manner. Too often, in a need to get things done quickly, adults may simply tell the child with ADD/ADHD what to do instead of allowing him to *think* of what he needs to do. While this seems to save time, it is at the expense of communicating to the child that he is competent; it says instead that he must depend on others to tell him what to do. By not allowing the child to come up with the answer or do a task simply because it will take a little more time, you may cause the child to feel inadequate, to perceive that he can't cope, and in general to develop a helpless, overly dependent attitude.

In the classroom, most teachers are aware that the child with ADD/ADHD needs more attention and is especially sensitive in situations where her "differences" are made known. You must use methods and materials that will hold the child's interest. Despite their sometimes rude and inappropriate behaviors, children with ADD/ADHD are quite sensitive to comments made in the classroom. Be very careful of what you say. If a child is misbehaving, it can be devastating to say, "Johnny, did you take your medicine this morning?" or "Beth seems to act so smart at times, let's see if she knows the answer to this question." Get and keep the child's attention; offer many opportunities for small successes, and praise, praise, praise! Emphasize and bring out the "good stuff" for everyone to see.

An Exercise Plan to Counteract Negative Themes

To help you learn to pay attention to this "good stuff," use a reminder system for cues to give more positive strokes. You may be cued by a watch that beeps on the hour or, preferably, on the half hour. Each time the beep is heard, look for something the child has done that could be considered an occasion for a positive comment or token. (Tokens are especially effective for younger children; theater-type tickets [available from school supply houses] seem to work well with older students.) The child is told that these tokens or tickets may be traded in no later than the end of the week for some special privilege; a specified number of tickets or tokens to give to the child each day is decided on in advance. The number of tokens or tickets may be increased as you see an increase in the overall number of times the good behaviors appear. When any good, appropriate, or improved behavior is shown, it is rewarded more often, thus bringing about an increase in the number of these behaviors per day. This exercise is designed to counteract the generally negative themes that pervade most of the attention given to children with ADD/ADHD.

3. Use a specific cue, preferably nonverbal, to get the child started on a task. For example, the teacher or parent may signal that it's time to get started by tugging on his or her own ear. Having the teacher and the parent use the same cue or signal will facilitate learning the meaning of that cue. It's important to avoid continually reminding the child to get to work; the child may then become excessively dependent on having others tell him when he needs to get started. The nonverbal cue also avoids potential embarrassment and labeling of the child in front of other children in the classroom. A good alternative when there is failure to respond to the nonverbal cue is to ask the child, "What are you supposed to be doing right now?" If he responds correctly, you may stroke and reinforce this, followed by further praise should the child get started by himself. As a last resort, the child may be directly told to "get busy on this assignment!"
4. A response-cost procedure may be employed to help keep the child on task—giving the child a number of tokens (younger child) or points (older child). He is told there will be a loss of tokens or points if off task, and completion of the task will bring about bonus points. As with any behavioral procedure, this should be set up using only one criterion—to be successful. Nothing will be gained by having the child repeatedly fail. Monitor the child on three similar assignments to determine about how many times he will get off task. Then set the number of tokens or points five higher than his worst performance. Thus, if he has lost five, eight, and ten points, assign him fifteen points. Also, give a bonus of five points when the task is completed within the allotted time. Be sure to remove the tokens or subtract points to give the child feedback. The token jar or card showing points or loss of points may be kept on the desk.
5. Homework assignments may parallel the child's work in school and be used to help develop appropriate work habits. The child can be monitored using the Homework Check Card as described in Chapter 6. Checks for "on-task" and "off-task" behavior may assist in developing more appropriate work habits.

Part B—Processing Control

Saliency Determination (B-1)—For the child with attentional weaknesses one may manipulate attention by varying the potency of the stimulus. Often this manipulation is done with bright colors.

1. Highlighting certain words will cause them to stand out from others. Using a brightly colored mat is also helpful; it may be easier to keep her attention focused on her work area.
2. Using differential reinforcement, it may also be possible to teach the child what is most relevant by using cues (colors, painting, etc.) to initially direct her attention to a certain stimulus, and then to reinforce that attention by verbal praise, tokens, or points.

Processing Depth and Detail (B-2)—It is difficult to process information and to learn it when there is insufficient neural activation in the brain. One must be in an alert state in order to function in learning situations.

1. One of the basic ways to enhance processing is through stimulant medication.
2. In lieu of medication, the teacher may enhance processing by using high-interest material, varying teaching approaches, using humor, maintaining involvement with an active and interactive learning approach, and using colorful materials and audiovisual techniques.
3. Alternate activities in class allow students to be active for a while (e.g., running in place, jumping jacks, and deep-breathing exercises). Insufficient oxygen results in failure to fuel the brain; inappropriate breathing may therefore result in slowing down of efficient mental processing. Thus, it is not unusual to find that asthma is frequently associated with attention and learning disorders.
4. If a student fails to get the message, the teacher must review the content, clarity, and complexity of instructions and then utilize inquiry to determine whether the message was received. Simply ask, "What did I ask you to do?" The cognitive searching involved will certainly activate the brain to some extent and focus the child's attention on the reception of future messages.

Mental Activation (B-3)—Again, this parameter is characteristic of a low level of arousal in the nervous system. Since the child with attentional weaknesses may frequently get distracted and off task, she is unable to become fully engaged in the task at hand, and cannot relate this new information to previously stored learned material.

1. Inappropriate daydreaming may be discouraged by having an active and interactive approach to learning. Also, when the child continues to think and to solve problems, she is less likely to daydream.
2. The response-cost program may be helpful here, since the child never knows when her behavior will be monitored.

Focal Maintenance (B-4)—This parameter is quite similar to the previous one. When children experience difficulty with sustained attention, they miss critical elements of conversation, and they may also fail to get all directions and explanations that are too complex.

1. First, verbal statements may be simplified and broken down into component parts.
2. Having the child repeat directions or explain them gives feedback on whether the information was received.

Satisfaction Control (B-5)—Children with attentioanl weaknesses satiate on materials and activities very quickly, and they attempt to search for new materials and activities that will satisfy them. Of course, this doesn't happen. With an incessant need for stimulation, a child may even engage in activities that are risky or that may create an uproar. Some inappropriate behavior may therefore relate to this factor of easy boredom. Clowning in the class may provide comic relief, attention from others, and certainly additional stimulation.

1. You must ensure that the inappropriate behavior does not pay off; use time-out, response-cost, or actively ignore (and reinforce others in the class who also actively ignore this behavior).
2. Attempt to provide stimulating learning situations. Use of computerized learning readily provides, with stimulating graphics, considerable stimulation that will keep the child interested. Also, by alternating stimulating segments with the less exciting ones, interest may be maintained.

Part C—Production Control

Previewing (C-1)—Difficulty in planning and using foresight is one of the hallmark characteristics of the child with attentional problems. The tendency to respond impulsively has been noted as a central feature of the clinical pattern and has been termed a general lack of behavioral inhibition. In the field of neuropsychology, this has been labeled as a problem or deficit in executive control functions.

1. Use of a cognitive mediation procedure such as self-talk may act as a slow-down technique that allows the child to consider possible outcomes. This requires some training in questioning or using prompts to guide behavior responses.
2. Offer general reinforcement for the child on those occasions when he does not respond impulsively. For example, "(name), you did really well at raising your hand and waiting to be called on."
3. Modeling can also be helpful. As in the previous example, it may be helpful to first comment on those children who do the appropriate thing (i.e., raise their hands) to answer a question, while ignoring those who blurt out the answer. A comment for the model might be: "(name), you did the appropriate thing by raising your hand when you wished to answer the question. I really appreciate that."

Facilitation and Inhibition (C-2)—Many inappropriate behaviors occur without conscious awareness on the part of the child with attentional difficulties. Many times, such behaviors involve deficiencies in social skills.

1. Attempt to develop and strengthen the appropriate social behaviors while discouraging inappropriate ones; use differential reinforcement.
2. Since social skills are often deficient, their development may require many repetitions after the appropriate skill is modeled and imitated. Use of "positive practice" techniques is therefore indicated.

Tempo Control (C-3)—A general lack of awareness of time constraints is also characteristic of children with attentional weaknesses. In part, this may be associated with distractions and off-task tendencies, but it is also a function of the problem of inadequate planning and foresight. Many repetitions or learning trials may be necessary to acquire the habits needed for organization and planning skills.

1. It is important to provide models for such planning, organizational, and time-management skills. Use of organizational charts to develop and teach sub-goals will help the child reach his ultimate overall goals.
2. Using self-monitoring checks on time estimation will allow the child to learn the concept of *pacing* in his work activity.
3. Knowing, in general, how much work the child can put out on a specific activity (e.g., number of math problems he can work) can be used in a type of "beat the clock" game. A time limit may be set to allow the child to win (i.e., beat the clock) in completing a specified amount of work. Knowing how quickly he can complete this work will then allow the teacher or parent to set a new goal (i.e., slightly less time), and to have the child try to "beat the clock" again. Times may be adjusted until he can complete the work in a reasonable amount of time. Also, each time the child is successful, this success should be reinforced (points or tokens along with praise). Maintain this success by reinforcing the child's completion of work within a reasonable time without using a "beat the clock" strategy.

Self-Monitoring and Self-Correcting (C-4)—In general, these problem areas center around lack of awareness. However, there is also a social skill deficit involved in that many times the child is unable to monitor his own behavior.

1. Self-monitoring is lost when the child gets off task or is distracted. Consequently, reinforcement should be provided when the child is on task. Use a response-cost procedure (i.e., subtract points or tokens) when he is off task.
2. Give continued feedback on mistakes the child makes. This is done as part of general awareness training—the child is asked to reflect on his behavior and to analyze it with regard to its appropriateness. If correctly assessed, the child is reinforced. If not, feedback on the problem behavior is given.
3. Use constant reminders employing "nag tapes" (Figure 7.7). These tapes—recorded by the father when possible or in a male's voice—remind the child, while he is doing a task, of various things to be aware of. Specifically, reminders to be careful and neat, to pace work according to the time allowed, to read each problem carefully, to keep focus on the task, and so forth, according to the child's needs.

Figure 7.7 NAG TAPE (Sample Narrative)

OK, now get ready to start this assignment. Listen or read the instructions carefully—make sure you understand the assignment—raise your hand to ask the teacher if you don't understand what to do. Once you understand, get started—know how long you have to complete this assignment so you can pace yourself and finish. Keep working—pay close attention to your work—make your work neat so the teacher can read it—stay on track—keep working—pay attention *only* to your work. Bring yourself back to your work if you get off track. Check your work—pay close attention to your work—keep working—keep it neat as you go—stay on track until you finish—keep working—be sure to check your work—each time you finish one thing, say, "Good, I did that one." When you're half finished, say, "Good, I'm halfway through." Keep working—keep working—stay on track—keep working—pay attention to your work.

Note: The above represents samples of statements that may be used in these tapes. Because each child may require a different emphasis, no universal tape is adequate. These tapes are most effective when made by a man and preferably the father; a personalized tape is the best approach with an identified child.

Reinforceability (C-5)—Children with attentional weaknesses are often seen as having a general problem with rewards and punishments. Such children seem to satiate more quickly on some rewards than children without attentional problems and physical punishment is ineffective.

1. Do a survey of reinforcers to determine which are useful for a certain child. The greatest variety would be found at home; however, use of the Survey of School Rewards (end of chapter, p. 243) is also helpful.
2. Mild punishments such as time-out or response-cost are most appropriate. In the school setting, both of these may be used, but the response cost procedure may be most effective.
3. Many children receive negative attention for misbehavior or problem behavior. To counteract this, the procedure called "time-in" may be employed. Basically, this involves attending to any appropriate behavior or any other behavior that is not inappropriate many times during the day. Sometimes the teacher may find it necessary to have a structured way of doing this. One approach is to have a signal or cue to remind the teacher to look for an appropriate reinforcement occasion. Use of the beeperlike device called the "motivator" or a watch that beeps on the half-hour would be useful. Alternatively, and for younger children, the teacher may have a bag of twenty tokens. Throughout the day, the teacher must give away all of the tokens to the child. As long as there are tokens in the teacher's pocket, he or she is reminded to pay attention to the child's appropriate behavior. Each time the teacher catches the child showing some appropriate behavior or *not* exhibiting an inappropriate behavior, a token is given to the child to place in a jar. The tokens are of course combined with verbal praise and feedback to the child concerning which appropriate behaviors were observed.

READY-TO-USE MATERIALS

EXAMPLES OF BEHAVIORAL CONTRACTS

SAMPLE COMPLEX BEHAVIOR CONTRACT

I, ______________________________, agree to do the following:
(Student's Name)

1. Complete written assignments with 80% accuracy or better before lunch time.
2. Remain quiet and keep my hands to myself when going out to recess or lunch.
3. Play cooperatively (i.e., no fights) at recess.
4. Write the assignment for homework for each period.

Each day that I do the above things, I may choose one of the following:

1. Use the class computer for 20 minutes for work or play at the end of the day.
2. Choose the next available class job (e.g., errand) the next day.
3. Twenty (20) minutes free time at the end of the day.

Completion of one week of the above daily list will earn one of the following:

a) having a friend sleep over

b) renting a selected movie

c) release from one weekend chore (i.e., folding clothes)

I agree to fulfill this contract.
Signed:

______________________________	______________________________
Student Signature	*Teacher Signature*
______________________________	______________________________
Parent Signature	*Date Completed*

This contract is in effect as of __________ (*Date*). It will expire on __________ (*Date*). At the end of this contract, a "new contract" may be written.

GENERAL BEHAVIOR CONTRACT

I, ______________________________, agree to ______________________________

____

(perform some task expected by parent/teacher). This is to be completed by (date) ____________*.

In return, I would like ____

(some wished-for reward). I therefore agree to the contract specified above.

______________________________   ______________________________

Parent/Teacher Signature   *Child's Signature*

*If no deadline is set for completion of the contract, put NA (Not applicable).

DAILY BEHAVIOR CONTRACT

Date ________________

My goal for today will be to ____

____

____.

When this goal is achieved, I will get ______________________________________

____.

Should I fail to achieve this goal today, I will accept the following consequence: ______________

____

____.

______________________________   ______________________________

Student's Signature   *Parent/Teacher Signature*

EXAMPLES OF HOME-SCHOOL NOTES

BEHAVIOR REPORT CARD

NAME ______________________________ DATE ______________

Dear Rater:

Please assess the child's behavior on the following items using the following scale. Excellent = 4, Good = 3, Fair = 2, Poor = 0 or N/A (Not applicable).

Observation #

BEHAVIOR ITEMS	1	2	3	4
1. Keeps hands to self (does not push, shove, pinch, or touch others inappropriately).				
2. Avoids fighting (does not hit, kick, or bite others).				
3. Avoids provoking fights (does not trip others or take things).				
4. Behavior appropriate to situation				
5. Plays cooperatively/gets along				
Time-outs				
Fines				
Rater's Initials				
Rating period code: Free time (FT); Lunchroom (LR); Recess (R); other (O)				

Daily School Note (Multiple Classes)

Name ______________________________ Date ______________

Dear Teacher:

Please rate this child in each class period in the areas listed on the following scale: Excellent = 4, Good = 3, Fair = 2, Poor = 0, or NA (Not applicable). Also indicate whether the class is in the morning or afternoon and initial at the bottom.

Note: IS = In-School Suspension, OS = Out-of-School Suspension.

Class Periods

AREA	1	2	3	4	5	6	7
Followed Instructions							
Completed Work							
Obeyed Class Rules							
Got Along With Others							
(write in)							
(write in)							
A.M./P.M. Class							
Time-outs							
Detentions							
Suspensions (IS/OS)							
Teacher Initials							
Lunchroom Behavior							
Recess Behavior							

WEEKLY SCHOOL NOTE

NAME ______________________________________ DATE ________________

Dear Teacher:

Please rate this child in the areas below in the following scale: Excellent = 4, Good = 3, Fair = 2, Poor = 0 or NA (Not applicable) for each day of the week, mornings and afternoons. IS = In-School Suspension, OS = Out-of-School Suspension

MORNING	MON	TUE	WED	THU	FRI
Followed Instructions					
Completed Work					
Obeyed Class Rules					
Got Along With Peers					
(write in)					
(write in)					
AFTERNOON					
Followed Instructions					
Completed Work					
Obeyed Class Rules					
Got Along With Peers					
(write in)					
(write in)					
Time-outs					
Detentions					
Suspensions (IS/OS)					
Lunchroom Behavior					
Recess Behavior					

Positive Comments: ____

____

____

____________________________________ *Teacher's Initials* ____________

SURVEY OF SCHOOL REWARDS

School Reinforcement Survey Schedule (C and A)

RATIONALE/PURPOSE

The School Reinforcement Survey Schedule was developed to determine to what degree a student finds attending class, doing homework, and socializing with school friends reinforcing.

ADMINISTRATION

Most adolescents should be able to complete this form on their own. Some adolescents and most children will need to have the therapist present to clarify some items.

GUIDELINES

1. Some of the items on the School Reinforcement Survey Schedule isolate one small event in the response chain of behaviors leading up to attending school, e.g., Question 3, "Entering the school building." It may be that some students have never stopped to evaluate their feelings about such a particular action. For such students, it is often helpful to have them close their eyes and imagine they are entering their particular school building in the morning and then describe their feelings upon doing so.
2. Question 19 on Form C and Question 23 on Form A list three school vacation times together. If a student wishes to differentiate feelings of anticipation for school after each of the three separate vacations listed, the information is apt to be helpful. This item was constructed as one idea because of the brevity of these holidays in contrast to the extended summer vacation and because all school systems don't give the same seasonal vacations.
3. Unlike the 5-point rating system on Form A, Form C has only a 3-point rating system. This shorter system is meant to make it easy for the younger client to rate degree of reinforcement.

ITEM BREAKDOWN

Form C
Number of questions: 31

Questions	*Topic*
1–4	Going to school
5–7	Participating in free-time activities
8, 9	Doing schoolwork
10–13	Talking about school to others
14, 15	Seeing the report card
16, 17	Participating in extracurricular activities
18–20	Looking forward to school after breaks
21–30	Learning subjects
31	Having enjoyable experiences in school

FORM A
Number of questions: 37

Questions	*Topic*
1-4	Going to school
5-7	Participating in free-time activities
8-10	Doing schoolwork
11-14	Talking about school to others
15, 16	Seeing the report card
17-21	Participating in extracurricular activities
22-24	Looking forward to school after breaks
25-36	Learning subjects
37	Having enjoyable experiences in school

USE OF THE INFORMATION

The School Reinforcement Survey Schedule can be utilized to discover what aspects of school attendance a student finds reinforcing. The student can then be taught to focus upon the reinforcing aspects of school and perhaps begin to spend more time participating in these activities. If, for example, an individual finds school generally aversive, he may be asked to complete this schedule and thus become aware of those aspects of school that *are* enjoyable to him. The client then can learn to focus on and improve upon these reinforcing aspects, possibly making the general school experience more rewarding. This may lead to increased school attendance.

In the treatment phase of therapy, some of the reinforcing items from the School Reinforcement Survey Schedule can be utilized as rewards to increase the frequency of behaviors that need to be increased or as response costs when inappropriate behaviors are emitted. Further, this form can be used in the behavioral analysis of school phobias.

COMPARISON TO OTHER FORMS

BEHAVIORAL RATING CARD: This card lists certain target behaviors; for short-term rewards for this program, the School Reinforcement Survey Schedule would be an excellent source.

PARENTS' AND CHILDREN'S REINFORCEMENT SURVEY SCHEDULE: This more general reinforcement form should give a comprehensive indication of what may be reinforcing to the client. It should also relate to some of the parent-child items on the School Reinforcement Survey Schedule.

REINFORCEMENT MENU: For the full-time student, pleasant school experiences may fulfill the criterion of immediate availability necessary for inclusion on the Reinforcement Menu.

REINFORCEMENT SURVEY SCHEDULES: There is often overlapping information in these more general reinforcement scales and the scales assessing reinforcement in particular settings (as this school schedule).

SCHOOL BEHAVIOR STATUS CHECKLIST: Once the therapist has determined the school behaviors to be targeted for change, the next step is to find possible reinforcers within the school environment.

RECOMMENDED READINGS

Homme, L., Csanyi, A. P., Gonzales, M. A., & Rechs, J. R. *How to use contingency contracting in the classroom.* Champaign, Ill.: Research Press, 1970.

Kazdin, A. E. *Behavior modification in applied settings* (rev. ed.). Homewood, Ill.: Dorsey Press, 1980.

School Reinforcement Survey Schedule (C)

Name ______________________________ Date ____________

Age ________ Sex: Boy ________ Girl ________

School ______________________________ Grade ____________

Put an X in the box that tells best how much you like each of these things about school.

	Not at all	A little	Very much
1. Leaving my home for school in the morning			
2. Riding or walking to school			
3. Going into the school building			
4. Going into my classroom and talking to my teacher alone			
5. Having recess			
6. Having lunch with the other children			
7. Playing with the other children			
8. Working with the other children in groups in my classroom			
9. Doing my homework			
10. Talking about school with my mother			
11. Talking about school with my father			
12. Talking about school with my friends after school			
13. Telling children who don't go to my school all about my school			
14. Seeing my report card			
15. Having my parents see my report card			
16. Being in or going to school sports events			
17. Going to special events like class trips, fairs, or school plays			
18. Being glad to go back to school at the end of summer vacation			
19. Being glad to go back to school at the end of Christmas, midwinter, and spring vacations			
20. Being glad to go back to school each Monday morning after the weekend			

continued . . .

Put an X in the box that tells best how much you like learning each of the following things.

	Not at all	A little	Very much	Do not learn that
21. Reading				
22. Language arts				
23. Math				
24. A foreign language				
25. Social studies				
26. Art				
27. Music				
28. Science				
29. Gym				
30. Religion				

31. Tell about the three things that happen in school that you like most:

 1. ______________________________

 2. ______________________________

 3. ______________________________

SCHOOL REINFORCEMENT SURVEY SCHEDULE (A)

NAME ______________________________ DATE ______________

AGE ________ SEX ________

SCHOOL ______________________________ GRADE ______________

Put a check mark in the column that best describes how much you like each of the following school-related activities.

	Not at all	A little	A fair amount	Much	Very much
1. Leaving your home for school in the morning					
2. Riding or walking to school					
3. Entering the school building					
4. Entering your home classroom and talking to your teacher alone					
5. Having recess or free time					
6. Having lunch with the other students					
7. Playing or socializing with the other students (sports, etc.)					
8. Doing classroom activities					
9. Studying with the other students in the study hall					
10. Doing your homework					
11. Talking about school with your mother					
12. Talking about school with your father					
13. Talking about school with your friends after school					
14. Talking about school with friends who attend a different school					
15. Seeing your report card					
16. Having your parents see your report card					

continued . . .

	Not at all	A little	A fair amount	Much	Very much
17. Going to school sports events					
18. Going to school dances or fairs					
19. Going to after-school clubs and meetings					
20. Going to school plays					
21. Going on class trips					
22. Looking forward to going back to school at the end of summer vacation					
23. Looking forward to going back to school at the end of the Christmas, midwinter, and spring vacations					
24. Looking forward to going back to school each Monday morning after the weekend					

Put a check mark in the column that best describes how much you like learning each of the following subjects.

	Not at all	A little	A fair amount	Much	Very much	Do not take
25. English						
26. Math						
27. A foreign language						
28. Social studies						
29. History						
30. Art						
31. Music						
32. Science						
33. Industrial arts						
34. Physical education (gym)						
35. Religion						
36. Reading (literature)						

37. Name the three things that happen in school that you like most:

1. ______________________________

2. ______________________________

3. ______________________________

CHAPTER 8

Effective Behavioral Techniques for Teachers

SPECIAL APPLICATIONS FOR TEACHERS

Teachers of ADD/ADHD children often encounter problem behaviors and situations quite similar to—and sometimes even more severe than—those faced by the parents. Additionally, teachers face some ADD/ADHD behavior that is unique to the classroom. When a teacher reports such a behavior problem, a parent may confront the teacher with a statement like, "Well, I don't have this kind of trouble with him at home; why is he such a problem in your class?" The implication is that there is something wrong with the ways in which the teacher structures and handles the class, and particularly in that teacher's interactions with the child. The teacher may resort to more drastic measures (i.e., punishing or ostracizing) to gain control, only to realize a continuing—or worsening—problem. Some teachers then become quite defensive, and feel inadequate, overwhelmed, and overstressed about such situations.

These problem situations can occur when a teacher operates from a poor understanding of ADD/ADHD and resultant behaviors, and when the teacher has little or no knowledge of strategies to effectively deal with such behavior. Teachers who do not have such knowledge and skills may feel that their competency is threatened; they develop feelings of inadequacy, depression, self-doubt, and ultimately a sense of hopelessness and failure. After a teacher has a good understanding of ADD/ADHD and accompanying behaviors and has learned effective techniques for dealing with such behaviors, however, he or she becomes more helpful and effective in interactions with the ADD/ADHD child, and experiences an enhanced sense of professional competence and a greater personal motivation for teaching children who manifest ADD/ADHD behaviors. Teachers are also encouraged to read the *C.H.A.D.D. Educators Manual* which covers general concepts about ADD/ADHD, along with school assessment procedures and treatment recommendations. Lastly, the manual covers some of the current legal issues about ADD/ADHD.

THE NATURE OF TEACHER-STUDENT INTERACTIONS

The three major factors regarding teachers that directly influence ADD/ADHD students are (1) the teacher's knowledge of ADD/ADHD, (2) the teacher's individual characteristics, and (3) the teacher's teaching style.

Teacher Knowledge

Teacher knowledge of ADD/ADHD is probably the most significant factor. Understanding ADD behavior is essential in effectively dealing with it. Here we emphasize some common misunderstandings that may unduly stress the ADD child and adversely affect his relationship with the teacher. *Inconsistency* is a primary characteristic seen in the work performance of the ADD child; the child may do well with a given learning task one day and perform poorly on the same type of task the next day. The child's inconsistency in performance may set him up for another problem: undue pressure. Teachers may say, "I know you can do this work because you did it all quite well yesterday." Dr. Russell Barkley has eloquently stated that when the child with ADD succeeds one time, we hold it against him for the rest of his life. However, when the teacher understands this characteristic and expects the ADD/ADHD child to be inconsistent in his work, then there can be more objective approaches to change, less emotional pressure and stress, and fewer derogatory comments, erroneously suggesting that "the child is just lazy—he can do better."

Other problems centering around the teacher's attitude and perceptions are also likely to be based on insufficient knowledge and a lack of understanding.

A general understanding of all of the basic characteristics of children with ADD/ADHD will be important here. These have been outlined in Chapter 1 in great detail. A few may be highlighted now. Rather than criticize or embarrass the child who is disorganized, teachers may help the child develop some skills and strategies to improve organization, such as the use of divided three-ring binders with color separation of subjects and a plastic pouch to keep pencils and other tools together. The teacher may also understand and recognize the child's need for stimulation by varying materials used for tasks while keeping the content consistent. Children with ADD/ADHD need the stability of routine but variation within that routine to maintain greater interest. Likewise, slow-down tasks may be utilized for these children who have problems with impulsive responding. Use of self-talk and reminders to raise hand to answer questions communicates an understanding of the child's basic problems. Furthermore, addressing attention problems and distractibility through the use of self-monitoring procedures acknowledges additional understanding of the child's difficulties in a manner that accommodates his/her problem and also considers potential emotional reactions.

Teacher's Characteristics

A teacher's individual characteristics constitute another influential factor in dealing with the ADD/ADHD child. The most obvious such characteristic is teacher *flexibility.* A teacher who is open to adjusting for the problems experienced by the ADD/ADHD child will have more success in dealing with these behaviors. On the other hand, if the teacher is rigid and inflexible, the ADD/ADHD child will have greater difficulty, and so will such a teacher.

> *Example:* An inflexible teacher gives an assignment and insists that all students must complete it in the same manner. A flexible teacher, in contrast, accommodates the ADD/ADHD child with regard to her short "work span" and divides the assignment into two or three shorter assignments.

Another individual characteristic is teacher *sensitivity.* A child with ADD/ADHD is already aware that she is somehow "different" from other students. Compounding this sense of being different, the child's self-esteem surely will suffer if the teacher also openly confronts her about test grades or medication, or embarrasses her over misbehavior. Any child's self-concept is seriously compromised by a history of ridicule and failure. A child with ADD/ADHD is a supersensitive child who needs a sensitive teacher.

Teaching Style

A teacher's style of teaching is the third main factor affecting a student. Teachers who have problems teaching an ADD/ADHD child are often the teachers with a teaching style that is not well suited for ADD/ADHD students. Such a style may reflect the following:

- a *hurried method* of teaching, speeding through lessons and assignments.
- a general *lack of organization* in presentation of lessons.
- a general *lack of attention to those quiet students* who don't stand out and thus attract the teacher's attention. (While a teacher certainly can't ignore disruptive students, he or she may often overlook the quiet, somewhat withdrawn, student with ADD without hyperactivity who mostly just daydreams.)
- an *authoritarian approach* that may result in considerable conflict with ADD/ADHD students who typically have many difficulties with rule-governed behavior. (A teacher using a more relaxed approach may face far fewer conflicts, depending, of course, on how these conflicts are handled.)

BRIEF HISTORY OF DEALING WITH ADD IN THE CLASSROOM

Many years ago, Strauss and Lehtinen (1947) developed a theory of the behaviors we define today as "ADD" (though the term "ADD" had not yet been coined). Their theory indicated that these children were overstimulated by complex environments; the overactive behavior was considered to be a direct result of this stimulation. This "overarousal theory" led to some "practical suggestions" for classroom environments as a potential means of dealing with the behavior.

Simply stated, it was thought that if the classroom was devoid of any bright colors or stimulating factors, the child would be able to sit quietly and do his work. These classrooms were thus sterile environments lacking exhibits and colorful walls; teachers were even encouraged to dress in drab clothing so as not to distract their students. This theory and implementation of these changes in the classroom were examined and tested by Cruickshank (1961) who found that such changes in classroom environment not only failed to help the child with ADD/ADHD but even made his problems worse. These children performed more poorly on academic tasks and either showed increased misbehavior or "fell asleep" in class due to the boredom of the sterile surroundings. While some of the original suggestions continue to appear in recommendations for classroom environments, the majority of teachers today no longer follow them.

Currently, classroom colors are being selected with the thought of *manipulating* the child's attention. As I noted in an early research study in 1969, various parameters of form, complexity, brightness, and color may be used to create optimal attending behavior as a function of the child's internal level of adaptation (i.e., his physiologically determined arousal level). Recent research from the Chesapeake Institute has provided additional support for this belief stating that by varying features of instructional activities or materials such as color, presentation rate and response activity has made a difference in the performance of ADD children. Adding color, varying presentation and level of detail reportedly serve to stimulate children with ADD/ADHD. Modern classrooms for ADD/ADHD students are often colorful and bright and exhibit a high level of visual complexity. However, today carrels are also used for work activity; these carrels mask visual distractions. Also, auditory distractions are sometimes masked by using music or "white noise" to help maximize work output.

THE TEACHER'S OPTIONS FOR ADAPTATION AND TRAINING

The focus on successful change in the school setting may involve the following:

- The classroom. *Focus* is on the (invisible) ADD/ADHD "handicap," treating it as a physical one. *Strategy* requires accommodation of the external environment (the classroom itself).

- The child. *Focus* is on the perceived internal deficiencies. *Strategy* is to change or modify some internal process in the child, allowing him to compensate for the perceived deficiency.
- The teacher. *Focus* is on teacher efforts to help the child successfully adapt to the classroom. *Strategy* involves teacher-initiated changes to facilitate the student's adaptation.

A combination of these elements works best.

Classroom Accommodations

Physical accommodations in the classroom are quite common, and even expected, whenever a child has a physical handicap or suffers a physically disabling injury (e.g., a broken leg). For example, a teacher may use preferential seating or may assign another student to help carry books for a child using crutches. If a student wears an eye patch or has had eye surgery, most teachers would agree to assign homework that could be tape recorded or would provide a peer "assistant" to help with reading and written work. These handicapping situations are temporary, but the ADD/ADHD child will probably have to compensate for his disorder for the rest of his life.

Now we will discuss in detail some common (environmental) classroom accommodations that can be greatly beneficial for the ADD/ADHD student.

Preferential Seating—Seat the ADD/ADHD child near you, or by students who model appropriate classroom behavior. The ADD/ADHD student should *not,* however, be seated by a noisy air conditioner or other equipment, or in or near a high-traffic or distracting area.

Use of Work Areas—Carrels lessen visual distractions and are available for all students to use for private work.

Seating Arrangements—These may be varied by the teacher as often as deemed helpful from the usual rows of desks to clusters or a semicircle or small groups at tables. However, some research has shown that the traditional desk arrangement in rows is better for children with ADD/ADHD compared with modular arrangement where several children share a table. Likewise, research has shown that classrooms with four walls are better than open classrooms (which are noisier).

Changes in Lighting—Changing the type of lights may make a positive difference; it may alleviate boredom and the annoyance of the "hum" of some fluorescent lights. Interestingly, introducing a strobe light periodically may also be beneficial.

Experimentation with Music—Some ADD/ADHD students may benefit from background music or from "white noise" (which may also help other students as well). For some students, a more highly rhythmic rock music may be of better help. (Of course, this would be played only with headphones and only for some children who work better with such a stimulus.)

Use of Headphones—Headphones may be necessary to present music, as noted above, or to block out distractions. They are also an integral part of some behavioral programs (e.g., self-monitoring procedures or the use of recorded "nag tapes").

Child-Centered Approaches

This category of strategies reflects attempts to change what the child does to deal with specific problems. It involves teaching the ADD/ADHD child various skills to help her change, or modify, an internal process which, in turn, helps her in the classroom (or other situations) where the ADD/ADHD behavior is problematic.

Modeling Instructions—When the child with ADD/ADHD is given simple, straightforward directions, it is helpful to teach the child to repeat and review the directions before starting on the task. This review and repetition of instructions counteracts the child's tendency to impulsively start an assignment without being certain of what is to be done. This procedure is taught simply by modeling (i.e., by asking the child what is to be done) and may be developed over time. Note that it is not always necessary to ask the identified ADD/ADHD child; the modeling procedure may be used with other children, too, so that the ADD/ADHD child is able to observe the imitation procedure.

Modeling Problem-Solving—This is an extension of the procedure of modeling instructions. After the process of repeating instructions to others and, ultimately, to himself, silently, the ADD/ADHD child may be taught an extension of this procedure whereby he continues self-talk with a problem-solving orientation. After gaining an understanding of the problem, the child must continue to ask himself questions about what he needs to do first. After knowing what to do, he must know *how* to do it (solve the problem), and, if there are alternative solutions, he must be able to discern which of these alternatives would be the most appropriate. Throughout this problem-solving process, the child will continue to engage in this self-talk, monitoring each step of the process and using the process to (mentally) check the accuracy of his work. This process is particularly helpful with math and writing assignments.

Teaching Organizational Structure—Learning structure and organizational skills will help the ADD/ADHD child avoid feeling overwhelmed by her classroom and homework assignments. Children who approach complex assignments with an organized plan certainly develop a greater sense of competency in their work. This, too, is an extension of the self-talk process as the child arranges work to be done in steps. The teacher can model these organizational approaches by showing the child how a large and complex assignment can be divided into a series of small assignments, with a logical progression from one to another, and leading to completion of the whole—or by approaching a simpler assignment one step at a time until completion. Then, when the child uses this approach, demonstrating it through her overt commentary, the teacher can reinforce the process (e.g., with verbal praise). Since many of these ADD/ADHD students have such significant problems with logical organization, learning such skills may develop quite slowly and only with much repetitive practice. However, once such habits are developed, they will serve the student in all learning processes throughout life.

Teaching Self-Monitoring—The child's work performance may be enhanced through the use of some periodic signal to help her develop the skill of self-monitoring. Such signals can be auditory (e.g., a tone heard via a tape recorder or a beep delivered by a watch) or inaudible, such as a vibratory signal (e.g., delivered by a device called the MotivAider®). These signals are designed primarily to teach the child self-monitoring skills and thus to increase her on-task behavior when performing a task. The overall effectiveness of the devices will be enhanced as the child develops increased awareness of on-task and off-task behavior. As with all of these skills, the ADD/ADHD child must practice many repetitions, and the general monitoring procedure itself must be reinforced for this skill to have lasting benefits. DuPaul has noted that the combination of "self-monitoring" with "self-reinforcement" has been effective in improving on-task behavior and academic accuracy, especially with older children.

Teacher-Centered Approaches

These strategies reflect changes that may be implemented by a teacher to facilitate adaptation of the ADD/ADHD child to the classroom and other school situations.

Providing Structure and Routine—Both are critically important for the child with ADD/ADHD. Often, difficulty is encountered by the ADD/ADHD child when moving from one class to another or from one activity to another. You will have to expend considerable effort planning and providing structure and routine in the classroom. Specifically, you must have a *written, planned sequence of daily classroom activities,* which must be *reviewed orally and left posted* (visual reminder of the routine). The basic daily structure of activities should remain consistent (e.g., pledge of allegiance, roll call, math class, recess, reading, lunchtime, art and music class, penmanship), but there should be variety within each daily activity to prevent boredom—another major problem for the ADD/ADHD child and other children as well. This way, the child knows to expect the same order of activities each day, but the component of an activity may vary (i.e., one time using audiovisual materials, another time a game activity, and another using real life or tangible materials as in a hands-on project). Providing such structure and routine and incorporating variation within the structure will certainly tax your creativity, but it will serve the needs of the ADD/ADHD child most effectively.

Avoiding Information Overload—This means *teaching to the capacity of the child's abilities to attend and accurately process information.* Be guided in this by an awareness of the child's general span of attention and with frequent checks to determine whether "the message sent" was, in fact, "the message received." The first step here is to focus on the communication needs of the ADD/ADHD child. Next, varying the length of the work period will give the child a greater probability of successful completion of the assigned work. As the child better handles small segments of an assignment or work activity, the work time span may gradually be increased, all the while reinforcing the child for successful work completion. If he has difficulty with an increased workload, drop back to an easier or smaller amount of work, allowing the child to experience success again. Then a slight increase may again be introduced and reinforced if successful. This way, a gradual approximation to a more desirable level of work output is developed. (In behavioral terms, this process is similar to the concept of "shaping.")

Establishing Behavioral Priorities—Focus on the behaviors of central importance for the ADD/ADHD child in the classroom. The greatest interference with the ADD/ADHD child's work output is not overactivity per se, but rather the child's impulsive style and distractibility. Establish (in writing) a list of those behaviors that interfere most with the child's abilities to attend, to learn, and to maintain work output. Note that many behaviors should be ignored. Minor activity problems like moving around in the seat, unusual postures, or humming and tapping, may not interfere with the child's work or even with the work of others around him. If such behaviors do receive attention (e.g., saying, "Stop that humming!"), they are then reinforced, will persist, and may even increase in frequency and intensity. Permitting the ADD/ADHD child some opportunity to move around, or to engage in some of the aforementioned behaviors, may actually be positively reinforcing after his work is completed. For example, the student may be told that he will be able to walk to the back of the room for free time *after* completing the assignment.

If noise is a general problem in the class (several children humming could be distracting), use a noise meter (available at some electronic supply centers) that gives a signal (ringing bell sound) if a certain level of noise is exceeded. The whole class may work together and receive a special privilege (e.g., popcorn party at end of week, field trip) if they keep the rings below a certain number—a number that allows for an almost guaranteed success. Then, once the class is successful, the criterion may be made more stringent. This framework encourages cooperative effort; all students will work with the ADD/ADHD child to help keep the noise level down by cues (e.g., verbal shushing) and by ignoring the noise generated by these peers. Again, this must be designed with initial success in mind—lenient at first and then more stringent.

If you are sufficiently flexible to allow some minor problem behaviors while focusing on dealing with these more critical behaviors, you will be most effective.

Selecting Relevant Consequences—All behavior is influenced by the consequence following that behavior. Here we will briefly discuss the "who, what, when, and where" of reinforcement and whether reinforcement should be positive or negative.

Who should provide consequences for behavior? The answer is simple: Anyone in a position to give it should provide feedback on behavior. In the school setting, this could include teacher, teacher's assistant, counselor, and peer tutor; at home it could be parents, tutors, relatives, friends, and outside counselors. Children—especially children with ADD/ADHD—need frequent feedback on their behavior and their academic work from multiple sources.

What are relevant consequences? This answer is fairly complex. ADD/ADHD children may be unique regarding effectiveness of consequences. While some of the more common positive reinforcers (Figure 8.1, Common Classroom Rewards) are effective with the ADD/ADHD child, other reinforcers—quite specific for a particular child—also must be determined and used on an individual basis. Also, rewards must be appropriate to developmental level (see Figure 8.2, Reinforcers by Age Group, on page 258).

Figure 8.1 COMMON CLASSROOM REWARDS

Homework reduction

Physical contact (hugs, pats, closeness)

Playing game with a friend

Computer access

Additional recess

Free time in class

Run errand/collect or distribute papers/other class job

Field trip

Class games

Tickets/stickers/a certificate/play money

Small toys (marble, car, doll, clay) or other prize

Breakfast or lunch with teacher

Time to finish homework in class

Reading special magazine or book

Food (cookies, raisins, banana chips, candy, gum, popcorn)

Listening to music on tape recorder (headphones)

Working with clay or play dough

Special pen or paper

Leading in a game

Being first in line

Skipping an assignment

Bringing something to class (Show and Tell)

Reduction of detention time

Figure 8.2 REINFORCERS BY AGE GROUP

SUGGESTED REWARDS FOR ELEMENTARY STUDENTS

1. Listening to stories or music on a tape recorder or phonograph with earphones.
2. Working in an art corner with special paper scraps and pieces of art materials, or at the easel.
3. Audiotaping a story for the class to listen to.
4. Being first in line.
5. Leaving class early for lunch.
6. Taking charge of a variety of activities, such as attendance taking, passing papers.
7. Getting a drink at any time without asking permission.
8. Being allowed to clean the chalkboards and erasers.
9. Arranging the toys on the game shelf, and being the first to pick a game to play.
10. Going to the library to work on a special project relating to a unit being studied.
11. Taking important messages to other teachers' rooms or to the office.
12. Tutoring a younger child in school.
13. Calling on students in the classroom. (Turn to the student and say, "Your turn to pick a student.")
14. Being able to look at magazines, special seasonal books, sports programs, etc., that are collected in a certain area in the room.
15. Being allowed to help the office secretary, custodian, cafeteria worker, or librarian for a 15-minute period.

SUGGESTED REWARDS FOR MIDDLE SCHOOL AND HIGH SCHOOL STUDENTS

1. Using a computer.
2. Doing extra-credit problems as an opportunity to raise grades.
3. Making up questions to appear on an upcoming test.
4. Choosing the display to go on a bulletin board.
5. Challenging the teacher or another student to a mind game, such as *Racko,* chess, or a computer game.
6. Reading magazines in a corner of the room.
7. Listening to selected tapes on a tape recorder.
8. Appearing as a guest lecturer in other classes.
9. Doing special crossword puzzles that involve skills related to the content areas.
10. Solving mystery problems involving situations that require application of math skills.
11. Being dismissed early from class in order to work in the office.
12. Audiotaping a story for a student who is having difficulty reading.

Since ADD/ADHD children satiate on consequences more rapidly than other students, they typically require many more potential (preferably positive) consequences in behavioral programs. For example, while playing a game that seems to be fun (positive reinforcers), after a time, an ADD/ADHD child may suddenly state, "I don't want to do this; let's do something else." (And to the person lacking information about ADD/ADHD, this abrupt change seems to occur without reason.) It has also been noted that, in general, the amount of reinforcement will influence the child's performance but has little effect on learning for the child with ADD/ADHD.

Regarding negative reinforcers (negative consequences to behavior), we consider both verbal (comments) and physical punishment (e.g., spanking). While there has been much controversy over the years about the usefulness of corporal punishment, the results of such negative reinforcers with the ADD/ADHD child are clear: Physical punishment is not effective and may even result in an increase in the frequency of behavior problems. Even negative verbal consequences, like critical scolding, can create embarrassment and cause deterioration of the child's self-concept and self-esteem. Only mild punishments—such as time-out and behavior-penalty (response-cost)—are recommended.

You can effectively use "soft reprimands" (quietly talking to the child so others will not hear the comment) as feedback for behavior that is only mildly aversive. When delivered without undue emotion, these "soft reprimands" are sometimes accompanied by a mild punishment (i.e., time-out or behavior-penalty).

When should consequences be provided? Another simple answer: *immediately and often*! ADD/ADHD children often have difficulty with delayed gratification. Thus, to be most effective, any reinforcement must be delivered as soon as possible after the behavior has occurred, and the reinforcements work best when they are provided frequently.

Many ADD/ADHD children have become accustomed to receiving negative reinforcers (i.e., criticism or other negative attention) for both misbehavior and lack of appropriate behavior. It is critically important to shift this emphasis and to give them frequent positive attention. Some clinicians estimate that it takes 10 positive comments to merely offset 1 negative one. In average home and school settings, consider how very often the child with ADD/ADHD receives negative comments or even punishment. (Parents and teachers may not even consciously register how often they give the child negative feedback.) This may give you an appreciation for how "stroke deficient" these children are. "Time-in" proponents recommend that the child be given positive comments or positive touches at least 100 times a day. Use a reminder system to help remember to provide frequent positive feedback. This reminder could be a watch that beeps; the MotivAider®, which provides an inaudible vibratory stimulus; or tokens that must be given to the child during class. Carrying these tokens in a waist pouch will also serve as a reminder to continue to give positive strokes to the child at the end of the period or day.

Positive consequences communicate to the child which behaviors are most desirable and which behaviors you want her to exhibit in the classroom or other situation. Negative attention, punishment, or critical comments, in general, only communicate to the child which behaviors are undesirable; they don't indicate which behaviors should be exhibited. Also, when the child knows which behavior is desired (i.e., appropriate), then punishment for the alternative inappropriate behavior is more effective.

Where should consequences be given? Again a simple answer: in as many situations and settings as possible. One problem with the results of many behavioral programs is transferring the learned skills from one setting to another (generalizing). Often, a skill developed in a specific context is exhibited only within that context. However, problem behavior in the classroom is more likely than not also problem behavior in the home, at the playground, at place of worship, and so forth. Plan for a behavior problem to be modified in several different situations. Combinations of negative consequences for the inappropriate behavior and positive consequences for the appropriate and desired behavior in multiple situations will result in changes that are most effective, long-lasting, and more generalized.

Using Response-Cost/Behavior-Penalty—(These two terms are used interchangeably.) Children with ADD/ADHD seem to be most influenced by this procedure. It is especially effective for young children up to adolescence. (Read carefully, for this is not negative reinforcement, but rather a creative twist on positive reinforcement.) Rather than doling out positive reinforcements one by one, in this procedure all reinforcements (e.g., points or tokens) are given at the beginning. The child's goal is to end with a prespecified minimum number of points or tokens in order to earn his reward. Inappropriate behavior results in points or tokens being taken. Goldstein and Goldstein (1990) have cogently stated that the child with ADD/ADHD so rarely gets all the rewards through positive behaviors that when all is provided up front, he has greater motivation not to lose these points (or tokens). This procedure has already been described; here we focus on several variations:

- *The individual case,* as described by Kendall and Braswell (1985): Here a child might initially be given twenty points or tokens. Whenever he makes a mistake, such as going too fast, omitting a step, or giving a wrong answer, a point or token is taken away as a cue for the child to stop and think before he answers. A brief explanation is provided as to why the point or token was taken away so that the child may learn and respond differently in the future.
- *The individual within a group:* Here the child begins with a set number of points determined by the range of a particular inappropriate behavior; for example, over a period of a week, blurting out answers up to a maximum of four times each day. Using this frequency as a guide, you can establish the criteria for success on a daily or weekly basis. (This depends on the age of the child and her need for immediate reward. For ages 8 or younger, a daily program may be sufficient.

However, design each child's program individually according to need.) If a daily program is acceptable, the child may receive six points or tokens in advance. Each time the child speaks out of turn, one point or token is subtracted. A 3″ × 5″ card may be placed on the desk with either the words, "Raise your hand to answer," or a drawing or picture of a child with hand raised (Figure 8.4), or both. When the child "blurts out," a slash mark, deleting one point, is put on the card. The child knows that the goal is to keep at least one point in order to receive some prearranged reward. A record is kept each day so that the criteria may be adjusted down to accommodate the child's improvement (e.g., when she blurts out only two times per day maximum). You may then give only four points or tokens. Of course, this procedure is always combined with immediate verbal praise when the child raises her hand, and praise for successful completion. Various behaviors may be selected that involve adherence to class rules in addition to the example given. Children who are able to work on more than one behavior or those who have prior experience working with individual behaviors (e.g., using picture cards described in Figure 8.4) may profit from use of a more complex "response-cost system," monitoring several of these behaviors. See Figure 8.4, Graphic Depiction of Rules, on page 262.

Figure 8.3 RESPONSE COST SYSTEM

Name:					*Date:*		
Behaviors	**Points**	M	T	W	TH	F	**Totals**
Out of Seat							
Talks Out							
Non Attending							
Noncompliance							
Disturbs Others							
Foul Language							
Fighting							
Off Task							
	Totals						

- *The response-cost lottery* (Wielkiewicz 1986): This program involves a small group of children within a class. In this program, the child is not required to compete with non-ADD children. Competing within a small group—and only with others who have similar problems—may allow for an increased probability

Name:	Response Cost Card					
Date:	M	T	W	Th	F	Total
Rule Above	Points Lost					

Name:	Response Cost Card					
Date:	M	T	W	Th	F	Total
waits turn						
Rule Above	Points Lost					

Name:	Response Cost Card					
Date:	M	T	W	Th	F	Total
works hard						
Rule Above	Points Lost					

Figure 8.4 Graphic Depiction of Rules (Note: A horizontal line may be used to divide each card so the upper portion may record points earned for compliance with the rule while the lower part may record points lost for non-compliance).

Name:	Response Cost Card					
Date:	M	T	W	Th	F	Total
pays attention						
Rule Above	Points Lost					

Name:	Response Cost Card					
Date:	M	T	W	Th	F	Total
quiets down						
Rule Above	Points Lost					

Name:	Response Cost Card					
Date:	M	T	W	Th	F	Total
raises hand						
Rule Above	Points Lost					

Figure 8.4 *(continued)*

Name:	Response Cost Card					
Date:	M	T	W	Th	F	Total
Is positive						
Rule Above	Points Lost					

Name:	Response Cost Card					
Date:	M	T	W	Th	F	Total
uses manners						
Rule Above	Points Lost					

Name:	Response Cost Card					
Date:	M	T	W	Th	F	Total
knows how to ignore						
Rule Above	Points Lost					

Figure 8.4 *(continued)*

of success for the child with ADD/ADHD. In this procedure, each child has a 3″ × 5″ card taped on his desk, with a specific number of blue slips (different color for each child) tucked under his card. Again, let's use the example of blurting out; it is determined that the child with the worst frequency of blurting out does so a maximum of up to four times per day. Then a total of six slips per child may be given, and each time a child blurts out, one slip is removed from under his card. At the end of the day, the slips remaining for each child are put in a box. At the end of the week, one slip is randomly drawn from the box, and the winner receives the predetermined reward. Each child knows that every time he loses a slip of his color paper, the chance for his color paper being drawn will be less. This provides an interesting variation of response-cost and introduces the concept of probability.

- *The attention training system:* This procedure, which is most frequently used to monitor off-task behavior, involves using a device that is placed on the student's desk and that is controlled remotely by the teacher. The student will receive points at regular intervals throughout the task with the device, which is set to deliver points at either one per minute or one per four minutes. However, whenever you see the student off task, no matter where in the classroom she is, you subtract a point. This reduction in points can be noted immediately by the student right at her desk, where a small red light is activated on top of the unit to cue the student and give feedback on her inappropriate off-task behavior. There are four buttons on the remote unit, which enable you to monitor four children at a time. At the end of the task, points are totaled and each monitored child receives rewards or free time according to the number of points that remain. Combined with verbal praise, this procedure can become a powerful aid. Interestingly, it is not disruptive to the class or the individual student involved. The only drawback for this procedure is that it may be too costly for most school budgets. The Attention Training System is available from the ADD Warehouse. A starter system will monitor one child ($318). A total of 4 children may be monitored (3 additional modules needed at $185 each).

  A similar program can be conducted using a flip card device (like a 3″ × 5″ holder for snapshots on a stand) on your desk, where each card is numbered. If a 20-minute assignment is given, the cards are turned to the number 20. Each time the child gets off task, one card is flipped to reduce the remaining points. At the end of the assignment, the card showing represents the child's points, which may be traded for some privilege. (The only drawback with this program is that it is probably limited to monitoring only one child, and that child must be seated close to your desk.)

Time-Out/Redirection—Time-out is a mild punishment and has been found to be quite effective with children who have ADD/ADHD. It is covered in detail in Chapter 4.

Time-out may be used primarily for the control of acting-out behaviors and persistent noncompliance. However, as Goldstein and Goldstein point out, teachers and parents must distinguish between noncompliance and incompetence. If the child with ADD/ADHD fails to comply with instructions in the classroom or in other school settings, you must look at how the instructions were given, whether the child received all of the message, or whether he responded impulsively or was misguided by distractions. Check to see if the child knew what to do and just didn't do it (oppositional and noncompliant), or if he really "missed the message" (incompetent, but consistent with behavior characteristic of ADD). Simply by asking, "(*Name*), what did I ask you to do?" you may be able to make this determination.

Another caution regarding use of time-out is that it is often overused and may become ineffective over time. Diminished effectiveness with time-out may also occur if the prime focus is on punishment, which never tells the child "what to do," only "what not to do." To maintain effective use of time-out, the procedure must be combined with a positive approach (see Chapter 4 on combining time-in with time-out).

While factors such as applications for time-out, use of a timer, rehearsal of time-out, and follow-up after time-out are all the same for school settings as for the home, two possible variations may change the procedure slightly in the school setting. The first involves the time criterion. Since time-out in the classroom may be used for several students, the time may vary from one to five minutes and not depend solely on the child's age. Use your judgment to determine whether a short (one minute) or long (five minute) time-out period should be used. This may vary with the child's age as well as according to the severity of the acting-out behavior.

Remember that time-out will work only if there is something positive for the child to return to. If a child has academic difficulty and continually experiences failure and criticism, she may actually come to enjoy longer and longer time-outs, because being removed from the classroom (where there is difficulty, failure and constant criticism) becomes desirable. Continual misbehavior would add time to the time-out (as the child is expected to behave more appropriately before being released). Should misbehavior continue, the child is told, "That's an additional five minutes" only twice, and—important to note—there is no lecturing or discussion about the misbehavior while the child is in time-out. All of her behavior while in time-out should be ignored, unless it becomes a danger to the child or others, or it makes it impossible for you to continue teaching. Should that be the case, the child should quickly be removed from the classroom.

The second variation is the place selected for time-out. Typically, the child will remain in the class and simply face a wall (not a window or a door or anyplace where he might find interesting things to look at). Note that for time-out, it is best not to send the child to a partitioned carrel, since that place should be associated with positive things and be reserved for use by any student who wishes to have a quieter place with fewer distractions.

Even though time-out is considered mildly punishing, it is perhaps best promoted as a time and place to "regain control" or "to bring oneself down" if emotionally upset or excited. If the child learns that when he becomes aware of his potential for acting out, he can voluntarily go to such a designated place in the classroom—or may briefly retreat to a mental "safe and quiet place" using a predetermined visualization—the time-out may be beneficial. Refrain from overusing time-out; excessive use may result in prolonged segregation of the child and may encroach upon his already fragile self-concept and diminished self-esteem. Overall, it is felt that time-out may be an intervention of "last resort," following implementation of generally more positive techniques as well as less restrictive aversive procedures such as response-cost.

Redirection as a substitute for time-out may be especially useful for younger children (below 8 years) and with older children whose mental age is within this range. Simply, redirection involves removing a child from one situation where acting out has started, or is about to occur, and placing that child in a different situation. If, for example, a child has become argumentative while participating in a classroom activity, she may be asked to join another group that is involved in a different activity. Very often, this change will interrupt the pattern of misbehavior. When more appropriate behavior appears in the alternate situation, this improved behavior may be reinforced with verbal praise and stroking (e.g., a pat on the shoulder).

Prevention Strategies—These intervention strategies are designed to ward off or prevent problems from occurring in the immediate or near future.

- *Employ success-oriented programs.* There is nothing better to promote future success than to focus on current success. The child with ADD/ADHD may experience so much failure that little is learned from yet another failure. About the only thing that occurs with failure is that self-esteem is further diminished, along with added deterioration of self-concept. Given sufficient loss, there is often associated depression and diminished motivation to achieve. It is critical that you build on small successes and changes rather than expecting large gains in the short term. Continue goal setting, allowing the child to set the pace for improvement. Often, parents and teachers become discouraged when behavioral programs fail to produce the immediate and dramatic changes that might occur with medication. While these behavioral changes are generally smaller, take comfort in the knowledge that what is being taught and maintained will result in lifelong skills that will aid the child repeatedly as he or she grows up and is faced with increasingly more challenging situations. Medication effects rapidly dissipate, but when these behavioral changes are maintained like other skills, the child's newly acquired adaptive behavior will become an asset for many years.
- *Review expectations regarding transitional situations.* As previously mentioned, it is difficult for the child with ADD/ADHD to move from one situation to the next. Situations that have different rules may present problems. Stoner and Green

(1992) found that less than 10% of children in the first three grades could state or identify rules pertaining to their own classroom. Going from the classroom to the playground or lunchroom may require a brief review of the primary rules that are appropriate to the new situation. Keep these rules simple, few in number, and posted for all to see during the review. Likewise, the child must be prepared for any unexpected changes in routine. Cuing behavior to prepare for the new situation may be helpful. Mental rehearsal, or role-playing what is required in the new situation, will greatly benefit the child. As Goldstein and Goldstein have noted, it is unwise to allow the child with ADHD to unwind and have free time before going to an assigned task. Instead, the child should be prepared to approach the task and free time becomes an appropriate consequence upon *completion* of the task.

WORKING WITH OR WITHOUT PARENT INVOLVEMENT

The most effective and powerful behavioral programs in the classroom will involve a child's parents. As DuPaul has noted, when both parent and teacher are actively involved in the treatment process, there is a greater probability of success. The use of a home-school approach gives you access to some of the most powerful reinforcers in the child's life. Selection of a combined home-school program, along with some of the classroom strategies already mentioned, provide you with the most powerful programs.

This is not an ideal world, however, and it will not always be possible—and sometimes not even recommended—that parents be involved in these programs. Why not? If you have noted that parents are especially harsh with their children, or a child reports almost daily spankings, you may decide that communication with the parents must be devoid of negative comments about the child; they could bring about further punitive actions from a parent. In such situations, it may be helpful to recommend a psychological evaluation, implement in-class strategies, and provide positive comments and praise about the child's successes wherever they can be found, while at the same time suppressing negative comments. Most parents, however, are interested, concerned, and cooperative when presented with observations about and requests for help with their child's problem behaviors in the classroom.

The recommended procedure for parent involvement may be first to implement some of the behavioral strategies directly in the classroom and in other school situations where the problem behavior occurs. For some children, this may be all that is needed. If you do not have adequate success, then parental involvement may be in order. The term "adequate success" is not synonymous with 100-percent behavioral control. In fact, 100-percent behavioral control is not only not required, it is perhaps not even desirable. With purely behavioral strategies, 100-percent control is simply not likely to occur; most teachers and most parents probably agree that improvement 80-to-90 percent of the time would be great. Teachers vary with regard to their individual tolerance for behavioral problems so judgments will be required for each ADD/ADHD child. With a little experimentation, you can decide which behaviors can be ignored, which ones will be priorities to target for behavior interventions, and to what degree improvement can be accepted without parental involvement before more formalized home-school programs are established.

Considerations of Developmental Levels

Developmental considerations play an enormous role in planning activities, learning, attention, and social-emotional reactions of children. The child with ADD/ADHD is often described as exhibiting characteristics of a "younger child," regardless of the actual chronological age of the child. Thus, just knowing that a child has been diagnosed as having ADD/ADHD is sufficient to warrant viewing that child's behavior from a different perspective. Often, the behavior exhibited is in direct contrast to the abilities demonstrated. Teachers will frequently remark that a child is quite bright, but that his or her behavior interferes with the realization of academic potential. A different perception of the child, allowing for the disorder, may influence your expectations of the child, communications with the child, allowances for misbehavior, reaction to misbehavior, and establishment of ultimate goals. Knowledge of appropriate behavior for children at various developmental levels is needed. An excellent resource is Piaget's *The Psychology of the Child.*

Baseline Level—Consider that a child's behavior at any point in development is the baseline level. Improvement may thus be geared toward slightly higher and higher levels using the concept of behavioral shaping. You, the teacher, must accept the child's behavior and set goals based on her baseline level. Expecting a child to make drastic changes and to conform to the behavioral level of a "normal" child of the same age causes significant stress and might certainly result in failure. Some teachers have established a policy that no exception will be made for the ADD/ADHD child, who is expected to assume the same responsibilities and exhibit the same behavioral organization as non-ADD peers. These teachers say, "She has to assume responsibility for writing homework assignments and bringing home necessary materials just like everyone else." Such expectations, though, may require a quantum leap in behavioral change in order for the ADD/ADHD child to achieve success (and this is often expected to occur without any guidelines or strategies offered by the teacher to help accomplish that leap). There are no magic changes for the ADD child. Strategic planning, many guidelines, and repetitive practice are needed for these behavioral changes to happen and for them to be reinforced gradually over time.

Age Variations—It is likewise clear that the younger ADD child will require different strategies, even within similar formats, compared with the older ADD child. Within the general sequence of antecedent events, behavior, and consequences (i.e., A-B-C), there are differences in each component for the younger versus older ADD child. First, communications, instructions, and expectations are modified for the younger child. Second, the behavior being considered is generally more simplified behavior with less stringent criteria. Third, reinforcers as consequences are different (see Figure 8.2). A change may typically be observed in structured behavioral programs. In home-school notes, faces (smiley, indifferent, and sad) may replace numerical ratings. Also, tokens may be used instead of points. Last, with many younger children, use a totally positive approach to behavior charts; older children may not only earn points but also lose them through fines for inappropriate behaviors.

Know the Normal Development of Attention—While there are many theories of attention and attention deficit, some developmental guidelines are needed for what is "normal" when attempting to deal with problem attentional behaviors that reflect deviance from normality. Some rough developmental guidelines have been reported by Jones (1994) based on research by Jean Regnell and published by Cooke and Williams (1987). These levels of normal development are reprinted with permission. (See Figure 8.5.)

Figure 8.5 THE LEVELS OF NORMAL DEVELOPMENT OF ATTENTION

Level 1 (birth to 1 year)
Level 1 is characterized by extreme distractibility, when the child's attention flits from one object, person, or event to another. Any new event (such as someone walking by) will immediately distract the child.

Level 2 (1 to 2 years)
Children can concentrate on a concrete task of their own choosing, but will not tolerate any intervention by an adult, whether verbal or visual. These children may appear obstinate or "willful," but in fact their attention is single-channeled, and all extraneous stimuli must be ignored in order to concentrate upon the task at hand.

Level 3 (2 to 3 years)
Attention is still single-channeled in that the child cannot attend to auditory and visual stimuli from different sources. A child cannot listen to an adult's directions while playing, but whole attention can be shifted to the speaker and back to the game, with the adult's help.

Level 4 (3 to 4 years)
The child must still alternate full attention (visual and auditory) between the speaker and the task, but now does this spontaneously without the adult needing to focus that attention.

Level 5 (4 to 5 years)
The child's attention is now two-channeled (that is, the child understands verbal instructions related to the task without interrupting the activity to look at the speaker). Concentration span may still be short, but the child can be taught in a group.

Level 6 (5 to 6 years)
Auditory, visual, and manipulatory channels are fully integrated and attention is well established and sustained.

These levels describe ages ranging from birth to 6 years. More complex levels of integrated auditory and visual attention modes, with the capacity for differential responding, are likely to occur beyond the age limits described. However, considerably more research is needed to delineate these more complex norms of attentional behaviors.

GENERAL SUGGESTIONS FOR WORKING WITH ADD/ADHD CHILDREN

A few general suggestions must be emphasized for teachers working with the child who has ADD/ADHD.

Verbal Praise

The child with ADD/ADHD rarely gets positive strokes or, when these are given, the ratio of positive to negative strokes is typically low. Positive strokes consist of rewards that may be classified as activity rewards, tangible rewards, and social rewards. Tangible rewards and activity-based reinforcers were discussed in Chapter 4. Here, examples of social rewards are presented (i.e., praise or verbal compliments). Perhaps the most complete list has been provided by Dr. Harvey Parker (1992) and is reprinted here with permission. (See Figure 8.6.)

Figure 8.6 EXAMPLES OF VERBAL PRAISE

Sample Compliments:

Great job!
You made it look easy.
Good thinking!
FANTASTIC!
I knew you could do it.
That's terrific.
That's good.
You figured that one out!
Keep at it.
I knew you could do it.
Right on!
Wow, you are good.
Keep up the good work.
GREAT!
Right on target.
You must be proud of yourself.
That's right.
Nice try.
You did very well today.
PERFECT!
I'm impressed with you.
UNBELIEVABLE!
Way to go!
Now you're cookin'!
Keep up the good work!
I like your style.
You really catch on quick.
I'm proud of you.
OUTSTANDING!
Much better.
Good for you.
A fine job.
Couldn't be better.
Good listening.
Well, aren't you something.
SENSATIONAL!
Looking great.
SUPERB!
Good answer.
You got it right!
You don't miss anything.
That was great.
You keep improving.
OUT OF SIGHT!

Reprinted with permission from *The ADD Hyperactivity Book of Schools* by Harvey Parker, 1992, Plantation, FL: Impact Publications.

Priming

Originally reported by Rapport (1978) and noted by DuPaul (1994), this procedure allegedly enhances the positive incentive of potential classroom reinforcers in behavioral programs. It requires that teacher and student review (which serves to remind the student of) the list of potential rewards for a behavioral intervention designed to improve the student's work output. Thus, if a behavioral contract is designed to allow the student "free time on the computer" after completion of a work assignment, the student is reminded of this reward *prior to* starting the assignment.

Proximity Control

Very often, you may obtain a desired behavior by simply assuming a quiet but stern facial expression standing with arms folded near the student. You act as a mildly aversive stimulus for the child, causing diminished misbehavior and perhaps stimulating a cognitive thought process that results in the child's beginning an appropriate behavior. For example, when the child is off task, playing with a pencil, your appearance and presence may suffice to cause the child to begin work without a word being uttered. Returning to work may then be reinforced with verbal praise or nonverbal touch from you. It must be emphasized that behavior change that occurs without verbal reminders must be reinforced, as it enhances independent functioning and assumption of responsibility.

Ignoring

Although this procedure was mentioned earlier, here we focus on the technique as a general suggestion. Active ignoring of some mildly inappropriate behavior is designed to withdraw attention and thus not reinforce the inappropriate behavior, nor to model to others (students in the class) that this behavior is worthy of attention. If this inappropriate behavior is a learned behavior, in the beginning of using the ignoring technique the behavior may temporarily increase (when attention is withdrawn), but it will eventually become weaker and extinguished. If this mildly annoying behavior does not change with the removal of all attention to it, then it is most likely one of the characteristic physiologically based activities shown by most children with ADD/ADHD. In the latter case, ignoring these behaviors may not remove them, but will prevent them from increasing in frequency or strength. Many teachers have found that a flexible approach to the child's excess movement, making noise, or playing with objects works best. Some teachers have even reported that allowing a child to hold something calming in his hand may not be disruptive and may actually result in the child's completing more work.

Several resources provide many more ideas for working with ADD/ADHD students in the classroom. These resources of books, videos, computer programs, etc. provide help for academic problems associated with ADD, as well as addressing the identified behavior problems often associated with ADD. The following reprint *101 Ways to Help Children With ADD Learn: Tips from Successful Teachers* may provide a fairly concise listing of various approaches. It is listed in the Appendix for resources.

Additional Suggestions*—Preferential seating* does not mean that the child should sit in the front of the class or even next to you. Sitting next to a child who models appropriate behaviors may be the best place—and of course the child should not be seated next to a busy doorway or near a noisy air conditioner.

A tape recorder or overhead projector may be very helpful for the ADD/ADHD child. The former may benefit the child who has difficulty writing or holding information in short-term ("working") memory long enough to write it down. The latter device may aid the child who gets distracted visually. It also allows the ADD/ADHD child to easily locate and follow important points that are emphasized with a pointer.

The Premack Principle dictates that the child do more unpleasant or more difficult work first, to be followed by easier work; the easier, more pleasant work then reinforces the prior, more difficult work and make it less aversive. In general, assign tasks deemed to be more difficult for ADD/ADHD students at the beginning of the class period.

With *self-monitoring*, you provide cues to signal the child to mark on a recording sheet whether she was on task or off task. Headphones may be used to present such cues as a beep or tone.

To use *response-cost*, a small (3″ × 5″) card may be taped to the child's desk. Periodically, while walking around the room, note when students are off task, marking their cards. Each child will begin with 50 points. You must know an approximate number of times a student will get off task to determine how many points will be needed to obtain a privilege. This procedure appears to be highly motivating for the child with ADD/ADHD.

Peer tutors are students who serve as "study buddies" or consultants for the ADD/ADHD child and can be very helpful in modeling appropriate behavior and providing information when possible.

Special materials. Several additional points are made by Rief (1996) in her video on inclusion procedures. It is worth emphasizing some of these in this section:

1. *Privacy boards*, made of heavy cardboard, provide partial isolation to lessen distractions and are an alternative to study carrels (which Rief refers to as office areas). Privacy boards are inexpensive and are easy to make. They are also available from the Center for Applied Psychology (see Resources for address).

2. *Graph paper* may be especially helpful for those students who have difficulty with math— and especially with visual-spatial alignment of numbers. It may also be useful for students who exhibit a significant variation in writing numbers. Initially, large-square graph paper may be used. The size of the squares may then be gradually reduced to allow the child to systematically reduce the size of his numbers and to write them more consistently.

3. *Computer paper*—the kind used in dot-matrix printers—may be helpful to those students who have general difficulty with handwriting. Lines are larger and the child may be encouraged to write only on the white spaces. Gradually the size of

paper may be reduced, and writing may be then done with special handwriting paper (i.e., larger lines separated by a dotted line across the middle). You can continue to reduce paper size as the child shows improved fine-motor coordination.

Special signals. Work out a nonverbal signal to use with a particular child to communicate a reminder that, in most cases, is designed to get the child to stop a certain activity (e.g., putting finger over lips when child is talking out of turn). A signal could likewise be used to remind a child to do something (e.g., tapping on nose to cue to return to work). A nonverbal signal may also be used as a positive nonverbal reinforcement (e.g., a "thumbs up" sign) when a child finishes a task but isn't close enough for you to give verbal reinforcement.

Multi-sensory instruction. Many children with ADD/ADHD also have learning disabilities. Instruction may be more effective for both of these groups of students when it is presented visually and auditorily; give instruction in written form, but also read the instructions prior to having the child begin the task. To optimize learning, it is best that information be processed in all three modes of a task (e.g., spelling: [1] read the word; [2] hear the word, and [3] write the word).

DEALING WITH PROBLEMS CHARACTERISTIC OF ADD/ADHD

Several of the problem behaviors commonly associated with ADD/ADHD may actually reflect underlying physiological processes. For example, the child with ADD/ADHD generally has a lower level of activation in the Reticular Activating System or RAS, creating a physiologically based low level of alertness. Likewise, hyperactivity and poor fine-motor coordination associated with ADD/ADHD are apparently neurophysiologically based and appear to be related to deficiencies in neurotransmitters. While some of these problem behaviors that are neurophysiologically based may be difficult to manage without medications, several other behavioral characteristics do respond to behavioral as well as other interventions. Here we discuss specific steps a teacher can take to improve such behaviors in the school setting.

Excess Motor Activity

Children with ADD, and especially those with ADHD, exhibit a lowered arousal level, and excessive motor activity is believed to represent the child's attempt to maintain a more alert aroused state. Without such activity, the child may become quite sleepy; in fact, many of the children do actually fall asleep in class. Generally such motor activity in girls tends to be excessive talking (which has greater social acceptance), while boys will fidget, get out of their seats, or act out (which is less socially desirable behavior). While talking and moving around are not, of themselves, bad behaviors, they can become inappropriate and undesirable in the classroom setting. Such excessive actions tend to garner negative attention and often allow them to avoid assignments that are perceived as difficult and mostly "boring." With ADD/ADHD kids, some of this motor activity may always be going on, so you must be somewhat flexible in this regard. Scheduling time for movement may be beneficially incorporated into the class schedule. Be aware also that this problem behavior may vary with medication effects, diet, stress, and emotional factors—some of which may remain unknown. However, some improvement in the classroom may be obtained with the following steps:

STEPS TO CONTROL EXCESS MOTOR ACTIVITY

1. Establish the rules and limits for these activities, keeping in mind the physiological basis for the behavior.
2. Develop predetermined signals that can cue students as to when to be quiet and when to talk (e.g., finger to lips or red light for quiet; green light for talking).
3. Establish a specific consequence for breaking the rule, such as loss of recess time or loss of points, tokens, or tickets.
4. Use students who obey the rules as models by reinforcing their quiet behavior with verbal praise. (Do not, however, compare the children.)
5. Practice using cognitive mediation by asking students who talk or who are out of their seats, "What should you be doing at this moment?"
6. Use many more positive consequences for appropriate quiet behavior, with (fewer) negative consequences for talking or being out of the seat.
7. You may use movement or talking as a positive consequence (i.e., privilege) for maintaining quiet or restricting movement at specified times or during certain activities. Also, other times for these behaviors may be prearranged (e.g., soft talking in designated areas allowed after work is completed).
8. Use stretch breaks, exercise, or brief relaxation exercises to assist in self-control of motor movements.
9. Integrate periods of active learning with seat work. Some teachers have students stand up for review of math facts (e.g., multiplication tables) and randomly call on students. This will help to maintain attention as well as allow for some movement.
10. Allow students to become more aware of their need to move; they can ask to move to a study carrel or to even work standing up.

Blurting Out Answers

Every teacher has at one time or another had problem children who blurt out answers instead of raising their hands and being called on to answer. This impulsive response style is one of the primary characteristics of ADD/ADHD. It is a basic lack of behavioral control. This characteristic is another one that has physiological undercurrents and may only be controlled to a degree.

STEPS TO CONTROL BLURTING OUT ANSWERS

1. Review and post rules regarding raising one's hand and being called on to obtain permissions (i.e., to answer a question, get assistance, go to the bathroom, etc.). In addition to posting written rules or verbalizing them, you may tape a card on the child's desk depicting the rule (see Figure 8.6).
2. Ignore those who blurt out answers and fail to raise their hands.
3. Praise those children who do raise their hands, and use them as models. Remember, never compare one child with another; simply give the praise to the child who does the right thing. Make the praise specific, as, "Charles, you followed the rule and raised your hand to answer—very good. Now what is . . .?"
4. When a child (who has blurted out before) does raise her hand, direct attention to her immediately.
5. Monitor the number of times each day that the ADD/ADHD child raises his hand to answer. Reward weekly improvement over each child's baseline levels and then over the previous week's performance. A simple count of the number of times the child raises his hand to answer may be kept from week to week. The count from the first week before the problem is addressed is used as the baseline. The intervention may start in the second week. For example, you may tape the card on the child's desk with a picture of a student raising his hand. In addition to counting the number of appropriate behaviors, give verbal praise and some back-up reward when a specific goal is reached.

Getting Off Task—Distractibility

Getting off task may be related to many factors. A novel stimulus (e.g., a siren) attracts attention. Children with ADD/ADHD satiate more rapidly even on interesting tasks. Boredom may turn these children to other interests, sometimes to things that have been brought with them to the class in anticipation of experiencing boredom. For those with additional learning disabilities (commonly associated with ADD/ADHD), there is the likelihood of experiencing frustration and difficulty in doing the work. As a result, a child may quickly lose motivation to continue working on an assignment.

STEPS TO CONTROL GETTING OFF-TASK

1. Use preferential seating in the class so that cues/signals may be given and the student's work may more easily be monitored.
2. Positively reinforce students who are on task. A soft pat on the shoulder (nonverbal reinforcer) may be sufficient. Be aware also of those students who respond poorly to verbal praise while they are on task. Elaborate verbal praise, in some cases, may actually cause those students to get off task.

3. Reinforce for completed work; this emphasizes the importance of continuing work to completion.
4. Divide assigned work into smaller work components to help the ADD/ADHD child. Knowing how long a child may maintain on-task work or about how many problems, sentences, and so on, he can do in one sitting will help you in dividing up the work. The more you know about how to structure success for the child, the better the outcome will be for you both.
5. Make it "OK" not to understand, to express frustration, and to ask for help. Many students get off task when they hit a snag—a segment of the assignment they perceive as being too difficult for them, or one they simply don't understand fully. The child must realize that he or she can communicate the difficulty to you, and then continue to work.
6. Utilize some of the self-monitoring procedures described earlier in this chapter.
7. Use privacy boards and allow the child to work in more isolated parts of the room or in study carrels.
8. Plan for more active involvement in learning tasks to reduce distractibility.
9. Use nag tapes or other devices to cue the child to stay on task, or to filter out excess, distracting noise.
10. As suggested by Dr. Mel Levine, teachers may use *reminder cards* taped to the desk or notebooks. Messages might include verbal reminders "Am I tuning out?" or "Am I listening to noise instead of the teacher?" Other reminder cards may simply have a nonverbal cue for appropriate behavior (e.g., cartoon picture of child doing work at desk).

Poor Attentional Skills (Visual/Auditory)

Difficulty in listening, difficulty in following directions, and difficulty in paying attention are all common problems for children with ADD/ADHD. The basis for all of these difficulties is poor attentional skills. Some children have most difficulty with information that is presented visually; others—a minority—have difficulty with material that is presented through the auditory sense modality.

STEPS TO CONTROL POOR ATTENTIONAL SKILLS (VISUAL/AUDITORY)

1. Actively involve the student in the learning process. Call out names randomly for answers. For example, in teaching multiplication tables, randomly name children to give answers.
2. Use high interest material and special projects related to concepts being taught to increase the student's interest.
3. Use frequent questions to ensure that specific bits of information are learned, or simply rephrase questions to foster better involvement.

4. Identify critical bits of information by actually stating, "This is something that you will need to pay attention to." Often, too, a great attention getting device is to stop talking completely and pause; on most occasions, students will stop what they are doing and turn their focus on you.
5. Repeat important information and present it in different sense modalities (e.g., written [visual] and oral [auditory]). Information is processed best with redundancy and repetition. In addition to your auditory and visual presentations, have the student write the material as well, to involve yet a third sense modality—kinesthetic.
6. Print critical information in bright colors, write on the board with colored chalk, and use bright-colored paper or highlighters to help draw attention.
7. Use prompts through teacher's aides or nag tapes via headphones to help the child with ADD/ADHD get started and continue working. In class, prompt with questions such as, "Joseph, what is it that you need to be doing right now?" to provide cognitive stimulation which should cue the child to start (or continue) work. Initially, avoid direct requests lest the child become dependent on your cue in order to begin work. It is far better if the idea to begin work comes from the child. Once this happens, you may say, "OK, you know what to do—now do it."
8. Provide frequent reinforcement—praise or a soft touch on the shoulder—for those who pay attention. Use statements such as "Joe, you listened really well and you got the answer—good for you" or "I'm really proud of the way everyone started working right after I gave the directions" or "I really appreciate the way everyone looked at me while I gave directions."
9. Use novelty to help elicit attention. Children with ADD/ADHD often respond and act like any other child in novel and challenging situations. In fact, novelties that might elicit mild anxiety in normal children may be beneficial to the ADD/ADHD child. There is, of course, a delicate balance that exists in choosing materials that are novel and stimulating and those that represent such a dramatic change that the child would have difficulty coping. Remember, the child with ADD/ADHD will have some difficulty adapting to drastic changes and transitions.
10. Use an overhead projector; it will allow you to use graphics and to visually emphasize points of instruction. It will also allow you to reveal only those portions of the material you are discussing at the moment. This helps the child to focus on what is relevant.
11. Use specific cues to denote where and when the child's attention is required. Rief (1993) terms these "point-and-go" signals.

Work Not Completed

This problem is intimately related to the problem of getting off task. Put simply, if the child gets off task to a significant degree, he will probably not complete the work assignment, whether it is classwork or homework. Once students develop poor work habits in class or at home, this pattern is likely to generalize to the other setting as well. To some extent, this problem may be resolved with the development of good class- and homework habits. Because of a poor sense of time, frustrations over the work, and various distractions, problems completing work may persist. However, establishing a consistent habit of appropriate work behavior will certainly be an important step toward successful work completion. Remember that children with ADD/ADHD have many problems with planning, organization, and time estimates. Remember, also, that habits develop slowly. Don't expect the child to "magically" develop these learning habits overnight. If you have ever tried to develop a new habit, you know it can be a very slow process with many setbacks along the way.

STEPS TO CONTROL WORK NOT COMPLETED

1. Monitor the input. Determine whether the child knows what to do by asking questions regarding class assignments or by using a homework monitoring system at home.
2. Teach the student (through modeling) how to self-monitor to plan and organize an assignment.
3. Teach the student how to self-monitor her progress toward a goal. Teach her to use sub-goals and a time schedule, and to check and see if she is "on course" and "on schedule." Use positive reinforcements as each sub-goal is reached to provide incentive and motivation to continue.
4. Provide periodic reminders (both visual and oral), so that the child is aware of the consequences for incomplete work and for work completed.

Confusion Over Directions

This problem centers around attention. When attention falters during the presentation of task instructions, there is a breakdown of the information processed, which may result in confusion and operation on incomplete facts.

STEPS TO CONTROL CONFUSION OVER DIRECTIONS

1. For each task, provide simple, clear, and concise directions whenever possible.
2. When directions are unnecessarily complex, involving sequential planning, break them down and present the task step-by-step, providing reinforcement for completion of each step.
3. Present directions both in writing (visual sense modality) and orally (auditory sense modality) and then post the written directions.
4. Check to be sure "the message sent" was indeed "the message received." Sometimes it is best to call on someone who usually *does* get directions correct-

ly, then praise that student for his accurate feedback of the assignment or task. This will demonstrate that knowing what to do is important, and it does pay off (child gets a positive stroke). And when the correct answer is given, the child with ADD/ADHD is then allowed to privately revise any initial misperception he may have had without the embarrassment of exposing his confusion aloud to the class.

5. You may find it beneficial to role-play and then rehearse what any child may do when he does not fully understand the directions for an assignment. Although this process might be obvious to most students, it well may not be obvious to the child with ADD/ADHD.

Disorganization

Many children who have ADD/ADHD are disorganized. Impulsivity, careless errors, and rushing through assignments lead to poorly organized work, confusion, and frequent forgetting of some part of the assignment. Such students may fail to complete all the work assigned because they have missed or misinterpreted what is needed to complete that assignment—or if they complete the work, they may forget to bring the work back to school!

STEPS TO CONTROL DISORGANIZATION

1. Model organizational behavior patterns that are critical for the child to develop. This might include a neatly organized desk, planned lessons and activities, and an "everything in its own place" routine for materials, supplies, and books in the classroom.
2. Post assignments and review them orally to aid the child in copying the assignment.
3. Use a "study buddy" system, so students can double-check homework assignments, due dates, and so forth, even after leaving school.
4. If at all possible, enlist the active cooperation of the parents for this vast problem and use a Homework Assignment Sheet or HAS. (See Chapter 6, Figure 6.2.)
5. In the classroom, initial on the HAS that the child has written the correct assignment and has the needed books and other materials to complete it.
6. Have the parent supervise completion of the work and initial on the HAS that the work was done and that it was filed in the appropriate place in the school bag.
7. Failure to comply with a step in this sequence should result in a specific negative consequence (e.g., no privileges when materials are not brought home one day).
8. By developing the kind of organizational routine illustrated on the HAS, the child will learn a pattern of habits that forces her to (self-)monitor her steps in organization of work, using a checklist procedure.

9. Using this type of monitoring system on the HAS will encourage the student to mark a calendar with due dates for special projects.
10. Focus on improvements in neatness and organization with compliments as often as possible.
11. Follow up regularly with participating parents. (They need positive feedback, too!)

Poor Handwriting

Children with ADD/ADHD also frequently have poor handwriting. This varies in degree from severe (dysgraphia) to mild (i.e., sloppy work, at times, where the child has shown in the past that he is capable of better work). In the latter case, the child's work may be sloppy because he rushes through it with a generally impulsive style.

STEPS TO CONTROL POOR HANDWRITING

1. Provide each student with his own sample of your rules for written work. This may include type of paper, the placement and sequence of identifying information (i.e., name, class, date), whether to use ink or pencil, whether proofreading is necessary, whether script or print is acceptable, as well as any other specific criteria you have for this level of instruction.
2. Use graph or computer paper to aid the child with fine-motor coordination problems. It may be especially helpful if the child starts with very large graph or computer pages; then gradually reduce the size of the squares or lines (using a copy machine with the enlargement-reduction feature). This will allow you to shape the size of the writing of letters or numbers gradually as coordination improves.
3. Help the student use a cognitive mediation approach while writing. This use of self-talk forces the student to slow down and pay closer attention to the details of her writing; it involves commenting on every movement involved in writing. While it is somewhat laborious at first, students who use this procedure do slow down and do generally produce neater work. Because of the verbal component (self-talk) correlated with visual and kinesthetic cues, there is more whole-brain involvement in the graphic writing process.
4. Of course, reinforce for those papers done neatly; also be alert for and reinforce noticeable improvements within a paper.
5. In addition to verbal praise for better fine-motor control in handwriting, posting the student's better work will provide a model for him as well as a reinforcement.
6. When a student has previously demonstrated better handwriting, sloppy papers may be returned to be redone.

7. Be flexible with students exhibiting dysgraphia. Note that students with severe problems who show little variation in their poor handwriting may function better using an alternative means to complete work, like a computer—or perhaps communicating some information using tape recorders. It may be necessary for you to drastically reduce the amount of written work, and tests may best be administered orally. According to Dr. Mel Levine these techniques are called "bypass strategies" to circumvent or work around a child's dysfunctions.

Homework Problems

Though these problems are discussed in detail in Chapter 6, it must be again that solving homework problems involves both teachers and parents helping the student.

STEPS TO CONTROL HOMEWORK PROBLEMS

1. Coordinate with parents the use of a Homework Assignment Sheet that is checked at school and at home.
2. Assign a "study buddy" to help double-check accuracy of recording the assignments and to provide back-up information when needed.
3. Write assignments on the board and review each one orally.
4. Develop an assignment sequence in advance and make it available to parents if needed.
5. You may need to individually modify assignments for those students who also have specific learning disabilities in reading, spelling, math, or writing. If the learning disability is in writing, a general reduction of written work assigned is needed—and perhaps you should allow that child to use a word processor to complete some assignments.
6. Many teachers do not wish to continue to check homework assignments, especially when there are several students in the class having problems getting assignments written down. A general solution is to teach the students how to do this task with training exercises conducted on a regular basis. An excellent resource for this is the "Skills for School Success" program by Archer and Gleason (1989).

Social Skill Problems

Although problems in peer relationships are not found with all children who manifest characteristics of ADD/ADHD, such difficulties are encountered with sufficient frequency to warrant their inclusion here. Considering the ADD/ADHD child's difficulty in controlling impulsive tendencies, problems with rule-governed behavior, and the often noted low-frustration tolerance, it is not surprising that many such children have problems with aggression. In social play, their characteristic difficulty playing by the rules, taking turns, and simply listening and following directions may result in some upsets on the playground, in the lunchroom, and while riding on the school bus. School problems related to ADD/ADHD behavior are not limited to the classroom; they are exhibited in other school-related activities as well.

Steps to Control Social Skill Problems

1. Post and orally review rules for the school-related activity or situation just prior to the child's going into that situation.
2. Also review the consequences for breaking those rules. Rules and consequences should be reviewed daily, especially during the beginning of the year and periodically thereafter.
3. Incorporate a "behavior report card" for recess, lunchtime, or on the bus as part of an overall behavior program (either solely school based or home-school based. (See the Behavior Report Card on p. 221, in Examples of School Notes.) This "report card" covers both appropriate and inappropriate behavior.
4. Generally focus positively on the more appropriate "alternative" behavior. (See Chapter 4 on the time-in concept.)
5. Set up more structured play activities wherein appropriate behaviors are more likely to occur, and then those more appropriate behaviors may be encouraged often.

MEDICATION ISSUES

As a treatment for the symptoms of ADD/ADHD, the use of stimulant medication has been—and continues to be—controversial. This book does not cover those issues; suffice it to say that for many years, stimulant medication has been used effectively as documented in volumes of clinical and scientific research. (See the section Medication Information for Clinicians in Chapter 2.)

Role of the Teacher

A child with ADD/ADHD is often first identified by referral from a teacher. Comparative analysis of the child's behavior within a developmental framework, such as the classroom, often provides critical information in the assessment process and ultimate diagnosis of the condition. Given the demands and expectations of the classroom, it is often the first place that ADD/ADHD symptomatology is manifested. Thus, teachers play an essential role in the assessment and diagnostic phase.

The question often arises, "Should teachers diagnose ADD/ADHD?" The answer, of course, is no, but their input is essential for such diagnostic impressions. Another question that one often encounters is, "Should teachers tell parents that the child needs medication?" Again, the answer is negative.

What you can say to a parent is, "I've noticed that your child has frequent difficulty staying on task, blurts out answers, and just cannot sit quietly very long. I think that these behaviors are a problem for him and may be preventing him from doing as well, academically, as he may be capable of performing. I really think that this is something you may wish to talk about with your pediatrician. I also think that a referral for psychological evaluation would give some additional information to see if he also shows evidence of a learning disability that could be affecting his performance." This type of narrative illustrates how you might communicate to the parent by *objectively focusing on* the child's *presenting problems behaviors* in the classroom *rather than suggesting a diagnosis* or a treatment for these problems.

After a child's condition has been assessed and determined to be ADD/ADHD, some potential interventions may be suggested to you. These may be coordinated by some professional outside the school (i.e., pediatrician, counselor), or by the in-house school psychologist. Whichever is the case, you may have continuing involvement in the treatment process in the following ways:

1. **Monitoring medication and behavioral program effectiveness:** Medication schedules often need several adjustments and can involve various combinations of medications. Since these dosage adjustments and introduction of or discontinuance of various medications often occur over a period of time (several weeks to several months), you are usually in the best position to rate the effectiveness of this medical component. (Several rating scales have already been mentioned and are listed in Appendix B.) The ultimate goal in using a medication regime is maximal behavioral control with minimal side effects and minimal interference with learning and social interactions. The current emphasis is not to find the highest dose for behavioral control, but to use a lesser level that still allows for adequate behavior management. In fact, with some of the mild-to-moderate cases, a behavior component without medications may be implemented first. Then, whatever behaviors remained to be addressed would be the target for a medication regime. Teacher ratings may be required to assess the impact of a behavioral management program without medical intervention, too.

2. **Monitoring medication side effects:** A reporting form for the teacher is provided in Figure 8.7. This form enables teachers to communicate with the child's physician regarding observations of the child. It is critical that any teacher who has a student on medication know:

   a. what medication(s) the child is taking

   b. the dose

   c. the overall medication schedule

   d. the name and phone number of the physician

   One primary concern when medications are used is side effects. An overmedicated child often appears drugged. Conversely, one of the most serious concerns

S-ADHD-RS MEDICATION MONITORING FORM

Name John School ______
Teacher Ms. Brown Grade 4 Age 9 yr 10 mo.
Physician Dr. Mach Date ______
Completed by Ms. Brown Parent ______ Teacher ✓
How long has this child been on medication? 1 month
Has there been a change in prescription or dosage? yes

Typically, children improve their behavior when placed on medication; however, not all behaviors respond favorably.

Behaviors
Rate the following current behaviors using the scale below:

1 = No longer a problem	4 = No improvement
2 = Lots of improvement	5 = Behavior is worse
3 = Good improvement	6 = Major deterioration
	N = Never a problem

Behavior	Rating	Total
ADHD Symptoms		
Attention	2	
Impulsivity	3	
Hyperactivity	3	8
Social Symptoms		
Peer Interaction	3	
Self Concept	2	
Social Skills	2	
Outbursts	2	9
Academic		
Reading	3	
Math	2	
Written Language	3	8
Classroom Behavior		
Complete Assignments	2	
Ability to Organize	3	
Noncompliant	3	
Out of Seat	3	
Verbal Interruptions	2	13

Side Effects (if any) Rate intensity: 1=none; 2=low; 3=mild; 4=moderate; 5=high; 6=very high

Appetitle Loss	1
Insomnia	1
Headaches	1
Stomach Ache	2
Tics	1
Irritability	2
Depression	2

Would you recommend that medication be continued? YES
Has the student made substantial gains since medication? YES
Comments:

Figure 8.7

S-ADHD-RS MEDICATION MONITORING PROFILE

Week(s) 5 After Medication

Name John Date ______ Grade 4

Physician Dr. Mach Teacher Ms. Brown

Behaviors Associated with ADHD

ADHD Symptoms				Social Symptoms				Academics			Classroom Behavior				
Score	AT	IP	HY	PI	SC	SS	Ob	RD	MA	WL	CA	AO	NC	OS	VI
6															
5															
4															
3															
2															
1															
N															

AT = Attention
IP = Impulsivity
HY = Hyperactivity

PI = Peer Interaction
SC = Self Concept
SS = Social Skills
OB = Outbursts

RD = Reading
MA = Math
WL = Written Language

CA = Complete Assignments
AO = Ability to Organize
NC = Non Compliant
OS = Out of Seat
VI = Verbal Interpretations

Medication Side Effects

Score	AI	IS	HA	SA	TI	IR	DP
6							
5							
4							
3							
2							
1							

AL = Appetite Loss
IS = Insomnia
HA = Headaches
SA = Stomach Ache
TI = Tics
IR = Irritability
DP = Depression

Figure 8.8

in using stimulant medication is the appearance of a tic disorder called Tourette's syndrome. Sometimes, when inappropriate medications are used (as with an incorrect assessment or diagnosis), a child may show an increase in inappropriate behaviors rather than fewer inappropriate behaviors.

3. **Cooperative behavioral programs:** In addition to ratings on the effectiveness of medications and possible side effects, the teacher of the child with ADD/ADHD is often asked to participate in cooperative home-school behavioral programs. While such programs do require time to complete forms and monitor behavior, clinical studies have shown that no additional time is required over and above that normally expended by the teacher in routine attempts to deal with the ADD/ADHD child's problems. There is no magic involved in behavioral programs; improvements typically are not dramatic but occur slowly and gradually over a period of time. However, what the child acquires is lifelong skills. Additionally, when asked about the most significant factor that helped them through school, many adults who suffered with ADD/ADHD as children replied that it was a special teacher who was supportive, understood the problem, and took the extra time to help the child accommodate to and to cope with the disability. These are the lasting benefits that come from a positive history of interactions within behaviorally structured programs. It stands in marked contrast to those children with a history of ADD/ADHD who received only medication. Long-term studies show a clear advantage for children who received both medication and behavior management. It is also believed that the enhanced interactions within behavioral interventions greatly contributed to the more positive outcomes.
4. **Inclusive Classroom Behavioral Program:** A program published by The Center for Applied Psychology, Inc., is entitled, "The AD/HD Classroom Kit" by Cheryl McNeil, Ph.D. In contrast to many programs for ADD/ADHD students that focus solely on these children, this program is designed is to be used with all children in the classroom, and according to the manual, "uses peer pressure to augment the behavioral expectations." Students are divided into four groups and each group has a name (picked by the students) and a leader (picked by the teacher). Throughout the day the groups (not individuals) can earn "happy face or sad face points" which are tracked on a "happy/sad face" chart. Then, at the teacher's discretion, the groups can play the Rewards Target Game if they have more "happy face" than "sad face" points. Those who don't meet this criterion simply watch. In the Rewards Target Game, a child (usually the leader of the group with the highest ratio of happy to sad face points) throws a Velcro ball at a target with various numbers. A correspondingly numbered reward card is selected and students get to play or have that reward. Some rewards may be tangible (e.g., a cookie); others involve an activity (e.g., acting like their favorite animal) or playing a short

game (e.g., charades). If a "balloon card" is drawn, a balloon is popped (two balloons, each having a *reward slip* inside, would have been blown up previously). When the balloon is popped, all students playing the game get the reward that was inside the balloon. After each game, the happy/sad face chart is erased and behavior is observed for the next round.

This type of behavioral procedure allows the teacher to

a. review all rules (that will get happy face points)
b. use peers to encourage good behavior
c. provide an incentive to work quietly on assignments
d. use modeling by other students for good example
e. work on appropriate behavior during transitions (difficult for ADD/ADHD kids) from game to work activity

Should a student show an unacceptable behavior he may be cued to change by the teacher (or by his group leader), who holds up two fingers, signaling that the child has two choices—either (a) follow the rules or (b) receive a sad face point for their group. While a group's solidarity is important to develop with this approach, if one child causes a group to obtain few rewards (i.e., always losing to other groups), this child may be rotated to other groups. This change may allow more than one group to function more adequately, with minimal negative effect upon the identified child. Other procedures may also then be utilized to assist this child in further development of appropriate behavior. With the exception of more severe forms of ADHD—and especially those with co-morbid oppositional defiant disorder or conduct disorder—this program appears to be an excellent one for general development and maintenance of appropriate behaviors.

COMPUTER-ASSISTED PROGRAMS

There has been an increasing number of computer-based programs to assist both parents and teachers with general information, diagnosis/treatment planning, education, and treatment of the child with ADD/ADHD. Two of these programs appear applicable for teachers in the school and classroom situation.

A program developed by Dr. Judy Wood is entitled, "Reaching the Hard to Teach." This computerized program uses the SAALE (Systematic Approach for Adapting the Learning Environment) model to identify "at-risk" students for special interventions and strategies. The Intervention Checklist appears especially helpful, covering characteristics of the setting and the student's present performance level in many different environments (e.g., classroom, cafeteria, library, P.E., etc.) and activities (e.g., note taking, tests, homework issues, etc.). It supports co-teaching, teaming, and inclusion as well as an individualized approach to the IEP (Individualized Educational Program). Many practical tips are provided for giving directions and using the chalkboard; the checklist for Rules and Routines is also very helpful. This program is available from Judy Wood, Inc.

Another program, available from the Center for Applied Psychology in King of Prussia, Pennsylvania, is entitled, "The Self-Controlled Classroom: A Breakthrough in Classroom Management." This program may be used by one child or the whole class in monitoring specific behaviors. The program sets and tracks progress toward goals, provides children with immediate reinforcement, sends progress reports to parents, and produces reward certificates.

CHAPTER 9

General Activities and Games

INFORMAL SKILL DEVELOPMENT

Many children with ADD/ADHD look forward to school's letting out. They rush home and can't wait to engage in some favorite activity in which they excel. This may be riding a bike, or playing Nintendo©, or perhaps engaging in some formal sport like football or basketball. Fine-motor coordination for these ADD/ADHD kids may be somewhat compromised, but many excel at sports that require good gross-motor coordination. However, some of these children have problems in social relationships and may prefer noncompetitive activities that allow for intermittent interaction with other children. In sports, this may be running track or swimming. A more casual activity might be bike riding. With optional social interaction, the ADD/ADHD child is free to make contact periodically and then move out on his own again. Being in charge of interactions allows the child to avoid undue social pressure and stress. Parents must be sensitive to what activities may be best suited for their ADD child.

The best recommendation for recreational activity for the child with ADD/ADHD is swimming. It is excellent exercise, a good outlet to dissipate energy, and an activity where the child mostly competes with himself or herself. While some of the initial training may be considered distasteful or even boring, it is probably the only thing that does turn them off to this activity. Even when they don't complete swimming lessons, many of these children may simply enjoy floating or splashing around in the water.

Fishing is an activity that has a calming effect on many children, but especially on the child with ADD/ADHD. It is an activity in which attention to a bobbing cork can be maintained for hours.

Football is another good sport for the ADD/ADHD child. Some of the training may be difficult, as there is a need to be still when the team is "set" prior to running a play, and there is a need for some coordinated movement (though minimally so for linemen). Attention training is inherent in the overall skill development, as the player must know when to start the play (e.g., listen for a specific cue in the quarterback's count). It requires a good deal of attention training and concentration for the child to perform adequately.

While children with ADD/ADHD may have some problems with safety, bike riding is good for exercise, socialization, and stress relief. Many of these children may also learn firsthand about mechanical work as they take apart, analyze, and put back together their bikes (often when nothing's broken).

An activity that is often overlooked for the child with ADD/ADHD is cooking. Many of these children may really enjoy this activity and should be encouraged by their parents. Cooking involves some critical components that provide excellent training experiences. For example, cooking involves measurement, timing, sequencing, and perhaps some creative judgment.

Involvement in organized groups for scouting and other outdoor activities may not be best for some of these children. Although a majority do prefer such outdoor activities, a large number do not. A parent must closely monitor such activities so that the child may be withdrawn if necessary.

The martial arts also provide some excellent experiences for the ADD/ADHD child. Besides being good exercise, this type of highly structured activity develops and reinforces attentional skills, coordination, self-control, and sequencing of movement. Initially, some children may be attracted to martial arts because of movies or TV, and the "aura" of participation in this activity may be sufficient to maintain their interest and discipline.

Monitoring the Child's Interest

Although the interest in various activities may vary from being extremely enthusiastic to being extremely bored, it is important to monitor the child's interest over time. Various hobbies and craft activities can be excellent pastimes that promote the development of concentration, fine-motor coordination, and work habits. Hobbies and other activities provide occasions for the ADD/ADHD child to focus attention and energies, and to achieve success and feelings of satisfaction. Remember to praise a child with ADD/ADHD when he is able to remain on task and complete projects; this is critical behavior that must be reinforced to increase the probability of generalization of these "hobby work habits" to other areas. Finding something that the child is good at helps to foster positive feelings and counteract many of the negative factors that contribute to poor self-esteem.

Children with ADD/ADHD also appear to enjoy playing with the computer. This will, for the most part, be limited to game activities as some educational programs may initially elicit some resistance. Nevertheless, developing an interest in and an affinity for working with the computer (for whatever reason) may provide positive benefits for the child in the future.

Many play activities also provide opportunities to reinforce appropriate behavior in general, like sharing and cooperating in play. Monitor and reward improved behaviors of cooperation and sharing in those game activities involving the identified child and sibs or peers. In addition, games have rules that must be followed; game activities may also be selected to focus on an area of need for the child. A few commonly available games can be used to deal with some specific problems or to help the child develop different ways of thinking.

Checkers—This is an excellent game that involves rules, visual-spatial and sequential judgment, thinking/planning before acting, and immediate feedback on mistakes of judgment. Additional components can be added; for example, each player has to say something nice about the other player (i.e., give a compliment) before each move or after getting a king. Alternately, each player could boast of some thinking process or move of which she was proud—something she did before getting each king. Adults monitoring this game, or while playing with the child, can provide tokens (poker chips or hand-made tokens of cardboard). These tokens can be saved or used as points to get some later privilege. You may also use the game of checkers as a procedure called "Think Ahead." Here you ask the child, "Where will you end up if you make that move?" After the child gives a mental guess, she may be shown the result of this move. Also, the child should ponder, "If I end up there, what can my opponent do?" These questions result in the child's learning to plan ahead mentally.

Legos®—This is an excellent activity that involves fine motor coordination, visual form judgment, sequencing, and planning skills. Frustration tolerance can also be reinforced when, in the face of frustration (i.e., can't find the right piece), the child is encouraged to persevere. When success is achieved, social praise and touch are delivered. Such activities can be performed alone, but are best done with the parent. You can provide verbal mediation and feedback on what the child is attempting to do. When the pieces do not match, questions can be suggested that may later be incorporated into the child's own cognitive thought sequences as a strategy for checking the accuracy of his own productions.

This activity is also good to reward the child for staying on task and for finishing his task. For children who have not experienced much success academically in completing tasks, finishing the Lego® production may result in a good feeling of accomplishment and success. When the child is successful at completing the production model, it allows you an opportunity to reinforce the child's completion by stating, "I really like the way you stayed with that until you finished." Also, you may comment (when the smiling child presents the completed model), "It really feels good when you work on something and finish it." The child thus has a good model for what awaits him when academic tasks are completed more often. These activities are fun and the child, in the context of play rather than in the demands and pressure of the classroom, learns many skills. (The child may be totally unaware of how these skills may affect his academic work.)

Other Activities—Other activities that may be used to help the child include:

- Crossword Puzzles—These are good for maintaining attention to words and sequencing.
- Picture Puzzles—The child may have to find what's wrong with the picture (i.e., something's out of place) or to find some detail in a complex pictorial (i.e., find all the ducks).
- Dot-to-Dot Drawings—These are excellent to work on sustained attention as well as sequencing and work completion.
- Mazes—These are excellent for planning ahead and controlling impulsive responding by using a form of "mental exploration."
- "Simon Says"—This has been around for some time and is excellent to help the child focus attention on verbal cues.
- "Flinch"—This is a two-person game where players face each other with palms touching (one's palms face up; the other's palms are down). The one with palms up (on bottom) then must try to slap the other's hand. If successful, palm positions are reversed. "Flinch" provides a good procedure for the ADD child to become more sensitive to subtle nonverbal movement cues. It has been described by Shapiro (1994) as "a game to measure AD/HD." However, this game must be monitored; should the intensity of slaps increase or other inappropriate behavior occur, this game should not be allowed to continue.

Games have intrinsic value in skill building for the child with ADD, and may also be used as general awards for completing other tasks, academic or otherwise.

Sometimes, the sense of urgency to deal with a child's problems may be so great that almost every waking moment is used in some type of training or activity. Don't overlook the normal free-play, unstructured time. All children need time for normal free play where there are no expectations other than to have fun.

FORMAL SKILL DEVELOPMENT

The difference between formal and informal skill development may be difficult to determine in some situations. The basic distinction is that formal skill development may involve activities and games that are not carried out primarily for fun, but to shape and establish some skills. In those informal activities and games, where the primary intent is recreational or participation is in a hobby or sport, some skill development may incidentally occur as part of the child's involvement with that activity.

In formal skill development, the selection of the game or activity depends upon the particular skill to be developed, and the primary purpose of the game or activity will be to shape, enhance, or establish that skill.

Each activity listed below addresses some lack of skill development and has some relevance to the child's overall problems and difficulties in adjustment. These activities and games are divided into specific areas that are critical for the child with ADD/ADHD to function well in the classroom, at home, and in society in general.

Specific skills, often deficient in children with ADD/ADHD, are the focus of formal training, which is most likely to be carried out by a teacher or mental health professionals; however, it is anticipated that such training will be available for parents to use in the home situation. (Attention training and the training of social skills are already available for home use.) By training across many different situations, the child learns more rapidly because of more learning trials, and she will also tend to generalize or apply her learned skills in more situations.

Although there is not a great deal of research on skill training of ADD/ADHD children in specific deficit areas, many training tools are available for clinical application to these problem areas of skill development:

1. Attention
2. Impulse Control
3. Activity Control
4. Organizational Skills
5. Social Skills
6. Anger Control
7. Self Concept
8. Cooperation/Sharing

Attention Training

Attentional processes are more complex than we sometimes think. Teachers tell parents, "Jimmy just needs to 'pay attention' in class; he doesn't keep his mind on his work." This all-too-common statement complains simplistically about a complex process. One may ask, "What does paying attention mean?" The teacher may believe that he has communicated a specific problem to the parent, but a host of questions arise from this general statement about not paying attention. Specifically, a parent may wish to know: When does the problem occur? In a specific class or in all? With one teacher or all? Only in one subject area (e.g., reading)? How long can the child attend? Does it matter where the child is seated? Does it matter how well the teacher is organized? How well he communicates? Are attentional problems only evident when changing from one type of task in a subject area to another? Did this problem just develop or has it been evident for some time? (While the focus is on attentional problems in this section, one might ask many of these same questions for other problem areas to be addressed.) At times, these difficulties with attention may be evident both at school and at home; for some children, however, they may appear only at school.

The complexity of attentional problems has been documented in neuropsychological research, and the breakdown of attentional processes into subtypes is based on the work of Sohlberg and Mateer (1987). The attention training games called Attend-O™ Attention Training Games developed by Dr. Flick at the ADD Clinic in Biloxi, MS, represent a hierarchically arranged set of increasingly more complex tasks which involve attentional processes as complex as those encountered in real-life situations. The Attend-O™ Attention Training Games evolved from a review of the neuropsychological rehabilitation literature in treating individuals who have sustained some type of brain injury, lesion, or dysfunction that has impacted upon their basic abilities including attention, memory, language, visual-motor, and other higher cognitive functions. The current emphasis is on the treatment of attentional deficits. (See Figure 9.1, Description of the Attentional Games.)

Theory-Based Attention Training—The model for attention training used here is that provided by Sohlberg and Mateer (1987). Their clinical model suggests that there are five subtypes, or varieties, of attention: (1) focused; (2) sustained; (3) selective; (4) alternating; and (5) divided attention (see Figure 9.1). Based on cognitive theories and clinical observations of individuals with traumatic brain injuries, Sohlberg and Mateer hypothesized that one may experience difficulties in attention at one or more levels within each of these hierarchically arranged categories of attention. The following provides a refined and modified description of each of these five attentional components as they are used in this AT Games program for treatment of Attentional Deficits in ADD/ADHD children and adults.

1. *Focused attention* is the most basic form of attention that involves the child's ability to respond to a specific stimulus (visual or auditory) event (e.g., one topic) without a shift in attention.
2. *Sustained attention* reflects a child's ability to maintain attention and persist on task until completion. This would also include the notion of vigilance and resistance to lapses in attention for an adequate period of time. Further, it is involved in the child's readiness to respond to some stimulus event. At the highest level, this also would incorporate the notion of holding and manipulating information as one might do in mental arithmetic.
3. *Selective attention* involves the child's ability to maintain a specific cognitive set in the face of competing distractions. For example, selective attention is involved when the child recognizes that the parent's voice during instructions is the main focus of attention and not others' comments or noises. It should also be noted that the distractors may be "external" (e.g., noise) or "internal" (e.g., one's thoughts or feelings).

Figure 9.1 DESCRIPTION OF THE ATTENTIONAL GAMES

THE ATTENTION TRAINING GAME		
Game Type	*Sensory Modality*	
	Visual	Auditory
FOCUSED ATTENTION	Every time you *see* a RED card, click the mouse.	Every time you *hear* the word RED, click the mouse.
SUSTAINED ATTENTION	Every time you *see* a RED card follow or come after a BLACK card, click the mouse.	Every time you *hear* the word RED follow or come after the word BLACK, click the mouse.
SELECTIVE ATTENTION	[A 3″ × 5″ array of colored cards is on the screen.] Every time a RED card follows a BLACK card, click the mouse. [Cards appear randomly in the 3″ × 5″ array. Various colors act as visual distractors.]	[A series of colors will be heard coming randomly from the right and left speakers.] Each time the word RED follows or comes after the word BLACK, click the mouse. [Various colors heard act as auditory distractors.]
ALTERNATING ATTENTION	Click the mouse every time a RED card follows a BLACK card (20″). Then click to BLACK-follows-RED (20″), then again click to RED-follows-BLACK (20″).	Click the mouse every time the word RED is heard to follow the word BLACK (20″), then click to BLACK-follows-RED (20″), then again click to RED-follows-BLACK (20″).
DIVIDED ATTENTION (I)	[Visual and Auditory presented at the same time.] Click the mouse when you *see* a RED card or *hear* the word RED (focus only on RED).	
DIVIDED ATTENTION (II)	[Visual and Auditory presented at the same time.] Click the mouse when you *see* a RED card follow a BLACK card or *hear* the word RED follow the word BLACK (more complex task).	
DIVIDED ATTENTION (III)	[Visual and Auditory presented at the same time.] Click the left mouse button when you *see* a RED card follow a BLACK card; click the right mouse button when you *hear* the word RED follow the word BLACK (the most complex task).	

4. *Alternating attention* includes the idea of "mental flexibility," as when there is a need to shift attention between tasks that access different modes of information processing or different response patterns—for example, the student who has to listen to the teacher and take notes alternately, while holding the information intact. This situation requires that the child switch from looking at the teacher (processing the information both visually and auditorally) and then transferring it in an abbreviated form through verbal expressive functions in writing. Some continuity of the flow of ideas and words must be maintained (i.e., a mental holding process) so that appropriate concepts, ideas, and facts may be reconstructed in notes.
5. *Divided attention* requires the ability to respond almost simultaneously to two or more tasks having different demands. This process may involve rapid alternation of attention or a somewhat automatic or almost unconscious processing and responsivity on one of the tasks. Attention may be divided into any combination of visual, auditory, or kinesthetic (movement) stimuli, but more commonly there is a visual and auditory combination. The task or response requirements may be as simple as a single unitary response or a complex one (e.g., two different visual-spatial [right versus left] response patterns). Such complex response patterns are not infrequently associated with complex attentional processes when one interacts with sophisticated machines (e.g., task demands of a pilot in the cockpit that is filled with gauges, auditory sounds, and multiple-response switches).

Training Program Applications—Before describing the Attend-O™ Attention Training Games, we must consider other available software and/or training programs for application with children with ADD/ADHD.

First, the Attention Process Training (APT) program developed by Sohlberg and Mateer (1987, 1989) has been used with children as young as 7 years of age. One study by Williams (1989) with a small group of children 8 to 11 years old showed improvements in attentional processes but with questionable generalization to their natural academic settings. Other successful training has been noted by Campbell (1990). However, Light and others (1996) have pointed out that the APT materials were not designed for children, and that some modules in the program would be difficult to apply as they assume skills that have not yet developed in the child.

Computer-based programs have been described by Bracy (*Soft Tools,* 1983), Sandford (*Captain's Log,* 1985), Williams (*Cool Springs Software,* 1992), and Podd (*neurXercise*™, 1989). According to a recent survey, only a few of these programs had been used with children who have ADD/ADHD. At present, only *Captain's Log* has been reportedly used in some preliminary studies with ADD children (Fine and Goldman 1994; Sandford 1995; Kotwal et al. 1994).

Over the last ten years, neuropsychologists have been developing these cognitive stimulation techniques primarily to rehabilitate adults who have experienced some type of brain insult that produced impairments in specific skill areas involving attention, memory, visual-motor skills, and other functions that have affected their adaptation to daily life routines. The emphasis in these techniques has been on rehabilitation as the attempt is made to repair or recover skills that have been lost or altered in some way. Some of these same techniques are beginning to be used with children who have ADD or LD (learning disabilities). While these children have not lost skills, they have failed to develop them. While no gross abnormalities of brain tissue or neurochemical processes have been fully documented, there is such a similarity of behavioral characteristics with these individuals who have sustained actual brain injury that the application of cognitive neuropsychological remediation techniques to the child with ADD or ADD/LD seems clearly worthwhile. In a recent study Kotwal and others (1994) have shown that training with the *Captain's Log* program with 20-35 training sessions resulted in some improvement on the Connors' Parent Rating Scale (for ADD) and a structured questionnaire, along with some general improvement in grades. A recent article in *CH.A.D.D.* magazine (Fall 1994) pointed out the value of using computers to help children with ADHD. Computerized training programs look quite promising and may become a useful tool in planning comprehensive treatment programs for children with ADD. Extension of some training exercises from the clinic into home and school settings would certainly help to increase generalization of learned attentional skills to those critical environments in which the child must function. Additionally, the increase in the number of practice trials would enhance the rapidity with which these skills were acquired.

Criteria for an Attentional Training Program—According to Sohlberg and others (1993), there are six basic tenets of the approach in addressing cognitive impairments.

1. *Use of a theoretical model.* The current attention training programs utilize the clinical model adopted by Sohlberg and Mateer (1989).
2. *Programs are hierarchically organized.* This guarantees a broad range of tasks and ensures a gradient of difficulty level that may be linked to real-life events.
3. *The necessity for repetition.* This series of programs is promoted to be used in a number of situations involving clinic, school, and eventually home use.
4. *The program series is data-driven.* Simply stated, progress through these programs extends from the simple to the most complex of attentional tasks, with movement determined by the person's performance (i.e., percent correct-percent errors).
5. *The program should plan for generalization.* The ultimate goal of this behaviorally based attention training system is to impact upon real-life attentional problems of the ADD child. Utilization of ratings that monitor changes in corresponding areas of attentional deficits will facilitate documentation of the effectiveness of the specific training components. Overall improvement in ancillary rating scales (e.g., Conners, ACTeRS, etc.) along with improvements in grades

and performance on specific neuropsychologically based attentional tasks will be monitored. The generalization factors will certainly be addressed by the use of extended training in different situations.

6. *Ultimate success will be determined by changes in school functioning.* This factor will simply represent the end process of training as reflected by improved functioning in real-life situations that are meaningful for the child with ADD/ADHD.

Plotting Improvement—First, a clinician must obtain baseline measures of performance (i.e., pretraining phase). This may be primarily rating scale information, but could also involve performance on a computerized test of attention. During the training phase, the clinician keeps a record of percentage of correct responses and the percentage of errors. These may be plotted (see Figure 9.2) to show improvement on each task and to show that the child is learning the skills. This graph also shows that each time the task is made more difficult (e.g., shifting from 1 card/2 sec to 1 card/sec and from there to 2 cards/sec) performance drops as expected. It is, in short, a good example of the learning process as applied to the acquisition of attentional skills. Post-training assessments, after a period of approximately three months, may reflect overall positive changes in ratings, psych and neuropsych test performance, and indirectly in classroom academic work.

If a general behavioral program is established at home, the child's scores may be translated into points (using a positive system only); this will provide additional motivation on these tasks. Improvement in attentional skills may be influenced by (1) the number of practice sessions, and (2) the number of situations in which practice occurs.

Like any habit development, and especially for children with ADD/ADHD, tasks must be repeated frequently. For this reason, it is desirable for the child to practice these tasks at home, at school, and at the clinician's office. In this way, the skills will be acquired faster and they will be better generalized across home and school situations. This means that the child will be better able to apply the learned skills in situations other than the one where they were learned.

Some of the work on other computerized programs, e.g., *Captain's Log* and *neurXercise*™ appeared in Chapter 2 in the section on Habilitation. However, note that there have been few studies in this area up to this point in time. This area is thus fertile grounds for research.

Complex Attention Training

Alphabet and Phonics Bingo are computerized training games developed by Dr. Joseph Sandford. *Auditory* Alphabet Bingo (for ages 4 to adult) trains listening skills, auditory attention, and discrimination, ability to follow spoken sequential instruction, focusing while ignoring distractions, and short-term memory. *Visual* Alphabet Bingo (for ages 6 to adult) trains reading comprehension, visual attention to detail, sequential visual processing, visual decoding, and discrimination. Both sets train response inhibi-

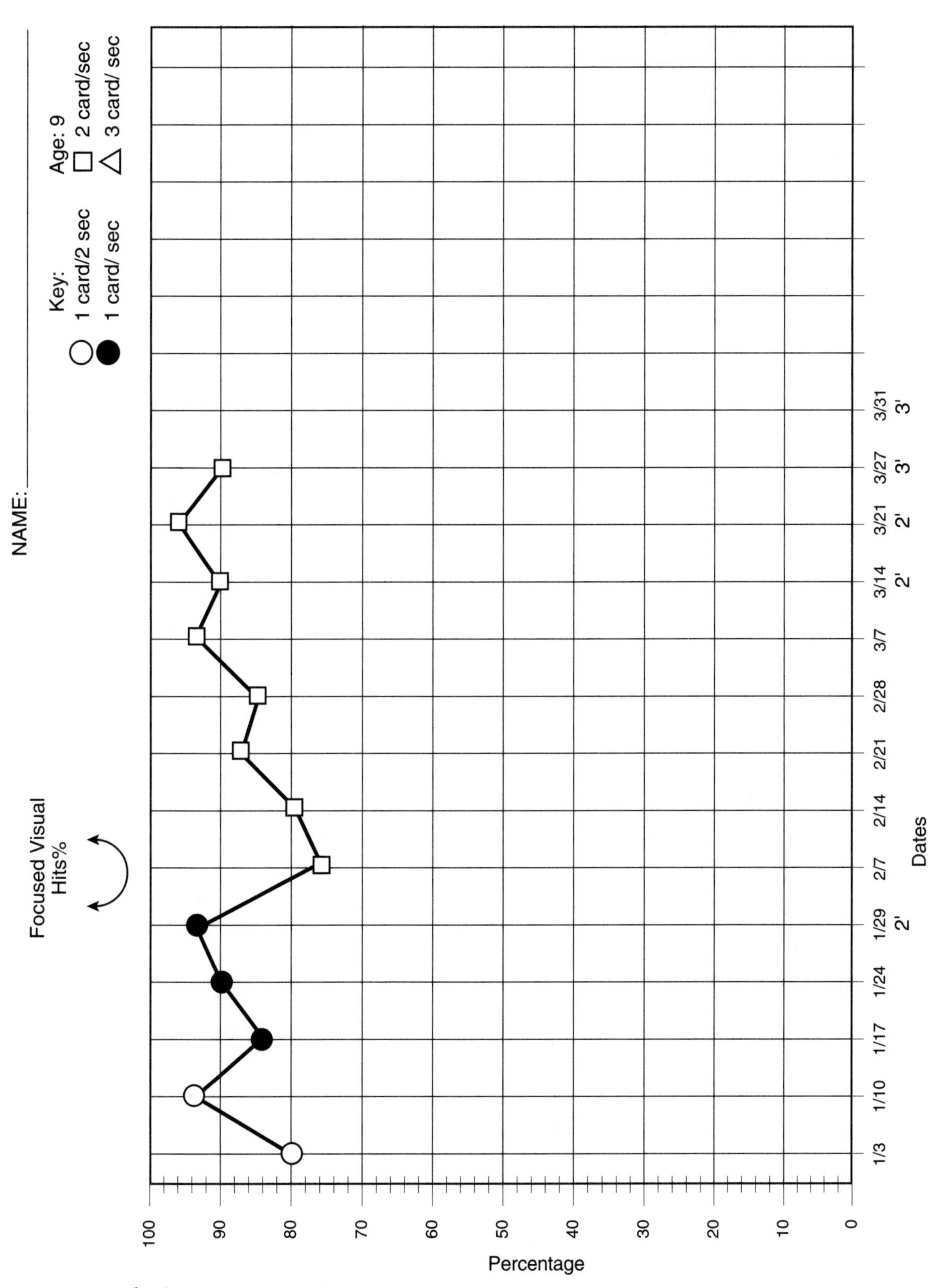

Figure 9.2 Plotting Improvement.

tion, spatial relationship concepts, and same/different concepts. The three Phonics Bingo programs are based on research showing that when target consonant sounds are "electronically stretched" there was enhanced learning of their basic phonemes. The programs automatically adapt to the age of the child (to present appropriate graphics) and also adapt to ability levels; at more advanced stages of training the exercises become quite challenging with numerous distractions built-in.

Impulse Control Training

An excellent board game format is provided by the "Stop, Relax, and Think" game (available from CAP or Center for Applied Psychology) which is played by the child(ren) and the counselor. This game combines some brief relaxation exercises with emphasis on awareness of inner sensations associated with various feeling states, and some problem-solving situations that prompt the child to think. All appropriate responses can be reinforced and feedback given to correct mistakes in thinking. However, one of the most useful aspects of this board game is the segment devoted to developing behavioral inhibition. When the child lands on STOP, he must roll a die. The number rolled determines what activity the child will be asked to perform. It might be a vocal-motor task (e.g., counting to ten over and over) or an overt complex motor activity (e.g., rubbing the stomach while patting the head). The child performs this task facing away from the therapist who will at some point say STOP. If the child continues on, no point (token) is earned; if he stops quickly ("freezes"), he gets the token. This appears to be a very useful format for training motor inhibition, by positive rewards (token) and praise for improving control. Control may gradually be shaped so the child is rewarded for better behavioral inhibition.

A maze drawing game is discussed by Dr. Lawrence Shapiro in his videotape "Self-Control Techniques in Child Psychotherapy." In this procedure, the therapist looks at issues of frustration for the child while he or she draws the maze and allows the therapist to teach the child to use language to solve the maze. This is essentially a self-instruction, self-talk procedure which does help the child to slow down and thus make fewer impulsive errors. The procedure easily lends itself to reinforcement for making good decisions, planning, and persistence toward completion.

Another maze game called "Stop Light" allows children to proceed to various points on the board (grid) with little cars that have small circular magnets inside (red on one side, green on the other). Underneath the board are similar magnets at intersections of the grid that will allow the child either to continue on or to stop (when the small magnet inside the car flips over to red). Even though the child may have rolled a high number on the die, she must stop when the "red light" appears. This game does not require any reading, allows for reinforcement of visual scanning (i.e., find the place to go), motor control, motor coordination (staying on the lines), planning and strategy (i.e., taking the shortest path to the place of destination on the board), and motor inhibition (a critical skill for ADD/ADHD children). The game is from CAP.

A third game that is useful in helping the child to develop planning and strategy, as well as to play by the rules, is "Look Before You Leap." Using frogs and a hidden wheel that changes the position of alligators, the child attempts to land on flies and avoid even touching his frog to an alligator square (where he would lose a card or a turn). Thus, foresight and planning are necessary. Such skills taught at this level may be directly applied to real-life problem solving. This game is available from ADD (ADD Warehouse) and CAP (Center for Applied Psychology).

Other games that focus on self-control can be found in *In Control: A Book of Games to Teach Children Self-Control Skills.* These games utilize a multimodal approach; they look at control problems from several different perspectives. The first game "You Hurt My Feelings" helps the child to understand how his behavior affects others. The "I'm In Control" game helps the child to look at consequences of her behavior, how to avoid people and situations that lead to problem behavior, and to develop strategies to deal with provocations (e.g., teasing). In the "Self-Coaching" game, the child learns self-talk to change from negative to positive statements. In the "Right On Time" game, the child learns the importance of making and keeping a schedule. The "Helping Others" game focus is on helping others and being selfless—developing good values. Last, the "Can I Play, Too" game concentrates on social skills of social entry, making friends, and group cooperation. This series of games might best be conducted in a small group, where the clinician works not just with specific motor impulse control, but also in a broader social context to provide real-life meaning for these skills. Developed by Dr. Lawrence Shapiro, the games are available from CAP.

Social Skill Training

There are a number of relevant social skills to concentrate on. Of course, just learning to play any of the games by the rules is helpful for the child who has relationship difficulty with peers and sibs. Several games and programs designed to teach social skills are available (and some overlap with other areas of skill training).

"The Prepare Curriculum" by Dr. Arnold Goldstein (1988) is a ten-course comprehensive program for use with elementary-level students and adolescents. It focuses on problem solving, interpersonal skills, anger control, moral reasoning, and stress management as major areas of problems for students who are aggressive, withdrawn, or generally weak in social competency. Games, role-play exercises, group discussion, and other activities are used in the training process (available from ADD).

An excellent game to foster and reinforce cooperation for children ages 7-12 is the "Mountaineering" game. Players must work together by sharing and cooperating as a team. Failure to do so results in no child's being successful on this task. This game provides excellent opportunity to teach the concepts of sharing and teamwork (available from CAP).

"You & Me: A Game of Social Skills" provides a good format for teaching everyday social skills including helping others, sharing, being polite, being a friend, and understanding another's point of view. Some role play may be used, but the interesting aspect of this game is that nonverbal feedback (in the form of cartoon drawings), as well as verbal feedback, is provided. Appropriate for kids ages 4-10 years (available from CAP).

The game "Listen Up" provides excellent opportunities to reinforce communication skills and listening skills. To win, players must go to each of four feedback corners of the board and report accurately on what other players say. A player picks up a happy face at each corner only if other players agree that the feedback was accurate. Appropriate for kids 7 years and up (available from CAP).

While not specifically addressing a type of social skill, "The Kindness Game" provides opportunities to teach specific actions that reflect cooperation with and consideration of others, with particular focus on feelings. Every time a player lands on a Kind Space on the board, she is asked to talk about a kind act and then color in a star. Landing on a Kindness Space, the unkind act must be turned into a kind act or the player loses (i.e., must erase) her star. The object of the game is to have all 25 stars colored in (available from CAP).

Self-Concept/Self-Esteem Training

A game called "Let's See—About Me" provides a format for the child to explore his self-image. Four areas of the board, from which questions are devised, correspond to Affect, Behavior, Cognition, and Social System. Each player needs five chips (i.e., must answer five questions) from each of the four areas before winning. Questions address feelings, thoughts, behavior, and the child's social system, as the child's ability to form loving attachments will be the basis for self-respect and for respect of others. Related games are "Let's See—About Me and My Friends" and "Let's See—About Me and My Family." (All are available from CAP.)

Another game entitled "POW! Personal Power" by Nancy Gajewski and Patty Mayo is designed to reinforce self-esteem in children ages 10-17 years of age. Players take turns responding to questions or engaging in activities designed to help them learn to evaluate themselves more positively, to more easily accept nonthreatening criticism from others, and to develop an understanding of the self-help skills needed to maintain a healthy self-esteem. The game also provides opportunities to teach players how to communicate positively with others (available from ADD Warehouse).

Organizational Study Skills

The "Skills for School Success" program developed by Anita Archer and May Gleason provides an excellent resource to teach several appropriate classroom behaviors as well as organizational and study skills. Rather than focusing on remediating their deficiencies, these procedures focus on developing skills that children with ADD/ADHD need to succeed in the classroom. Behavior appropriate before and after class, and time and materials management are covered. Learning strategies that focus on completing assignments, memorizing, proofreading, and taking notes are just a few of the areas discussed. In addition, study strategies and discussions about how to take tests are covered. Using reference material, and reading and interpreting graphs and tables are also highlighted. This program covers grades 3 through 6 with guidelines for a downward extension to grades 1 and 2. Advanced programs for grades 7-12 are now offered. This program is available from Curriculum Associates.

A workbook program is also available, entitled "Study Strategies Made Easy: A Practical Plan for School Success" by Leslie Davis and Sandi Suotowitz with Harvey C. Parker. The focus of this series of exercises is on grades 6-12. It covers organization, learning styles, reading comprehension, communication, note taking, homework, stress management, memorization, and test taking. It is designed to be used as a program, but the clinician may wish to focus on specific sections that are critical for an individual child (available from ADD Warehouse).

Anger Control Training

"The Anger Solution" game helps children learn effective and socially acceptable conflict management. Used by a clinician, the game provides the child with a format where she can learn that she can have control over behavioral responses to anger and that she can make decisions that result in positive solutions. In this game, the child may learn to become more aware of when she first begins to feel angry and to use some prevention strategies she will learn as part of this game. Combined with relaxation techniques and positive self-talk, affirmations focusing on good qualities and traits may allow the child to spend more time in what is termed the "success cycle." This reflects improved feelings about the self and others when control is used and stands in contrast to those times the child is in the "victim's cycle," when control is lost through explosive anger—making others victims, too. Use of strategies associated with the success cycle may be reinforced while those that contribute to the victim's cycle are not rewarded. Overall, this game provides a basis for developing alternative solutions to aggressive behaviors (available from CAP).

Goldstein (1988) cites a refinement of Novaco's (1975) three stage sequence into a chain where the child learns (1) cues—both physiological and kinesthetic that signal anger arousal, (2) triggers—both internal and external factors that provoke anger, (3) reminders—self-instruction statements to reduce anger arousal (e.g., "I can work out a plan to handle this."), (4) reducers—techniques in combination with reminders to reduce anger (e.g., deep breathing, backward counting), and (5) self-evaluation—the opportunity to self-reinforce and/or self-correct (depending on the success of the preceding steps).

There are also a number of books and workbooks with stories, story metaphors, and various exercises and games that address the problem of excess anger from the point where it originates (i.e., triggers) to its behavioral consequences. Several resources focus on awareness and prevention while others simply address the need for alternative solutions in a problem-solving mode. Some of these resources include "Everything I Do You

Blame on Me," "The Very Angry Day That Amy Didn't Have," "Sometimes I Like to Fight, But I Don't Do It Much Anymore" (available from CAP) and "Don't Rant and Rave on Wednesday! The Children's Anger Control Book" (available from ADD Warehouse). "Anger Control Problem-Solving Cards" and the "Anger Control Tool Kit" (available from CAP) also have many useful formats for the clinician in working with the angry and aggressive child.

Training in Problem Solving

The "Think Aloud" small-group program by Bonnie Camp and Mary Ann S. Bash is actually a series of programs for children of varying age groups. It combines cognitive training and problem solving, utilizing verbal mediation (i.e., language) to achieve problem resolution. Putting the focus on acting *after* thinking more carefully results in academic improvements and better social behavior. "Think Aloud" is designed for elementary-age children and uses different materials at different levels. The child is first taught the basic approach of asking a series of questions, as follows: What is my problem? What is my plan? Am I using the best plan? How did I do? In addition to the four basic questions, the other procedures include looking for alternatives, interpreting emotional responses, planning, using foresight in context, and engaging in logical inductive reasoning processes to handle different situations. Role-playing has a major part in this program. *Note:* This program clearly has limited usefulness and applicability because of problems with generalizations and difficulty utilizing it with children who may have a broad range of developmental cognitive or emotional problems.

Another game, titled "The Road to Problem Mastery," is based on similar approaches. Its concept of roadblocks and hazards reflects problems that are encountered on the road through life. It covers a six-step problem-solving approach:

1. "Can Do!" (develop a problem-solving attitude)
2. "What's the problem?" (defining a goal)
3. "What could you do?" (brainstorming)
4. "What would happen if?" (considering the consequences)
5. "Do it!" (carry out the solution)
6. "How did it work?" (conduct an evaluation of the effectiveness of the solution)

This game provides a format similar to the "Think Aloud" program and it is much easier to maintain cooperation with this type of format. Suitable for kids 7 years and older, it provides enjoyable and challenging tasks that allow for feedback, shaping of behavioral responses, and increased flexibility in thinking (available from CAP).

ADJUNCTIVE TRAINING MATERIALS

Several games and books don't really fit into any of the above training modalities. Nonetheless, these materials may be helpful in several areas.

The "Classroom Behavior Game" is quite helpful in teaching twelve appropriate behaviors important to adequate functioning in the classroom—including raising your hand, taking turns, ignoring inappropriate behavior of others, having a positive attitude, and listening. The behaviors involved are associated with roles that are applicable to most classrooms. An excellent feature of this game is the provision of nonverbal cartoon pictures that depict the appropriate behavior for the role involved in each question the child answers. Playing this game may also reinforce use of the pictorial cartoons (e.g., raising hand) that may be placed on the child's desk to cue appropriate behavior of raising hand to answer questions in class. The game is set up to allow emphasis of those rules that are the most difficult for a child and those that might be included in a home-school behavioral program as well (available from CAP).

The "Coping Skills" game covers several areas of training including self-concept/self-esteem, problem solving, relaxation and stress management training, and anger and impulse control. Nine coping skills are incorporated into this game format. When a situation card is drawn, the child must put herself in another child's shoes, say how she might feel and which coping skill would be most helpful in that situation. Dealing with feelings, adjusting attitudes, accepting imperfections, planning ahead, and asking for help are just a few of the coping skills addressed. This game is suitable for ages 7 through 12 years (available from CAP).

"Stress Strategies" allows the clinician to use a game format to introduce and teach basic and brief relaxation techniques. This is a game that may best be combined with other relaxation procedures such as biofeedback and taped relaxation exercises.

"The Stress-Less Game" teaches children six ways to handle stress and includes relaxation techniques, positive thinking, time management, creating a less stressful environment, handling relationships better, and caring for one's own body. A useful anti-stress chart for use at home allows the child to apply and monitor newly acquired stress-coping skills; this clearly aids in the generalization of these skills, which also may be reinforced at home with the home behavioral system (point system). This game is appropriate for kids 7 through 12 years (available from CAP).

Several books are helpful in teaching stress management and relaxation concepts. These include *Take a Deep Breath: The Kid's Play-Away Stress Book* and *Ready, Set, Relax* (both available from CAP). Another excellent resource is *Don't Pop Your Cork on Mondays: The Children's Anti-Stress Book* by Adolph Masa, as well as the book *Don't Feed the Monster on Tuesdays: The Children's Self-Esteem Book* by the same author. (Both of these books are available from ADD Warehouse.)

An almost universally accepted therapeutic game that is often used in introductory therapy sessions is "The Talking, Feeling, and Doing Game." It is a good procedure to determine just how well a child verbalizes about certain issues. Varying in degree of cognitive and emotional difficulty, this game also gives the child the option of not responding to certain questions. However, as the clinician models self-disclosure, the child may experience greater freedom to engage in therapeutic dialogue. Partly diagnostic and partly therapeutic, this game often provides a vehicle to further explore areas of concern for the child. It is suitable for ages 4 through 11 years (available from CAP).

CHAPTER 10

Survival Training for Parents and Teachers

Parents and teachers experience a significant degree of stress in dealing with the child with ADD/ADHD. Parents may suffer marital distress, and sometimes separation and divorce. ADD/ADHD is clearly a family problem; everyone is affected, including non-ADD siblings.

In the classroom, one of the greatest sources of stress for the teacher involves discipline of difficult-to-manage children. Here too, other ADD and non-ADD children may be affected. It is a common observation that when children with ADD/ADHD are grouped together, in a family or in a classroom, there is a kind of synergistic effect. In short, behavior problems may increase exponentially.

It's helpful to be aware that additional problems are created when the parent or teacher of a child with ADD/ADHD also manifests residual symptoms and characteristics. In such cases, the child with ADD/ADHD is faced with a parent or teacher who may be disorganized, inconsistent, impulsive, quick tempered, and poorly tuned in to the child's needs. Such parents and teachers may have adopted a somewhat rigid routine, and will therefore lack flexibility in coping with difficult behavior. Interaction between these parents and/or teachers with children who have ADD/ADHD will thus be fraught with tension and prove to have explosive consequences.

CHANGING YOUR COPING STRATEGY

Don't attempt to deal with too many problems at one time; you'll only feel overwhelmed by the task and give up or frantically try to cope with all problems at once. Focus on one or perhaps two problems at a time. Break larger tasks into smaller units.

Prioritize problem behaviors. This does not mean dealing with the most severe behavior first; at times, you will find that once a mild or moderate behavior problem is handled, others may not be so severe.

Just like the child with ADD/ADHD, parents and teachers need breaks in the routine. Behavior problems will not be resolved overnight, and when some behavioral procedure seems not to be working, it may be helpful to stand back—retreat, if you will—and take a look at what's going on. On occasions, parents and teachers become overfocused—concentrating on one aspect of a problem while failing to see the overall picture. It is important to use breaks in your routine to incorporate pleasurable activities. Excessive pressure to perform may not only fail to achieve desired results but may also lead to the child's becoming depressed, possibly even suicidal, over failure to meet your expectations. Problems with depression appear most often in adolescents with ADD/ADHD.

What can you do to counteract and deal with the stress associated with managing the child with ADD/ADHD?

Relaxation and Stress Management

Learn simple relaxation and stress management techniques. There are many relaxation tapes; short five- to 10-minute tapes may be used on a daily basis. Relaxation tapes are available in bookstores and tape centers, as well as through the ADD Clinic in Biloxi. Even shorter relaxation exercises may be integrated within a hectic schedule. Some of these include (1) shrugging the shoulders and rotating them forward and backward in a circular motion three times each way, (2) rotating the head (for neck muscles) in a circular movement to the right (three times) and to the left (three times), (3) taking a slow, deep breath (from the abdomen) in through the nose and breathing out through the mouth, (4) repeating the procedure in (3) and saying "one" slowly as you breathe out, and (5) sitting very quiet and still while visualizing yourself in a calm, soothing, relaxing place (a kind of short mental vacation).

Another alternative is to use a kind of "stress inoculation" procedure that involves the self-talk method, described in Chapter 4, to aid in actively ignoring some behavior. This procedure may serve to reduce stress and at the same time maintain the proper course in working with the child.

When a behavior is selected to be ignored, much additional stress will be created as the child becomes frustrated that he is not getting the usual attention. The result is a general escalation of the intensity of effect associated with that behavior. In other words, you must be prepared to "ride out" more severe behaviors. If it is whining, the whining becomes louder. If it is drumming a pencil on the desk, the drumming becomes louder. Prepare in advance to deal with this more intense behavior by using a self-talk exercise that is designed to keep your attention focused on something other than the child. This may involve attempting to read a book or newspaper, work on a project, or grade papers. You must, however, realize that no work will be accomplished during this time. The time is to be used to eventually weaken the child's response. Be prepared not to give in, as this would certainly make the child even more persistent in the behavior, showing it at a more intense level. Keep the following internal dialogue in mind—and use it!

> Okay, I know this is going to get worse, but I can handle it. It's important for me to keep my attention on this newspaper (or grade book). I know I won't be able to concentrate very well, so I'm not concerned about getting anything accomplished—I just need to keep my attention on these materials.

Typically, the intensity of the behavior will increase.

> Okay, I know his behavior is getting worse now. I expected that so it's no surprise to me. What I need to do is continue my deep breathing and bring my attention back to my materials. I'm prepared for this to continue for a while and to even get worse. I can handle this. I can continue to allow my muscles around my neck and shoulders to relax and let go. I can imagine the relaxation spreading to other muscles in my body. I'll just have to wait this out. I know that if I give in, he'll just be more persistent next time—and even more intense. I can handle this. I can remain calm and relaxed.

With a little practice, you can devise a self-talk procedure that best suits your style of conversation and your unique situation. Ignoring was discussed in detail in Chapter 4. Take a few moments now to reflect on a situation where such a procedure would be helpful and write your own narrative script to use while ignoring some behavior, using Exercise 10.1. Remember that the child with ADD/ADHD exhibits many behaviors that may be physiologically determined and may never be totally removed or extinguished. It is, however, important to avoid adding a learned component to that behavior that makes it even more difficult to handle. In short, many of these behaviors (e.g. wiggling, tapping, humming, etc.) might be diminished but never removed by this procedure. Try your hand at the self-talk exercise now.

Exercise 10.1 NARRATIVE SELF-TALK PROCEDURE FOR IGNORING SOME BEHAVIOR

____

____

____

____

____

____

____

____

____

____

Writing Daily Affirmations

Using daily affirmations may be useful. While some affirmations have a religious content, others simply reaffirm your desire to change the way you respond to the child with ADD/ADHD. These statements may be repeated several times each day. It is therefore helpful to have them posted within view or easily accessible in your wallet or pocket. Some simple examples of these affirmations for parents and teachers are provided here.

PARENTS

"I have the knowledge and the strength to deal with my child's difficult behavior."

"In the past, I have been too harsh with my child's behavior. I can use other techniques that would be less emotional for both my child and myself."

TEACHERS

"I can now better understand the ADD child's behavior and I can be more flexible in dealing with it."

"I now know that I don't have to respond to every inappropriate behavior from the ADD child; I can ignore some of these behaviors even though they may be annoying."

A book of affirmations by Tian Dayton (1991) is suggested as an additional reference. It is important that you develop your own affirmations (Exercise 10.2) that are specific to your situation and the problem behaviors you face. Use the previous affirmations as a guide and be sure to begin your statement with the pronoun "I".

Exercise 10.2 WRITE AT LEAST TWO AFFIRMATIONS THAT MAY HELP YOU AS A TEACHER OR PARENT

____

____

____

____

____

Developing an Assertive Style

Many children with ADD/ADHD firmly believe that they are in control—and in many cases they are. When misbehavior garners attention, the attention is reinforcing. Even though much of this attention is negative or seemingly unpleasant, most attention to the child with ADD/ADHD is negative and so, over time, negative attention is rewarding. It's simple—negative attention is better than no attention at all. Thus, many children with ADD/ADHD learn which buttons to press to elicit attention from their parents or teachers. After years of such experience, this pattern becomes almost like a game. Remember, the child with ADD/ADHD comes from a state of low-arousal and may be actively seeking to create some excitement or an uproar. Sometimes the "punishment" may be well worth the laughs or upheaval created by the behavior. For many, "punishment" in school means being sent out of the classroom, which has little meaning to the child who thinks the class is boring. Escape further reinforces such behavior as does the teacher's reaction.

Children with ADD/ADHD can almost predict when they will get in trouble, and some parents and teachers have learned to recognize some of these signs as well. The main point here is that both parents and teachers must be able to resist attempts by the child to be manipulated and controlled. One such procedure that is important to parents and teachers who wish to survive parenthood or teacherhood with the child is to be assertive with regard to behavioral procedures.

Writing "Broken Record" Statements—As you probably know by now, some behaviors of the child with ADD/ADHD can be quite resistant to change. You must be just as resistant and persistent in not giving in to demands made by the child or to behaviors that are clearly manipulative in nature. A technique known as the "broken record," as described by Cynthia Whitman (1991), can be used when the child makes repetitive annoying requests or shows some other irritating behavior. The procedure is simple—*just say NO*! Repeating this statement and saying, "I'm sorry—you can't have what you want," may bring about an escalation of the intensity of the request (i.e., louder whining and perhaps temper tantrums depending on the child's age) or repetition of some other annoying behavior designed to "punish you" for not giving in to the demands.

It is important to state here that assertiveness is also needed in not allowing the child to name call, curse, or threaten you. Being assertive is requesting the respect you deserve as a parent or teacher. If such behaviors occur, it is important to state firmly, "I will not allow you to abuse me in that manner. It's OK to express your feelings; it's not OK to say what you said." Depending on the nature and severity of the "abuse," you may wish to simply turn away from the child and leave. Alternatively, a more formal punishment (i.e., time-out, behavior penalty, or the overcorrection procedure) may be used. It is, however, important to consider the occasion for the child's verbal outburst. If you used harsh words with the child, it is not unusual that the child will retaliate in a similar manner. It is again important for both parents and teachers to avoid harsh words or embarrassing language; in short, be positive and model generally appropriate behavior.

Exercise 10.3 on page 314 is designed to familiarize you with statements that can be used for certain behaviors—statements that would be appropriate for an "assertive stance." It is important to be prepared with these statements. They can be rehearsed so that when the behavior occurs they will become almost automatic.

Exercise 10.3 WRITE "ASSERTIVE" TYPE STATEMENTS FOR TWO OR THREE BEHAVIORS.

____

____

____

____

____

SUMMING UP PARENT-TEACHER MENTAL HEALTH

To reduce and control the emotional stress associated with behavior management of the ADD/ADHD child—for you *and* for the child—parents and teachers must address the following issues:

1. **Accept the child.** ADD/ADHD is a neurobiological problem, just like asthma or epilepsy. It can be controlled or managed but never (at this point in time) eliminated. Use of appropriate medications and/or behavioral strategies may result in improvement 80 percent of the time or better.
2. **Know about ADD/ADHD and treatments that will make things better.** Knowing and understanding the nature of ADD/ADHD is an important first step. You must also understand which behavioral techniques, used consistently, will make a difference in how the child responds. Medication often results in quick and sometimes dramatic behavior change, yet old behaviors return when the medication wears off. It is equally important to teach the ADD/ADHD child "skills that take the place of pills." Skills may be used as the child grows older and needs to cope with situations without medication. It is critical that the child learn to rely on his or her own resources, and not turn to medication as a primary solution to problems. Keep in mind that the best outcomes determined from long-term studies of ADD/ADHD children as adults relate to use of behavioral techniques combined with medication.
3. **Remain calm in crisis.** Utilize your relaxation and stress inoculation procedures. Calm creates the environment most conducive to maintaining close relationships and keeping children under control. Erect filters to allow you to focus on critical behaviors while ignoring the annoying ones.
4. **Maintain a routine.** Maintain structure at home and in the classroom. Knowing what to expect—and when—is critical. So, too, is the development of habits. The

trick is to have an established routine in which the components change to heighten and maintain the child's interest. Also included here is allowance for transitions. Extensive planning and discussion of transition times will allow you to avoid considerable stress.

5. **Keep communications clear.** This sounds simple, but may be the source of turmoil in families and classrooms. Remember that communications provide the basic structure at home and in class. When these are unclear, the child may become confused. Be clear and concise giving instructions step-by-step, orally and—when possible—in writing. Mumbling, nagging, arguing, yelling, and trying to talk over "noise" will be ineffective.

6. **Be aware of triggers to crisis events.** Most parents and teachers are aware of those situations or occasions that are associated with, or directly bring about, an eruption of misbehavior. Restructuring such situations or occasions may be all that is needed to avoid escalation of misbehavior.

7. **Stay positive.** More than any other recommendation, this one is crucial in maintaining relative calm at home or at school. When negative attention is given, everyone becomes more tense. As behavior escalates, relationships are stressed, and the situation culminates in a sometimes violent interchange.

8. **Use appropriate behavioral techniques.** Parents and teachers are exposed to numerous variations of behavioral procedures. Sometimes inappropriate conclusions may be drawn when some techniques fail to work as they should. Many times, however, the procedure was used inappropriately or perhaps not long enough to get results, or this may simply be one of those occasions when nothing will work (i.e., the 20 percent of the time previously referred to). If you have a thorough knowledge of the techniques in this book, you will be better prepared to meet challenges at home or in the classroom. However, any change in behavior occurs slowly; knowing what to do and actually doing it are two completely different things. It will require some practice and feedback to assure that changes in the approach to behavior management have actually occurred.

9. **Join a support group.** Many local and national organizations allow parents and teachers to share information and to realize that they are not alone in dealing with the behavior of a child with ADD/ADHD. You may benefit greatly by being able to exchange ideas, and share feelings and common concerns. Typically, these support groups will also have some of the latest information on new procedures, products and services. The largest organization is CH.A.D.D. (See the address and phone number listed in Appendix F).

10. **General resources.** All parents and teachers must stay abreast of new products, services, books, and so on. A list of centers that provide resources for parents and teachers, as well as the children, is listed in Appendix F.

11. **Consider adult ADD.** Many parents and some teachers, as well as other professionals, may recognize characteristics of ADD/ADHD in themselves as they read and learn about problematic behavior in their children. For parents, this may not be at all unusual, since there is a strong genetic component that is well documented for this disorder. While adult ADD has not been a primary focus in this book, there are many books, checklists, workbooks, and tests oriented toward the adult with ADD/ADHD. Since this disorder may either be co-morbid with or serve as a potential catalyst for several other significant clinical disorders, it may be an excellent way for parents to begin looking at sources of problems they have encountered along with their children. It is reasonable to assume that when a parent is treated or becomes aware of such problems, orientation to and manner of coping with the child with ADD/ADHD often changes. As a result, the overall relationship changes and the child's behavior may improve, even if nothing else does. A list of resources for adults with ADD is provided in Appendix F.
12. **Specific resources.** Refer to the information provided in the appendixes of this book to aid you on the evaluation and treatment of ADD/ADHD.

APPENDIX A

A Neuropsychological Report

NEUROPSYCHOLOGICAL REPORT

NAME:	Male Child	AGE:	7 years, 3 months
DATES TESTED:		BIRTH DATE:	
REFERRED BY:	X. Y., M.D.	GRADE:	2nd

TESTS ADMINISTERED

Wechsler Intelligence Scale for Children—III
Wechsler Individual Achievement Test
Wide Range Achievement Test—Revised
Peabody Picture Vocabulary Test—Revised
Jordan Left-Right Reversal Test
Wisconsin Card Sorting Test
Trail Making Test
Finger Tapping
Grooved Pegboard
Strength of Grip Test
Wide Range Assessment of Memory and Learning
Beery Developmental Test of Visual-Motor Integration
Screening Test for Auditory Processing Disorders (SCAN)
Drawings on Command
Alphabet and Numbers
Human Figure Drawing
Kinetic Family Drawings
Sentence Completion Test
Conners Teacher Rating Scale
Conners Parent Rating Scale
ACTeRS Profile
Dyslexia Screening Test
Gordon Diagnostic Assessment of Attention
Intermediate Visual & Auditory Continuous Performance Test
Personality Inventory for Children
Pediatric Questionnaire
Behavioral Observations
Developmental History Questionnaire
Review of Records
Clinical Interview with mother, father, and stepmother

REFERRAL INFORMATION

This child is a 7-year, 3-month-old right-handed white male who was referred by neurologist X. Y., M.D. This child has reportedly had episodes of difficulty in concentration, which started during preschool and has continued throughout his current 2nd grade placement. Occasional staring spells were also described, but without any apparent loss of consciousness or tonoclonic disorders. In addition to difficulty concentrating, he has been disruptive in class by running around and being hyperactive. A tentative diagnosis of Attention Deficit Hyperactivity Disorder was given by his neurologist, Dr. Y. However, other neurological diagnoses have been considered, including a seizure disorder. In addition to the current neuropsychological evaluation, an EEG and an MRI have been scheduled. The purpose of this evaluation was to assist in providing a more complete overall clinical picture providing some elucidation of strengths and weaknesses, and recommendations for behavioral interventions.

Developmental History

Information regarding this boy's developmental history was provided by his mother, his father, and his stepmother. According to his natural mother, "My son had a rough birth." His mother took Inderal for her diagnosed Mitral Valve Prolapse. His mother also noted, "I had to premedicate with antibiotics for delivery. During the 7th month, I tried to start labor early and was given medication." She reports that she had two weeks of false contractions (2-5 minutes apart) with pains in her back. The delivery was very stressful, and affected both mother and the baby's heart rate. She noted, "My son's heart rate had slowed due to the Inderal, and I was told that the baby had died and was being revived. This was within 6 hours of the birth due to low blood sugar." Earlier there were breathing difficulties at birth and the child weighed 8 lbs, 11 ozs, delivered full term. No Apgar scores were available. Jaundice was reported at birth.

According to this child's mother, he was very active as a baby and she reported that he had to be constantly walked: "He wouldn't stay in one place." Feeding was also very difficult, and he was very resistant to new foods. Sleep was another problem area as he reportedly was up at about 4 A.M. His pediatrician, Dr. P. put him on 5 mgs. of Catapres. The child reportedly withdrew when strange people appeared. It was also noted that he did not adapt very well to changes in routine. He cried very loudly and drank his bottle quickly.

Developmental milestones were generally within normal limits. His mother reported that he crawled at approximately 6 to 7 months of age, sat up around 5 to 6 months of age, and walked around 10 months of age. Toilet training occurred at 3 years of age with no significant problems. Bed wetting continued until approximately 3 years of age with no subsequent problems. There was no significant developmental delay in speech, as noted by his mother. However, developmental estimates of language acquisition were not available. Further, she did report that "as a toddler, he frequently became angry while playing and often threw his toys."

General Health and Medical History

This child has never had a significant head injury or a broken bone, nor has there been any problem with ingestion of a poison or medicine. In fact, it was reported that he has never had a major illness. He has not been hospitalized. In addition, his parents noted that there was no history of ear infections with high fevers, no use of tubes, nor has he had a fever over 102 degrees.

In August this year, Dr. Y. conducted a neurological examination. On his physical exam, he reports that this boy's "face is notable for possible mild hypertelorism, somewhat flattened philtrum. Cranial nerves were essentially intact and visual fields were full to finger confrontation." Fundoscopic exam was within normal limits, and he reports "normal sensation on the face with normal hearing to finger rub." "Motor exam showed no drift and strength was 5/5 in the upper and lower extremities. Reflexes were 2 and symmetric in the biceps, triceps, brachial radialis, knees, and ankles. Finger-nose-finger was intact. He could do normal hopping on one leg and normal tandem gait." The overall report was a normal neurological exam, but to rule out for absence seizures, an EEG and an MRI were recommended.

An EEG conducted at the city's hospital, this year, was reportedly within normal limits for this patient's age. While there was a basic background rhythm of 9 1/2 to 10 hertz alpha, predominantly posteriorly, there was also intermittent frontal beta, as well as intermittent frontal rhythmic low frequency activity noted in the theta range. Hyperventilation induced a marked diffuse high amplitude delta and theta activity which was symmetric. Photic stimulation produced no abnormalities.

An MRI was also conducted, this year, with the impression of a "normal MRI of the brain," along with "inflammation in the maxillary sinuses, bilaterally."

Also, this year, it was noted that this child had started on treatment of Ritalin 20 mgs. po at 9 a.m. and Catapres, and Ritalin at lunch, and 10 mgs. Ritalin po at 3 p.m. His mother reports that the Catapres helps with his apparent behavioral dyscontrol and his sleeping problems. However, the Ritalin, on the dose scheduled, does not appear to modify his classroom behavior. In the past, this boy had seen Dr. Y., a neurologist, who gave him a trial of Dexedrine, which did not appear to help him significantly at that time.

According to his parents, this child does have some continuing sleep problems. On occasions, he even appears to have been "sleepwalking," as he reportedly goes from his bottom bunk to his mother's room. This boy also reportedly falls asleep in the car when he is riding for long periods of time. He goes to bed at approximately 8 P.M. and takes about 30 minutes to unwind. During his sleep, he has been noted to kick, toss, and talk; he also reportedly grinds his teeth.

FAMILY SITUATION

This child's parents had problems in their relationship during the pregnancy, and the boy's early infancy. Subsequently, they have separated and divorced. The child's father has remarried, and brief biological family history reveals a positive incidence of emotional problems, suicide, and learning problems. In addition, his father has noted that he seemed to be "hyperactive" as a youngster. This youngster has a brother, age 10, who reportedly has "no problems." For the most part, this brother "gets honors in school and the client says he would like to be like his brother." Currently, this patient lives with his mother and goes to live with his father every other weekend. Mother, father, and stepmother all appear to get along well, and stated this fact in the interview.

EDUCATIONAL HISTORY

According to his mother, this child did attend kindergarten, but not nursery school. During these early grades, he was described as happy, hard to leave, and fearful. At present, his parents believe that he is unenthusiastic about school, and tries less than average. His best subject is reported to be spelling, while his worst subject is math. The biggest difficulty regarding school work is that "he will not complete his work." This boy has reportedly had most of his trouble in school, and gets angry with himself about some of the difficulties he experiences. In particular, he has had difficulty writing, and his father noted that "he has had some problems reversing letters like b's and q's."

SOCIAL BEHAVIOR

This boy has had no trouble with friendships. However, at times, he reportedly "seems to be in a world of his own." His father notes that "he looks through you." Sometimes he can answer questions about what is said, but on most occasions, he seems to miss the point. His father also notes that his son has a "problem with aggressiveness. He is very stubborn and hardheaded—it's his way, or no way." He continues to explain that he is "aggressive with his brother. He angers easily and gets angry with himself when he is frustrated." However, it is also observed that his emotions change rather quickly; as his father says, "the next minute he can be loving you." Despite the aggression noted, he also seems to "have more patience when his brother shows him things." This child is described as a "picky eater—he often wants hot dogs and pizza all the time." He reportedly gets hungry during the night, and while he eats, "he plays with everything." His parents report that they have no problems in social situations, such as church, as he will often take something with him to play with (e.g., cards). He enjoys athletic games and according to his parents, has few problems in this area.

Behavioral Observations

This child is a 7-year, 3-month-old white male who has blonde hair and green eyes. He is of average height and weight for his age, and he is right-handed. He appeared for this first session of this evaluation wearing a blue, green, and white shirt, green shorts, white socks, with black athletic shoes. His only distinguishing physical feature consists of freckles sprinkled across his nose.

Initial contact with this boy was unremarkable. He showed excellent cooperation, with good eye contact, yet at times appeared slightly depressed. Attention and concentration were good on most tasks, but only fair on some of the specific attentional tests. He appeared to be distracted by outside noises. Overall activity was considered within normal limits. He showed a normal degree of fidgeting, as well as normal persistence on tasks. However, on the attentional tasks, he did need continuous praise and encouragement. Moderate impulsivity was noted in general, with a high level of impulsivity on specific attentional measures. His motivation appeared to be generally average. On occasions, he appeared to distract himself with pencil tapping. In fact, whenever he had a pencil, he would play with it. In general, he showed fairly good self-confidence in his responses, and he was able to maintain some level of conversation with the examiner. Comprehension to task appeared to be fairly good on most tasks. On one occasion, this child noted, "I almost died at birth, but the doctor saved me." When he was asked to elaborate on this unusual comment, he stated, "Ask my mom about it; I'm stupid—I don't know all that stuff." He continued stating, "I'm not very smart; I almost failed first grade."

This child was alert and oriented on most tasks, and smiled only occasionally during the evaluation. Overall rapport was considered fair. He looked around the room quite a bit. After given some test instructions, he would indicate that he understood. However, when questioned, he would be unable to explain what he was asked to do.

The obtained results from this evaluation appear to adequately reflect this child's abilities and achievements, as well as his behavioral and emotional characteristics.

Assessment of Classroom Behavior

On the ACTeRS Profile, this boy's teacher rated him as having moderate difficulties with regard to attention, hyperactivity, and social skills; little difficulty was noted with regard to oppositional behavior in the morning sessions. In the afternoon, his teacher noted some deterioration of his behavior with severe problems in the areas of attention, hyperactivity, and social skills. These ratings were obtained during a period of time when he was on his initial medication schedule.

His teacher, Ms. Z, noted, "I have found in observing him that there is a certain time that he seems to come out of his quiet and most well-behaved period. The time seems to be right around 9:40 A.M. It's almost as though he has been asleep and all of a sudden, he is aggressive, and sometimes hostile. For example, when I see he isn't doing his work right, he gets mad and will say "I don't care." Ms. Z continues to note, "He cannot attend to any group directions, or stay still long enough to complete an assignment."

Classroom behavioral problems include fidgeting, making noises, being easily frustrated, restless, excitable, inattentive, and easily distracted. He also reportedly disturbs other children, and shows mood changes that are quick and dramatic.

Overall, this child is noted to be easily led by others, lacks a sense of fair play, and teases others or interferes with their activities. In relationship to authority figures, he is noted to be defiant and imprudent, as well as stubborn. He shows an excessive demand for the teacher's attention. Overall, his behavior is noted to be worse than that of many others in the class.

On the Dyslexia Screening Instrument, completed by his teacher, his score is most similar to the scores of students in the development sample who were identified as having dyslexia.

Assessment of Intelligence and Achievements

On the Wechsler Intelligence Scale for Children—III, this child achieved a verbal IQ of 111, a performance IQ of 100, and a full-scale IQ of 106. Overall, he is currently functioning within the AVERAGE RANGE OF MENTAL ABILITIES and is at the 66th percentile, compared with other children his age. The difference between his verbal and performance IQs is statistically significant at the 85% confidence level. This indicates less than a 15% possibility that the difference represents a chance variation, rather than an actual difference between verbal and performance skills. The following are his subtest scores:

Wechsler Intelligence Scale for Children—III

	SS		SS
INFORMATION	9	PICTURE COMPLETION	13
SIMILARITIES	14	CODING	7
ARITHMETIC	14	PICTURE ARRANGEMENT	12
VOCABULARY	13	BLOCK DESIGN	9
COMPREHENSION	9	OBJECT ASSEMBLY	9
DIGIT SPAN	8	SYMBOL SEARCH	12

On the Verbal Comprehension Factor, this boy's performance was within the AVERAGE RANGE with a corresponding Index Score of 108. This suggests that his ability to apply verbal skills and information to the solution of new problems is AVERAGE and reflects average ability to process verbal information. His ability to think and solve problems in nonverbal, abstract, and conceptual terms was also within the AVERAGE RANGE. His Perceptual Performance Index score was 106, and measures his ability to form abstract-visual concepts without the use of words, as well as his ability to manipulate objects and to perceive relationships between them. His Freedom From Distractibility Factor measures his ability to sustain attention and maintain concentration and effort on task. His performance on these measures suggests an AVERAGE ABILITY with an Index Score of 106. Speed of Mental Processing, which reflects his short-term visual and nonverbal memory, is a measure of how quickly he can grasp and retain visual information. His index score of 99 suggests an adequate ability to learn material within an average amount of time compared to other students his age.

Compared with other students his age, this child's performance on the Ability Tasks suggests strengths in the areas of verbal concept formation, vocabulary, and verbal fluency. However, he also showed weaknesses relative to his peers with regard to short-term visual memory and perceptual motor integration.

This boy's reasoning index is greater than that of his recall. This suggests strengths in abstraction, relational thinking, and insight, despite his relatively weak memory or limited educational experience. His performance on the Digits Span Subtest ranks at the 25th percentile, which is moderately weak relative to other verbal measures. Consequently, problems involving immediate memory, mental alertness, and attention are all characteristic. It is also important to note that these basic types of functions may influence more complex cognitive skills. His performance on the Coding Subtest falls at the 16th percentile, which is also moderately weak relative to other performance measures. This performance measure reflects visual-motor coordination with emphasis upon psychomotor speed.

On the Wide Range Achievement Test—Revised, this boy obtained the following test scores in basic skill areas of reading, spelling, and arithmetic:

WRAT—R

TEST RESULTS:	STANDARD SCORE	PERCENTILE	GRADE EQUIVALENTS
READING	102	55	Middle 2nd Grade
SPELLING	81	10	Middle 1st Grade
ARITHMETIC	93	32	End of 1st Grade

His performance on the reading subtest was generally within NORMAL LIMITS for his grade placement, and also consistent with his ability test measures. He was slightly low with regard to his achievements in spelling and arithmetic, with spelling being significantly discrepant from his ability test measures. His difficulties are most clearly manifested in his handwriting, which appears labored at times, and is also characterized by poor letter formation, as well as significant tendencies to reverse certain letters. His problems are consistent with visual-spatial dysfunction and difficulty with fine-motor coordination. Overall, this gives the impression of mild to moderate dysgraphia.

On the Wechsler Individual Achievement Test, this child obtained the following test scores in the table below. Again, his performance on the basic reading test was within the expected range, with a Standard Score of 107. Reading Comprehension was also average for his grade placement. His performance on arithmetic calculations yielded a Standard Score of 103, which reflects average ability to perform basic pencil and paper math. However, on the Math Reasoning subtest, his Standard Score of 82 suggests that his ability to utilize math skills when applied to real-life situations was BELOW AVERAGE.

Executive Functions

On the Trail Making Test, this boy's performance was impaired for both Part A (67 seconds) and Part B (205 seconds). His performance reflected deficiencies with regard to both visual scanning and searching and visual-spatial sequencing. His performance on Part A may be considered POOR, while his performance on Part B was VERY POOR. It is most notable that he had much difficulty shifting from one mental set to another; this was particularly evident on Part B.

WIAT

	G.E.	S.S.	%
Reading	2.0	107	68
Reading Comprehension	2.2	107	68
Math Calculation	1.9	103	58
Math Reasoning	K.3	82	12
Written Language	2.8	116	86
Listening Comprehension	—	108	70
Oral Expression	—	105	63

This boy also had some difficulty on the Wisconsin Card Sorting Test. However, these deficiencies reflected only mild impairment with regard to the degree of perseveration noted. It should, however, be emphasized that his performance was fairly good overall, with the exception of his perseverative responses. This would suggest only mild difficulty on this task that is also indicative of problems in cognitive flexibility.

On the Maze Test of the WISC—III, he did experience some difficulty with visual-motor coordination and became slightly confused at times. However, his overall performance on this task was essentially within NORMAL LIMITS (Scale Score = 11).

Language Functions

Receptive language skills are quite good for this child's age (PPVT-R: Standard Score = 108, 70th percentile, Age Equivalent = 8 years, 0 months). On a Screening Test for Auditory Processing Disorders, his performance is essentially within NORMAL LIMITS (Scan Composite: Standard Score = 95, 37th percentile, Age Equivalent = 6 years, 9 months). His performance on the Vocabulary Subtest of the WISC—III (Expressive Language Functions) ranks at the 84th percentile and may be considered slightly strong relative to other verbal measures. In addition to being an estimate of word knowledge and language development, this performance also indicates adequate long-term memory, concept formation, acquired knowledge, and comprehension.

Motor Skills Assessment

On the Finger Tapping Test, this boy's average right-hand performance over 5 trials was 31.2, while his performance on the left hand was 29.2 taps. There was essentially no right-hand advantage on this task, and his performance must be considered SOMEWHAT SLOWED for both hands. The lack of right-hand dominance reflects poorer performance on the preferred right hand. Likewise, his strength of grip averaged 13.0 kilograms on the preferred right hand, compared with 15.0 kilograms on the left hand. While his right hand is within NORMAL LIMITS, it is clearly poorer than his left when the dominance factor is considered.

On the Grooved Pegboard, a more complex task of manual dexterity and visual-motor coordination, his performance was slow on both hands with yet another indication of the lack of advantage for the right hand (Right Hand: 125 seconds; Left Hand: 121 seconds). This overall pattern suggests mild motor difficulty, but primarily with his preferred right hand.

Visual Motor/Visual Perceptual Skills

On the Beery Developmental Test of Visual Motor Integration, this child's performance was POOR for his age (Beery VMI: Age Equivalent = 5 years, 7 months, 6th percentile). This task reflects poor visual motor integrative skills and may also relate to his poorly developed expressive writing skills. In his graphic reproduction of the alphabet and numbers from 1-10, he not only had difficulty forming the letters, but also committed reversals in both letters and numbers. In addition, it was quite clear that his performance was labored and he experienced considerable frustration on this task.

On the Jordan Left-Right Reversal Test, his performance was BELOW NORMAL LIMITS with a development age of less than 5 years. This would suggest some difficulty in actual discrimination of the visual-spatial orientation of letters. While this characteristic has been noted in certain patterns of dyslexia, many of the characteristics as rated by his teacher on the Dyslexia Screening Instrument refer to behavioral manifestations of Attention Deficit Disorder, along with his difficulty in his handwriting, copying, and general organization of work. A few of his rated characteristics do appear to reflect underlying problems that may affect his reading and math performances, and unless remediated, may have a greater impact in higher grade levels.

Learning and Memory

On the Wide Range Assessment of Memory and Learning, this boy obtained the following index scores:

WRAML INDEX SCORES

	INDEX	PERCENTILE
Verbal Memory Index	98	45
Visual Memory Index	107	68
Learning Index	91	27
General Memory Index	98	45

His poor performance on the Sound Symbol Subtest (Learning Scale) suggests a major area of weakness in associating sounds and visual symbols. At times, his answers are completely unrelated to any of the sounds of the subtest, indicating that he is not only having some difficulty matching sounds to symbols, but also difficulty remembering the group of sounds that are introduced. Also, even when he does remember a given sound, he may not retain that association on the next trial. Following the delay, he may forget all sound-symbol associations. In addition to this area of difficulty, it is also clear that he has more general problems dealing with visual stimuli. For example, on one of the verbal memory subtests, his only difficulty encountered was on the number-letter memory task, which involves sequencing, attention, immediate memory, and cognitive shifting. On the visual memory index, his only problem was on visual sequencing tasks, and on the general memory index, his difficulty on delayed recall of visually learned material was the only one falling within the LOW AVERAGE RANGE. All other subtests were within the AVERAGE RANGE. While he may not have a memory problem per se, he does seem to have some difficulty remembering sounds and visual symbols associated with those sounds, which has a characteristic "dyslexic" quality. Results from other subtests would suggest that once this child learns a word, his comprehension skills should increase. Consequently, there is a need to develop more automatic word attack skills. He also performs more poorly on tasks requiring that spontaneous organizational demands be combined with short-term memory. Essentially, he may reach a point of "information overload." Although he may have the ability to hold some information in short-term memory, he lacks the ability to apply internal organizational strategies. Consequently, learning may proceed quite slowly and laboriously as material that has previously been processed may be neglected as new material is added. In short, this boy is experiencing difficulties with organization of material such that he may have problems remembering larger quantities of new and unrelated information. His impulsive and inefficient attentional skills may also result in problems of learning and memory as he encounters greater amounts of rote material to learn.

Attention and Concentration

On the Gordon Diagnostic Assessment of Attention, this child's performance on the Delay Task falls within the NORMAL RANGE. This demonstrates adequate capacity for delay and inhibition on this basic self-control measure. However, on the Vigilance Task, his correct responses fall within the ABNORMAL RANGE, indicating significant lapses in sustained attention. Errors fall within the BORDERLINE RANGE, reflecting a moderate level of impulsivity. His performance was also inconsistent on this task, reflecting a fluctuating level of self-control. It should also be noted that during the early stages of this task, his performance was quite disorganized, but he was able to adjust somewhat and did become better controlled. On the Distractibility Task, his correct responses fall within the NORMAL RANGE yet errors are within the ABNORMAL RANGE, reflecting a high level of impulsivity. This overall pattern reflects a somewhat random pattern of responding to the stimuli as his performance was quite erratic over time. It is also clear that while his initial performance was marginal, he tended to deteriorate rather quickly with regard to both his correct responses and errors (impulsivity).

On the IVA (Intermediate Test of Visual and Auditory Attention), this boy's performance was consistent with ADHD (predominantly inattentive type). Experiencing difficulty in processing visual stimuli, he literally ignored one half of the visual targets presented. Thus, he was unable to "pay attention" to visual and auditory stimuli at the same time. It was significant that he had difficulty shifting sets trying to respond to auditory stimuli while randomly responding to the visual stimuli. In short, he was extremely inattentive to auditory stimuli, while his attention was better toward visual stimuli (although he ignored about 50% of these visual targets). It is also significant that his reaction times were significantly slowed for both auditory (435 ms) and visual (250 ms) stimuli on the sensory/motor scale. This reflects poor processing, especially for visual stimuli, and is consistent with neuropsychological dysfunction.

On the ADHD Test, the boy's mother rated him as having significant ADHD problems (ADHD Quotient = 121, 92nd percentile). This rating falls within the HIGH PROBABILITY RANGE for having ADHD. Significant problems are noted with regard to hyperactivity and impulsivity, with secondary problems related to inattention.

Behavioral and Emotional Assessment

According to information supplied by his mother, this child appears to have a very high degree of adjustment problems. Temper tantrums, sassing, destruction of property or toys, fighting and yelling, are all characteristically seen, along with general noncompliance. Some sleep difficulties have been noted to include restlessness, along with awakening during the night. Muscular twitches, jerking and shaking movements have also been observed. In addition, significant headaches have been reported to occur pretty much of the time. Overall, his level of physical complaints appears excessive. He is also noted to cry easily and to act in an overly dependent manner, at times, even clinging to his parents. This child is emotionally sensitive, restless, excitable, and impulsive. He also experiences some temper outbursts, along with pouting and sulking behavior. According to his mother, there is an excessive tendency to deny wrongdoing, or to blame others for his mistakes. He also confabulates stories about what has happened to account for his actions. Emotionally labile, he appears to have difficulty controlling his behavior and is described as having a low level of frustration tolerance. In addition to problems controlling his temper, he at times has some difficulty with depression. On occasions, he has had some difficulty appropriately identifying his feeling states. This child also appears to exhibit a poor self-concept with a low level of self-esteem. He is quite critical of himself for his poor school performance. Comparisons are often made to his brother and he openly admits to wanting to be like him.

Considerable frustration also appears to be associated with school. According to his mother, some of his difficulties involve excess talking in class and being out of his seat.

Interpretive Summary and Recommendations

This boy is currently functioning with the RANGE OF AVERAGE INTELLIGENCE with slightly better developed verbal as opposed to nonverbal visual-spatial skills. He also shows relatively poor ability to grasp and retain visual information. Visual discrimination, visual-spatial sequencing, visual searching, and visual motor difficulties have all been noted. He even experiences some greater difficulty in recall of visually learned material. In particular, there is difficulty with sound-symbol learning, i.e., the association of phonetic sounds and visual symbols. This may clearly impair his memory and learning processes. Although he does not exhibit a significant delay in the development of basic reading skills at this time, he reportedly does experience greater difficulty with oral reading and does exhibit some "dyslexic-type characteristics." Letter reversals, along with difficulties in handwriting, characterized by poor letter formation, letter reversals, and considerable frustration are associated with his graphic writing difficulty, but described as a mild dysgraphia. On attentional tasks, he certainly does have difficulty with lapses in attention and does manifest a considerable amount of impulsivity. He is slow to process information, especially in the visual mode, and is significantly slow in his motor reaction times. He may easily become overwhelmed by complex tasks commonly completed by most 7-year-old children.

His overall test pattern is consistent with an ATTENTION DEFICIT HYPERACTIVITY DISORDER, which is compounded by his significant dysgraphia and a mild visual-spatial "dyslexic-type pattern" associated with difficulties involving the orthographic features of written language. Neuropsychologically, these characteristics would not be unusual in consideration of the residual effects of anoxia at birth that is often associated with ADD and LD characteristics. This diffuse pattern is also not atypical considering recent findings pointing to additional involvement of subcortical brain structures that are implicated and associated with allocating and focusing attentional resources on linguistic tasks. In general, there is evidence of significant chronic, but static, neuropsychological dysfunction which may involve multiple cortical and possibly subcortical sites. In particular, there is evidence of mild dysfunction with regard to motor functions and a clear lack of advantage with his dominant right hand. In addition, this child presents difficulties in adaptive behavior that further impair his overall adjustment.

This child is emotionally immature, emotionally sensitive, and emotionally labile; he has much difficulty controlling anger and is easily aroused with a low level of frustration tolerance. At times, he's depressed and exhibits a poor self-concept and low self-esteem. Some of his feelings of inadequacy are brought out even more when he compares himself to his brother, who is doing well in school.

Notwithstanding, the following recommendations are offered in this case:

1. Targeted medication to address his Attention Deficit Hyperactivity Disorder, as well as associated aggressive tendencies.
2. A cognitive neuropsychological habilitation approach to foster the development of attentional skills. In addition, both attention and concentration may be facilitated through everyday practice in areas such as drawing, painting, computer programming, and woodworking.
3. Because handwriting is an extremely difficult skill to develop, his written assignments may need to be modified and his examination for acquired knowledge in tests may either need to be much shorter or orally based.
4. While he is working on the development of handwriting skills, along with the remediation of mild dysgraphia, use of some type of assisted devices like dictation machines, mnemonic devices, or a computer would be most beneficial. Further development of manual dexterity may include everyday activities such as writing, drawing, painting, completing crafts, working with various types of hand tools, typing, video games, and other computer programs.
5. This child would also appear to benefit from learning how to organize material that is to be memorized. Review of chapter headings, noting the content of pictures, and reading chapter summaries may help to organize material for retrieval of such information in future assignments. In addition, mnemonic aids such as associating pictures with words, along with descriptive labels, may utilize both auditory-phonetic and the visual-spatial aspects of reading.
6. In an attempt to teach to his strengths, teachers would be well advised to emphasize an auditory-phonetic approach to the development of word attack skills or more emphasis on phonetics in general. He will clearly need much tutoring and remedial work in the areas of reading and spelling, as well as handwriting, even though his current achievements do not, at this time, reflect significant problems.
7. A comprehensive visual examination to rule out any basic visual defects would also be essential.
8. An individualized therapy program focusing on the development of adaptive control of social-emotional behavior. This program should target areas of impulse control, stress management, and anger control.
9. A comprehensive behavior management program for his parents and stepparent. This would be designed to insure consistency in dealing with his behavior across various situations. Additional involvement of his teacher(s) in a home-school system could also allow for enhanced communication regarding his school behavior in a behaviorally based program.
10. Periodic consultation with this child's teacher(s) to promote the use of the most effective techniques of behavior management in the classroom.
11. A repeat neuropsychological evaluation within one year to assess his developmental status and the effectiveness of his therapy program.

Respectfully,

____

Clinical Psychologist

APPENDIX B

Rating Scales

TEACHER RATING FORM

ACTeRS® 2nd Edition

Rina K. Ullmann, M. Ed.
Esther K. Sleator, M.D.
Robert L. Sprague, Ph.D.

Below are descriptions of behavior. Please read each item and compare the child's behavior with that of his or her classmates. Circle the number that most closely corresponds with your evaluation. Transfer the total raw score for each of the four sections to the profile sheet to determine normative percentile scores.

Child's Name: Chris Student
Rater: Mrs. Truitt
ID#: 60952
Date: 9-11-97

ATTENTION	Almost Never				Almost Always
1. Works well independently	1	**2**	3	4	5
2. Persists with task for reasonable amount of time	**1**	2	3	4	5
3. Completes assigned task satisfactorily with little additional assistance	1	**2**	3	4	5
4. Follows simple directions accurately	1	2	**3**	4	5
5. Follows a sequence of instructions	1	**2**	3	4	5
6. Functions well in the classroom	1	**2**	3	4	5

ADD ITEMS 1-6 AND PLACE TOTAL HERE 12

HYPERACTIVITY	Almost Never				Almost Always
7. Extremely overactive (out of seat, "on the go")	1	2	3	**4**	5
8. Overreacts	1	**2**	3	4	5
9. Fidgety (hands always busy)	1	2	**3**	4	5
10. Impulsive (acts or talks without thinking)	1	**2**	3	4	5
11. Restless (squirms in seat)	1	2	3	**4**	5

ADD ITEMS 7-11 AND PLACE TOTAL HERE 15

SOCIAL SKILLS	Almost Never				Almost Always
12. Behaves positively with peers/classmates	1	2	**3**	4	5
13. Verbal communication clear and "connected"	1	2	3	**4**	5
14. Nonverbal communication accurate	1	2	3	**4**	5
15. Follows group norms and social rules	1	**2**	3	4	5
16. Cites general rule when criticizing ("We aren't supposed to do that")	1	2	3	**4**	5
17. Skillful at making new friends	1	**2**	3	4	5
18. Approaches situations confidently	1	2	3	4	**5**

ADD ITEMS 12-18 AND PLACE TOTAL HERE 24

OPPOSITIONAL	Almost Never				Almost Always
19. Tries to get others into trouble	1	**2**	3	4	5
20. Starts fights over nothing	**1**	2	3	4	5
21. Makes malicious fun of people	1	**2**	3	4	5
22. Defies authority	1	**2**	3	4	5
23. Picks on others	1	**2**	3	4	5
24. Mean and cruel to other children	1	**2**	3	4	5

ADD ITEMS 19-24 AND PLACE TOTAL HERE 11

MetriTech, Inc.

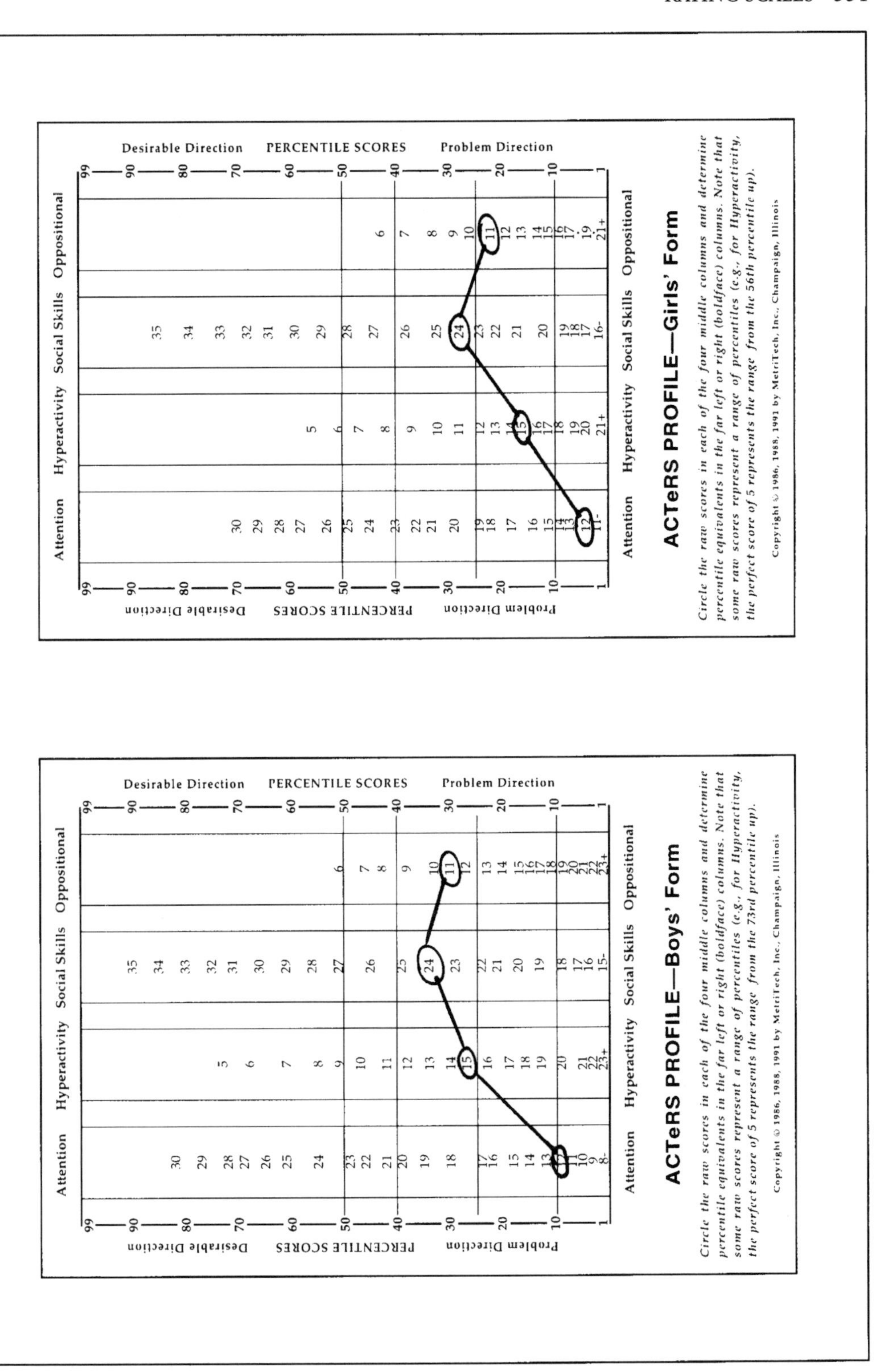
TEACHER RATING PROFILE
Attention Hyperactivity Social Skills Oppositional
Desirable Direction PERCENTILE SCORES Problem Direction
ACTeRS PROFILE—Boys' Form
Circle the raw scores in each of the four middle columns and determine percentile equivalents in the far left or right (boldface) columns. Note that some raw scores represent a range of percentiles (e.g., for Hyperactivity, the perfect score of 5 represents the range from the 73rd percentile up).
Copyright © 1986, 1988, 1991 by MetriTech, Inc., Champaign, Illinois
ACTeRS PROFILE—Girls' Form
Circle the raw scores in each of the four middle columns and determine percentile equivalents in the far left or right (boldface) columns. Note that some raw scores represent a range of percentiles (e.g., for Hyperactivity, the perfect score of 5 represents the range from the 56th percentile up).
Copyright © 1986, 1988, 1991 by MetriTech, Inc., Champaign, Illinois

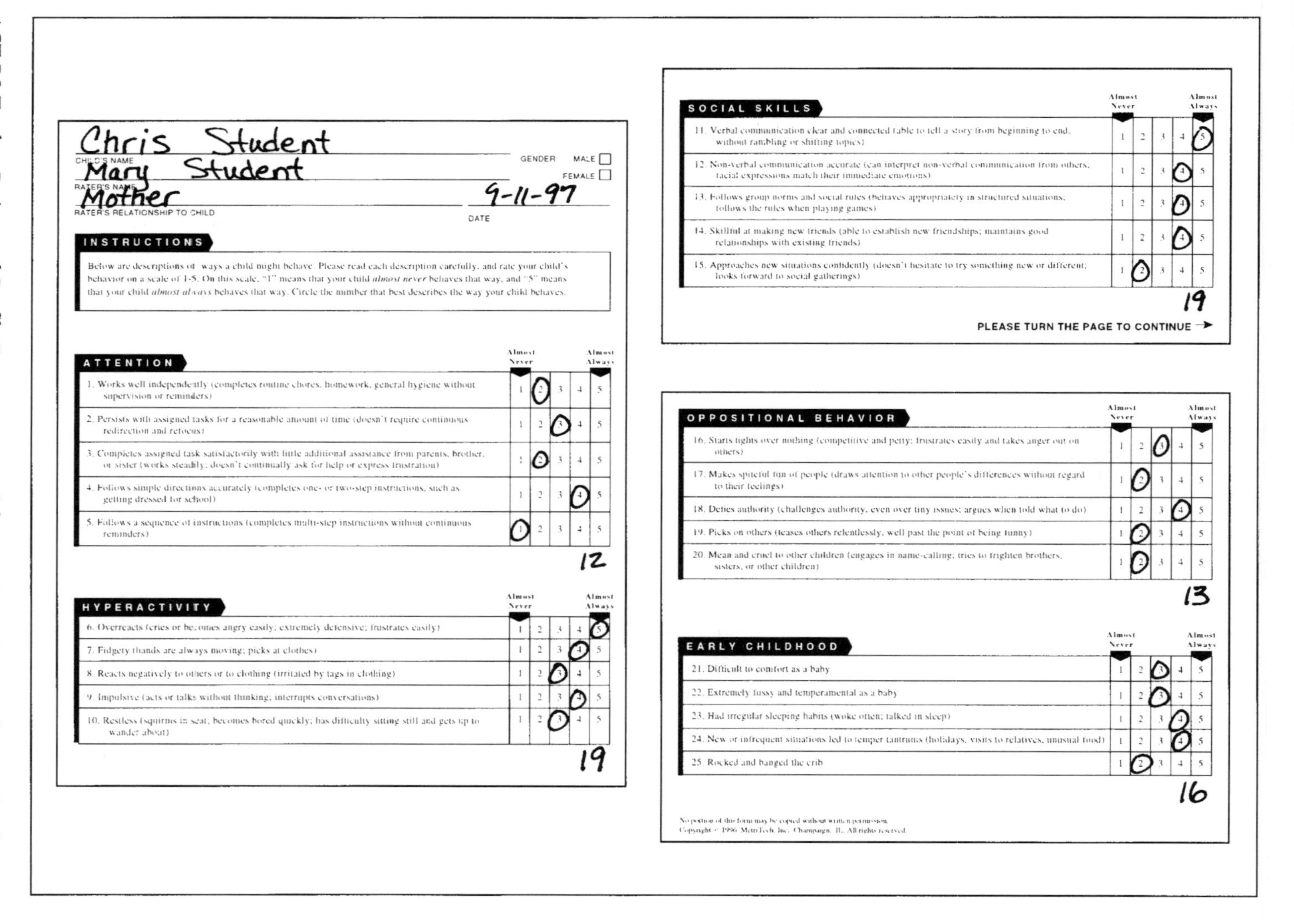

PARENT RATING FORM

Chris Student
CHILD'S NAME

Mary Student
RATER'S NAME

Mother
RATER'S RELATIONSHIP TO CHILD

GENDER MALE ☐ FEMALE ☐

9-11-97
DATE

INSTRUCTIONS

Below are descriptions of ways a child might behave. Please read each description carefully, and rate your child's behavior on a scale of 1-5. On this scale, "1" means that your child *almost never* behaves that way, and "5" means that your child *almost always* behaves that way. Circle the number that best describes the way your child behaves.

ATTENTION	Almost Never				Almost Always
1. Works well independently (completes routine chores, homework, general hygiene without supervision or reminders)	1	(2)	3	4	5
2. Persists with assigned tasks for a reasonable amount of time (doesn't require continuous redirection and refocus)	1	2	(3)	4	5
3. Completes assigned task satisfactorily with little additional assistance from parents, brother, or sister (works steadily; doesn't continually ask for help or express frustration)	1	(2)	3	4	5
4. Follows simple directions accurately (completes one- or two-step instructions, such as getting dressed for school)	1	2	3	(4)	5
5. Follows a sequence of instructions (completes multi-step instructions without continuous reminders)	(1)	2	3	4	5

12

HYPERACTIVITY	Almost Never				Almost Always
6. Overreacts (cries or becomes angry easily; extremely defensive; frustrates easily)	1	2	3	4	(5)
7. Fidgety (hands are always moving; picks at clothes)	1	2	3	(4)	5
8. Reacts negatively to others or to clothing (irritated by tags in clothing)	1	2	(3)	4	5
9. Impulsive (acts or talks without thinking; interrupts conversations)	1	2	3	(4)	5
10. Restless (squirms in seat; becomes bored quickly; has difficulty sitting still and gets up to wander about)	1	2	(3)	4	5

19

SOCIAL SKILLS	Almost Never				Almost Always
11. Verbal communication clear and connected (able to tell a story from beginning to end, without rambling or shifting topics)	1	2	3	4	(5)
12. Non-verbal communication accurate (can interpret non-verbal communication from others; facial expressions match their immediate emotions)	1	2	3	(4)	5
13. Follows group norms and social rules (behaves appropriately in structured situations; follows the rules when playing games)	1	2	3	(4)	5
14. Skillful at making new friends (able to establish new friendships; maintains good relationships with existing friends)	1	2	3	(4)	5
15. Approaches new situations confidently (doesn't hesitate to try something new or different; looks forward to social gatherings)	1	(2)	3	4	5

19

PLEASE TURN THE PAGE TO CONTINUE →

OPPOSITIONAL BEHAVIOR	Almost Never				Almost Always
16. Starts fights over nothing (competitive and petty; frustrates easily and takes anger out on others)	1	2	(3)	4	5
17. Makes spiteful fun of people (draws attention to other people's differences without regard to their feelings)	1	(2)	3	4	5
18. Defies authority (challenges authority, even over tiny issues; argues when told what to do)	1	2	3	(4)	5
19. Picks on others (teases others relentlessly, well past the point of being funny)	1	(2)	3	4	5
20. Mean and cruel to other children (engages in name-calling; tries to frighten brothers, sisters, or other children)	1	(2)	3	4	5

13

EARLY CHILDHOOD	Almost Never				Almost Always
21. Difficult to comfort as a baby	1	2	(3)	4	5
22. Extremely fussy and temperamental as a baby	1	2	(3)	4	5
23. Had irregular sleeping habits (woke often; talked in sleep)	1	2	3	(4)	5
24. New or infrequent situations led to temper tantrums (holidays, visits to relatives, unusual food)	1	2	3	(4)	5
25. Rocked and banged the crib	1	(2)	3	4	5

16

PARENT PROFILE FORMS

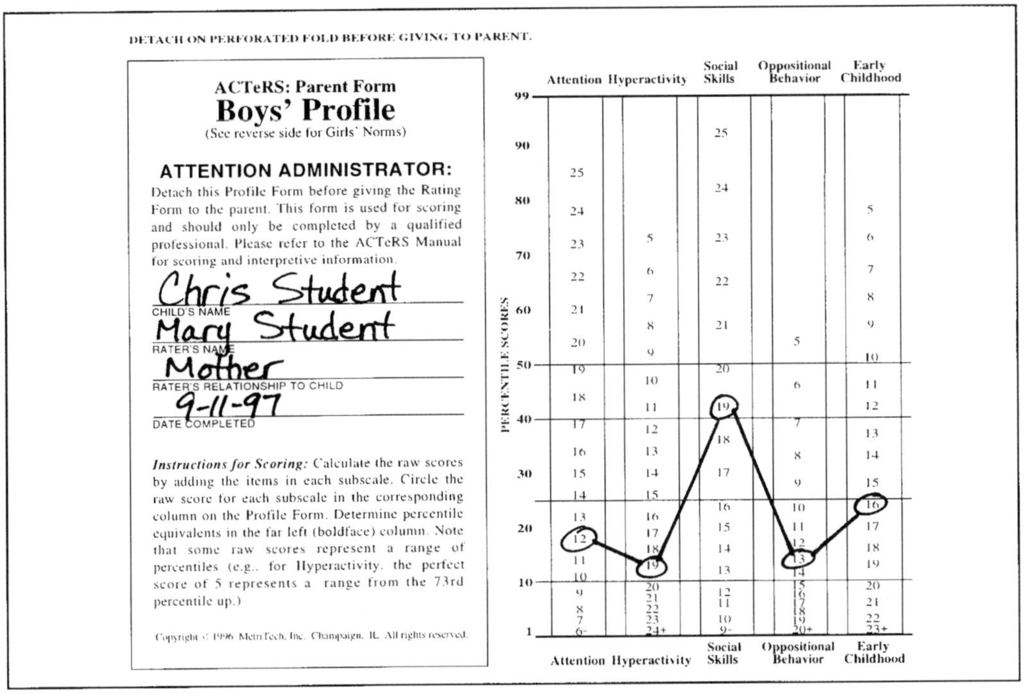

DETACH ON PERFORATED FOLD BEFORE GIVING TO PARENT.

ACTeRS: Parent Form

Boys' Profile

(See reverse side for Girls' Norms)

ATTENTION ADMINISTRATOR:

Detach this Profile Form before giving the Rating Form to the parent. This form is used for scoring and should only be completed by a qualified professional. Please refer to the ACTeRS Manual for scoring and interpretive information.

Chris Student
CHILD'S NAME

Mary Student
RATER'S NAME

Mother
RATER'S RELATIONSHIP TO CHILD

9-11-97
DATE COMPLETED

Instructions for Scoring: Calculate the raw scores by adding the items in each subscale. Circle the raw score for each subscale in the corresponding column on the Profile Form. Determine percentile equivalents in the far left (boldface) column. Note that some raw scores represent a range of percentiles (e.g., for Hyperactivity, the perfect score of 5 represents a range from the 73rd percentile up.)

PERCENTILE SCORES: 99, 90, 80, 70, 60, 50, 40, 30, 20, 10, 1

- Attention: 25, 24, 23, 22, 21, 20, 19, 18, 17, 16, 15, 14, 13, (12), 11, 10, 9, 8, 7, 6-
- Hyperactivity: 5, 6, 7, 8, 9, 10, 11, 12, 13, 14, 15, 16, 17, 18, (19), 20, 21, 22, 23, 24+
- Social Skills: 25, 24, 23, 22, 21, 20, (19), 18, 17, 16, 15, 14, 13, 12, 11, 10, 9-
- Oppositional Behavior: 5, 6, 7, 8, 9, 10, 11, 12, (13), 14, 15, 16, 17, 18, 19, 20+
- Early Childhood: 5, 6, 7, 8, 9, 10, 11, 12, 13, 14, 15, (16), 17, 18, 19, 20, 21, 22, 23+

Attention Hyperactivity Social Skills Oppositional Behavior Early Childhood

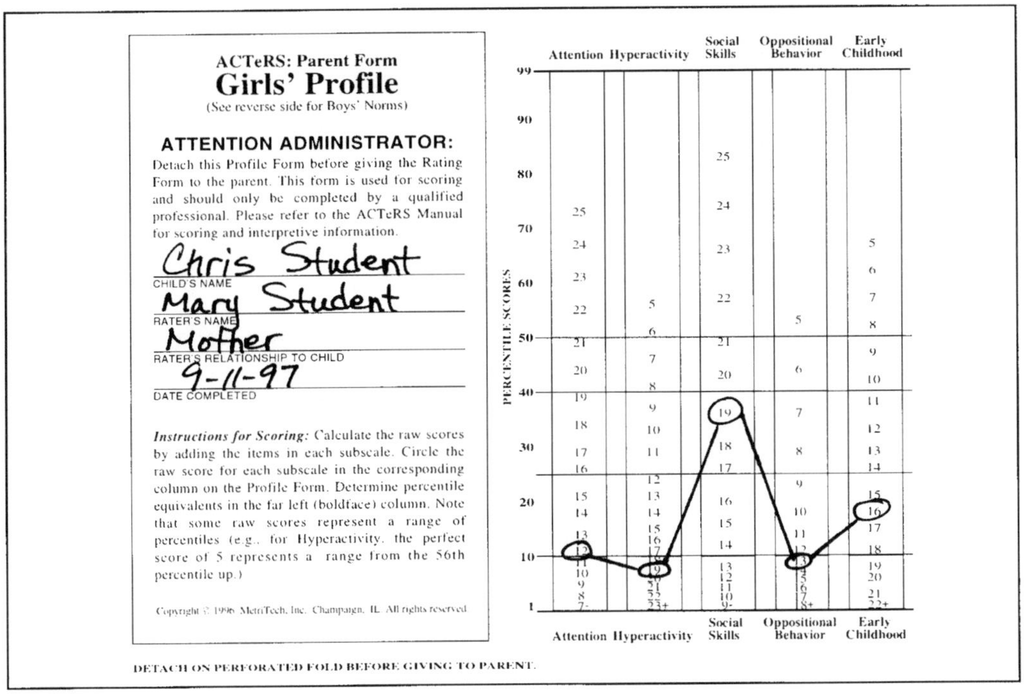

ACTeRS: Parent Form

Girls' Profile

(See reverse side for Boys' Norms)

ATTENTION ADMINISTRATOR:

Detach this Profile Form before giving the Rating Form to the parent. This form is used for scoring and should only be completed by a qualified professional. Please refer to the ACTeRS Manual for scoring and interpretive information.

Chris Student
CHILD'S NAME

Mary Student
RATER'S NAME

Mother
RATER'S RELATIONSHIP TO CHILD

9-11-97
DATE COMPLETED

Instructions for Scoring: Calculate the raw scores by adding the items in each subscale. Circle the raw score for each subscale in the corresponding column on the Profile Form. Determine percentile equivalents in the far left (boldface) column. Note that some raw scores represent a range of percentiles (e.g., for Hyperactivity, the perfect score of 5 represents a range from the 56th percentile up.)

PERCENTILE SCORES: 99, 90, 80, 70, 60, 50, 40, 30, 20, 10, 1

- Attention: 25, 24, 23, 22, 21, 20, 19, 18, 17, 16, 15, 14, 13, (12), 11, 10, 9, 8, 7-
- Hyperactivity: 5, 6, 7, 8, 9, 10, 11, 12, 13, 14, 15, 16, 17, 18, (19), 20, 21, 22, 23+
- Social Skills: 25, 24, 23, 22, 21, 20, (19), 18, 17, 16, 15, 14, 13, 12, 11, 10, 9-
- Oppositional Behavior: 5, 6, 7, 8, 9, 10, 11, 12, (13), 14, 15, 16, 17, 18+
- Early Childhood: 5, 6, 7, 8, 9, 10, 11, 12, 13, 14, 15, (16), 17, 18, 19, 20, 21, 22+

Attention Hyperactivity Social Skills Oppositional Behavior Early Childhood

DETACH ON PERFORATED FOLD BEFORE GIVING TO PARENT.

ACADEMIC PERFORMANCE RATING SCALE

STUDENT ______________________________ DATE ____________

AGE ________ GRADE ________ TEACHER ______________________

For each of the below items, please estimate the above student's performance over the **PAST WEEK.** For each item, please circle **one** choice only.

Item					
1. Estimate the percentage of written **math** work *completed* (regardless of accuracy) relative to classmates.	0-49% 1	50-69% 2	70-79% 3	80-89% 4	90-100% 5
2. Estimate the percentage of written **language arts** work *completed* (regardless of accuracy) relative to classmates.	0-49% 1	50-69% 2	70-79% 3	80-89% 4	90-100% 5
3. Estimate the *accuracy* of completed written **math** work (i.e., percent correct of work done).	0-64% 1	65-69% 2	70-79% 3	80-89% 4	90-100% 5
4. Estimate the *accuracy* of completed **written language** arts work (i.e., percent correct of work done).	0-64% 1	65-69% 2	70-79% 3	80-89% 4	90-100% 5
5. How consistent has the quality of this child's academic work been over the past week?	Consistently poor 1	More poor than successful 2	Variable 3	More successful than poor 4	Consistently successful 5
6. How frequently does the student accurately follow teacher instructions and/or class discussion during *large-group* (e.g., whole class) instruction?	Never 1	Rarely 2	Sometimes 3	Often 4	Very Often 5
7. How frequently does the student accurately follow teacher instruction and/or class discussion during *small-group* (e.g., reading group) instruction?	Never 1	Rarely 2	Sometimes 3	Often 4	Very Often 5
8. How quickly does this child learn new material (i.e., pick up novel concepts)?	Never 1	Rarely 2	Sometimes 3	Often 4	Very Often 5

continued . . .

9. What is the quality or neatness of this child's handwriting?	Poor 1	Fair 2	Average 3	Above Average 4	Excellent 5
10. What is the quality of this child's reading skills?	Poor 1	Fair 2	Average 3	Above Average 4	Excellent 5
11. What is the quality of this child's speaking skills?	Poor 1	Fair 2	Average 3	Above Average 4	Excellent 5
12. How often does the child complete written work in a careless, hasty fashion?	Never 1	Rarely 2	Sometimes 3	Often 4	Very Often 5
13. How frequently does the child take more time to complete work than his/her classmates?	Never 1	Rarely 2	Sometimes 3	Often 4	Very Often 5
14. How often is the child able to pay attention without you prompting him/her?	Never 1	Rarely 2	Sometimes 3	Often 4	Very Often 5
15. How frequently does this child require your assistance to accurately complete his/her academic work?	Never 1	Rarely 2	Sometimes 3	Often 4	Very Often 5
16. How often does the child begin written work prior to understanding the directions?	Never 1	Rarely 2	Sometimes 3	Often 4	Very Often 5
17. How frequently does this child have difficulty recalling material from a previous day's lessons?	Never 1	Rarely 2	Sometimes 3	Often 4	Very Often 5
18. How often does the child appear to be staring excessively or "spaced out"?	Never 1	Rarely 2	Sometimes 3	Often 4	Very Often 5
19. How often does the child appear withdrawn or tend to lack an emotional response in a social situation?	Never 1	Rarely 2	Sometimes 3	Often 4	Very Often 5

Note: From "Teacher Ratings of Academic Skills: The Development of the Academic Performance Rating Scale" by George J. DuPaul, Mark D. Rapport, and Lucy M. Perriello, 1991, *School Psychology Review, 20,* 284-300. Reprinted with permission.

SCHOOL SITUATIONS QUESTIONNAIRE

CHILD'S NAME ______________________________ DATE ______________

NAME OF PERSON COMPLETING THIS FORM ______________________________

Instructions: Does this child present any behavior problems for you in any of these situations? If so, indicate how severe they are.

Situations	*Yes/No* *(Circle one)*		*Mild*		*If yes, how severe?* *(Circle one)*						*Severe*
While arriving at school	Yes	No	1	2	3	4	5	6	7	8	9
During individual deskwork	Yes	No	1	2	3	4	5	6	7	8	9
During small-group activities	Yes	No	1	2	3	4	5	6	7	8	9
During free play time in class	Yes	No	1	2	3	4	5	6	7	8	9
During lectures to the class	Yes	No	1	2	3	4	5	6	7	8	9
At recess	Yes	No	1	2	3	4	5	6	7	8	9
At lunch	Yes	No	1	2	3	4	5	6	7	8	9
In the hallways	Yes	No	1	2	3	4	5	6	7	8	9
In the bathroom	Yes	No	1	2	3	4	5	6	7	8	9
On field trips	Yes	No	1	2	3	4	5	6	7	8	9
During special assemblies	Yes	No	1	2	3	4	5	6	7	8	9
On the bus	Yes	No	1	2	3	4	5	6	7	8	9

Office Use Only: No. of problems ____ Mean severity ____

ADHD RATING SCALE

CHILD'S NAME ______________________ AGE ______ GRADE ______

COMPLETED BY ______________________

Circle the number in the *one* column which best describes the child.

	Not at all	*Just a little*	*Pretty much*	*Very much*
1. Often fidgets or squirms in seat.	0	1	2	3
2. Has difficulty remaining seated.	0	1	2	3
3. Is easily distracted.	0	1	2	3
4. Has difficulty awaiting turn in groups.	0	1	2	3
5. Often blurts out answers to questions.	0	1	2	3
6. Has difficulty following instructions.	0	1	2	3
7. Has difficulty sustaining attention to tasks.	0	1	2	3
8. Often shifts from one uncompleted activity to another.	0	1	2	3
9. Has difficulty playing quietly.	0	1	2	3
10. Often talks excessively.	0	1	2	3
11. Often interrupts or intrudes on others.	0	1	2	3
12. Often does not seem to listen.	0	1	2	3
13. Often loses things necessary for tasks.	0	1	2	3
14. Often engages in physically dangerous activities without considering consequences	0	1	2	3

SNAP RATING SCALE

CHILD'S NAME ______________________________ AGE _______ GRADE _______

COMPLETED BY ____

Check the one column which best describes the child.

	Not at all	*Just a little*	*Pretty much*	*Very much*
Inattention				
1. Often fails to finish things he or she starts	____	____	____	____
2. Often doesn't seem to listen	____	____	____	____
3. Easily distracted	____	____	____	____
4. Has difficulty concentrating on school work or other tasks requiring sustained attention	____	____	____	____
5. Has difficulty sticking to a play activity	____	____	____	____
Impulsivity				
1. Often acts before thinking	____	____	____	____
2. Shifts excessively from one activity to another	____	____	____	____
3. Has difficulty organizing work (this not being due to cognitive impairment)	____	____	____	____
4. Needs a lot of supervision	____	____	____	____
5. Frequently calls out in class	____	____	____	____
6. Has difficulty awaiting turn in games or group situation	____	____	____	____
Hyperactivity				
1. Excessively runs about or climbs on things	____	____	____	____
2. Has difficulty sitting still or fidgets excessively	____	____	____	____
3. Has difficulty staying seated	____	____	____	____
4. Moves about excessively during sleep	____	____	____	____
5. Is always "on the go" or acts as if "driven by a motor"	____	____	____	____
Peer Interactions				
1. Fights, hits, punches, etc.	____	____	____	____
2. Is disliked by other children	____	____	____	____
3. Frequently interrupts other children's activities	____	____	____	____
4. Bossy, always telling other children what to do	____	____	____	____
5. Teases or calls other children names	____	____	____	____
6. Refuses to participate in group activities	____	____	____	____
7. Loses temper often and easily	____	____	____	____

SNAP Rating Scale. Used with permission from William E. Pelham, Jr., Ph.D., University of Pittsburgh Medical Center and James Swanson, Ph.D., University of California, Irvine.

FLICK'S SURVEY OF "SKILLS FOR SCHOOL SUCCESS"
Parent/Teacher Form
Research Edition / Copyright Pending

CHILD'S NAME ______________________ BIRTH DATE __________ AGE _______

GRADE ______ SCHOOL ______________________ HOMEROOM TEACHER ________________

NAME OF RESPONDENT ______________________________ DATE ____________

___PARENT ___TEACHER ___OTHER ______________

Information obtained by this survey will be used to determine your child's strengths and weaknesses with reference to the "Skills For School Success Program"

Please reply to the following statements, giving your perceptions about this child's school behavior, work and study habits.
Please reply for each statement.

RESPONSE KEY:

N/A = Does not apply
1 = YES
2 = MOSTLY YES
3 = SOMETIMES
4 = MOSTLY NO
5 = NO

About CLASS BEHAVIOR, this child:	N/A	1	2	3	4	5
Uses time wisely to prepare for class (e.g., getting pencils, papers and materials ready).						
Spends the time in class listening to the teacher and completing assignments.						
At the end of a class period, spends time getting ready for the next subject.						
If required to change classes, does so quietly and goes directly to the next class.						
Writes the homework assignments down in Homework Assignment Book.						

RESPONSE KEY: 1 = YES 2 = MOSTLY YES 3 = SOMETIMES 4 = MOSTLY NO 5 = NO

About ORGANIZATIONAL BEHAVIOR, this child:	N/A	1	2	3	4	5
Brings all needed supplies to school.						
Keeps all papers and work in a divided binder with pockets, and uses a plastic pouch for pencils, erasers, etc.						
Has a Homework Assignment Book to record all assignments.						
Keeps a routine schedule of study time and other activities.						
Has a calendar for long-range projects and assignments.						
Hands in work "on time."						
Keeps desk neat and organized.						

RESPONSE KEY: 1 = YES 2 = MOSTLY YES 3 = SOMETIMES 4 = MOSTLY NO 5 = NO

About LEARNING AND STUDY STRATEGIES, this child:	N/A	1	2	3	4	5
Makes sure of the directions for each assignment.						
Studies a little bit each night several days before a test.						

LEARNING AND STUDY STRATEGIES *(continued)*	N/A	1	2	3	4	5
Checks over work after completing an assignment.						
Looks over the content of an assignment before doing it.						
Asks self-questions during process of reading assigned material.						
Uses visual (seeing), auditory (hearing), or touch (feeling/sensation) as a help to learn things.						
Notes the kind of test to study for (e.g., true-false, essay, multiple-choice, fill-in-the-blanks).						
Practices taking tests by making up questions.						
Records notes by seeing and hearing the information presented in class.						

RESPONSE KEY: 1 = YES 2 = MOSTLY YES 3 = SOMETIMES 4 = MOSTLY NO 5 = NO

About NOTE TAKING, this child:	N/A	1	2	3	4	5
Writes notes about materials presented.						
Reviews notes to pick out important points.						
Compares notes with others when there are questions about accuracy.						
Has learned to use various symbols and abbreviations in notes.						
Tries to relate information in the text to note taking.						
Reviews notes in advance of tests.						

RESPONSE KEY: 1 = YES 2 = MOSTLY YES 3 = SOMETIMES 4 = MOSTLY NO 5 = NO

About TEST TAKING, this child:	N/A	1	2	3	4	5
Re-reads test instructions to be sure to know what to do.						
Keeps old tests for review.						
Reviews recent tests to correct errors and learn from mistakes.						
Knows how to approach different kinds of tests.						
Recognizes the components of a test which may be worth more points toward the test grade.						
Uses old (corrected) tests to prepare for the final exam.						
Seems satisfied with the kinds of grades earned on tests.						
Knows which kind of tests s/he can do well on and which kind s/he does poorly on.						
Can do equally well on a written test as compared to one given orally.						
Handwriting speed is adequate during test-taking and especially on tests requiring long answers.						

RESPONSE KEY: 1 = YES 2 = MOSTLY YES 3 = SOMETIMES 4 = MOSTLY NO 5 = NO

About USING REFERENCE MATERIAL, this child:	N/A	1	2	3	4	5
Looks at the Table of Contents before reading a book.						
Uses the Index and Glossary.						
Is familiar with pie, bar, and line graphs.						

USING REFERENCE MATERIAL *(continued)*	N/A	1	2	3	4	5
Has practiced reading tables to obtain information.						
Can compare tables and graphs to determine similarities and differences.						
Can locate words quickly in a dictionary.						
Has used an encyclopedia to obtain information.						

RESPONSE KEY: 1 = YES 2 = MOSTLY YES 3 = SOMETIMES 4 = MOSTLY NO 5 = NO

About INFORMATION PROCESSING, this child:	N/A	1	2	3	4	5
Can read and identify main ideas in stories.						
Understands what is read and can relate the information to others.						
Sees how material is organized (chapter, title, and paragraph headings).						
When encountering unknown words, writes them down or looks them up and notes the definition in the book.						
Reads best and retains the information when relaxed but alert.						

RESPONSE KEY: 1 = YES 2 = MOSTLY YES 3 = SOMETIMES 4 = MOSTLY NO 5 = NO

About INFORMATION RETENTION, this child:	N/A	1	2	3	4	5
Knows other methods to remember information different than re-reading it over and over.						
Knows memory strategies to help remember things.						
Can remember a general theme as well as details in a story.						
Can remember things best after review by seeing, hearing, and writing informational facts.						
Remembers information best when given a signal or cue as a reminder that something is important and will probably be on a test.						

RESPONSE KEY: 1 = YES 2 = MOSTLY YES 3 = SOMETIMES 4 = MOSTLY NO 5 = NO

About HOMEWORK, this child:	N/A	1	2	3	4	5
Uses a Homework Assignment Book.						
Checks off things that will be needed at home for assignments.						
Has a routine place and time for homework.						
Does most difficult homework first; then, the easier, more liked things.						
Files completed homework and checks it off the list.						
Checks over homework for mistakes.						

RESPONSE KEY: 1 = YES 2 = MOSTLY YES 3 = SOMETIMES 4 = MOSTLY NO 5 = NO

About RELATIONSHIP WITH TEACHERS, this child:	N/A	1	2	3	4	5
Believes the teacher understands his or her problems.						
Is aware of the teacher's expectations of him or her.						
Knows the class rules.						

RELATIONSHIP WITH TEACHERS *(continued)*	**N/A**	**1**	**2**	**3**	**4**	**5**
Feels free to ask questions.						
Can always go to the teacher for help with some assignment or subject.						

OTHER OBSERVATIONS OR COMMENTS: ______________________________

____

____

____

____

____

____

____

____

APPENDIX C

ADD/ADHD Diagnostic Checklist and Treatment Organizer

ADD/ADHD DIAGNOSTIC CHECKLIST AND TREATMENT ORGANIZER

(Grad L. Flick, Ph.D. Copyright Pending)

CHILD'S NAME ________________________ AGE _____ BIRTH DATE _____ GRADE _____

CLINICIAN ____ DATE ____________

I. DIAGNOSTIC PHASE

A. Assessment—Psychological

	Relevant	*Date Started*	*Date Completed*	*Defer to*
1. Background Information and Developmental History (Parent/Guardian)				
2. Behavioral Observation				
3. Rating Scales—Parent				
4. Rating Scales—Teacher				
5. Assess Ability/Achievements				
6. Assess Executive Control				
7. Assess Visual-Motor				
8. Assess Memory				
9. Assess Attentional Skills				
10. Assess Self Concept/Self-Esteem				
11. Assess Social Skills				
12. Assess Visual-Spatial Skills				
13. Assess Language				
14. Assess Behavioral/Emotional				
15. Assess Inclusion Potential				

B. Assessment—Medical

	Relevant	*Date Started*	*Date Completed*	*Defer to*
1. Medical History				
2. Medical Exam				
3. Neurological Exam (optional)				

C. Assessment—Other (optional)

	Relevant	*Date Started*	*Date Completed*	*Defer to*
1. Vision				
2. Hearing				
3. Speech and Language				

continued . . .

D. Differential Diagnosis

	Relevant	Date Started	Date Completed	Defer to
1. Meets DSM-IV Criteria for:				
(a) 314.01 ADHD—Combined Type				
(b) 314.00 ADHD—Predominantly Inattentive Type				
(c) 314.01 ADHD—Predominantly Hyperactive—Impulsive Type				
2. Co-Morbid/Mimic Syndromes Considered				
Learning Disability				
Mental Retardation				
Oppositional Defiant Disorder				
Conduct Disorder				
Dysthymic Disorder (Depression)				
Anxiety Disorder				
Bipolar Disorder				
Obsessive Compulsive Disorder				
Head Injury				
Other Psychological Condition				
Medical Condition Considered				

II. Treatment Phase

A. Medical Intervention

1. Medical Test Needed				
2. Pre-Treatment/Baseline Teacher Ratings Obtained				
3. Medication Trial on				
(a)				
(b)				
(c)				

continued . . .

B. Classroom Accommodations	Relevant	Date Started	Date Completed	Defer to
1. School Consultation with Teachers				
2. IEP Discussed/Implemented				
3. Special Education Resources for				
(a)				
(b)				
4. Special Education Placement in				
5. Inclusion Strategies:				
Proximity Control				
Preferential Seating				
Tape Recorder				
Overhead Projector				
Self-Monitoring				
Special Materials				
Special Signals				
Study Carrels				
Display Clear Rules				
Review Clear Rules				
Homework Assignments Written Down/Reviewed				
Day Schedule Posted/Reviewed				
Alternate Work Activity				
Multi-sensory Instruction				
Reduction Homework/Assignments				
Use of Peer Tutors				
Extended Time for Tests				
Oral Examinations				
Use of Computer				
Monitor Homework Assignment Sheet/Check Backpack				
Premack Principle (Schedule Hard Work Before Easy Work)				

continued . . .

B. Classroom Accommodations *(cont'd)*

	Relevant	Date Started	Date Completed	Defer to
Adjust Schedule for Peak Performance				
Use of Electronic Assist Devices				
Establish Set Routine with Variation Within Routine				
Designated Quiet Zone in Class				
Use of Self-Instruction Procedure				

C. Behavioral Intervention

	Relevant	Date Started	Date Completed	Defer to
1. In Class				
(a) Verbal Praise/Positive Approach				
(b) Ignoring				
(c) Response Cost Procedure to Develop: ____________				
(d) Time-out for ____________				
(e) Time-in for ____________				
(f) Inclusive Classroom Behavioral Program				
(g) Point/Token System				
2. Home-School Program				
(a) Periodic Communication Established				
(b) Check on Consistency in Both Settings				
(c) Teacher/Parent Roles Defined				
3. Parent/Teacher Training				
(a) Parents/Teachers have at least one full day of behavioral training				
(b) Parent/Teacher knowledge of ADD/ADHD and behavioral techniques assessed				
(c) Appropriate educational resources available to Parent/Teacher on ADD/ADHD and behavioral techniques				
(d) Mechanism in place for communication about problems in behavioral program				
4. Parent Behavioral Program				
(a) General Positive Orientation				

continued . . .

C. Behavioral Intervention *(cont'd)*

	Relevant	Date Started	Date Completed	Defer to
(b) Alternative Behaviors Listed				
(c) Balanced Program Established				
(d) Point/Token System				
(e) Response Cost				
(f) Time-out/Time-in				
(g) Positive Practice				
(h) Grounding				
(i) Simulated School Behaviors				
Impulse Control				
Listening Skills				
Following Directions				
Work Completion				
Sustaining Attention				
Social Skills				

D. Supplementary Remedial Program

	Relevant	Date Started	Date Completed	Defer to
1. Tutoring				
(a) One-on-One				
(b) Computerized				
2. *Skills for School Success* Program				
3. *Homework Helpers* Program				
4. Speech/Language Therapy				
5. Motor Coordination Therapy				
(a) Gross Motor				
(b) Fine Motor/Handwriting				
6. Attentional Skills Training				
(a) Home				
(b) School				

continued . . .

E. Legal Resources

	Relevant	Date Started	Date Completed	Defer to
Parents/Guardians have understanding of:				
1. Section 504 Rehabilitation Act				
2. Individuals with Disabilities Act (IDEA)				
3. Advocacy Needed for ________________				

F. Clinic/Therapy Programs

	Relevant	Date Started	Date Completed	Defer to
1. Parent Centered Programs				
(a) General Discussion of the A-B-C of Behavioral Programs				
(b) Antecedents				
Review /Development of Rules				
Expectations Discussed				
Communication Style Addressed				
Meta-Communication Considered				
(c) Behaviors Discussed				
Inappropriate Behaviors Listed				
Alternative Behaviors Listed				
Can Ignoring Be Used?				
(d) Consequences				
Types of Consequences Discussed				
Instrumental Behavior Analysis				
Shaping Discussed				
Concept of Balanced Behavior Program				
(e) Managing Behaviors				
Time-out Discussed				
Time-in Discussed				
Behavior Penalty Discussed				
Grounding Applications				
Point/Token System				

continued . . .

F. Clinic/Therapy Programs *(cont'd)*

	Relevant	Date Started	Date Completed	Defer to
2. Child-Centered Programs				
(a) Skill Development				
Attention Training				
Impulse Control Training				
Social Skill Training				
Self-Concept/Self-esteem Focus				
Organizational and Study Skills				
Anger Control Training				
Problem Solving Training				
Handwriting Program				
(b) Cognitive Mediation				
Self-instruction				
Self-monitoring				
Positive Self-talk				
Problem Solving Exercises				
(c) Counseling				
Understanding of ADD/ADHD				
Understanding Medications				
Understanding and Focusing on Strengths				
Social Group Interaction Structured				

III. FAMILY FUNCTIONING

A. Relationships with Parents

	Relevant	Date Started	Date Completed	Defer to
1. Child provided structured activities based on strengths and abilities				
2. Some time (preferably 1 hour) set aside for "pure fun" activity				
3. Parents are consistent and model appropriate behavior				
4. Rules/chores written down and reviewed				

continued . . .

B. Relationship with Siblings

	Relevant	Date Started	Date Completed	Defer to
1. Encourage cooperation and sharing				
2. Discourage discrimination (i.e., scapegoating) and name-calling				
3. Sibling(s) understand nature of ADD/ADHD				
4. Balance time for ADD and non-ADD sibling(s)				

C. Parent Survival Techniques

1. Knowledge and Acceptance of ADD/ADHD				
2. Use Relaxation/Stress Reduction				
3. Maintain a Routine				
4. Stay Positive				
5. Maintain Clear Communication				
6. Join a Support Group				
7. Continue Education About ADD				
8. Be Aware of Adult ADD Characteristics				
9. Use Affirmations				
10. Use Broken Record Technique				

D. Other Factors

1. Diet				
2. Sleep				
3. Assist Devices				
4. Homework Habit Development				
5. Use Simulated School Behaviors in Home Behavioral Program				

continued . . .

E. Additional Considerations	Relevant	Date Started	Date Completed	Defer to
1. Parent Behavior Management Workshops				
2. Educational Consultation/Tutoring				
3. Speech and Language Therapy				
4. Occupational Therapy/Motor Coordination				
5. Psychiatric Consultation				
6. Home Computer Training				

IV. Planning and Review

A. Who will coordinate it? ________________________

B. How often? ________________________

C. Who will be involved? ________________________

D. Future Considerations (list)

____

____

____

____

V. Comments

____

____

____

____

____

____

____

____

____

____

APPENDIX D

Treatment Options for ADD/ADHD Using a Problem-Oriented Approach

(flow chart)

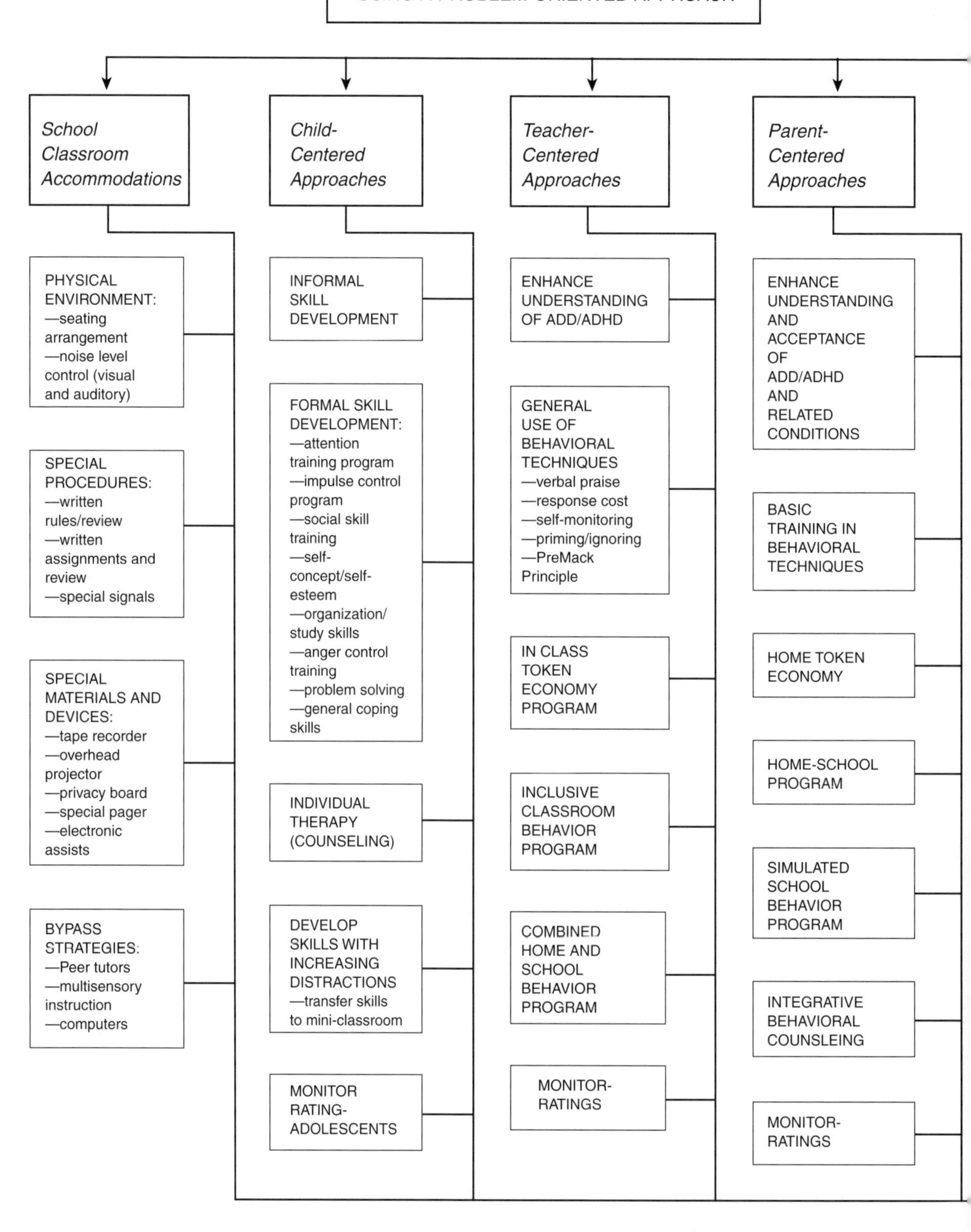
TREATMENT OPTIONS FOR ADD/ADHD
USING A PROBLEM-ORIENTED APPROACH
School Classroom Accommodations
PHYSICAL ENVIRONMENT: —seating arrangement —noise level control (visual and auditory)
SPECIAL PROCEDURES: —written rules/review —written assignments and review —special signals
SPECIAL MATERIALS AND DEVICES: —tape recorder —overhead projector —privacy board —special pager —electronic assists
BYPASS STRATEGIES: —Peer tutors —multisensory instruction —computers
Child-Centered Approaches
INFORMAL SKILL DEVELOPMENT
FORMAL SKILL DEVELOPMENT: —attention training program —impulse control program —social skill training —self-concept/self-esteem —organization/ study skills —anger control training —problem solving —general coping skills
INDIVIDUAL THERAPY (COUNSELING)
DEVELOP SKILLS WITH INCREASING DISTRACTIONS —transfer skills to mini-classroom
MONITOR RATING-ADOLESCENTS
Teacher-Centered Approaches
ENHANCE UNDERSTANDING OF ADD/ADHD
GENERAL USE OF BEHAVIORAL TECHNIQUES —verbal praise —response cost —self-monitoring —priming/ignoring —PreMack Principle
IN CLASS TOKEN ECONOMY PROGRAM
INCLUSIVE CLASSROOM BEHAVIOR PROGRAM
COMBINED HOME AND SCHOOL BEHAVIOR PROGRAM
MONITOR-RATINGS
Parent-Centered Approaches
ENHANCE UNDERSTANDING AND ACCEPTANCE OF ADD/ADHD AND RELATED CONDITIONS
BASIC TRAINING IN BEHAVIORAL TECHNIQUES
HOME TOKEN ECONOMY
HOME-SCHOOL PROGRAM
SIMULATED SCHOOL BEHAVIOR PROGRAM
INTEGRATIVE BEHAVIORAL COUNSLEING
MONITOR-RATINGS

Medical Approaches

- STIMULANTS
- ANTI-DEPRESSANTS
- ANTI-HYPERTENSIVES
- COMBINED PHARMACO-THERAPY
- OTHER SPECIFIC MEDICATIONS
- MONITORING EFFECTS AND SIDE EFFECTS

Other Therapies

- TREAT VISUAL IMPAIRMENT
- TREAT HEARING IMPAIRMENT
- TREAT MOTOR IMPAIRMENT
- SPEECH AND LANGUAGE THERAPY

Special Education Resources

- RESOURCE ROOM
- SELF-CONTAINED CLASSROOM
- SPECIAL SCHOOL
- SPECIAL PROGRAMS:
  - —reading
  - —spelling
  - —math
  - —handwriting
- MONITOR-EVALUATE

RE-EVALUATE CHILD'S NEEDS WITH IMPROVEMENT AND/OR AS ADDITIONAL PROBLEMS MAY DEVELOP

APPENDIX E

Model Clinic for ADD/ADHD

A Model ADD Clinic

The ADD Clinic provides comprehensive programs for children, adolescents, and adults who present attentional, learning, or behavioral-emotional problems. Following a neuropsychological assessment, a multi-component treatment program is structured to address each person's individual needs. For children/adults who have had a previous evaluation only minimal testing may be required. While behavioral counseling is the primary orientation for parents of children with ADD, cognitive/behavioral strategies are used with the ADD child, adolescent, or adult. Additional cognitive neuropsychological remediation is employed for the identified person with ADD/LD.

Assessment of Attention Behavior

Attention behavior is evaluated in three ways. First, an objective computer-based procedure is used to assess the child's general level of self-control, his/her sustained attention, and his/her ability to attend in the presence of distractions. This provides valid information regarding a person's ability to focus attention (i.e., vigilance) over time and his/her ability to inhibit or suppress responses (i.e., avoiding impulsive responding)—two fundamental features characteristic of ADD. A person's scores, objectively recorded by the computer, are compared to those of a normative group of same-aged peers. Both auditory and visual attention are assessed. This data would then be combined with historical background information and parent/teacher ratings on ADD behavior to provide a comprehensive assessment of attentional behavior.

Neuropsychological Assessment and Diagnosis

A comprehensive psycho-educational evaluation involves assessment of the child's basic abilities, achievements, social skill, executive control functions, emotions, and behavior. In addition to an objective assessment of attentional behaviors, particular emphasis is placed upon the child's classroom behavior where attention, activity level, social skills, oppositional behavior and other potential behavior problems are rated by the teacher.

Diagnostic impressions are therefore based on data obtained from several sources—parent, teacher and child. When evaluating a child, it is also important to determine which factors—attention, learning, or behavior—may be the primary problem and those that are secondary and tertiary in the overall diagnostic impression. Treatment programs of the ADD Clinic are designed within the framework of this diagnostic sequence.

ADD Clinic Treatment Program

Cognitive Behavioral Program: Initially the individual is introduced to various strategies of attentional control using a variety of techniques directed at those ADD characteristics that are of primary importance for the child. Included in this array of techniques are self-awareness training and cognitive mediation procedures involving self-instruction, self-monitoring, and the basic strategies of "stop, look, listen, and think" before acting.

The First Phase of Treatment

The first phase of treatment typically focuses upon strengthening or enhancing attention, concentration, and memory skills. Without adequate levels of functioning in each of these areas, other aspects of the habilitation or rehabilitation process are often frustrated.

The Focus of Subsequent Treatment

After the initial phase, the focus turns to the establishment of restoration of verbal language skills. The amount of attention paid to these skill areas depends upon the nature of the individual's deficits or weaknesses. A critical aspect with respect to the habilitative provision for training in the areas of reasoning, abstraction, and logical analysis. When these higher level cognitive functions are emphasized they seem to have an impact effect upon the rest of the neuropsychological rehabilitation process.

How the Goals of Treatment Are Achieved

The programs in this system are designed to provide enjoyable and motivating practice material that give immediate feedback on performance within an individualized behavioral therapy format for both children and adults. Through a behavioral procedure called "shaping," the patient is able to gradually develop those cognitive functions that have either been delayed in maturation or impaired by genetic factors. An individual's progress will therefore build upon success achieved on each task. This is accomplished by beginning each task at a level the person can handle successfully. Once that performance is strengthened through reinforcement the task may be made slightly more difficult until all deficit areas are covered and the patient has achieved maximum gains.

Social Skills Group Program

Many children with ADD have problems in their social relationships. The social skills program is behaviorally-based and designed to establish and/or enhance further development of a variety of social skills that relate to problem areas in the child's classroom, as well as in his/her play activities.

Child Behavior Management for Parents

Concurrent with the child's program, behavior management techniques are taught to those caregivers (e.g., parents/grandparents) who must deal directly with ADD behavior in the home situation, as well as in other outside situations. The most effective behavioral strategies for use with ADD behaviors are discussed.

Mini-Classroom Program

One of the most difficult problems in the treatment of ADD behaviors involves the transfer of what the child learns during individual therapy to the classroom setting. This program was therefore initiated to assist in the child's utilization of the various strategies of coping with distractions and to strengthen his/her "on task" behavior in a small classroom-type environment. This would ultimately bridge the gap between his/her individual acquisition of coping strategies to their utilization in the regular classroom. A second situation in which these skills could be potentially transferred is during homework sessions. A special "Skills for School Success" program is conducted in a small group format to further develop organization and study skills as well as other skills needed in the classroom.

Home Training

A series of attention training games are currently under development at the ADD Clinic. Software for computerized exercises will be available initially for all those who participate in the program. Since most ADD children may acquire relevant attention skills more gradually, the additional computer exercises for use by parents at home will facilitate development of these attentional skills.

THE SUMMER PROGRAM

The Summer Program at the ADD Clinic in Biloxi, Mississippi, allows for more intensive work on those behaviors that are most troublesome and problematic for the child with ADD/ADHD. Using activities that are enjoyable and stimulating, the major focus is on further development of social skills. Improved ability to share and cooperate is central to this behaviorally-based program. In addition, individualized and/or group programs may involve emphasis on impulse-control, attentional processes, relaxation and stress management, problem-solving and general coping strategies. Parent behavior management and follow-up sessions with parents will assist in fostering generalization of such therapeutic training to other situations. In addition, at some point in the child's training program, distractions of recorded classroom noise may be introduced. At a more advanced stage, children may be grouped to form a mini-classroom.

SUMMER CAMP

A more extensive and comprehensive Summer Camp is also offered outside of the Clinic. Both residential (boarding) and day (local) programs are planned. These therapeutic programs provide learning experiences designed to improve attention, learning and behavior while enhancing self-confidence and self-esteem. An overall behavioral format is used that will offer success experiences for the child with ADD/ADHD. For three weeks the child will participate in many unique recreational and outdoor activities at the beach and in many other planned activities (e.g., swimming, fishing, cooking, and various sports). All field trips and activities will be monitored behaviorally. In addition, all routine activities covering mealtime, bedtime and group participation will also be monitored. In addition to the general focus on social skill development, there are small group programs focusing on anger management and coping skills, relaxation skills, listening skills, problem-solving and organizational skills, as well as study skills (a portion of the time is devoted to some basic academic work). This latter work may be presented via the computer as would the Attention Training exercises. Parents are involved during the beginning and ending phases of this Summer Camp. Some basic behavioral techniques are discussed in the beginning and at the end; some suggestions are offered to assist in maintaining and further enhancing skills developed during the camp as well as to provide recommendation for their generalization and integration into the child's classroom and home environments.

The ADD Clinic offers year-round assessment and treatment of ADD behaviors in children, adolescents and adults. For more information about an intensive Summer Program, Summer Camp, resources materials, workshops for parents of children with ADD, as well as regular year-round programs, call 1-800-962-2673, or write the ADD Clinic, 983 Howard Avenue, Biloxi MS 39530.

APPENDIX F

Recommended Resources

Additional sources of help are listed here and are organized in these categories:

- Recommended Resources for Kids (Also see Videos & Newsletters categories.)
- Recommended Resources for Teens and Adults
- Recommended Resources for Parents
- Recommended Resources for Teachers (Also see Videos category.)
- Recommended Professional Resources
- Additional Resources

    Books
    Legal Resources
    Videos
    ADD Resource Catalogues
    Newsletters
    Computer Software Resources
    Internet Resources
    Organizations/Support Groups
    Advocacy Resources

RECOMMENDED RESOURCES FOR KIDS

Bauer, K. *Active Andy: An Elementary School Child's Guide to Understanding ADHD.* Wauwatusa: IMDW Publications, 1993.

Corman, C. and Trevino, E. *Eukee the Jumpy Jumpy Elephant.* Plantation: Specialty Press, 1995.

Galum, M. *Otto Learns About His Medicine.* New York: Imagination Press, 1988.

Gehret, J. *I'm Somebody, Too!* New York: Verbal Images, 1992.

Gehret, M. *Eagle Eyes: A Child's Guide to Paying Attention.* New York: Verbal Images Press, 1991.

Gordon, M. *I Would If I Could: A Teenager's Guide to ADHD/Hyperactivity.* New York: GSI, 1991.

Gordon, M. *Jumpin' Johnny Get Back to Work: A Child's Guide to ADHD/Hyperactivity.* New York: GSI, 1991.

Gordon, M. *My Brother's a World Class Pain: A Sibling's Guide to ADHD.* New York: GSI, 1992.

Lite, L. *A Boy and a Bear: The Children's Relaxation Book.* Plantation: Specialty Press, 1996.

Moss, D. Shelby. *The Hyperactive Turtle.* Rockville: Woodbine House, 1989.

Nadeau, K. and Dixon, E. *Learning to Slow Down and Pay Attention* (Revised Edition). Ammandale: Chesapeake Psychological Publications, 1993.

Parker, R. *Making the Grade: An Adolescent's Struggle with ADD.* Plantation: Specialty Press, 1994.

Parker, R. *Slam Dunk: A Young Boy's Struggle with ADD.* Plantation: Specialty Press, 1995.

Quinn, P. and Stern, J. *Putting on the Brakes: Young People's Guide to Understanding Attention Deficit Hyperactivity Disorder (ADHD).* New York: Magination Press, 1991.

Quinn, P. and Stern, J. *The "Putting on the Brakes" Activity Book: For Young People with ADHD.* New York: Magination Press, 1993.

Shapiro, L. *Jumpin' Jake Settle Down: A Workbook to Help Impulsive Children Learn to Think Before They Act.* King of Prussia: The Center for Applied Psychology, 1994.

Shapiro, L. *Sometimes I Drive My Mom Crazy, But I Know She's Crazy About Me.* King of Prussia: The Center for Applied Psychology, 1993.

Shore, H., Marcozzi, B.A., and Shapiro, L.E. *Anybody Can Bake a Cake: A Motivational Workbook for Kids.* King of Prussia: The Center for Applied Psychology, 1995.

RECOMMENDED RESOURCES FOR TEENS AND ADULTS

Dendy, C.A. *Teenagers with ADD: A Parent's Guide.* Rockville: Woodbine House, 1994.

Hallowell, E. and Ratey, J. *Driven to Distraction: Reorganizing and Coping with Attention Deficit Disorder from Childhood through Adulthood.* New York: Pantheon, 1994.

Hartmann, T. *Attention Deficit Disorder: A Different Perception.* Penn Valley: Underwood Books, 1993.

Hechtman, L. and Weiss, G. *Hyperactive Children Grown Up.* New York: Guilford Press, 1986.

Kelly, K. and Ramundo, P. *You Mean I'm Not Lazy, Stupid, or Crazy? A Self-Help Book for Adults with Attention Deficit Disorder.* Cincinnati: Tyrell and Jerem Press, 1993.

Levine, M.D. *Keeping Ahead in School.* Cambridge, MA: Educators Publishing Service, 1990.

Murphy, K. and LeVert, S. *Out of the Fog: Treatment Options & Coping Strategies for Adult Attention Deficit Disorder.* New York: Hyperion, 1995.

Nadeau, K. *A Comprehensive Guide to Attention Deficit Disorder in Adults.* New York: Brunner Mazel, 1995.

Nadeau, K. and Biggs, S.H. *Schools' Strategies for ADD Teens.* Annandale, VA: Chesapeake Psychological Publications, 1993.

Quinn, P. *ADD and the College Student: A Guide for High School and College Students with Attention Deficit Disorder.* New York: Magination Press, 1994.

Weiss, L. *Attention Deficit Disorder in Adults: Practical Help for Sufferers and Their Spouses.* Dallas: Taylor Publishing Co., 1992.

Weiss, L. *"Attention Deficit Disorder in Adults" Workbook.* Dallas: Taylor Publishing Co., 1994.

Wender, P. *Attention Deficit Hyperactivity Disorders in Adults.* New York: Oxford University Press, 1995.

Wender, P. *The Hyperactive Child, Adolescent and Adult: Attention Deficit Disorder Through the Lifespan.* New York: Oxford University Press, 1987.

RECOMMENDED RESOURCES FOR PARENTS

Books

Alexander-Roberts, C. *The ADHD Parenting Handbook.* Dallas: Taylor Publishing Co., 1994.

Anderson, W., Chitwood, S. and Hayden, D. *Negotiating the Special Education Maze: A Guide for Parents and Teachers.* Rockville: Woodbine House, 1990.

Bain, L. *Attention Deficit Disorders.* New York: Dell Publishing Co., 1986.

Barkley, R. *Attention Deficit Hyperactivity Disorder: A Handbook for Diagnosis and Treatment.* New York: Guilford Press, 1990.

Christenson, S.L. and Conoley, J.C. (eds.). *Home-School Collaboration.* Silver Spring, MD: National Association of School Psychologists, 1992.

Colemann, W. *Attention Deficit Disorders, Hyperactivity and Associated Disorders: A Handbook for Parents & Professionals,* 6th Ed. Madison: Calliope Books, 1993.

Conner, C. *Feeding the Brain: How Foods Affect Children.* New York: Plenum, 1989.

Copeland, E. and Love, V. *Attention, Please!* Plantation: Specialty Press, 1995.

Cutler, B. *You, Your Child and Special Education: A Guide to Making the System Work.* Baltimore: Paul H. Brooks, 1993.

Flick, G.L. *Power Parenting for Children with ADD/ADHD: A Practical Parent's Guide for Managing Difficult Behaviors.* New York: The Center for Applied Research in Education (Simon & Schuster), 1996.

Fontenelle, D. *Understanding and Managing Overactive Children.* Englewood Cliffs: Prentice-Hall, Inc., 1983.

Fowler, M. *Maybe You Know My Kid: A Parent's Guide to Identifying, Understanding and Helping Your Child With Attention-Deficit Hyperactivity Disorder.* New York: Birch Lane Press, 1990.

Friedman, R. and Dogal, G. *Management of Children and Adolescents with Attention Deficit Hyperactivity Disorder.* Dallas: Pro-Ed, 1992.

Garber, S. W. et al. *If Your Child is Hyperactive, Inattentive, Impulsive, Distractible* . . . . New York:

Goldberg, R. *Sit Down and Pay Attention: Coping with ADD Throughout the Life Cycles.* Washington, D.C.: The PIA Press, 1991.

Goldstein, S. and Goldstein, M. A *Parent's Guide: Attention Deficit Disorder in Children.* Salt Lake City: Neurology Learning and Behavior Center, 1995.

Green, C. and Chee, K. *Understanding Attention-Deficit Disorder: A Parent's Guide to ADD in Children.* London: Vermilion, 1995.

Goldstein, S. and Goldstein, M. *Hyperactivity: Why Won't My Child Pay Attention.* New York: Wiley-Interscience, 1992.

Greenberg, G. and Herm, W. *Attention Deficit Hyperactivity Disorder: Questions and Answers for Parents.* Champaign: Research Press, 1991.

Hallowell, E. and Ratey, J. *Driven to Distraction: Recognizing and Coping with Attention Deficit Disorder from Childhood through Adulthood.* New York: Pantheon, 1994.

Hartmann, T. *Attention Deficit Disorder: A Different Perception.* Navato: Underwood-Miller, 1993.

Hechtman, L. and Weiss, G. *Hyperactive Children Grown Up.* New York: Guilford Press, 1986.

Ingersoll, B. *Your Hyperactive Child: A Parent's Guide to Coping with ADD.* New York: Doubleday, 1988.

Isaacs, S. and Ritchey, W. *I Think I Can, I Know I Can.* New York: St. Martin's Press, 1989.

Kelly, K. and Ramundo, P. *You Mean I'm Not Lazy, Stupid, or Crazy? A Self-Help Book for Adults with Attention Deficit Disorder.* Cincinnati: Tyrell and Jerem Press, 1993.

Kennedy, P., Terdal, L. and Fusetti, L. *The Hyperactive Child Book.* New York: St. Martin's Press, 1993.

Latham, P. S. *Succeeding in the Workplace: Attention Deficit Disorder & Learning Disabilities in the Workplace.* Grawn: JKL Communications, 1994.

Levine, M. *Keeping A Head In School.* Cambridge: Educator Publishing Service, 1990.

Maxey, D. *A Different Way of Dealing with ADHD: 365 Daily Meditations for Encouragement.* Roanoke: AAAD Support Groups, 1993.

Maxey, D. *How to Own and Operate an Attention Deficit Kid.* Roanoke: AAAD Support Groups, 1993.

Moss, R. *Why Johnny Can't Concentrate.* New York: Blanton Books, 1990.

Paltin, D. *The Parent's Hyperactivity Handbook: Helping the Fidgety Child.* New York: Plenum Press, 1993.

Phelan, T. *All About Attention Deficit Disorder (Revised).* Glen Ellyn: Child Management, 1993.

Robin, A.L. and Weiss, S.K. *Managing Oppositional Youth: Effective, Practical Strategies for Managing the Behavior of Hard to Manage Kids and Teens!* Plantation, Specialty Press, Inc. 1997

Shure, M. and Oparah, D.C. with Anderson, B. *How to Raise and Teach a Thinking Child: Helping Young Children Think About What They Do and Why.* Plantation: Specialty Press, Inc., 1997.

Silver, L. *Dr. Larry Silver's Advice to Parents on Attention Deficit Disorder.* Washington: American Psychiatric Press, 1993.

Sloane, H. *The Good Kid Book: How to Solve the 16 Most Common Behavior Problems.* Champaign: Research Press, 1988.

Taylor, J. *Helping Your Hyperactive Child.* Rochlin: Prima Publishing, 1994.

Weiss, G. and Hechtman, L.T. *Hyperactive Children Grown Up, Second Edition.* New York: Guilford Press, 1993.

Zeigler Dendy, C.A. *Teenagers with ADD: A Parent's Guide.* Bethesda: Woodbine House, Inc., 1995.

RECOMMENDED RESOURCES FOR TEACHERS

Barkley, R. *ADHD in the Classroom: Strategies for Teacher (Video).* New York: Guilford Press, 1994.

Copeland, E. and Love, V. *Attention Without Tension.* Atlanta: 3 C's of Childhood, 1990.

Davis, L., and Sirotowitz, S. with Parker, H.C. (1996). *Study Strategies Made Easy.* Plantation: Specialty Press Inc.

DuPaul, G. G., and Stoner, G. (1994). *ADHD in the Schools: Assessment and Intervention Strategies.* New York: The Guilford Press.

Goldstein, S. and Goldstein, M. *A Teacher's Guide: Attention Deficit Hyperactivity Disorder in Children.* Salt Lake City: Neurology Learning and Behavior Center, 1987.

Goldstein, S. and Goldstein, M. *Educating Inattentive Children (Video).* Salt Lake City: Neurology Learning and Behavior Center, 1990.

Nadeau, K. G., Dixon, E. B., and Biggs, S. H. (1995). *Schools' Strategies for ADD Teens.* Annandale: Chesapeake Psychological Publications.

Parker, H. ADAPT: *Attention Deficit Accommodation Plan for Teaching.* Plantation: Specialty Press, 1992.

Parker, H. *The ADD Hyperactivity Handbook for Schools.* Plantation: Impact Publications, 1992.

Pierangelo, R. and Jacoby, R. *Parents' Complete Special Education Guide: Tips, Techniques, & Materials for Helping Your Child Succeed in School and Life.* New York: The Center for Applied Research in Education, 1996.

Rhode, G., Jenson, W. R., and Reavis, H. K. (1992). *The Tough Kid Book: Practical Classroom Management Strategies.* Longmont: Sopris West.

Rief, S. *ADHD Inclusive Instruction and Collaborative Practice (Video).* New York: National Professional Resources, 1993.

Rief, S. *How to Reach and Teach ADD/ADHD Children.* New York: The Center for Applied Research in Education, 1993.

Rief, S. and Heimburge, J. *How to Reach and Teach All Students in the Inclusive Classroom.* New York: The Center for Applied Research in Education, 1996.

Shapiro, E. S., and Cole, C. L. (1994). *Behavior Change in the Classroom: Self-management Interventions.* New York: The Guilford Press.

Swanson, J. *School-based Assessments and Interventions for ADD Students.* Irving: KC Publishing, 1992.

Wielkiewicz, R. M. *Behavior Management in the Schools: Principles and Procedures.* New York: Pergamon Press, Inc., 1986.

RECOMMENDED PROFESSIONAL RESOURCES

Benoit, M., Parker, H. C., Penrod, J. C., Restin, A., and Schmidt, C. *Why Can't Bobby Pay Attention? Current Issues and Answers in Attention-Deficit/Hyperactivity Disorder (Video).* Plantation: Specialty Press, Inc., 1995.

Biederman, J., Spencer, T., and Wilens, T. *Medical Management of Attention-Deficit/Hyperactivity Disorder. (Video)* (Parts I and II), Plantation: Specialty Press, Inc., 1997.

Conners, C. K. *Attention-Deficit/Hyperactivity Disorder: Assessment and Treatment for Children and Adolescents.* New York: Multi-Health Systems, & Inc., 1996.

Copeland, E. D. *Medications for Attention Disorders.* Atlanta: SPI Press, 1991.

Copps, S. C. *The Attending Physician.* Plantation: Specialty Press, Inc., 1996.

Davis, L., and Sirotowitz, S. *Study Strategies Made Easy Video: A Practical Plan for Schools Success Grades 6-12.* Plantation: Specialty Press, Inc., 1997.

Davis, L., and Sirotowitz, S. with Parker, H. C. *Study Strategies Made Easy: A Practical Plan for Schools' Success.* Plantation: Specialty Press, Inc., 1996.

Shapiro, L. E. *Tricks of the Trade: 101 Psychological Techniques to Help Children Grow and Change.* King of Prussia: The Center for Applied Psychology, Inc., 1994.

Trower, T. *The Self-Control Patrol Workbook: Exercises for Anger Management.* King of Prussia: The Center for Applied Psychology, Inc., 1995.

Zimmerman, T. *The Cooperation Workbook.* King of Prussia: The Center for Applied Psychology, Inc., 1995.

ADDITIONAL RESOURCES

LEGAL RESOURCES

Horovitz, I., King, T., and Meyer, E. *"Legally Mandated Options Available to Children with ADHD within Public Education," Clinical Pediatrics, 1993, Vol 32(11) 702-704.*

Latham, O.S. and Latham, P.H. *Attention Deficit Disorder and the Law.* Washington: JKL Communications, 1993.

VIDEOS (THOSE WITH * ARE FOR KIDS; THOSE WITH ** ARE FOR TEACHERS)

Barkley, R. *ADHD in Adults.* New York: Guilford Press, 1994.

**Barkley, R. *ADHD in the Classroom: Strategies for Teachers.* New York: Guilford Press, 1994.

Barkley, R. *ADHD—What Can We Do?* New York: Guilford Press, 1992.

Barkley, R. *ADHD—What Can We Know?* New York: Guilford Press, 1992.

**Goldstein, S. and Goldstein, M. *Educating Inattentive Children.* Salt Lake City: Neurology Learning and Behavior Center, 1990.

*Goldstein, S. and Goldstein, M. *It's Just Attention Disorder.* Salt Lake City: Neurology Learning and Behavior Center, 1991.

Goldstein, S. and Goldstein, M. *Why Won't My Child Pay Attention?* Salt Lake City: Neurology Learning and Behavior Center, 1989.

*Gordon, M. *Jumpin' Johnny Get Back to Work: The Video.* New York: GSI, 1991.

Phelan, J. *Adults with Attention Deficit Disorder: ADD Isn't Just Kids Stuff.* Glen Ellyn: Child Management, 1994.

Phelan, J. *Attention Deficit Hyperactivity Disorder.* Glen Ellyn: Child Management, 1990.

Phelan, T. and Bloomberg, J. *Medication for Attention Deficit Disorder: All You Need to Know.* Glen Ellyn: Child Management, 1994.

**Reif, S. *ADHD Inclusive Instruction and Collaborative Practices.* New York: National Professional Resources, 1993.

Rief, S. *How to Help Your Child Succeed in School.* San Diego: Educational Resource Specialists, 1997. (1-800-682-3528)

Robin, A. *ADHD in Adolescence: The Next Step—A Video Guide for Clinical Description, Diagnosis and Treatment of Adolescents with ADHD.* Worcester: Madison Avenue Marketing, 1993.

Robin, A. *ADHD in Adulthood: A Clinical Perspective.* Worcester: National Professional Resources, 1992.

ADD Resource Catalogues

ADD Books
P.O. Box 157
Dexter, MI 48130
(313) 662-2778

ADD Clinic
Resources for Parents
983 Howard Avenue
Biloxi, MS 39531
1-800-962-2673

ADD Discount Books
312 Riley Circle
Gadsden, AL 35901
(334) 543-1170

ADD Warehouse
300 Northwest 70th Avenue
Suite 102
Plantation, FL 33317
(305) 792-8944

Attention Deficit Resources Center
1344 Johnson Ferry Road
Suite 14
Marietta, GA 30068

National Professional Resources, Inc.
Dept. C95, 25 South Regent Street
Port Chester, NY 10573
914-937-8879, FAX: 914-937-9327

The FRIC Clearinghouse on Disabilities and Gifted Education

The Council for Exceptional Children
1920 Association Drive
Reston, Virginia 20191-1589
1-800-328-0272
TTY 703/264-9449
E-mail: ericec@cec.sped.org

Newsletters (Those with * Are for Kids)

ADD Forum (CompuServe)
800-524-3388 (Representative 464)

ADD-ONS
P.O. Box 675
Frankfort, KY 60423

The ADHD Report
Russell Barkley, Editor
Guilford Publications
72 Spring Street
New York, NY 10012
800-365-7006

The ADDed Line
3320 Creek Hollow Drive
Marietta, GA 30062
800-982-4028

ADDult News
c/o Mary Jane Johnson
ADDult Support Network
2620 Ivy Place
Toledo, OH 43613

Advance, a publication of ADDAG
8091 S. Ireland Way
Aurora, CO 80016
303-690-7548

ATTENTION (magazine)
CH.A.D.D. National Headquarters
499 Northwest 70th Ave., Suite 308
Plantation, FL 33317
305-587-3700, FAX: 305-587-4599

Attention Please, Newsletter for children with Attention Deficit Disorder
2106 3rd Avenue, N.
Seattle, WA 98109-2305

***BRAKES: The Interactive Newsletter for Kids with ADHD**
Magination Press
19 Union Square West
New York, NY 10003
800-825-3089

CHADD Newsletters (CHADDER/ CHADDER BOX)
CH.A.D.D. National Headquarters
499 Northwest 70th Ave., Suite 308
Plantation, FL 33317
305-587-3700, Fax: 305-587-4599

Electronic Bulletin Boards
(a) American On-line
(b) Prodigy
(c) Disabilities Forum
(d) ADD Bulletin Board

HAAD ENOUGH (Bi-Monthly)
HAAD Support Groups
P.O. Box 20563
Roanoke, VA 24018

Kids Getting You Down?
Learning Development Services
3754 Clairemont Drive
San Diego, CA 92117

The Rebus Institute Report
1499 Bayshore Blvd., Suite 146
Burlingame, CA 94010

COMPUTER SOFTWARE RESOURCES

ABLEDATA
National Rehabilitation Information Center
Catholic University of America
4407 Eighth St., NE
Washington, D.C. 20017
(202) 635-5822

"Following Directions" (Grades 3-6)
Lawrence Productions
1800 S. 35th Street
Galesburg, MI 49053
(800) 645-6564

Miranker, C. and Elliot, A.
The Computer Museum Guide to the Best Software for Kids
New York: Harper Collins Publishers, Inc., 1995

"Test Taking Made Easy" (Grades 2-5)
Lawrence Productions
1800 S. 35th St.
Galesburg, MI 49053
(800) 645-6564

Kids Works 2
Davidson and Associates
P.O. Box 2961
Torrance, CA 90509
(800) 545-7677

INTERNET RESOURCES

One ADD Place
(http://www.greatconnect.com/oneaddplace)
A "virtual neighborhood" that consolidates information and resources.

ADD Webnet
(http://members.aol.com/addwebney/index.html)
A central directory of links that connects you to sites of individuals or groups that provide information, offer support, or share insights on ADD.

ADD and ADHD Infoline
(http://www.alcasoft.com/add)
Information and resources put together by a family's personal experience with ADD.

ORGANIZATIONS/SUPPORT GROUPS

ADDA (Attention Deficit Disorder Association)
P.O. Box 972
Mentor, OH 44060
(800) 487-2282

ADDAG (Attention Deficit Disorder Advocacy Group)
8091 South Ireland Way
Aurora, CO 80016
(303) 690-7548

ADDIEN (ADDult Information Exchange Network)
P.O. Box 1701
Ann Arbor, MI 48106

ADDult Support Network (for ADD Adults)
Mary Jane Johnson
2620 Ivy Place
Toledo, OH 43613

Adult ADD Association
1225 East Sunset Drive, Suite 640
Bellingham, WA 98226-3529
(206) 647-6681

Attention Deficit Information Network (AD-IN)
475 Hillside Avenue
Needham, MA 02194
(617) 455-9895

Attention Deficit Resource Center (Special Focus on ADD Adults)
Lawrence L. McLear, Ph.D, Director
1344 Johnson Ferry Rd., Suite 14
Marietta, GA 30068
(800) 537-3784

Children with Attention Deficit Disorders (CHADD)
499 Northwest 70th Ave., Suite 101
Plantation, FL 33317
(305) 587-3700

The Council for Exceptional Children
1920 Association Drive
Reston, VA 20191
(800) 328-0272

Learning Disabilities Association (LDA)
4156 Library Road
Pittsburgh, PA 15234
(412) 341-1515

National Network of Learning Disabled Adults (NNCDA)
808 West 82nd St., F-2
Scottsdale, AZ 85257

Professional Group for ADD and Related Disorders (PGARD)
28 Fairview Road
Scarsdale, NY 10583
(914) 723-0118

ADVOCACY RESOURCES

- Learning Disabilities Assocation of America (LDA) (PA) (412) 341-1515 (State LDA Ofice and Local LDA Chapter)
- Orton Dyslexia Society (MD) 1-800-222-3123
- National Center for Learning Disabilities (NY) (212) 545-7510
- CH.A.D.D. (Children & Adults with Attention Deficit Disorders) National Office (FL) 1-800-233-4050 (Ask for local chapters.)
- TAPP/PTI Office (Technical Assistance for Parent Programs Project/Parent Training & Information Projects) Check with your state or local LDA office or call the Federation for Children with Special Needs (MA) (617) 482-2915
- National Association of Protection & Advocacy Systems (legal information & support) (202) 408-9514
- HEATH (National Clearinghouse on Post-secondary education for Individuals with Disabilities) (Washington, D.C.) 1-800-544-3284
- NICHCY (National Information Center for Children and Youth with Disabilities (Washington, D.C.) 1-800-695-0285
- ERIC Clearinghouse for Handicapped and Gifted Children, Council for Exceptional Children (VA) (703) 264-9474
- Office for Civil Rights (Contact your state LDA or TAPP/PTI Office)
- Local Special Education Attorney
- Local School Psychologist, Personnel and Superintendent

TV ALLOWANCE™

To order this device, call 1-800-231-4410 or write to TV Allowance™, 5605 SW 74th St., South Miami, FL 33143. The manufacturer will offer purchasers a discount if they mention they read about the device in this book.

REFERENCES

American Psychiatric Association. *Diagnostic and Statistical Manual of Mental Disorders (4th edition).* Washington, D.C.: Author, 1994.

Anesko, K. M., and Levine, F. M. (1987). *Winning the Homework War.* New York: ARCO/Simon & Schuster.

Archer, A., and Gleason, M. (1989). *Skills for School's Success (Grades 3–6).* North Billerica, MA: Curriculum.

Aylward, G. P. (1994). *Practitioner's Guide to Developmental and Psychological Testing.* New York: Plenum Medical Book Company.

Azrin, H.H., and Holz, W.C. (1966). "Punishment," in W.K. Homig (Ed.) *Operant Behavior: Areas of Research and Application.* New York: Appleton Century Cross.

Baren, M. (1996). "Advanced Pharmacotherapy for the Treatment of Children and Adolescents with ADD." Presentation at the 8th Annual Conference, CH.A.D.D., Chicago, Ill.

Barkley, R. A. (1987). *Defiant Children: A Clinician's Manual for Parent Training.* New York: Guilford Press.

Barkley, R.A. (1990). *Attention-Deficit Hyperactivity Disorder: A Handbook for Diagnosis and Treatment.* New York: Guilford Press.

Barkley, R.A. (1994). *Can Neuropsychological Tests Help Diagnose ADD\ADHD? ADHD Report, 2(1).* New York: Guilford Press.

Barkley, R.A. (1995). *Taking Charge of ADHD: The Complete Authoritative Guide for Parents.* New York: Guilford Press.

Biederman, J., Faraone, S.V., Keenan, K., et. al. (1992). "Further Evidence for Family-Genetic Risk Factors in Attention-Deficit\Hyperactivity Disorder: Veterans of Co-morbidity and Probands and Relatives in Psychiatrically and Pediatrically Preferred Samples." *Archives of General Psychiatry,* 49, 728, 728-738.

Borland, B.L., and Hechtman, H.K. (1976). "Hyperactive Boys and Their Mothers: A 25 Year Follow-up Study." *Archives of General Psychiatry,* 33, 669-675.

Bracy, B.L. (1983-1993). *Soft Tools,* Indianapolis: Neuroscience Publishers.

Burd, L., Kerbeshian, J., and Fisher, W. (1987). "Does the Use of Phenobarbital as an Anti-Convulsant Permanently Exacerbate Hyperactivity?" *Canadian Journal of Psychiatry,* 32, 10-13.

Burte, J.M., and Burte, C.L. (1994). "Ericsonian Hypnosis Pharmacotherapy and Cognitive-Behavioral Therapy in the Treatment of ADHD." *Australian Journal of Clinical Hypnotherapy and Hypnosis* 15(1), 1-13.

Campbell, S.B. (1985). "Hyperactivity in Preschoolers: Carlics and Prognostic Implications." *Clinical Psychology Review,* 5, 405-428.

Campbell, S.B. (1990). *Behavior Problems in Preschool Children: Clinical and Developmental Issues.* New York: Guilford Press.

Cantwell, D.P. (1972). "Psychiatric Illness in the Families of Hyperactive Children," *Archives of General Psychiatry,* 27, 414-417.

Carlson, C.L., Pelham, W.E., Milich, R., Dixon, J. (1992). "Single and Combined Effects of Methylphenidate and Behavior Therapy of the Classroom Performance of Children with Attention-Deficit\Hyperactivity Disorder," *Journal of Abnormal Child Psychology,* 20:213-232.

CH.A.D.D. May Issue (Fall 1994).

Chelune, G.J., Ferguson, W., Koon, R., and Dickey, T.O. (1986). "Frontal Lobe Disinhibition in Attention-Deficit Disorder." *Child Psychiatry and Human Development,* 16, 221-234.

Childers, A.T. (1935). "Hyper-activity in Children Having Behavior Disorders." *American Journal of Author Psychiatry,* 5, 227-243.

Clark, Lynn S. (1985). *S.O.S.! Help for Parents.* Bowling Green: Parents Press.

Colby, C.L. (1991). "The Neuro Anatomy and Neurophysiology of Attention," *Journal of Child Neurology,* (6), 90-118.

Conners, C.K., and Son March, J.S. (1994). *Conners-March Developmental Questionnaire.* Toronto: Multi-Health Systems, Inc.

Cooke, J., and Williams, D. (1987). *Working with Children's Language.* Tucson, AZ: Communication Skill Builders.

Cripe, F.F. (1986). "Walk Music as Therapy for Children with Attention-Deficit Disorder: An Exploratory Study," *Journal of Music Therapy,* 23(1), 30-37.

Cruickshank, W.M., Bentzen, F.A., Tatzeburg, F.H., and Tannhauser, M.T. (1961). *A Teaching Method for Brain Injured and Hyperactive Children.* Syracuse: Syracuse University Press.

Dayton, Tian (1991). *Affirmation for Parents: How to Nurture Your Children.* Deerfield Beach: Health Communications.

Douglas, V.I. (1972). "Stop, Look and Listen: The Problem of Sustained Attention and Impulse Control in Hyperactive and Normal Children," *Canadian Journal of Behavioral Science,* 4, 259-282.

DuPaul, G.J., and Stoner, G. (1994). *ADHD in the Schools: Assessment and Intervention Strategies.* New York: Guilford Press.

Faraone, S. V., Biederman, J., Keenan, K., and Tsuang, M. T. (1991). "A Separation of DSM-III Attention-Deficit Disorder and Conduct Disorder: Evidence from a Family-Genetic Study of American Child Psychiatric Patients." *Psychological Medicine,* 21 (1), 109-121.

Fennell, E.B. (1995). "The Role of Neuropsychological Assessment in Learning Disabilities," *Journal of Child Neurology,* 10(1), 36-41.

Findley, L. J., Barth, J. T., Powers, M. E., et. al: (1986). "Cognitive Impairment in Patients with Obstructive Sleep Apnea and Associated Hypoxemia." *Chest* 90, 686-690.

Fine, A., and Goldman, L. (1994). "Innovative Techniques in the Treatment of ADHD: An Analysis of the Impact of EEG Biofeedback Training in a Cognitive Computer Generated Training." Paper presented at the American Psychological Association Annual Meeting, Los Angeles.

Flick, G.L. (1969). "Attention to Colorful Stimuli as a Function of Stimulus Parameters and the Level of Adaptation in Normal and Mentally Retarded Children." Unpublished Doctoral Dissertation, University of Miami, Coral Cables, FL.

Flick, G.L. (1996). *Power Parenting for Children with ADD/ADHD: A Practical Parents' Guide for Managing Difficult Behaviors.* New York: Center for Applied Research in Education/Simon and Schuster.

Ford, M.J., Poe, V., and Cox, J. (1993). "Attending Behaviors of ADHD Children in Math and Reading Using Various Types of Software," *Journal of Computing in Childhood Education,* 4(2), 183-196.

Fowler, M. (1992). *CH.A.D.D. Educator's Manual.* Fairfax, VA: CASET Associates.

Garber, S. W., Garber, M. D., and Spizman, R. F. (1990). *If Your Child is Hyperactive, Inattentive, Impulsive, Distractible . . . Helping the ADD (Attention-Deficit Disorder) Hyperactive Child.* New York: Villard Books.

Gaultheria, T. (1991). "Childhood Hyperactivity," in *Thomas Gaultheria (Ed.) Neuropsychiatry and Behavioral Pharmacology.* Berlin: Springer-Verlag.

Goldstein, A.P. (1988). *The Prepared Curriculum: Teaching Pro-social Competencies.* Champaign, Ill: Research Press.

Goldstein, J., and Cornacchio, J. (1996). *ADD Mazement,* Portsmouth, NH: Octoba Software.

Goldstein, S., and Goldstein, M. (1985). *The Multi-disciplinary Evaluation and Treatment of Attention-Deficit Disorders in Children: Symposium Handbook.* Salt Lake City, UT: Neurology, Learning and Behavior Center.

Goldstein, S., and Goldstein, M. (1990). *Managing Attention Disorders in Children.* New York: John Wiley & Sons, Inc.

Goodwin, S.E., and Mahoney, M.J. (1975). "Modification of Aggression Through Modeling: An Experimental Probe," *Journal of Behavior Therapy and Experimental Psychiatry,* 6, 200-202.

Gordon, M., Thomason, D., Cooper, S., & Ivers, C.L. (1991). "Nonmedical Treatment of ADHD/Hyperactivity: The Attention Training System," *Journal of School Psychology,* 29, 151-159.

Graham, S., and Harris, K. R. (1996). "Addressing Problems in Attention, Memory and Executive Functioning." An Example from Self-Regulated Strategy Development, in Lyon, G. R., Krasnegor, N. A. (Eds.): *Attention, Memory, and Executive Functions.* Baltimore, MD: Paul H. Brooks Publishing Company, 349 & 365.

Hagerman, R.J., Kemper, M., & Hudson, M. (1985). "Learning Disabilities and Attentional Problems in Boys with Fragile-X Syndrome," *American Journal of Diseases of Children,* 139, 674-678.

Hanf, C. (1969). *A Two-Stage Program for Modifying Maternal Controlling During Mother/Child Interaction.* Paper presented at the meeting of the Western Psychological Association, Vancouver, British Columbia.

Hauser, T., Zametkin, A.J., Martinex, P., Vitiello, B., Matochik, J.A., Mixson, A.J., & Weintraub, B.D. (1993). "Attention-Deficit/Hyperactivity Disorder in People with Generalized Resistance to Thyroid Hormone," *New England Journal of Medicine,* 328, 997-1001.

Hechtman, L. (1994). "Genetic and Neurobiological Aspects of Attention-Deficit/Hyperactive Disorder: A Review," *Journal of Psychiatry and Neuro Science,* 19(3), 193-201.

Heilman, K. M., Voeller, K. K. S., and Nadeau, S. E. (1991). "A Possible Pathophysiologic Substrate of Attention-Deficit/Hyperactivity Disorder." *Journal of Child Neurology*, 6th, S76-S81.

Jones, C.B. (1994). *Attention-Deficit Disorder: Strategies for School-Age Children.* San Antonio: Communication Skill Builders.

Kendall, T.C, and Braswell, L. (1985). *Cognitive-Behavioral Therapy for Impulsive Children.* New York: Guilford Press.

Kotwal, D., Montgomery, D., and Burns, W. (1994). "Computer Assisted Cognitive Training for ADHD: A Case Study." Presented at the Annual Convention of the APA.

Leventhal, B. (1996). "ADHD: An Update of Psycho-pharmacotherapy." Presented at the CH.A.D.D. 8th Annual Conference, Chicago.

Levine, M. (1994). *Educational Care.* Cambridge: Educators' Publishing Service.

Levinson, S., Kopari, J., and Fredstrom, J. (1995). *The MotivAider® Method of Queue Directed Behavior Change: Manual for Teachers.* Three River Falls: Behavioral Dynamics.

Light, R., Satz, P., Asarnow, R.F., Lewis, R., Ribbler, A., and Neumann, E. (1996). "Disorders of Attention" in *Pediatric Neuropsychology: Interfacing Assessment and Treatment for Rehabilitation.* Batchelor, E.S., and Dean, R.S., (Eds.), Needham Heights, MA: Allyn & Bacon.

Lubar, J.F. (1991). "Discourse on the Development of EEG Diagnostics and Biofeedback Treatment for Attention-Deficit/Hyperactivity Disorders," *Biofeedback and Self-Regulation,* 16, 201-225.

McCraken, J.A. (1991). "A Two-Part Model of Stimulant Action on Attention-Deficit/Hyperactivity Disorder in Children," *Journal of Neuropsychiatry,* 3, 201-209.

Miller, K.J. (1996). "Medication in Attention-Deficit/Hyperactivity Disorders." Presentation at the CH.A.D.D. 8th Annual Conference, Chicago.

Mirsky, A.F. (1987). "Behavioral and Psychophysiological Markers of Disordered Attention," *Environmental Health Perspectives,* 74, 191-199.

Molitch, M., and Eccles, A.K. (1937). "Effects of Benzedrine Sulfate on Intelligence Scores of Children," *American Journal of Psychiatry,* 94, 587-590.

Morrison, J.R., and Stewart, M.A. (1974). "Bilateral Inheritance as Evidence for Polygenicity in the Hyperactive Child Syndrome," *Journal of Nervous and Mental Disease,* 158, 226-228.

Novaco, R. W. (1975). *Anger Control: A Development and Evaluation of an Experimental Treatment.* Lexington, MA: Lexington.

Pelham, W.E., Bender, M.E., Caddell, J., Booth, S., and Moorer, S.H. (1985). "Methylphenidate in Children with Attention-Deficit Disorder," *Archives of General Psychiatry*, 42, 948-952.

Pelham, W.E., and Murphy, H.A. (1986). "Attention-Deficit and Conduct Disorders" in M. Hersen (Ed.), *Pharmacological and Behavioral Treatments: An Integrative Approach.* (pp. 108-148) New York: Wiley.

Piaget, J., and Inhelder, B. (1969). *The Psychology of the Child.* New York: Basic Books.

Podd, M.H., Mills, M.W., and Seelig, D.P. (1989). *A Manual for NeuroXercise*™. Published and distributed by Dr. Podd.

Rapoport, J. (1996). "Neurobiological Research Updates on Attention-Deficit Disorders." Presented at the CH.A.D.D. 8th Annual Conference, Chicago.

Roberts, M.L., and Landau, S. (1895). "Using Curriculum-based Data for Assessing Children with Attention-Deficits" in *The Journal of Psychoeducational Assessment.* Monograph series, Special ADHD Issue, pp. 74-87.

Robin, A. L., Schneider, M., and Dolnick, J. (1976). "The Turtle Technique: An Extensive Case Study of Self-Control in the Classroom." *Psychology in the Schools,* 1, 449-459.

Roizen, N.J., Blondis, T.A., Rubinoff, I.M., Kieffer, A., Stein, J. (1996). "Psychiatric and Developmental Disorders in Families of Children with Attention-Deficit/Hyperactivity Disorder." *Archives of Pediatric Adolescent Medicine,* 150, 203-208.

Rossiter, T.R., and LaVague, T.J. (1995). "A Comparison of EEG Biofeedback and Psychostimulants in Treating Attention-Deficit/Hyperactivity Disorders," *Journal of Neurotherapy,* (1), 48-59.

Ross, D.M., and Ross, S.A. (1976). *Hyperactivity: Research, Theory and Action.* New York: John Wiley & Sons.

Rosvold, H. E., Mirsky, A. F., Sarason, I., Bransome, E. D., and Beck, L. H. (1956). "A Continuous Performance Test of Brain Damage." *Journal of Consulting Psychology,* 20, 343-350.

Rourke, B.P. (1994). "Neuropsychological Assessment of Children with Learning Disabilities: Measurement Issues" in G.R. Lyon (Ed.), *Frames of Reference for the Assessment of Learning Disabilities: New Views on Measurement Issues* (pp. 475-514), Baltimore, MD: Paul H. Brookes.

Sandford, J.A., and Browne, R.J. (1988). *Captain's Log Cognitive System.* Richmond, VA: Brain Train, Inc.

Sandford, J.A. (1995). "Improving Cognitive Behavioral Psychotherapy Treatment of ADHD and ADD Disorders with the *Captain's Log*: Cognitive Training System." Newsletter of the Society for Cognitive Rehabilitation (Fall-Winter Issue).

Satterfield, J.H., and Dawson, M.E. (1971). "Electrodermal Carlics of Hyperactivity in Children," *Psychophysiology,* 8, 191-197.

Shaywitz, B.A., Cohen, D.J., and Bowers, M.B. (1977). "CSF Monoamine Metabolites in Children with Minimal Brain Dysfunction: Evidence for Alteration of Brain Dopamine," *Journal of Pediatrics,* 1, 67-71.

Shaywitz, S.E., and Shaywitz, B.A. (1991). "Attention-Deficit Disorder: Diagnosis and Role of Ritalin in Management," in L.L. Greenhill and B.B. Osman (Eds.), *Ritalin: Theory in Patient Management* (pp. 45-67). New York: Marianne Liebert.

Sohlberg, M.M., and Mateer, C.A. (1989). *Introduction to Cognitive Rehabilitation: Theory and Practice.* New York: Guilford Press.

Sohlberg, M.M., Johnson, L., Panle, L., Raskin, S., Mateer, C.A. (1993). *Manual for Attention Process Training—II.* Tuyallup: Association for Neuropsychological Research and Development.

Spencer, P. "Current Concepts in Pharmacotherapy and Issues on Co-Morbidity in the Treatment of ADD in Children and Adolescents." Panel Presentation at CH.A.D.D. 8th Annual Conference, Chicago.

Spreen, O., Risser, A.H., and Edgell, D. (1995). *Developmental Neuropsychology.* New York: Oxford University Press.

Still, G.F. (1902). "Some Abnormal Psychological Conditions in Children," *Lancet,* 1, 1007-1082.

Stoner, G., and Greene, S. K. (1992). "Reconsidering the Scientist-Practitioner Model for School Psychology Practice." *School Psychology Review,* 21, 154-165.

Stoudemire, A. (1994). *Clinical Psychiatry for Medical Students (2nd ed.).* Philadelphia: J.B. Lippinscott Co.

Strauss, A.A., and Lehtinen, L.E. (1947). *Psychopathology and Education of the Brain-Injured Child.* New York: Grune and Stratton.

Tredgold, A.F. (1908). *Mental Deficiency (Amentia).* New York: W. Wood.

VanZomeren, A.H., and Brouwer, W.H. (1994). *Clinical Neuropsychology of Attention.* New York: Oxford University Press.

Walker, H.M. (1979). *The Acting-Out Child: Coping with Classroom Disruptions.* Boston: Allyn & Bacon.

Weinberg, W.A., and Emslie, G.J. (1991). "Attention-Deficit/Hyperactivity Disorder: The Differential Diagnosis" (Supplement), *Journal of Child Neurology,* 6, S21-S34.

Weiss, G., and Hechtman, L.T. (1986). *Hyperactive Children Growing Up.* New York: Guilford Press.

Welner, Z., Welner, A., Stewart, M.A., Palkes, H., and Wish, E. (1977). "A Controlled Study of Siblings of Hyperactive Children," *Journal of Nervous Mental Disease,* 165, 110-117.

Whitman, C. (1991). *Win the Whining War and Other Skirmishes: A Family Peace Plan.* Pasadena: Perspective Publishing.

Wielkiewicz, R.M. (1986). *Behavior Management in the Schools: Principles and Procedures.* Elmsford, New York: Pergamon Press, Incorporated.

Wilens, T. "Chart Concepts in Pharmacotherapy and Issues in Co-Morbidity in the Treatment of ADD in Children and Adolescents." Panel Presentation at CH.A.D.D. 8th Annual Conference, Chicago.

Williams, D.J. (1989). *A Process-Specific Training Program in the Treatment of Attention-Deficits in Children.* Unpublished Doctoral Dissertation, University of Washington.

Williams, J.M. (1992). *Software for Psychological Testing in Education.* Walkersville, MD: Cool-Spring Software.

Zametkin, A.J., et. al. (1990). "Cerebral Glucose Metabolism in Adults with Hyperactivity of Childhood Onset," *New England Journal of Medicine,* 323, 1361-1366.

INDEX

A

D

E

F

G

I

J

K

L

M

N

O

P

T